Lecture Notes in Computer Science   15183

Founding Editors

Gerhard Goos
Juris Hartmanis

Editorial Board Members

Elisa Bertino, *Purdue University, West Lafayette, IN, USA*
Wen Gao, *Peking University, Beijing, China*
Bernhard Steffen ⓘ, *TU Dortmund University, Dortmund, Germany*
Moti Yung ⓘ, *Columbia University, New York, NY, USA*

The series Lecture Notes in Computer Science (LNCS), including its subseries Lecture Notes in Artificial Intelligence (LNAI) and Lecture Notes in Bioinformatics (LNBI), has established itself as a medium for the publication of new developments in computer science and information technology research, teaching, and education.

LNCS enjoys close cooperation with the computer science R & D community, the series counts many renowned academics among its volume editors and paper authors, and collaborates with prestigious societies. Its mission is to serve this international community by providing an invaluable service, mainly focused on the publication of conference and workshop proceedings and postproceedings. LNCS commenced publication in 1973.

Sabrina Kirrane · Mantas Šimkus · Ahmet Soylu · Dumitru Roman
Editors

Rules and Reasoning

8th International Joint Conference, RuleML+RR 2024
Bucharest, Romania, September 16–18, 2024
Proceedings

 Springer

Editors
Sabrina Kirrane
Vienna University of Economics
and Business
Vienna, Austria

Ahmet Soylu
OsloMet – Oslo Metropolitan University
Oslo, Norway

Mantas Šimkus
TU Wien
Vienna, Austria

Dumitru Roman
SINTEF AS/OsloMet – Oslo Metropolitan University
Oslo, Norway

ISSN 0302-9743　　　　　　　　ISSN 1611-3349　(electronic)
Lecture Notes in Computer Science
ISBN 978-3-031-72406-0　　　　ISBN 978-3-031-72407-7　(eBook)
https://doi.org/10.1007/978-3-031-72407-7

© The Editor(s) (if applicable) and The Author(s), under exclusive license
to Springer Nature Switzerland AG 2024, corrected publication 2024

This work is subject to copyright. All rights are solely and exclusively licensed by the Publisher, whether the whole or part of the material is concerned, specifically the rights of translation, reprinting, reuse of illustrations, recitation, broadcasting, reproduction on microfilms or in any other physical way, and transmission or information storage and retrieval, electronic adaptation, computer software, or by similar or dissimilar methodology now known or hereafter developed.
The use of general descriptive names, registered names, trademarks, service marks, etc. in this publication does not imply, even in the absence of a specific statement, that such names are exempt from the relevant protective laws and regulations and therefore free for general use.
The publisher, the authors and the editors are safe to assume that the advice and information in this book are believed to be true and accurate at the date of publication. Neither the publisher nor the authors or the editors give a warranty, expressed or implied, with respect to the material contained herein or for any errors or omissions that may have been made. The publisher remains neutral with regard to jurisdictional claims in published maps and institutional affiliations.

This Springer imprint is published by the registered company Springer Nature Switzerland AG
The registered company address is: Gewerbestrasse 11, 6330 Cham, Switzerland

If disposing of this product, please recycle the paper.

Preface

These are the proceedings of the 8th International Joint Conference on Rules and Reasoning (RuleML+RR 2024). RuleML+RR joined the efforts of two well-established conference series: the International Web Rule Symposia (RuleML) and the Web Reasoning and Rule Systems (RR) conferences.

The RuleML symposia have been held since 2002 and the RR conferences since 2007. The RR conferences were a forum for discussion and dissemination of new results on Web Reasoning and Rule Systems, with an emphasis on rule-based approaches and languages. The RuleML symposia were devoted to disseminating research, applications, languages, and standards for rule technologies, with attention to both theoretical and practical developments, to challenging new ideas, and to industrial applications. Building on the tradition of both, RuleML and RR, the joint conference series RuleML+RR aims to bridge academia and industry in the field of rules, and to foster cross-fertilization between the different communities focused on the research, development, and applications of rule-based systems. RuleML+RR aims to be the leading conference series for all subjects concerning theoretical advances, novel technologies, and innovative applications of knowledge representation and reasoning with rules.

To leverage these ambitions, RuleML+RR 2024 was organized as part of the event *Declarative AI 2024: Rules, Reasoning, Decisions, and Explanations*, Which was held between the 16th and the 18th of September 2024. This event was hosted by the Bucharest University of Economic Studies (ASE), Romania. With its general topic *"Declarative Artificial Intelligence,"* a core objective of the event was to present the latest advancements in AI and rules, rule-based machine learning, reasoning, decisions, and explanations and their adoption in IT systems. To this end, *Declarative AI 2024* brought together co-located events with related interests. In addition to RuleML+RR, this included the Reasoning Web Summer School (RW 2024) and DecisionCAMP 2024.

The RuleML+RR conference moreover included several subevents:

1. *Doctoral Consortium* – an initiative to attract and promote student research in rules and reasoning, with the opportunity for students to present and discuss their ideas, and benefit from close contact with leading experts in the field.
2. *International Rule Challenge* – an initiative to provide competition among work in progress and new visionary ideas concerning innovative rule-oriented applications, aimed at both research and industry.
3. *Industry Track* – an initiative to present work from all areas of rules–and reasoning–based technologies specifically for solving real industry problems.
4. *Project Networking Session* – an initiative to bring together relevant projects working in the area of data and AI with particular focus on, but not limited to, the event topics: rules, reasoning, decisions, and explanations

The program of the main track of RuleML+RR 2024 included the presentation of 12 full research papers and 4 short papers. These contributions were carefully selected by the Program Committee from 35 submissions, two of which were desk rejected; thus 33 high-quality submissions were sent for review. Each paper was carefully reviewed by at least three reviewers and all borderline papers were discussed in detail. The technical program was then enriched with the additional contributions from its subevents as well as from DecisionCAMP 2024, an event aimed at practitioners which was virtual this year.

At RuleML+RR 2024, three keynote speakers were invited:

- Jan Van den Bussche, Hasselt University (Belgium): *Shapes Constraint Language: Logic, Queries, and Provenance*
- Alessandra Mileo, Dublin City University (Ireland): *Neuro-Symbolic AI and Human-Centred Explainability*
- Stefan Borgwardt, TU Dresden (Germany): *Explaining Description Logic Reasoning*

The chairs sincerely thank the keynote speakers for their contribution to the success of the event. The chairs also thank the Program Committee members and the additional reviewers for their hard work in the careful assessment of the submitted papers. Further thanks go to all authors of contributed papers for their efforts in the preparation of their submissions and the camera-ready versions within the established schedule. Sincere thanks to the chairs of the Doctoral Consortium, Rule Challenge, Industry Track, and Project Networking Session, and to the chairs of all co-located Declarative AI 2024 events. The chairs finally thank the entire organization team including the Publicity, Proceedings, and Sponsorship Chairs, who actively contributed to the organization and the success of the event.

A special thanks goes to all the sponsors of RuleML+RR 2024 and Declarative AI 2024: Springer, Bucharest University of Economic Studies, Bucharest Business School, OsloMet, SINTEF, RuleML Inc, and RR Association. Special thanks also go to the publisher, Springer, for their cooperation in editing this volume and publication of the proceedings. We are grateful to the sponsors of RuleML+RR 2024 as they also contributed towards the awards: RuleML+RR Harold Boley Distinguished Paper award, RuleML+RR Best Student Paper award, RuleML+RR Best Rule Challenge paper award, and RuleML+RR Best Doctoral Consortium Paper award.

August 2024

Sabrina Kirrane
Mantas Šimkus
Ahmet Soylu
Dumitru Roman

Organization

General Chairs

Ahmet Soylu — Oslo Metropolitan University, Norway
Dumitru Roman — SINTEF AS/Oslo Metropolitan University, Norway

Program Chairs

Sabrina Kirrane — Vienna University of Economics and Business, Austria
Mantas Šimkus — Vienna University of Technology, Austria

Rule Challenge Chairs

Anisa Rula — University of Brescia, Italy
Emanuel Sallinger — TU Wien, Austria

Doctoral Consortium

Ognjen Savkovic — Free University of Bozen-Bolzano, Italy
Ioana Georgiana Ciuciu — Babeş-Bolyai University, Romania

Industry Track Chairs

Ioan Toma — Onlim, Austria
Josiane Xavier Parreira — Siemens, Austria

Networking Session Chairs

Radu Prodan — University of Klagenfurt, Austria
Hui Song — SINTEF AS, Norway

Proceedings Chairs

Dumitru Roman   SINTEF AS/Oslo Metropolitan University, Norway
Ahmet Soylu   Oslo Metropolitan University, Norway

Publicity Chairs

Tomáš Kliegr   Prague University of Economics and Business, Czechia
Ines Akaichi   Vienna University of Economics and Business, Austria

Local Chair

Strat Vasile Alecsandru   Bucharest University of Economic Studies (ASE), Romania

Sponsorship Chairs

Cristina Marcu   Bucharest University of Economic Studies (ASE), Romania

Local Team

Mihai Gheorghe   Bucharest University of Economic Studies (ASE), Romania
Cosmin-Adrian Proscanu   Bucharest University of Economic Studies (ASE), Romania

Web Chair

Ahmet Soylu   Oslo Metropolitan University, Norway

Finance Chair

Strat Vasile Alecsandru   Bucharest University of Economic Studies (ASE), Romania

Program Committee

Albin Ahmeti	Vienna University of Technology, Austria
Alisa Kovtunova	TU Dresden, Germany
Andrea Cimmino Arriaga	Universidad Politécnica de Madrid, Spain
Andrea Mazzullo	Free University of Bozen-Bolzano, Italy
Anelia Kurteva	TU Delft, Netherlands
Angelo Montanari	University of Udine, Italy
Anisa Rula	University of Brescia, Italy
Anni-Yasmin Turhan	TU Dresden, Germany
Antonino Rotolo	University of Bologna, Italy
Antonis Bikakis	University College London, UK
Bernardo Cuenca Grau	University of Oxford, UK
Chang Sun	Maastricht University, Netherlands
Cristina Feier	University of Warsaw, Poland
Davide Sottara	Mayo Clinic, USA
Diego Calvanese	Free University of Bozen-Bolzano, Italy
Dörthe Arndt	TU Dresden, Germany
Domenico Lembo	Sapienza University of Rome, Italy
Egor V. Kostylev	University of Oslo, Norway
Emanuel Sallinger	Vienna University of Technology, Austria
Federico Scafoglieri	Sapienza University of Rome, Italy
Francesca Alessandra Lisi	University of Bari, Italy
Francesco Ricca	University of Calabria, Italy
Francesco Santini	Università di Perugia, Italy
Francesco M. Donini	Università della Tuscia, Italy
Frank Wolter	University of Liverpool, UK
Franz Baader	TU Dresden, Germany
George Konstantinidis	University of Southampton, UK
Giorgos Flouris	FORTH-ICS, Greece
Gong Cheng	Nanjing University, China
Guido Governatori	Charles Sturt University, Australia
Horatiu Cirstea	Loria, France
Jan Rauch	Prague University of Economics and Business, Czechia
Jan Vanthienen	KU Leuven, Belgium
Jesse Heyninck	Open Universiteit, Netherlands
Jessica Zangari	University of Calabria, Italy
Johannes Fürnkranz	Johannes Kepler University Linz, Austria
Joost Vennekens	KU Leuven, Belgium
Jorge Martinez-Gil	Software Competence Center Hagenberg, Austria
Josiane Xavier Parreira	Siemens AG Österreich, Austria

Juliana Küster Filipe Bowles	University of St Andrews, UK
Kia Teymourian	University of Texas at Austin, USA
Konstantin Schekotihin	Alpen-Adria Universität Klagenfurt, Austria
Leopoldo Bertossi	Carleton University, Canada
Livio Robaldo	University of Swansea, UK
Loris Bozzato	Fondazione Bruno Kessler, Italy
Manolis Koubarakis	National and Kapodistrian University of Athens, Greece
Marco Maratea	University of Genoa, Italy
Maria Vanina Martinez	Artificial Intelligence Research Institute (IIIA-CSIC), Spain
Markus Krötzsch	TU Dresden, Germany
Maurizio Lenzerini	Sapienza University of Rome, Italy
Michaël Thomazo	Inria, France
Nico Potyka	Cardiff University, UK
Nicoletta Fornara	Università della Svizzera Italiana, Switzerland
Ognjen Savkovic	Free University of Bozen-Bolzano, Italy
Patrick Koopmann	Vrije Universiteit Amsterdam, Netherlands
Paul Krause	University of Surrey, UK
Piero Bonatti	University of Naples Federico II, Italy
Rafael Peñaloza	University of Milano-Bicocca, Italy
Rolf Schwitter	Macquarie University, Australia
Roman Kontchakov	Birkbeck, University of London, UK
Sebastian Rudolph	TU Dresden, Germany
Sergio Tessaris	Free University of Bozen - Bolzano, Italy
Sotiris Moschoyiannis	University of Surrey, UK
Stefan Schlobach	Vrije Universiteit Amsterdam, Netherlands
Theresa Swift	Universidade Nova de Lisboa, Portugal
Thom Frühwirth	University of Ulm, Germany
Thomas Lukasiewicz	University of Oxford, UK
Thomas Meyer	University of Cape Town, South Africa
Timotheus Kampik	Umeå University, Sweden
Tomas Kliegr	Prague University of Economics, and Business, Czechia
Umberto Straccia	ISTI-CNR, Italy
Umutcan Serles	University of Innsbruck, Austria

Additional Reviewers

Lucas Larroque	École Normale Supérieure de Paris, France
Sascha Rechenberger	Ulm University, Germany

RuleML+RR 2024 Sponsors

Invited Talks

Neuro-Symbolic AI and Human-Centred Explainability

Alessandra Mileo

Dublin City University, Ireland
alessandra.mileo@dcu.ie

Abstract. Neuro-Symbolic AI is becoming a fast-growing area of research; however, there is still a lot of potential for leveraging neurosymbolic approaches to address the need for explainability and confidence. These are key requirements when it comes to using AI to support human experts in high-stake decision making. In this talk, I will discuss how Deep Representations, Knowledge Graphs, Cognitive Reasoning and Human Experts can be used as key ingredients in the design of a Neuro-Symbolic cycle for human-centred explainability. I will discuss challenges in the design of such a cycle as well as opportunities for the adoption of Neuro-Symbolic AI in real world scenarios.

Keywords: Neuro-symbolic · AI Explainability · Knowledge graphs

Explaining Description Logic Reasoning

Stefan Borgwardt

Institute of Theoretical Computer Science, Technische Universitat Dresden, Germany
`stefan.borgwardt@tu-dresden.de`

While logic-based reasoning is explainable in theory, understanding the explanations often requires expert training and a lot of time. For explaining consequences entailed by description logic ontologies, the main form of explanations are so-called justifications that pinpoint the axioms responsible for an entailment. However, with large justifications or expressive logics, it can be hard to see why the entailment follows from the justification. In recent years, we have studied approaches for computing proofs, which consist of simple steps for explaining an entailment, but may contain many such steps. We investigated different methods of computing proofs that are optimized according to some quality criteria, such as the size of the proof [1–3, 6]. In addition to evaluating these ideas on existing description logic ontologies, we have conducted a series of user studies to find out how to best present proofs to users of description logic ontologies [5]. Moreover, we implemented our algorithms in the Protege plug-in Evee, which can not only explain why an entailment holds, but also why an expected entailment does not follow from the ontology [4].

Acknowledgments. The research reported here was funded by DFG grant 389792660 as part of TRR 248–CPEC, see https://perspicuous-computing.science.

References

1. Alrabbaa, C., Baader, F., Borgwardt, S., Koopmann, P., Kovtunova, A.: Finding small proofs for description logic entailments: Theory and practice. In: LPAR (2020). https://doi.org/10.29007/NHPP
2. Alrabbaa, C., Baader, F., Borgwardt, S., Koopmann, P., Kovtunova, A.: Finding good proofs for description logic entailments using recursive quality measures. In: CADE (2021).https://doi.org/10.1007/978-3-030-79876-5_17
3. Alrabbaa, C., Baader, F., Borgwardt, S., Koopmann, P., Kovtunova, A.: Combining proofs for description logic and concrete domain reasoning. In: RuleML+RR (2023)https://doi.org/10.1007/978-3-031-45072-3_4
4. Alrabbaa, C., Borgwardt, S., Friese, T., Hirsch, A., Knieriemen, N., Koopmann, P., Kovtunova, A., Kruger, A., Popovič, A., Siahaan, I.: Explaining reasoning results for OWL ontologies with Evee. In: KR (2024), to appear.

5. Alrabbaa, C., Borgwardt, S., Hirsch, A., Knieriemen, N., Kovtunova, A., Rothermel, A.M., Wiehr, F.: In the head of the beholder: Comparing different proof representations. In: RuleML+RR (2022). https://doi.org/10.1007/978-3-031-21541-4_14
6. AAlrabbaa, C., Borgwardt, S., Koopmann, P., Kovtunova, A.: Explaining ontology-mediated query answers using proofs over universal models. In: RuleML+RR (2022). https://doi.org/10.1007/978-3-031-21541-4_11

Contents

What's in a Neighborhood? Describing Nodes in RDF Graphs Using Shapes ... 1
   Maxime Jakubowski and Jan Van den Bussche

Using Answer Set Programming for Integrity Maintenance in a Smart
Home System 14
   Mario Wenzel

Collaborative Benchmarking Rule-Reasoners with B-Runner 23
   *Federico Ulliana, Pierre Bisquert, Akira Charoensit, Renaud Colin,
Florent Tornil, and Quentin Yeche*

Rule Confidence Aggregation for Knowledge Graph Completion 32
   *Patrick Betz, Stefan Lüdtke, Christian Meilicke,
and Heiner Stuckenschmidt*

RIFF: Inducing Rules for Fraud Detection from Decision Trees 50
   *Lucas Martins, João Bravo, Ana Sofia Gomes, Carlos Soares,
and Pedro Bizarro*

Ontology-Based Update in Virtual Knowledge Graphs via Schema
Mapping Recovery 59
   Romuald Esdras Wandji and Diego Calvanese

Reevaluation of Inductive Link Prediction 75
   Simon Ott, Christian Meilicke, and Heiner Stuckenschmidt

Judicial Explanations 91
   Cecilia Di Florio and Antonino Rotolo

OntoRaster: Extending VKGs with Raster Data 108
   Arka Ghosh, Albulen Pano, Guohui Xiao, and Diego Calvanese

Complete Approximations of Incomplete Queries 124
   Julien Corman, Werner Nutt, and Ognjen Savković

Reasoning in Rough Description Logics with Multiple Indiscernibility
Relations 142
   Rafael Peñaloza and Anni-Yasmin Turhan

A Benchmark for Rule Induction in Automated Business Decisions 159
   Hagen Völzer, Daniel Horn, Yusik Kim, and Greger Ottosson

Revising Defeasible Theories via Instructions 176
   *Mihai Pomarlan, Maria M. Hedblom, Laura Spillner,
and Robert Porzel*

FaithEL: Strongly TBox Faithful Knowledge Base Embeddings for $\mathcal{EL}$ 191
   Victor Lacerda, Ana Ozaki, and Ricardo Guimarães

RDF Surfaces as a First-Order Language for the Semantic Web 200
   *Dörthe Arndt, Jos De Roo, Patrick Hochstenbach, Rebekka Martens,
Femke Ongenae, and Mathijs van Noort*

Ambiguities in Defeasible Logic: A Computational Efficient Framework
and Algorithm 217
   Guido Governatori and Francesco Olivieri

Legally-Guided Automated Decision-Making System Using Language
Model Agents for Autonomous Driving 234
   *Ya Wang, Daniel Barta, Julian Hesse, Philip Buchwald,
and Adrian Paschke*

Correction to: Legally-Guided Automated Decision-Making System
Using Language Model Agents for Autonomous Driving C1
   *Ya Wang, Daniel Barta, Julian Hesse, Philip Buchwald,
and Adrian Paschke*

Author Index 249

What's in a Neighborhood? Describing Nodes in RDF Graphs Using Shapes

Maxime Jakubowski and Jan Van den Bussche(✉)

Data Science Institute, Universiteit Hasselt, Hasselt, Belgium
jan.vandenbussche@uhasselt.be
https://www.mjakubowski.info, https://vdbuss.github.io/

Abstract. There are several situations where it is desirable to be able to extract a subgraph from an RDF graph, based on a node in the graph, and given a shape that the node conforms to. Such a subgraph can be called a neighborhood. We discuss desiderata for neighborhoods, and compare different possible definitions. We show connections with data provenance and causality. We also show how to obtain provenance polynomials for the shape constraint language SHACL from the work of Dannert and Grädel.

1 Introduction

A lot of data on the Web is present in the form of RDF graphs [1,23]. For our purposes, we can think of an RDF graph simply as an edge-labeled, directed graph [25]. In reality the RDF data model is more general [11]; notably, it does not distinguish between nodes and edge labels.

RDF graphs can be interpreted from two perspectives. One perspective considers an RDF graph to be a description of knowledge: a logical theory. Thereto, appropriate vocabularies have been introduced for representing logical constructs: RDFS for relationships and class hierarchies, and OWL for more expressive description logic formulas [3]. The other perspective is not in opposition to the first, but is more primitive in that it does not really try to interpret the graph. The only interpretation that is still done is that the graph nodes are not only merely abstract (blank nodes) but can also represent concrete data values (literal nodes) or can identify actual resources on the Web (IRI nodes).

Here we are taking this second perspective. In this perspective, RDF is a schemaless data model: unlike in classical data modeling, one does not first design and prescribe a complex schema, and then only considers instances conforming to that schema. Instead, every edge-labeled graph is a potential instance. Of course, there are still many advantages to having a schema, or structural information about the data, even if it is only partial. These advantages are well known and lie in efficiency, usability, data quality, etc.

For this reason, schema languages were soon proposed for RDF graphs, notably, SHACL and ShEx [7,21,23,26]. The emphasis is on *descriptive* rather than *prescriptive* schemas: not the form or structure of the entire data is intended to be prescribed completely, but rather, one describes various *shapes* that can be expected to be present in the data.

Shapes can be thought of as possibly complex conditions on nodes v in a graph: which labels can, or must, appear on edges involving v? Which atomic data types should literal nodes have when they are linked to v? Which further shapes should the neighbors of v satisfy? Indeed, in SHACL, shapes are essentially logic formulas, which are always evaluated on nodes, as in description logics [5,24]. In ShEx, shapes are expressed more in a manner reminiscent of regular expressions and tree automata. In this paper, we will work with the convenient logical formalisation of SHACL started by Corman et al. [10] and extended to full SHACL in our work with Delva and Dimou [14].

We note that a SHACL schema (known as a shapes graph) does not only contain definitions of shapes, but it also allows to pair these shapes to simply node-selecting queries (so-called targets). An RDF graph G is then said to conform to a schema if for each shape–target pair σ–τ, every node v selected by τ in G satisfies σ in G. The task of checking this (known as validation) will be less of a focus in the present paper; we will focus more on shapes in themselves.

2 Neighborhoods

In various situations, it is desirable to be able to extract, from an RDF graph G, a *subgraph* B of G, based on some given node v, and in accordance to some given shape σ. We discuss some of these next.

DESCRIBE Queries. The RDF query language SPARQL has a DESCRIBE query form which, given a node v, returns some RDF graph purporting to describe that node. Such queries are used often in practice (e.g., [8]). The SPARQL standard leaves open how these queries should actually be answered. Yet, most engines return all edges of the graph G in which v is involved, effectively returning a subgraph of G which is often called the *neighborhood* of v. We might denote it by $B^G(v,1)$.

The 1 in the above notation stands for the distance the edges go from v in the graph, which indeed equals one; the B stands for ball, following terminology and notation from metric topology. More generally, for any natural number k, we could define $B^G(v,k)$ to be the subgraph of G consisting of all edges lying on paths of length at most k that contain v.

It seems more useful, however, if we could use a describing shape σ instead of just some distance k, something that has been discussed within the community [27]. The idea would be to have a notion of neighborhood $B^G(v,\sigma)$, defined for any given node v that satisfies σ in graph G. Intuitively, we would like this to be a subgraph of G, containing the relevant edges from G that cause v to satisfy σ, but preferably not more.

As a simple example, suppose σ is the shape "v has at least one outgoing email edge, and at most one outgoing name edge". If v satisfies σ, it seems intuitively clear that $B^G(v,\sigma)$ will need to contain at least one of the email edges emanating from v. Should the neighborhood contain additional edges as well? That is less clear.

Provenance. Beyond giving a semantics to DESCRIBE queries using shapes, neighborhoods can also serve to provide *provenance* for shapes. In databases, many notions of provenance have been considered [9,15]. The common pattern to all approaches is that given a database D, a query Q, and a query result ν, the provenance should explain why ν is indeed a result of Q in D. Our setting clearly matches this pattern, with G, v and σ playing the role of D, ν and Q, respectively.

With this motivation of providing provenance for SHACL, we proposed a concrete definition of neighborhoods in our work with Delva and Dimou [14]. We will indicate that definition by $B_{\text{prov}}^G(v,\sigma)$, to discriminate it from the general idea of neighborhood, and from other concrete proposals.

Knowledge Graph Subsets. Many large knowledge graphs consulted in practice are presented in RDF format and support a SPARQL endpoint. In principle, any desired graph or subgraph, including one's favorite definition of neighborhoods, could be constructed from a large data graph using a SPARQL query. Yet, it may be easier and more natural to extract subgraphs using shapes: given a shape σ, retricve all nodes satisfying σ, together with their neighborhoods.

With this motivation of subset extraction, Labra Gayo and collaborators have proposed another concrete definition of neighborhoods, this time using shapes expressed in ShEx rather than SHACL [20,22].

Shape Fragments. Independently, the same idea of using shapes as a retrieval mechanism was proposed in our above-cited work on provenance for SHACL; we called it *shape fragments* to make the link with the already known mechanism of triple pattern fragments [29]. We proved the following correctness property for B_{prov}: when a graph conforms to a SHACL schema, then so does the shape fragment formed by taking the neighborhoods of all target nodes of all shapes in the schema. Informally speaking, this means that the shape fragment still contains all information that is important for the schema; yet, the fragment can be much smaller than the original graph.

Repairs. When a graph is validated against a schema, a violation report is generated, listing all target nodes that do not satisfy the shape associated to the target. When we are faced with a node v in a graph G that does not satisfy a shape σ, we want an *explanation* of this violation, so that we may repair it in the data. Since v satisfies the negation $\neg\sigma$, the neighborhood $B^G(v,\neg\sigma)$ might serve as such an explanation.

Here, however, we have a problem, since so far we have been thinking of neighborhoods as subsets of the data, consisting of facts (edges) that are present in the data (graph). When dealing with negative conditions, missing facts are equally important for explanations as present facts. For example, let σ be the shape "v has a colleague that is also a friend" (expressible in SHACL, using sh:not and sh:disjoint). When v does not satisfy σ in graph G, this can conceivably be repaired by adding a friend-edge to one of v's colleagues (or vice versa). However, if $B^G(v, \neg\sigma)$ is a subgraph of G, it cannot include such a missing edge. As a matter of fact, B_{prov} is even defined to be just empty for disjointness constraints.

Indeed, a proper notion of repair in databases should contain missing facts as well as present facts [4]. For SHACL, this was pursued by Ahmetaj et al. [2]. They define an explanation[1] of a node v in a graph G for a shape σ to be a minimal pair (A, D), where A is a set of edges missing in G, and D is a set of edges present in G, such that inserting A into G and deleting D from G would cause v to no longer satisfy σ.

This notion of explanation may be considered as an alternative definition for neighborhoods. It differs however in two important aspects from the previous proposals. Not only does it involve negative information, as already discussed; it is also no longer *deterministic*, due to the minimality requirement. For example, continuing the above example, suppose v has exactly two colleagues c_1 and c_2, but no friends. Then each of the two missing friend-edges $v \nrightarrow c_1$ and $v \nrightarrow c_2$ are equally valid minimal explanations for v not having any colleagues that are also friends.

3 Provenance Polynomials

At this point we have seen that several approaches exist to defining exactly what should be in a neighborhood, and there may be others. Is there a unique principled approach? Given the connection to data provenance, we should look at *provenance polynomials*, which are at the heart of most approaches in data provenance [9, 15].

In the context of databases, the provenance polynomial of a result ν of a query Q to a database D is a compact representation of all the proofs why ν indeed belongs to $Q(D)$. Provenance polynomials were first considered for queries expressed in positive-existential first-order logic [17]; later they were extended to full first-order logic [16, 28].

Since SHACL (without recursion) can be translated into first-order logic, in principle, we could use this to obtain provenance polynomials for SHACL. However, given the affinity of SHACL to description logic, here we adopt the provenance polynomials developed by Dannert and Grädel for modal logics, guarded logics, and description logics [12, 13].

To see how this works, we must recall the formalisation of SHACL as a logic, already mentioned in the Introduction. We make a few simplifications for what follows. We omit inverse properties and property paths. We also omit the

---

[1] They actually define explanations for non-satisfaction, but we present the same idea for satisfaction, so as to fit our story better. For logics closed under negation, as indeed SHACL is, this makes no difference.

constraints sh:lessThan, sh:lessThanEq, and sh:uniqueLang. We omit recursion (which has no standardized meaning) and therefore can also omit shape names and the sh:hasShape constraint.

Under the above simplifications, the syntax of *shapes* ϕ is then given by the following grammar:

$$\phi ::= \top \mid \bot \mid \mathit{hasValue}(c) \mid \mathit{test}(t) \mid \mathit{eq}(p,r) \mid \mathit{disj}(p,r) \mid \mathit{closed}(P)$$
$$\mid \phi \wedge \phi \mid \phi \vee \phi \mid \neg \phi \mid \geq_k p.\phi \mid \leq_k p.\phi \mid \forall p.\phi$$

Here, c stands for node constants; t for tests; p and r for property names; P for finite sets of property names; and k for natural numbers. By *tests*, we mean any of the tests on single node values that are provided in SHACL, such as typechecking of a literal, regex matching of an IRI, etc.

Shapes are evaluated in RDF graphs; we formalize an RDF graph as a finite set of *edges*, where an edge is a triple of the form (s,p,o), where s and o are nodes and p is a property name. We often abbreviate "RDF graph" to "graph".

Let ϕ be a shape, let G be a graph, and let a be a node in G. Table 1 now gives the definition of when a *satisfies* ϕ in G, denoted by $G, a \models \phi$. The table omits the obvious logical meanings of $\top$ (true), $\bot$ (false), and the boolean connectives (and, or, not). In the table we use the notation $[\![p]\!]^G(a)$ to denote the set $\{b \mid (a, p, b) \in G\}$.

Table 1. Semantics of shapes.

ϕ	$G, a \models \phi$ if:
$\mathit{hasValue}(c)$	$a = c$
$\mathit{test}(t)$	a satisfies t
$\mathit{eq}(p,r)$	the sets $[\![p]\!]^G(a)$ and $[\![r]\!]^G(a)$ are equal
$\mathit{disj}(p,r)$	the sets $[\![p]\!]^G(a)$ and $[\![r]\!]^G(a)$ are disjoint
$\mathit{closed}(P)$	for all triples $(s,p,o) \in G$ with $s = a$ we have $p \in P$
$\geq_k p.\psi$	$\#\{b \in [\![p]\!]^G(a) \mid G, b \models \psi\} \geq k$
$\leq_k p.\psi$	$\#\{b \in [\![p]\!]^G(a) \mid G, b \models \psi\} \leq k$
$\forall p.\psi$	every $b \in [\![p]\!]^G(a)$ satisfies $G, b \models \psi$

We introduce provenance polynomials as multivariate polynomials over the boolean semiring,[2] with edges playing the role of indeterminates. If e is an edge, we will write $[e]$ when it is used as an indeterminate. We will refer to these indeterminates as *provenance tokens* (or simply tokens). To deal with negation, we assume (without loss of generality) that shapes are in negation normal form.

Now, let ϕ be a shape in negation normal form, let G be a graph, and let a be a node in G. Table 2 defines the provenance polynomial $pol(G, a, \phi)$ for

---

[2] The boolean semiring has two elements 0 and 1 with logical or as addition and logical and as multiplication. Note that, since $1 + 1 = 1$, any polynomial p is equal to $p + p$, also $p + p + p$, etc.

the SHACL logical operators. Since these operators are standard in description logics, our definition is in line with the definition given by Dannert and Grädel [12] for the description logic $\mathcal{ALC}$. Their definition is generalized here to deal with counting quantifiers.

Table 2. Definition of provenance polynomials for SHACL logical operators.

ϕ	$pol(G, a, \phi)$
$\top$	1
$\bot$	0
$hasValue(c)$	1 if $a = c$ and 0 otherwise
$\neg hasValue(c)$	0 if $a = c$ and 1 otherwise
$test(t)$	1 if a satisfies t and 0 otherwise
$\neg test(t)$	0 if a satisfies t and 1 otherwise
$\phi_1 \wedge \phi_2$	$pol(G, a, \phi_1) \cdot pol(G, a, \phi_2)$
$\phi_1 \vee \phi_2$	$pol(G, a, \phi_1) + pol(G, a, \phi_2)$
$\forall p.\psi$	$\prod_{b \in \llbracket p \rrbracket^G} [a, p, b] \cdot pol(G, b, \psi)$
$\geq_k p.\psi$	$\sum \{ \prod_{b \in X} [a, p, b] \cdot pol(G, b, \psi) \mid X \subseteq \llbracket p \rrbracket^G(a) \ \& \ \#X = k \}$
$\leq_k p.\psi$	$\prod \{ \sum_{b \in X} [a, p, b] \cdot pol(G, b, \neg\psi) \mid X \subseteq \llbracket p \rrbracket^G(a) \ \& \ \#X = k+1 \}$

Example 1. Consider the shape ϕ expressing "v has at most one author who is not a student":

$$\phi = \leq_1 \text{auth}. \leq_0 \text{rdf:type}.hasValue(\text{stud})$$

Consider graph G:

$$G = \begin{array}{|lll|} \hline c & \text{auth} & a_1 \\ a_1 & \text{rdf:type} & \text{prof} \\ c & \text{auth} & a_2 \\ a_2 & \text{rdf:type} & \text{stud} \\ \hline \end{array}$$

Node c satisfies ϕ in G, since only a_1 is not a student.

To compute $pol(G, c, \phi)$, let $\sigma = hasValue(\text{stud})$ and let $\psi = \leq_0 \text{rdf:type}.\sigma$, so that $\phi = \leq_1 \text{auth}.\psi$. Note that $\neg\psi$ in negation normal form equals $\geq_1 \text{rdf:type}.\sigma$. We calculate:

$$\begin{aligned} pol(G, c, \phi) &= [c, \text{auth}, a_1] \cdot pol(G, a_1, \neg\psi) + [c, \text{auth}, a_2] \cdot pol(G, a_2, \neg\psi) \\ &= [c, \text{auth}, a_1] \cdot [a_1, \text{rdf:type}, \text{prof}] \cdot pol(G, \text{prof}, \sigma) \\ &\quad + [c, \text{auth}, a_2] \cdot [a_2, \text{rdf:type}, \text{stud}] \cdot pol(G, \text{stud}, \sigma) \\ &= [c, \text{auth}, a_1] \cdot [a_1, \text{rdf:type}, \text{prof}] \cdot 0 \\ &\quad + [c, \text{auth}, a_2] \cdot [a_2, \text{rdf:type}, \text{stud}] \cdot 1 \\ &= [c, \text{auth}, a_2] \cdot [a_2, \text{rdf:type}, \text{stud}]. \end{aligned}$$

Recall that the triples in square brackets are provenance tokens.

Now suppose we would add to G a triple (c, auth, a_3), so that c no longer would satisfy ϕ. Then, due to $X = \{a_1, a_3\}$, the above result would be multiplied by 0 and the entire polynomial would become 0. □

The above example illustrates the following fundamental property, which is straightforward to prove formally.

Theorem 1. $G, a \models \phi$ if and only if $pol(G, a, \phi) \neq 0$.

3.1 Neighborhoods from Polynomials

Theorem 1 suggests at least two principled approaches to defining a neighborhood $B^G(a, \phi)$:

All tokens: Simply collect the edges from all tokens in $pol(G, a, \phi)$. We denote this by $B^G_{\mathrm{tok}}(a, \phi)$.
One monomial: Every polynomial is a sum of monomials. Now collect the edges from the tokens in just one of the monomials. We denote this by $B^G_{\mathrm{mon}}(a, \phi)$. This is a non-deterministic approach, since there may be many monomials in a polynomial.

Note that, if $G, a \not\models \phi$, the polynomial is 0, so by both approaches above, the neighborhoods would be empty, which is reasonable since the node does not satisfy the shape describing the neighborhood.

Example 2. In Example 1, there is only one monomial, and we have
$$B^G_{\mathrm{tok}}(a, \phi) = B^G_{\mathrm{mon}}(a, \phi) = \{(c, \mathsf{auth}, a_2), (a_2, \mathsf{rdf{:}type}, \mathsf{stud})\}.$$

For a simple example involving multiple monomials, let ϕ now denote the shape $\geq_1 \mathsf{auth}.\top$, simply expressing that v has at least one author. For the same graph G, we have $pol(G, c, \phi) = [c, \mathsf{auth}, a_1] + [c, \mathsf{auth}, a_2]$, so
$$B^G_{\mathrm{tok}}(c, \phi) = \{(c, \mathsf{auth}, a_1), (c, \mathsf{auth}, a_2)\}.$$

For $B^G_{\mathrm{mon}}(c, \phi))$, there are two possible outcomes, namely the two singletons $\{(c, \mathsf{auth}, a_1)\}$ and $\{(c, \mathsf{auth}, a_2)\}$. □

What with the constraints *eq* and *disj* and their negations? These go beyond description logic-like constraints, in that they independently test the presence or absence of edges in the graph. To deal with them, we must introduce explicit atomic edge formulas of the form $E(e)$, where e is an edge. These formulas do not belong to SHACL but help defining the polynomials. Essentially, the polynomial of $E(e)$ in G equals the token $[e]$ if e is present in G, and equals 0 otherwise.

Moreover, to deal with *disj* and $\neg eq$ we must also introduce *negated* edge formulas and allow negative tokens, of the form $[\bar{e}]$. The polynomial of $\neg E(e)$ equals $[\bar{e}]$ if e is absent from G, and 0 otherwise. This then leads to the definitions in Table 3. One can verify that Theorem 1 continues to hold.

Table 3. Provenance polynomials for *eq*, *disj*, and their negations.

ϕ	$pol(G, a, \phi)$
$E(e)$	$[e]$ if $e \in G$ and 0 otherwise
$\neg E(e)$	$[\bar{e}]$ if $e \notin G$ and 0 otherwise
$eq(p, r)$	$\prod_{b \in [\![p]\!]^{G}(a)} [a, p, b] \cdot pol(G, a, E(a, r, b))$ $\cdot \prod_{b \in [\![r]\!]^{G}(a)} [a, r, b] \cdot pol(G, a, E(a, p, b))$
$disj(p, r)$	$\prod_{b \in [\![p]\!]^{G}(a)} [a, p, b] \cdot pol(G, a, \neg E(a, r, b))$ $\cdot \prod_{b \in [\![r]\!]^{G}(a)} [a, r, b] \cdot pol(G, a, \neg E(a, p, b))$
$\neg disj(p, r)$	$\sum_{b \in [\![p]\!]^{G}(a)} [a, p, b] \cdot pol(G, a, E(a, r, b))$
$\neg eq(p, r)$	$\sum_{b \in [\![p]\!]^{G}(a)} [a, p, b] \cdot pol(G, a, \neg E(a, r, b))$ $+ \sum_{b \in [\![r]\!]^{G}(a)} [a, r, b] \cdot pol(G, a, \neg E(a, p, b))$

Example 3. To illustrate the four new constraints, consider the three graphs in Fig. 1. We have:

$$pol(G_1, a, eq(p, r)) = [a, p, b]^2 [a, r, b]^2$$
$$pol(G_2, a, disj(p, r)) = [a, p, b_1] \overline{[a, r, b_1]} [a, r, b_2] \overline{[a, p, b_2]}$$
$$pol(G_3, a, \neg disj(p, r)) = [a, p, b_2] [a, r, b_2]$$
$$pol(G_3, a, \neg eq(p, r)) = [a, p, b_1] \overline{[a, r, b_1]} + [a, r, b_3] \overline{[a, p, b_3]}$$

□

$$G_1 = \boxed{\begin{array}{ccc} a & p & b \\ a & r & b \end{array}} \qquad G_2 = \boxed{\begin{array}{ccc} a & p & b_1 \\ a & r & b_2 \end{array}} \qquad G_3 = \boxed{\begin{array}{ccc} a & p & b_1 \\ a & p & b_2 \\ a & r & b_2 \\ a & r & b_3 \end{array}}$$

Fig. 1. Graphs used in Example 3.

We may choose to extend the notion of a neighborhood by also allowing *negated edges* $\bar{e}$ to be present, indicating that their absence is important for the satisfaction of the shape. In this case, we can generalize the definitions of B_{tok} and B_{mon}, taking edges from positive tokens as well as negated edges from negated tokens. We refer to such neighborhoods as *3-valued neighborhoods*.

Example 4. In Example 3, for $B_{\text{tok}}^{G_3}(a, \neg eq(p, r))$, we would obtain the 3-valued neighborhood
$$\{(a, p, b_1), \overline{(a, r, b_1)}, (a, r, b_3), \overline{(a, p, b_3)}\}.$$
For 3-valued $B_{\text{mon}}^{G_3}(a, \neg eq(p, r))$ there would be the two possibilities
$$\{(a, p, b_1), \overline{(a, r, b_1)}\} \quad \text{and} \quad \{(a, r, b_3), \overline{(a, p, b_3)}\}.$$

□

For other applications, one may want to insist that a neighborhood really is a subgraph, so consists only of edges present in the graph. In that case we can define variants B_{postok} and B_{posmon} which take only the edges from positive tokens and disregard negative tokens in the polynomial. Interestingly, with one exception, one can verify that the neighborhood definition proposed for provenance for SHACL [14], which we denote here by B_{prov}, coincides with B_{postok}. The only exception is for $disj(p, r)$, for which B_{prov} defines the neighborhood to be empty, while $B^G_{\text{postok}}(a, disj(p, r))$ consists of all p- and r-edges emanating from a in G.

4 Causality

A quite different, purely semantic approach to neighborhoods is through causality. In this realm, the notion of *actual cause* proposed by Halpern and Pearl [19] has been very influential. Adapting their more recent definition [18] to our setting, this amounts to the following. Let $G, a \models \sigma$ as before. A *supercause* for $G, a \models \sigma$ is a set S of positive and negated edges such that all positive edges belong to G; all negated edges are missing from G; and in the graph resulting from G by deleting the positive edges and inserting the negated edges, a no longer satisfies ϕ. Now a *cause* is a minimal supercause.

Example 5. Take $G_2, a \models disj(p, r)$ from Example 3. The set $\{(\overline{a, p, b_2}), (a, r, b_2)\}$ is a supercause but not a cause. Indeed, $\{(\overline{a, p, b_2})\}$ alone is already a cause, since inserting this missing edge would make p and r no longer disjoint at a. Similarly, $\{(\overline{a, r, b_1})\}$ is a cause. The two causes for $G_1, a \models eq(p, r)$ are $\{(a, p, b)\}$ and $\{(a, r, b)\}$ since deleting either of them causes equality to be no longer satisfied. □

Of course, causes are exactly the explanations introduced by Ahmetaj et al. [2] in their work on repairs, already discussed in Sect. 2. It is tempting to use causes as neighborhoods. However, we will see soon that they may violate a fundamental property that we likely want from neighborhoods.

5 Desiderata for Neighborhoods

At this point we understand that there are a variety of possible definitions of precisely what should be in a neighborhood. There is no single best definition, since there are different desiderata one may have about neighborhoods, and these desiderata are not all compatible with each other. We discuss this next, taking some of our work with Bogaerts [6] done in the setting of first-order logic, and adapting it slightly to the SHACL context.

Determinism has been mentioned a number of times already. B_{tok} is deterministic; B_{mon}, and also causes, are not. It depends on the application whether nondeterminism is acceptable. When using neighborhoods as a retrieval mechanism, as discussed in Sect. 2, we probably want determinism.

Sufficiency. One desideratum seems so fundamental that it probably should be a hard requirement: given that v satisfies shape σ in graph G, then $B(G, v, \sigma)$ should be such that v still satisfies σ in $B(G, v, \sigma)$.[3] When a neighborhood definition has this property for all B, v, σ, we call it *sufficient*. This terminology was coined by Glavic [15] in the context of data provenance.

Example 6. Consider G, c and ϕ from Example 1 where we calculated $pol(G, c, \phi)$ showing that

$$B^G_{\text{tok}}(c, \phi) = \{(c, \text{auth}, a_2), (a_2, \text{rdf:type}, \text{stud})\}.$$

We see that c also satisfies ϕ in this neighborhood.

Next let us continue Example 3. From the polynomials given there we obtain:

$$B^{G_1}_{\text{postok}}(a, eq(p, r)) = \{(a, p, b), (a, r, b)\}$$
$$B^{G_2}_{\text{postok}}(a, disj(p, r)) = \{(a, p, b_1), (a, r, b_2)\}$$
$$B^{G_3}_{\text{postok}}(a, \neg disj(p, r)) = \{(a, p, b_2), (a, r, b_2)\}$$
$$B^{G_3}_{\text{postok}}(a, \neg eq(p, r)) = \{(a, p, b_1), (a, r, b_3)\}$$

We again see that a still satisfies the respective constraint in each of the neighborhoods. □

The above example is no coincidence: it can be proven [14] that B_{prov}, which we have seen earlier is almost the same as B_{postok}, is indeed a sufficient provenance definition. Also B_{posmon} can be shown to be sufficient, adapting proof techniques used in the context of first-order logic [6].

Causes (Sect. 4) are typically not sufficient. For a simple example, let σ be the shape $\geq_1 p.\top \wedge \geq_1 r.\top$. Node a satisfies σ in graph $G = \{(a, p, b), (a, r, c)\}$. There are two causes, namely the which node a satisfies in the two singleton subsets of G. In neither of them, a satisfies σ.

Causal Relevance. While a single cause may not provide a sufficient notion of neighborhood, interesting notions can still be obtained based on causality. Indeed, a natural desideratum on neighborhoods can be that it exclusively consists of edges that come from causes (where different edges may come from different causes). We call such edges *causally relevant*. For example, it can be shown [6] that restricting B_{tok} to only causally relevant edges still yields a sufficient notion of neighborhood.

Minimality. Given some set X of desiderata, we may naturally require neighborhoods to be *minimal for X*. Minimality almost always leads to nondeterminism, as there will be typically multiple minimal candidates. For example, just take sufficiency, and the shape $\geq_1 p.\top \vee \geq_1 r.\top$ requiring that v has a p-edge or an r-edge. When v has both, we can keep only one of them and have a minimally sufficient neighborhood.

---

[3] When using 3-valued neighborhoods, we should be careful about what we mean by satisfaction [6].

6 Conclusion

Coming back to our initial motivation for studying neighborhoods in Sect. 2, what, if any, should the standard semantics of DESCRIBE USING a shape be in SPARQL? As there is no "best" definition, it is probably best left unstandardized. Yet, B_{postok} seems to be a very reasonable semantics. When we want something smaller, we can further restrict to causally relevant edges, but, the computational complexity may be high. The computational complexity of finding causes for SHACL shapes is already known to be high [2]. Perhaps, the complexity of finding the causally relevant edges in the provenance polynomial may be lower; this may be a direction for further research.

Computing neighborhoods, especially in the presence of property paths in shapes (which we have omitted here for simplicity) can be a challenge [14]. That also seems to be a good direction for further research.

In this paper, we have worked with SHACL, but neighborhoods for ShEx have already been investigated [20,22]. A comparison between the approaches, in particular comparing nonrecursive ShEx to provenance polynomials for nonrecursive SHACL, would be interesting.

Finally, we mention that RDF is more than just labeled graphs; edge labels can be nodes by themselves. Designing an extension of SHACL that treats properties on equal footing as subjects and objects is another interesting direction for further research.

Acknowledgments. We thank Bart Bogaerts, Thomas Delva, and Anastasia Dimou for fruitful collaborations on the topics discussed in this paper.

References

1. Abiteboul, S., Manolescu, I., Rigaux, P., Rousset, M.C., Senellart, P.: Web Data Management. Cambridge University Press, Cambridge (2012)
2. Ahmetaj, S., David, R., Ortiz, M., Polleres, A., Shehu, B., Simkus, M.: Reasoning about explanations for non-validation in SHACL. In: Bienvenu, M., Lakemeyer, G., et al. (eds.) Proceedings 18th International Conference on Principles of Knowledge Representation and Reasoning, pp. 12–21. IJCAI Organization (2021)
3. Allemang, D., Hendler, J., Gandon, F.: Semantic Web for the Working Ontologist: Effective Modeling for Linked Data, RDFS, and OWL. ACM (2020)
4. Bertossi, L.: Database Repairing and Consistent Query Answering. Synthesis Lectures on Data Management, Springer, Cham (2011)
5. Bogaerts, B., Jakubowski, M., Van den Bussche, J.: SHACL: a description logic in disguise. In: Gottlob, G., Inclezan, D., Maratea, M. (eds.) LPNMR 2022. LNCS, vol. 13416, pp. 75–88. Springer, Cham (2022). https://doi.org/10.1007/978-3-031-15707-3_7
6. Bogaerts, B., Jakubowski, M., Van den Bussche, J.: Postulates for provenance: instance-based provenance for first-order logic. Proc. ACM Manage. Data **2**(2), 95:1–95:16 (2024)

7. Boneva, I., Labra Gayo, J.E., Prud'hommeaux, E.G.: Semantics and validation of shapes schemas for RDF. In: d'Amato, C., et al. (eds.) ISWC 2017. LNCS, vol. 10587, pp. 104–120. Springer, Cham (2017). https://doi.org/10.1007/978-3-319-68288-4_7
8. Buil-Aranda, C., Ugarte, M., et al.: A preliminary investigation into SPARQL query complexity and federation in Bio2RDF. In: Calì, A., Vidal, M.E. (eds.) Proceedings 9th Alberto Mendelzon International Workshop on Foundations of Data Management. CEUR Workshop Proceedings, vol. 1378 (2015)
9. Cheney, J., Chiticariu, L., Tan, W.C.: Provenance in databases: why, how and where. Foundations and Trends in Databases **1**(4), 379–474 (2009)
10. Corman, J., Reutter, J., Savkovic, O.: Semantics and validation of recursive SHACL. In: Vrandecic, D., et al. (eds.) Proceedings 17th International Semantic Web Conference. Lecture Notes in Computer Science, vol. 11136, pp. 318–336. Springer (2018). extended version, technical report KRDB18-01. https://www.inf.unibz.it/krdb/tech-reports/
11. Cyganiak, R., Wood, D., Lanthaler, M.: RDF 1.1 concepts and abstract syntax. W3C Recommendation (2014)
12. Dannert, K.M., Grädel, E.: Provenance analysis: a perspective for description logics? In: Lutz, C., Sattler, U., Tinelli, C., Turhan, A.-Y., Wolter, F. (eds.) Description Logic, Theory Combination, and All That. LNCS, vol. 11560, pp. 266–285. Springer, Cham (2019). https://doi.org/10.1007/978-3-030-22102-7_12
13. Dannert, K.M., Grädel, E.: Semiring provenance for guarded logics. In: Madarász, J., Székely, G. (eds.) Hajnal Andréka and István Németi on Unity of Science. OCL, vol. 19, pp. 53–79. Springer, Cham (2021). https://doi.org/10.1007/978-3-030-64187-0_3
14. Delva, T., Dimou, A., Jakubowski, M., Van den Bussche, J.: Data provenance for SHACL. In: Stoyanovich, J., Teubner, J., et al. (eds.) Proceedings 26th International Conference on Extending Database Technology, pp. 285–297. OpenProceedings.org (2023)
15. Glavic, B.: Data provenance: origins, applications, algorithms, and models. Found. Trends Databases **9**(3–4), 209–441 (2021)
16. Grädel, E., Tannen, V.: Semiring provenance for first-order model checking. arXiv:1712.01980 (2017)
17. Green, T., Karvounarakis, G., Tannen, V.: Provenance semirings. In: Proceedings 26th ACM Symposium on Principles of Database Systems, pp. 31–40. ACM (2007)
18. Halpern, J.: A modification of the Halpern-Pearl definition of causality. In: Yang, Q., Wooldridge, M. (eds.) Proceedings 24th International Joint Conference on Artificial Intelligence, pp. 3022–3033. AAAI Press (2015)
19. Halpern, J., Pearl, J.: Causes and explanations: a structural-model approach. part i: causes. Br. J. Philos. Sci. **56**, 843–887 (2005)
20. Iglesias Préstamo, A., Labra Gayo, J.: Using pregel to create knowledge graphs subsets described by non-recursive shape expressions. In: Ortiz-Rodríguez, F., Villazón-Terrazas, B., et al. (eds.) KGSWC 2023. LNCS, vol. 14382, pp. 120–134. Springer, Cham (2023). https://doi.org/10.1007/978-3-031-47745-4_10
21. Knublauch, H., Kontokostas, D.: Shapes constraint language (SHACL). W3C Recommendation (2017)
22. Labra Gayo, J.: Creating knowledge graph subsets using shape expressions. arXiv:2110.11709 (Oct 2021)
23. Labra Gayo, J., Prud'hommeaux, E., Boneva, I., Kontokostas, D.: Validating RDF Data. Semantics, and Knowledge. Synthesis Lectures on Data. Springer, Cham (2018)

24. Ortiz, M.: A short introduction to SHACL for logicians. In: Hansen, H., Scedrov, A., et al. (eds.) WoLLIC 2023. LNCS, vol. 13923, pp. 19–32. Springer, Cham (2023). https://doi.org/10.1007/978-3-031-39784-4_2
25. Schreiber, G., Raimond, Y.: RDF 1.1 primer. W3C Working Group Note (2014)
26. ShEx—shape expressions. https://shex.io
27. SPARQL 1.2 community group: DESCRIBE using shapes. https://github.com/w3c/sparql-12/issues/39
28. Tannen, V.: Provenance analysis for FOL model checking. ACM SIGLOG News **4**(1), 24–36 (2017)
29. Verborgh, R., Vander Sande, M., Hartig, O., et al.: Triple pattern fragments: a low-cost knowledge graph interface for the web. J. Web Semant. **37–38**, 184–206 (2016)

Using Answer Set Programming for Integrity Maintenance in a Smart Home System

Mario Wenzel(✉)

Martin-Luther-Universität Halle-Wittenberg, Institut für Informatik,
Von-Seckendorff-Platz 1, 06099 Halle (Saale), Germany
mario.wenzel@informatik.uni-halle.de

Abstract. Smart homes are usually programmed using Event-Condition-Action rules, which is problematic for integrity maintenance, as the user needs to know which events may lead to an invalid state, and which actions – depending on the event – to take to repair the system. This paper describes an approach for integrity maintenance in a smart home system using Answer Set Programming.

Using the popular open source home automation platform "Home Assistant" as a framework, we allow users to specify desired integrity constraints for their home in a familiar syntax, i.e. Python Boolean expressions with some special functions.

By rewriting the user's system invariant to goal descriptions and adding ASP rules for planning service calls to change device states where possible, the system tries to restore itself to a desired state, whenever necessary.

Keywords: Answer Set Programming · Integrity Maintenance · Home Automation

1 Introduction

The growing presence of smart devices in homes, often acquired incidentally through routine purchases of modern appliances, has made the "smart home" increasingly relevant for the general population. Despite not needing these smart features, people tend to try them out, purchase other compatible appliances, and create some convenient automations for everyday tasks. Users interact with the system first by integrating the different appliances and then by writing rules about their behaviour. The smart home systems are programmed – by convention and as industry standard – as event-driven systems.

The rules are generally[1] event-condition-action (ECA-rules) rules, often called "automations" or "routines". In the simplest case, a user selects an event

---

[1] Examples include but are not limited to: Amazon Alexa, Apple HomeKit, Google Home, Home Assistant, openHAB, Domoticz, Shelly Smart Control, Tuya Smart, Samsung SmartThings.

(the sun goes down), a condition (the user is at home), and an action (a light gets turned on). When the user comes home after dark, as the sunset event has already happened earlier that day, the routine does not work as expected. They now implement a second routine: coming home (event) when the sun is already down (condition) turns on the light (action). The light also needs to turn off both when the user leaves and when it gets light outside again.

Adding a bedtime routine of turning down the light when their phone or smart watch activates sleep tracking works well in winter. As summer approaches and one day they need to get up early in the morning, the user decides to go to bed before sundown. As the user is sleeping, the sun sets and the lights at home come on and wake the user.

The user continues adding more conditions to their routines and generally wrangle with the state of the light, as they try to enforce a simple invariant: the light should be on if and only if they are at home and it is dark and they are not sleeping. ECA-rules do not lend themselves to enforcing such invariants, as the user 1. needs to specify which events may occur that violate that invariant and 2. needs to specify which actions are needed to achieve a desired state of the smart home system. Not a very smart home after all.

While ECA-rules are a useful tool to *react to events*[2], it is an inadequate tool to maintain complex invariants of the smart home system over time, as it leaves state management and maintenance to the user. Our proposal is to give smart home users an additional tool that allows them to precisely describe complex invariants of their smart home that are automatically maintained by the system. The smart home domain is ideal for goal-oriented reasoning, but we know of no other implementation for actual home automation systems using classical AI techniques.

We have chosen the open source smart home framework "Home Assistant" (HA) as a target for our implementation. Users write invariants as Python expressions using functions they are familiar with, as they are used within HA's template engine already. We normalize some Python-specific constructs, transform the invariant to conjunctive normal form and rewrite the disjunctions to Answer Set Programming (ASP) integrity constraints.[3] Using traditional planning approaches, [3,8] we add rules that describe the state transitions of our smart devices depending on called services (actions), and add the current device states as facts. The models of the answer set program correspond to possible sets of actions to perform in order to restore the smart home system to a valid state.

Section 2 gives a short overview over the HA architecture and useful abstractions. Section 3 recapitulates how ASP integrity constraints are obtained from a system invariant written as a Python expression. Section 4 contains the planning rules for maintaining the invariants and describes the execution of the planned invariant enforcement actions. The implementation of our approach is evaluated in Sect. 5.

---

[2] For example, this author's home automation systems flashes multiple lights when the door of their toddler's bedroom is being opened at night.

[3] We will call the user-supplied expression the "invariant". After translation into a logic program we call it the "integrity constraint".

The main contributions of this paper are the rewriting of a Python expression into integrity constraints, the translation of the HA architecture into ASP rules, and finally an actual implementation to evaluate the approach. The implementation is available at https://github.com/maweki/ha-decl-tk.

2   Home Assistant Architecture

Ignoring some of the intricacies, the fundamental organizational unit in the HA data model is an "entity", representing a controllable or monitorable aspect within the system, such as a light, sensor, or switch. All changes to entities are recorded in the HA database. The "states" table is at the centre of the HA database. The table contains, ignoring some optimisations and normalisations, the "entity", a value (the "state"), a JSON object "attributes" for a set of key-value-pairs containing additional information, and a timestamp for that state change.

While the database contains historic values that are used to present diagrams, statistics, etc., only the most recent state for each entity is the one accessible to the user via interface functions, like `states(entity)`[4], that is also implemented as a predicate `is_state(entity, state)`.

Which states an entity may have depends on its "domain". While sensors can have single strings, timestamps, or numbers as their state (units are stored in attributes), binary sensors, lights, and switches can only be "on" or "off". Buttons have the last timestamp they were pressed at as their state. As an absolute timestamp does not make sense in terms of an integrity constraint, each timestamp state is always internally converted to a time difference in seconds to the current time.

Only atomic values are allowed as sensor states. Complex information is either stored in the attributes or distributed across multiple entities. It is not unusual for devices, collections of entities that together represent a single physical or virtual piece of hardware, to bundle dozens of entities. A device representing a dryer might have sensor entities for estimated finishing time, start time, current power draw, cumulative energy usage, filter durability, a select entity to select the current program, and a switch entity for internal lighting and enabling notification sounds. An entity's domain also determines which service calls it accepts, like "turn on" and "turn off" for lights and switches, "press" for buttons, and none for sensors. Entities can be viewed as state machines and service calls are a way to force a transition between states, usually reflecting the state change in the real world. As the user can also interact with the physical device, the changed entity state is reflected within the home automation system and entities can change states "by themselves" that way without a service call.

While many HA features are "no-code" available through the web-frontend, for many advanced use cases users define "templates" to encode specific mathematical operations, comparisons, or complex logic, for conditions, service data

---

[4] This naming is due to the broad internal usage of the `states` object. The called function returns just a single value.

(for ECA rules), output text (for UI), or derived entity states (both). A template describing the invariant from the introduction may be, given appropriate entities:

```
is_state('light.l', 'on') is
  (is_state('person.usr', 'home') and
  is_state('binary_sensor.dark', 'on') and
  not is_state('sensor.st', 'sleeping'))
```

Problematically, HA (and smart home systems generally) does not have a concept of transactions or consistency that goes outside the boundaries of a single entity. Therefore all state changes have to be viewed in isolation and there is no additional information about valid state transitions within any subset of entities. Each state change of relevant entities has to be reacted to individually.

A system state S is an interpretation for the `is_state` predicate, mapping all entities to a state value. A user-defined invariant c is a quantifier-free formula in predicate logic that should be true with every S and $S \cdot \delta = S'$ after an augmented state value mapping δ (i.e., state change or sequence thereof). We call a state $S \models c$ "consistent". If some δ leads to $S \cdot \delta \not\models c$ then, traditionally, a database system would roll back the transaction (i.e., δ does not happen, returning to S) using the reverse operation $\tilde{\delta}$ with $S \cdot \delta \cdot \tilde{\delta} = S$. But in general, we can not reverse δ as the state changes effected by the integrity maintenance must be consistent with the entity's accepted service calls. The home automation system usually can not un-open a door, or un-rise the sun. This is in contrast to traditional integrity maintenance approaches for database systems where tuple deletion and transaction rollback are always "fair game" [1] for a repair, or the repair is highly manual, interactive, or uses very domain-specific knowledge [2,4,9]. Let r be a set of actions and s be a function that maps sets of actions to a (partial) interpretation for `is_state` after applying these actions. We call such an r with $S \cdot \delta \cdot s(r) \models c$ a "repair".

3 Conversion of User Formulas

As we are limited to specific sets of actions with generally known consequences, a traditional planning approach using Answer Set Programming [3,8] with the goal of not violating the integrity constraint is suitable. The user gives their invariant as a Python expression, while the logic program contains integrity constraints in the form of $\bot$:- $L_1, \ldots, L_n$. The entered expressions are not completely arbitrary, as only the `states` and `is_state` functions are allowed (and only with entity names and state values as constants), and we expect the general comparison operators to only be used between state-values and not between Boolean values. The user should slightly misuse the `is` operator (used for instance equality) for logical equivalence, instead of `==`, and, conversely `is not` instead of `!=`. This gives disjoint sets of operators for "value" comparison and Boolean connectives. Integrity constraints are obtained from the given Python expression with the following three steps:

1. **Normalization:** Python is syntactically very rich. Python expressions need to be normalized in such a way that
    - every comparison is binary. A comparison a == b == c is rewritten to a == b and b == c.
    - is, is not, and if-else only use and and or. a is b is rewritten to a and b or not a and not b, and a if c else b is rewritten to c and a or not c and b.
    - in for set or list containment is not used. a in [e1, e2] is rewritten to a == e1 or a == e2 and only allow containers that are static, i.e., without function calls in their definition. not in is rewritten accordingly.
2. **Conversion:** After normalization,
    - the formula is rewritten to CNF using an algorithm from literature [10] to obtain a formula like (a or b) and (c or d).
    - the disjunctions are rewritten into goal clauses, obtaining a formula (false :- not a and not b) and (false :- not c and not d).
    - the outer conjunction is split into seperate integrity constraints to obtain :- not a and not b. and :- not c and not d.
3. **Defunctionalization:** The integrity constraint may still contain constructs using function calls like not states("light.l1") == states("light.l2") and not states("sensor.temp1") - states("sensor.temp2") > 10.
    - the not is pushed into the comparison to obtain
      states("light.l1") != states("light.l2") and
      states("sensor.temp1") - states("sensor.temp2") <= 10.
    - the is_state predicate is used instead of the states function, introducing and binding fresh variables to retain the original semantics, to get
      is_state("light.l1", V1) and is_state("light.l2", V2) and V1 != V2 and
      is_state("sensor.temp1", V3) and is_state("sensor.temp2", V4) and V3 - V4 <= 10.

This process allows Python expression containing 1. the states function (with string constants as entity names) and constants, 2. arithmetic and Boolean operations and comparisons between them, and 3. constant lists/sets and the inclusion operation as invariants. Disallowed are tuple construction, dictionaries, list/set comprehensions, generator expressions, other function calls, and non-atomic arguments for the allowed functions.

To integrate the invariant maintenance with the HA architecture and taking hints from other integrations that continually monitor and change entity states the following additional entities are created for each user-supplied invariant:

- A binary sensor that returns the state of the invariant, re-evaluating the state whenever the state of a used entity changes.
- A switch that allows the user to enable or disable invariant enforcement. Automations are also switches (though with their own domain), that can be enabled or disabled. The invariant enforcement is active iff the switch is on and the invariant tracking binary sensor is off.

4 ASP Based Planning and Setting Plans in Action

Answer Set Programs are logic programs that are designed to generate answer sets – particular solutions to the problem defined by the program – adhering to the stable model semantics [8]. ASP has a very accessible syntax and is often used as a convenient front-end for SAT [7]. The stable model semantics allows us to generate multiple possible solutions (i.e., repairs). Pragmatically, the answer set solver clingo can readily be used within a HA integration and its optimization feature allows us to weigh different repairs [5] by various criteria.

The planning procedure describes one step of deductive reasoning for each supported domain, encoding the entities' behaviours according to the possible actions (service calls). While sensors allow no actions, lights can be turned on and turned off, and buttons can be pressed:

```
% sensor - no action allowed
:- action(E, _), domain(sensor, E).
% light - turn_on/turn_off allowed
{action(E, turn_off); action(E, turn_on)} :- domain(light, L).
is_state(E, "on") :- domain(light, E), was_state(E, "off"),
  action(E, turn_on).
is_state(E, "off") :- domain(light, E), was_state(E, "on"),
  action(E, turn_off).
% button - press allowed
{action(E, press)} :- domain(button, E).
is_state(E, 0) :- domain(button, E), was_state(E, _),
  action(E, press).
```

Some general behaviour is also encoded: if there is no action for an entity its state does not change, there should not be an action that changes nothing, there should not be two actions affecting the same entity.

```
is_state(E, S) :- not action(E, _), was_state(E, S).
:- is_state(E, S), was_state(E, S), action(E, _).
:- action(E, A1), action(E, A2), A1!=A2.
```

For each entity used in the invariant the following facts are added to the Answer Set Program:

- A fact for its domain.
- A fact for its current state as `was_state`.
- A fact for duration since this entity last changed state.

Together with the converted user formula as integrity constraints, this logic program is passed on to clingo [6][5]. All answer sets contain one or multiple actions that constitute a "repair".

---

[5] As clingo is distributed as a Python package, it is only necessary to add it as a dependency for the integration and HA installs it automatically, when needed.

It is possible that there are multiple answer sets. For example, when a group of lights should track each other's state: `states("light.light1") == states("light.light2") == states("light.light3")`. When one light is manually switched to make it differ from the other two, one of the two repairs is just the reversal of the manual (and presumably desired) change. This is also the repair with the least number of actions. The default optimisation scheme is to maximize for changing the entities that have not changed the longest: `#maximize { C@1 : action(E, _), last_changed(E, C)}`. This is useful in multiple ways: 1. It tries to maintain the recent (manual) changes that violated the invariant, and 2. if the set of actions did not work (e.g., because an entity is unresponsive or behaves otherwise unexpectedly) and the invariant is still violated, for the next "try" other entities are least recently changed, putting them in a kind of queue.

For the best answer set – the selected repair – all derived actions are executed. If everything worked as expected, the invariant tracking binary sensor is now on again and invariant enforcement is suspended. Otherwise, HA will call the invariant enforcement again after 30 s.

Multiple invariants should, if possible, use disjoint sets of non-sensor entities, as there is no global coordination between the invariants. Of course, it is always possible to write them in a single invariant as a conjunction. Though the separate switches for selectively enforcing the invariants may be desired.

5 Conclusion and Future Work

Home automation systems are usually programmed using ECA rules. While this is useful for some kinds of rules, specifically those reacting to events, it is impractical for invariant maintenance. ECA rules are, in some sense, not very "smart". By using traditional planning approaches we can make our smart home system much smarter by automatically selecting actions to attain a desired state.

We allow users to encode their invariants using functions and syntax they are already familiar with. By declaring the invariants, writing complicated and interleaving automations can be avoided. The architecture and domains already defined in Home Assistant allow us to access and change device states without "reinventing the wheel" and preclude any discussion about modelling the smart home system and its components itself. The interfaces for the devices supported by HA already conform to the Home Assistant specification, which gives us a consistent set of services to affect our smart home, independent of device manufacturer.

Since we do not syntactically translate state and state changes into event calculus or some other formalism, it possible for users to add additional rules without also learning about and adhering to said formalism. The predefined rules are clear and obvious for advanced HA users, as we stick to HA's nomenclature when modeling the system's behaviour.

From personal experience the presented approach works quite well for certain cases: a single non-sensor entity tracking the state of a complex condition `(is_state("light.light1", "on") is (states("zone.home") > 0 and is_state("sun.sun", "below_horizon")))` is often needed and easily defined. Similarly, entities (that can be switched manually) synchronizing their states (`states('light.ledstrip') == states('switch.spotlight')`) is a useful application that is not well supported by HA. The case where there are multiple possible repairs (to achieve a lit room, either opening a window shutter during daytime or turning on a light) has yet to be evaluated. One of the open question is, whether a single repair or class of repairs is – from an inhabitant's perspective – consistently more desirable than the other ones and whether the case of multiple substantially different but equally desirable repairs actually exists.

While the project is stable and we are aiming at inclusion into the unofficial community integration repository, there is room for improvement:

- In further work we would like to implement access to attributes and the services that affect them, like light-level for lights, or target temperature for thermostats.
- Which additional costs can be associated with the predefined services? Additional optimisation strategies could be useful on a case by case basis. Opening shutters is more costly in time and mechanical stress than turning lights on, for example.
- Ideally, we would like the planning not to end at the entity-boundary. Neither HA nor our toolkit "knows" the relation of different entities' states, like the temperature inside approaching the temperature outside if the window is open, or the temperature going up if the heating system is engaged. Disregarding including these effects in the planning procedure, how would users even enter these relations and effects in a manner accessible to the layperson with a suitable flexibility?
- Additionally, the engaged heating has a delayed effect. How well does our approach cope with changes that do not happen immediately?
- In HA entities can be organized into "areas" (rooms) and floors and we would like users to be able to access all lights in an area using queries like `domain(light, E)`, `area(kitchen, E)`, or generally use aggregates over multiple entities (as a burglary deterrent, there should always be exactly one light on when nobody is home) but it is unclear what a suitable syntax is and how it could be made accessible to the user.

With the Home Assistant Declarative Toolkit we aim to bring more declarative tools to the home automation field in the future.

References

1. Bertossi, L.E.: Causality in databases: answer-set programs and integrity constraints. In: Olteanu, D., Poblete, B. (eds.) Proceedings of the 12th Alberto Mendelzon International Workshop on Foundations of Data Management, Cali, Colombia, May 21–25, 2018. CEUR Workshop Proceedings, vol. 2100. CEUR-WS.org (2018). https://ceur-ws.org/Vol-2100/paper7.pdf

2. Ceri, S., Widom, J.: Deriving production rules for constraint maintainance. In: McLeod, D., Sacks-Davis, R., Schek, H. (eds.) 16th International Conference on Very Large Data Bases, August 13–16, 1990, Brisbane, Queensland, Australia, Proceedings, pp. 566–577. Morgan Kaufmann (1990). http://www.vldb.org/conf/1990/P566.PDF
3. Dimopoulos, Y., Nebel, B., Koehler, J.: Encoding planning problems in nonmonotonic logic programs. In: Steel, S., Alami, R. (eds.) ECP 1997. LNCS, vol. 1348, pp. 169–181. Springer, Heidelberg (1997). https://doi.org/10.1007/3-540-63912-8_84
4. Fraternali, P., Paraboschi, S., Tanca, L.: Automatic rule generation for constraint enforcement in active databases. In: Lipeck, U.W., Thalheim, B. (eds.) Modelling Database Dynamics. Workshops in Computing, pp. 153–173. Springer, London (1992). https://doi.org/10.1007/978-1-4471-3554-8_10
5. Gebser, M., Kaminski, R., Kaufmann, B., Schaub, T.: Clingo = ASP + control: Preliminary report. CoRR **abs/1405.3694** (2014). http://arxiv.org/abs/1405.3694
6. Gebser, M., Kaminski, R., Kaufmann, B., Schaub, T.: Multi-shot ASP solving with clingo. Theory Pract. Log. Program. **19**(1), 27–82 (2019). https://doi.org/10.1017/S1471068418000054
7. Lierler, Y.: What is answer set programming to propositional satisfiability. Constraints An Int. J. **22**(3), 307–337 (2017). https://doi.org/10.1007/S10601-016-9257-7
8. Lifschitz, V.: Answer Set Programming. Springer, Cham (2019). https://doi.org/10.1007/978-3-030-24658-7
9. Moerkotte, G., Lockemann, P.C.: Reactive consistency control in deductive databases. ACM Trans. Database Syst. **16**(4), 670–702 (1991). https://doi.org/10.1145/115302.115298
10. Russell, S.J., Norvig, P.: Artificial Intelligence - A Modern Approach, Third International Edition. Pearson Education (2010). http://vig.pearsoned.com/store/product/1,1207,store-12521_isbn-0136042597,00.html

Collaborative Benchmarking Rule-Reasoners with B-Runner

Federico Ulliana[1]($^{\boxtimes}$), Pierre Bisquert[2], Akira Charoensit[1], Renaud Colin[2], Florent Tornil[1], and Quentin Yeche[2]

[1] Inria, LIRMM, Univ Montpellier, CNRS, Montpellier, France
`{federico.ulliana,akira.charoensit,florent.tornil}@inria.fr`
[2] INRAE, Montpellier, France
`{pierre.bisquert,renaud.colin,quentin.yeche}@inrae.fr`

Abstract. Conducting experimental analysis on rule reasoners is a mainstream task for validating novel algorithms and systems. Nevertheless, providing robust, verifiable, and reproducible experiments can still raise a sensible challenge. This paper introduces B-Runner, an open library for *collaborative benchmarking* focusing on the deployment of extended tests for *knowledge and rule-based systems* with low cost and high robustness. B-Runner reduces the benchmarking setup time while guaranteeing experiment repeatability. Also, it improves the scrutability of experimental protocols thereby enhancing the fairness of system comparisons.

1 The Benchmarking Issue

Scientific experiments are essential for validating and improving systems, but they come with numerous challenges. These can be classified depending on whether they are related to planning, reporting, or conducting experiments.

Planning consists in writing down all design choices for the experiments. Notably, the benchmarks to use, the competitors to consider, the testing environment (hardware/software) and the target measures.

Reporting includes retrieving and analyzing the results, then choosing the most meaningful data as well as the most informative and succinct graphical representations.

Conducting consists in faithfully implementing what has been planned. This includes setting up the test environment, coding (and verifying) the experimental protocols, and then running the tests while handling potential failures.

While all phases of experimental analysis can cause issues, the experiment conduction is perhaps the least accessible part. Accessibility here is intended as the *time and effort it takes a user to conduct a robust experimental analysis*. Of course, with high accessibility experimental analysis can be deeper, which directly translates to more thoughtful validation of novel approaches.

Conducting is also intimately related to *repeatability*. Repeatability means that another user equipped with the appropriate software and hardware can repeat the same experiments [14]. Repeatability is easily attained when experiment conduction is simple, reliable, and documented. Conversely, it may be a burden to prepare a test suite and write sophisticated instructions on how to configure and run a benchmark starting from ad-hoc scripts, not to mention debugging them to make them portable on different systems. Experiment repeatability has become increasingly relevant during the last decades. Nowadays many conferences have established reproducibility[1] tracks.

Independent vs Collaborative Benchmarking

In this work, we argue that the underlying issue with benchmarking conduction and repeatability lies in the lack of a platform for *collaborative benchmarking*. Indeed, the most common benchmarking scenario is one where activities are conducted *independently*, which in practice results in a plethora of hard-to-maintain scripts and ad hoc methods for running tests. While this consideration may apply to many fields, we emphasize that our focus is on the case of benchmarking *knowledge and rule-based reasoners* for which we introduce a dedicated library.

Independent Benchmarking. Figure 1.a) illustrates a set of users (here A, B, C) conducting an experimental analysis to understand the performances of a given reasoning system (which may or may not have been coded by one of the users). The system supports multiple query answering (QA) tasks on a knowledge base. In particular, users B and C want to test the performances of QA via query rewriting while user A is interested in the performances of QA via the chase.

Let us explain this scenario in detail. A knowledge base (KB) is composed of a *factbase* and a set of *rules* modelling semantic constraints on the data (ontologies, data-dependencies, etc.) used to both enrich it and ensure its consistency [15]. The reasoner can be commanded through an API. The API also offers a number of basic features. For instance, *loading* and *building* the knowledge base starting from plain data and/or data-integration mappings [10]. But also, using a certain type of internal *storage* for the data (graph, relational, triplestore, in-memory/disk, etc.). And, finally, being able to *evaluate* queries on a factbase (without considering the rules). The API also includes a number of advanced features. These includes techniques which accounts for rules using *saturation* (also called *chase*) and *query rewriting*. The chase approach essentially consists at extending the factbase with the result of the application of rules [6]. Query rewriting in contrast compiles the rules into the input query thereby yielding a *reformulated* query which provides the same answers (as the input rules and query) on any database [9]. Query answering via the chase consists in evaluating the input query on the saturated knowledge base. Query answering via rewriting consists in evaluating the reformulated query on the input data.[2]

---

[1] reproducibility is stricter than repeatability: not only it ensures that the experiment can be re-run, but that it also yields the same result.

[2] To illustrate, consider the factbase $F = \{P(a)\}$, the rule $\forall x.P(x) \rightarrow R(x)$, and the boolean query $Q = \exists y.R(y)$. The chase yields $\{P(a), R(a)\}$ where Q answers true. Query rewriting yields reformulation $\exists y.R(y) \vee P(y)$ answering true on F.

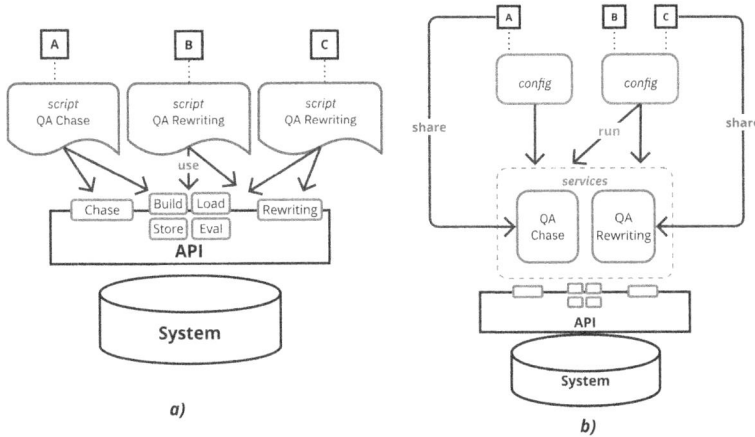

Fig. 1. Benchmarking: *a)* Independent vs *b)* Collaborative.

As Fig. 1.a) shows, to conduct the test, every user writes a script coding an experimental protocol by leveraging on the API. Typically, this is done *from scratch*. Firstly, this is *time consuming*, as it requires learning the API and internals of the system as well as coding the measurements for the API calls. Secondly, this is *error prone*. Indeed, since scripts are *independently* written, for more complex tests it is not uncommon for the test protocols to even diverge, at the point measuring different operations.[3] All of this makes that setting up an experiment can have a significant cost and compromised robustness, resulting in low accessibility.

Collaborative Benchmarking. A principled solution to this issue is to provide users with a platform for collaborative-benchmarking, which simplifies the conduction of extended test trials. Collaborative benchmarking captures the idea that robust and repeatable experimental analysis can be achieved if *a community of users work together* on *i)* consolidating a set of *test protocols* which *ii)* can run on a *reliable framework* and *iii)* without *unnecessary complexity* at the user level. Figure 1.b) illustrates the case for collaborative benchmarking. Again, we consider users *B* and *C* testing QA via rewriting and user *A* testing QA via the chase. The first characteristic of this approach is that it allows users to share *benchmarkable services* (or simply services) coded in a common programming language, which very much improves protocol readability. Every such service implements a self-contained *testing protocol* which allows one to measure the performances (time, throughput, etc.) of a certain task. This test protocol is meant to be deployed on a variety of input scenarios and algorithm configurations - and not on a single one. By definition, sharing test implementations can benefit from code reviews in a collaborative environment, thus increasing

---

[3] typical errors are including/omitting optimizations and/or parsing time, writing on disk or standard output (logging, result export), improper cold/warm measures [14].

the robustness of the experimental analysis and avoiding the divergence of testing protocols. Figure 1.b) illustrates user A sharing a service for running QA via the chase, while user C shares a service for QA via rewriting. By fostering test reuse, user B can perform an experimental analysis without coding by reusing the service shared by C. This results in significant time savings. Besides test sharing, another key characteristic of this approach is that test trials are specified by users via *configurations*. This makes the specification of test trials more *declarative* than programmatic, and hence independent from any programming languages. In this aspect, collaborative benchmarking is strongly opposed to independent benchmarking, the latter allowing each script to be potentially written in a different language. Crucially, configuration files can also be shared, as illustrated for users B and C. Not only does this save time, but it allows users to *communicate* and *document* the content and aim of their experiments in a more standard and intelligible way.

1.1 Novelty and Contributions

We introduce B-Runner: *a Java tool for collaborative benchmarking on knowledge and rule-based reasoners.* The distinctive elements of the tool are the following.

1) Collaborative B-Runner allows users to share and reuse experimental protocols and test configurations. The notion of collaborative benchmarking has been little regarded for rule-based reasoners. To the best of our knowledge, B-Runner is the first attempt to systematize this approach for rule-based reasoners.

2) Simple and Robust B-Runner allows to define trial specifications through declarative configurations which require minimal coding and learning of test systems. B-Runner proposes a design pattern for writing test protocols that favors their scrutability. The execution of tests is controlled via the Java Microbenchmarking Harness (JMH) library. This favors converging towards robust error-free testing protocols and measures.

3) Extensible and Portable. B-Runner's generic architecture allows to easily include novel systems and testing protocols. B-Runner is Java-based, which makes it portable, yet still able to support benchmarking of non-Java systems.

1.2 User Groups and Paper Organization

B-Runner can be used by two types of users: *testers* and *providers*. Testers define experiments from available services using configuration files (for instance, user B in Fig. 1.b). Providers share benchmarking services (for instance, users A and C in Fig. 1.b that share services for testing respectively QA chase and QA rewriting). In the remainder of this paper, Sect. 2 presents how a tester can declare a benchmarking activity through a configuration file. Section 3 shows the provider side of offering a benchmarking protocol. Section 4 delves into features and limits of B-Runner.

2 Benchmarking in a Hurry!

The first key feature of B-Runner is the possibility of doing benchmarking at small cost for *tester* users. Let us define the benchmarking activities we consider. A benchmarking activity B is a sequence of service executions $B = (e_1, \ldots, e_k)$. Every service execution is a triple $e = (s, c, r)$ where s is a service, c is a configuration for the service, and r the repetition parameters. A configuration $c = (n, a, d)$ is a combination of an execution environment n on top of which the service s is executed by taking as input an algorithm configuration a and an input scenario d. The repetition parameter is a pair $r = (f, i)$ where f is the number of forks and i the number of the iterations for the execution of s given c.

```
#      Reasoner
reasoner = integraal

#      Scenarios (fixed rules and queries)
### 10M data
scenario.s10M.data          = data10.dlgp
scenario.s10M.rules         = ontology.dlgp
scenario.s10M.workload      = queries.dlgp

### 100M data
scenario.s100M.data         = data100.dlgp
scenario.s100M.rules        = ontology.dlgp
scenario.s100M.workload     = queries.dlgp

#      Algorithms
### chase (in-memory)
tool.inmem_chase.service    = QAChase
tool.inmem_chase.dbType     = inMemoryGraphStore
tool.inmem_chase.checker    = semiOblivious

### rewriting (postgres)
tool.postgres_rew.service   = QARewriting
tool.postgres_rew.driver    = postgreSQL
tool.postgres_rew.driverURL = jdbc:postgresql://...

#      Environment
execution.basic_env.maxMemory  = 16g
execution.basic_env.timeout    = 10m
execution.basic_env.fork       = 2
execution.basic_env.iterations = 3

#      Export
export = json
```

Fig. 2. Trial Configuration Example

Figure 2 illustrates a benchmarking activity made of four service executions (with their corresponding configurations and repetitions parameters). The goal of a *fork* is twofold. Firstly, it creates a "cold" execution environment. Secondly, it sets up the reasoning system for running a number of repetitions (of the same service). An *iteration* takes places within a fork, and consists in the actual execution of the service itself. It is worth pointing out that every fork in B-Runner triggers the creation of a new Java Virtual Machine (JVM) where the test runs. More specifically, this is accomplished by leveraging on Java Microbenchmark Harness (JMH), and happens to be useful to eliminate measure bias (due to cache, Just-In-Time compilation, etc.).

Figure 2 shows a configuration written by a tester and inspired by the example given in the introduction (Fig. 1). The syntax represents a collection of properties which stands as a notation for *trees*.[4] In the example, reserved keywords for B-Runner are highlighted in blue. As indicated by line 2, the configuration applies to the InteGraal reasoner [3]. Keywords proper to the configuration of the reasoner are highlighted in red. The configuration then continues with the specification of two test scenarios "s10M" (lines 6–8) and "s100M" (lines 11–13). To declare different datasets, we use the reserved keyword `scenario`. Both scenarios consider the same ontology-rules and queries but differ in terms of data.[5] Then, two different algorithmic strategies for query answering are used. This is done with properties prefixed by the keyword `tool`. The first is via the chase procedure (line 17). Note also that the data is stored in a native InteGraal in-memory graph store (line 18) and that a specific variant of the chase, called *semi-oblivious* [7] is chosen (line 19). Similarly, a second strategy based on rewriting is defined (line 22). In this case, note that the data is stored on a (local or remote) PosgtreSQL server (line 23) which is accessible via the given connection URL (line 24). These options illustrate the richness and simplicity of the algorithm configuration that can be achieved. Finally, the execution environment for the tests is set. This is done to properties prefixed by the keyword `execution`. Options include setting the maximum JVM size to 16GB (line 27), setting the timeout for the execution of a *single* iteration to 10 min (line 28), and the number of forks and repetitions (lines 29–30). The last command (line 33) exports the results in JSON.

From this specification file, B-Runner automatically conducts a benchmarking activity on a sequence of configurations generated by combining *every* input scenario with *every* algorithm and *every* environment configuration. The resulting benchmarking activity is illustrated in Fig. 2. Note that selective test execution (useful for example to restart failures) is also possible in B-Runner [1].

3 Sharing a New Benchmarkable Service

The second distinctive feature of B-Runner is the possibility of sharing new testing protocol for *provider* users. In contrast to configuration files, protocols must be *programmatically written*. B-Runner adopts Java, yet the methodology we present here is transposable to other programming languages.

In a nutshell, B-Runner proposes a design pattern for implementing protocols which aims at making a *service equivalent to an array of method references*. Below, we present a testing protocol for query answering via query rewriting, which measures time for each step of the task. Let us present the B-Runner API for specifying new testing protocols. (1) A new protocol can be specified by simply implementing the `serviceOperations` method. (2) In turn, this uses two methods for specifying the test steps: `setup` and `operation`. The method

---

[4] To illustrate, lines 6–8 of Fig. 2 can be written in JSON as the record {scenario: {s10M: {data:data10.dlgp, rule:ontology.dlgp, workload:queries.dlgp}}}.
[5] In the example, the .dlgp extension stands for the Datalog-Plus language [4].

`setup` corresponds to a step that has to be performed *for every fork*. The method `operation` corresponds to a step that has to be performed *for every iteration*.

```
public void serviceOperations() {

  setup(DATA_LOADING,     this::setData);
  setup(RULE_LOADING,     this::setRules);

  operation(QUERY_LOADING,    this::setQuery);
  operation(BUILD_REWRITER,   this::buildRewriter);
  operation(QUERY_REWRITING,  this::rewrite);

  operation(BUILD_EVALUATOR,  this::buildEvaluator);
  operation(QUERY_EVALUATION, this::evalRewriting);
}
```

As the example illustrates, typical examples of setup steps include the loading of the scenario, notably data and rules which are considered fixed (lines 3–4). Then, operation steps include creating objects and executing query rewriting (lines 6–8), followed by evaluation (lines 10–11). Note that describing a step via `setup` and `operation` systematically requires two inputs. The first is a description of the step, which is mandatory to associate a measure to an operation. The second is a *method reference* (e.g., `this::setData` refers to the `setData` method of the class implementing the protocol). Each method includes a compound block of instructions. As already said, the goal of this design pattern is to see a protocol as an array of method references. As a side effect, this results in code which is free from ad-hoc timers for measuring (as this code can be factorized).

We understand that this discussion mostly concerns engineering aspects of the tool, but we believe them to be critical to be able to share intelligible protocols. For space reasons, we refer to [1] for more details on B-Runner architecture.

4 Effective Experiment Conduction

We conclude by discussing two key aspects: outputs and limitations of the tool.

Interpreting Benchmark Results. The goal of benchmarking is to yield data to be analyzed. B-Runner provides results in a structured format (XML or JSON) which suit routines for data aggregation. Monitoring test execution must also not be underestimated as tests can take a long time and/or fail. Benchmarking progress as well as errors are visible via logging and exported results [1].

Recognizing and Overcoming Limitations. While B-Runner provides a flexible and extensible setting to automate testing scenarios, it also has some limitations. We will discuss how to circumvent some points that mainly pertain to the use of Java.

Monitoring Memory. This is a feature that B-Runner does not currently handle but which is planned for future releases. The strategy we pursue consists in using the JMH library facilities to plug a profiler for reporting custom metrics.

The API Wall. The measurement possibilities depend on the granularity of the methods exposed by the API of the tested system. B-Runner integrates seamlessly with Java APIs but it can still be used for tools implemented in other languages either via Java Native Interface (JNI) or system calls.

Comparing Versions. Comparing the performance of a tool to one of its previously published versions may raise a conflict of Java dependencies. To avoid this, two separate executions of the benchmarking activity are required (see [1]).

5 Related Work

Collaborative benchmarking has been little regarded for rule-based reasoning. The closest work to ours is [2] which provides an API and an implementation for testing Java reasoners inspired by the OpenRuleBench benchmark [11]. However, our system differs by proposing a more general and scalable architecture, which introduces a methodology for writing and sharing configurations and test protocols, as well as the use of JMH for controllable experiment conduction. Collaborative benchmarking is important in the context of *scientific workflows* [8]. These have been introduced for the reproducibility and automation of large scale scientific computations in domains such as genomics, biology, and astronomy [5]. These are expressed as a directed graph whose nodes are computations and edges dependencies. Research work in this area concerns the design of languages for workflow specification, as well as the reproducibility of experiments (or part of experiments) involving large data masses. The optimization of scheduling computations across distributed and cloud platforms has also been considered, with the goal to obtain results faster and with less cloud computation [12,13].

6 Conclusion and Outline

Principled benchmarking paradigms can be instrumental to perform robust experimental analysis at small cost. In particular, we advocate for the development of collaborative benchmarking for knowledge and rule-based reasoners. As an answer to this need, we introduced B-Runner, an open library for testing rule-based reasoners. B-Runner leverages on Java Microbenchmarking Harnessing (JMH) for experiment conduction. B-Runner is Java-based, which makes it portable, yet still able to support non-Java systems.

Our library implements an architecture for collaborative benchmarking which is service-oriented and configuration-driven. We argue that sharing reusable services dramatically reduces experiment setup thereby increasing their reproducibility. More generally, this provides testing accessibility to larger audiences. Also, making test protocols transparent through a simple yet well-defined design pattern enhances their robustness and scrutability. Crucially, this can contribute to increase the fairness of comparisons when these span across different tools. Using a configuration-based approach, as opposed to scripting, constitutes a simple way to plan extended benchmarking activities, which also improves readability. Finally, note that while B-Runner focuses on reasoning systems, the principles it implements can be applied to a larger extent.

B-Runner is available online [1]. The tool supports a number of reasoners and is currently under active development. Future work also involves the creation of a library for automatic chart creation from trial results.

References

1. B-runner repository (2024). https://gitlab.inria.fr/rules/brunner
2. Angele, K., Angele, J., Simsek, U., Fensel, D.: RUBEN: a rule engine benchmarking framework. In: Rule Challenge @ RuleML+RR 2022 (2022)
3. Baget, J.F., et al.: InteGraal: a tool for data-integration and reasoning on heterogeneous and federated sources. In: BDA 2023. Montpellier, France (2023)
4. Baget, J., Gutierrez, A., Leclère, M., Mugnier, M., Rocher, S., Sipieter, C.: Datalog+: formats and translations for existential rules. In: RuleML (2015)
5. Barker, A., van Hemert, J.: Scientific workflow: a survey and research directions. In: Wyrzykowski, R., Dongarra, J., Karczewski, K., Wasniewski, J. (eds.) PPAM 2007. LNCS, vol. 4967, pp. 746–753. Springer, Heidelberg (2008). https://doi.org/10.1007/978-3-540-68111-3_78
6. Beeri, C., Vardi, M.Y.: A proof procedure for data dependencies. J. ACM (1984)
7. Benedikt, M., et al.: Benchmarking the chase. In: PODS (2017)
8. Cohen-Boulakia, S., et al.: Scientific workflows for computational reproducibility in the life sciences: status, challenges and opportunities. Futur. Gener. Comput. Syst. **75**, 284–298 (2017)
9. König, M., Leclère, M., Mugnier, M., Thomazo, M.: Sound, complete and minimal UCQ-rewriting for existential rules. Semantic Web **6**(5), 451–475 (2015)
10. Lenzerini, M.: Data integration: a theoretical perspective. In: PODS (2002)
11. Liang, S., Fodor, P., Wan, H., Kifer, M.: Openrulebench: an analysis of the performance of rule engines. In: WWW (2009)
12. Liew, C.S., Atkinson, M.P., Galea, M., Ang, T.F., Martin, P., Hemert, J.I.V.: Scientific workflows: moving across paradigms. ACM Comput. Surv. (2016)
13. Liu, J., Lu, S., Che, D.: A survey of modern scientific workflow scheduling algorithms and systems in the era of big data. In: 2020 IEEE International Conference on Services Computing (SCC), pp. 132–141. IEEE (2020)
14. Manegold, S., Manolescu, I.: Performance evaluation in database research: principles and experience. In: EDBT (2009)
15. Mugnier, M., Thomazo, M.: An introduction to ontology-based query answering with existential rules. In: RR Summer School (2014)

Rule Confidence Aggregation for Knowledge Graph Completion

Patrick Betz[1(✉)], Stefan Lüdtke[2], Christian Meilicke[1], and Heiner Stuckenschmidt[1]

[1] University of Mannheim, Mannheim, Germany
{patrick,christian,heiner}@informatik.uni-mannheim.de
[2] University of Rostock, Rostock, Germany
stefan.luedtke@uni-rostock.de

Abstract. Rule learning approaches for knowledge graph completion are efficient, interpretable and competitive to purely neural models. The rule confidence aggregation problem aims to find a single plausibility score for a candidate fact predicted by multiple rules. Despite its ubiquity due to noisy and large rule sets from data-driven learning, the problem is underrepresented in the literature and lacks a theoretical foundation. In this work, we demonstrate that existing aggregation approaches can be expressed as marginal inference operations over the predicting rules. In particular, we show that the common Max-aggregation strategy, which scores candidates based on the rule with the highest confidence, has a probabilistic interpretation. Finally, we propose an efficient and overlooked baseline that is slightly superior over the simple strategies.

1 Introduction

Knowledge Graphs (KGs) describe certain domains by *relation(subject, object)* facts. Most of the real-world KGs are incomplete and only contain a fraction of the true facts in the respective domain. The problem of knowledge graph completion (KGC) aims to derive the missing facts by using the information in the existing graph [27,28].

The proposed model classes in the literature for KGC are data-driven. For instance, a model might learn the regularity that people which appear in movies tend to be actors and can use it to make new predictions. Although the dominating paradigm in the literature lies on models based on latent representation, a KG is symbolic in its nature. Symbolic approaches for KGC learn human readable rules from the KG and their predictions are therefore inherently interpretable. They are shown to be competitive to latent based approaches [27] and can achieve state-of-the-art results on large graphs [14]. To perform KGC with a symbolic approach, a previously learned set of rules has to be applied to the KG to derive plausibility scores for unseen target facts. Whenever multiple rules predict a candidate fact, the question arises of how to aggregate individual rule confidences, as demonstrated in the following running example.

Example 1. *Let locIn denote the relation locatedIn. Consider the following clauses or rules.*

c_1 [0.64] : *worksFor(X,Y)* ← *internAt(X,Y)*
c_2 [0.44] : *worksFor(X,Y)* ← *studentAt(X,A), locIn(A,B), locIn(Y,B)*
c_3 [0.41] : *worksFor(X,Y)* ← *studentAt(X,A), cooperatesWith(A,Y)*

The numbers in brackets denote the standard rule confidences, i.e., the proportion of correct predictions on a training KG [8]. The first and third rule are quite intuitive. The second rule expresses that a person might work for a company if that company is located at the same place where this person went to university. Now assume that all three rules predict Anna to work for Google. The confidence aggregation problem is concerned with finding a final score derived from the three confidence values. The aggregation will also reflect if, e.g., Anna is more likely to work for Google than a person for which only the first two rules made the prediction.

While combining logical reasoning and probabilistic uncertainty is a fundamental aspect of statistical relational learning [1,11,25], the aggregation problem is often not expressed explicitly. Additionally, these approaches perform model theoretic entailment, which is too expensive in our settings. KGs can consist of a large number of facts with millions of learned rules. Similarly, in the field of association rule mining, rule quality is often estimated for individual rules independently without considering the problem of aggregation [3,6,8,20].

The predictive quality of a mined rule set depends to a large extend on the aggregation decision and surprisingly there exists a theoretical and empirical gap in the recent KGC literature between techniques to learn rules and their successful application. To the best of our knowledge, there only exist few works which are primarily concerned with the aggregation problem for KGC [2,21,22]. While they improve upon simple strategies, the theoretical foundations are not discussed.

In this work, we close this gap and develop the formal foundations of the problem. We present a probabilistic model in which the aggregation reduces to performing marginal inference over a joint distribution of the rules (Sects. 4.1–4.3). We show that the common Max-aggregation strategy can exactly be recovered from this model when the correlation of the rule variables is assumed to be maximal: If the correlation matrix is set to the upper Fréchet-Hoeffding bound for the correlation of two random variables, then target inference is equivalent to Max-aggregation (Sect. 4.4).

We also establish the connection to performing inference under model-theoretic entailment. We demonstrate that, when considering large rule sets and KGs, the problem is more intricate than simply being solved by using full reasoning (Sect. 4.5).

Finally, we investigate a simple aggregation baseline, Noisy-or top-h, which can be understood as a mixture of the simple aggregation functions (Sects. 4.6–5) and is slightly superior over the simple strategies.[1]

2 Related Work

Rule mining approaches learn datalog rules from a KG. In the context of association rule mining, AMIE [8] and the respective improved versions AMIE+ [7] and AMIE3 [12] show how to mine rules when data is incomplete. AnyBURL [15] is the successor of RuleN [16]. It is shown to be competitive to neural approaches regarding predictive performance and runtime [14,27]. Evoda learns rules based on genetic programming [34]. Other approaches are tailored towards large graphs [3,6] or to learn negative rules [20]. There also exist attempts to improve rule quality by providing more advanced confidence computations [8,24]. The rule quality is evaluated by calculating the precision of the individual rules independent from the remaining rules on a gold standard KG. In this work, we regard rule quality from the viewpoint of the predictions made by all of the rules, which allows comparisons to other model classes such as neural models.

The combination of logic and uncertainty has a rich history in the statistical relational learning literature. For instance, Stochastic Logic Programs [1,31] and Bayesian Logic Programs (BLP) [11] augment inductive logic programming [18] with probability. Rules are represented as conditional probabilities and a joint probability distribution is modelled over the least Herbrand base of an underlying logic program. Here, the aggregation problem becomes explicit. In particular, when multiple conditionals have the same effect variable, they are collapsed into one by the use of a *combining rule*. Nevertheless, this heuristic is applied on top of the formal framework whereas we model the problem directly. A difficulty for BLPs is that the probability distribution is only well defined when the underlying graph does not contain cycles [25].

Markov Logic Networks (MLNs) are proposed to overcome the cycle problem as well as the requirement to define the *ad hoc* combining rule [25]. MLNs subsume many of the approaches from the statistical learning literature. Each possible ground fact is associated with a binary random variable and every possible grounding of every rule with a weight and a binary feature. The aggregation of clauses is performed implicit for MLNs and can not be modelled easily. We show an example regarding MLNs in the additional report. The focus of this work are settings where model theoretic entailment is not feasible. For instance, an MLN would need to define $15k \cdot 237$ random variables on the dataset FB15k-237 and a feature for every possible rule grounding with a rule set size of 5 million. If we only try to calculate the immediate consequences of all learned rules on this dataset, this already takes more than 600 GB of memory.

A similar note can be made for neural theorem proving, where the forward-chaining algorithm is relaxed to a smooth differentiable function [17,26]. To

---

[1] The additional report to this paper, containing proofs, can be found here or by request to the authors.

the best of our knowledge, these approaches have not shown yet to scale to datasets of the size used in our experiments. This also holds for ProbLog [4] which combines probabilistic inference with model theoretic entailment and has the strongest resemblance to our approach. We discuss the details in Sect. 4.4.

The confidence aggregation problem is discussed explicitly by SAFRAN [22] where a clustering of the rules is learned. Other works represent rules with embeddings or learn their confidences [2,21]. These works show improvements in regard to simple strategies but they do not consider a fundamental treatment of the problem and the models exhibit some computational overhead.

3 Background

3.1 Knowledge Graph Completion

A KG $\mathcal{G}$ is a set of *relation(subject, object)* facts which are often equivalently written as triples in the form $(subject, relation, object)$. We let $\mathcal{E} \times \mathcal{P} \times \mathcal{E}$ denote the set of all possible triples, which contains $\mathcal{G}$. Here, $\mathcal{E}$ is a set of entities and $\mathcal{P}$ a set of binary predicates which we term relations. We make two assumptions about KGs throughout the work. First, we use the open-world assumption [19]. A fact $t \in \mathcal{G}$ contained in a KG represents a true statement. We also say that the fact is observed. An unobserved fact $t^{(u)} \notin \mathcal{G}$, on the other hand, does not necessarily represent a false statement; its truth value is unknown. The second assumption states that the KG is incomplete and gives practical relevance to the open-world assumption. For an incomplete KG, it holds that there exist facts that are not contained in the KG but are indeed true.

KGC is concerned with finding facts that are unobserved and true. In this work, we focus on the mostly used evaluation protocols which are defined by ranking based evaluation metrics. The derivations of this work are, however, independent of the evaluation protocol as long as scalar scores for candidate predictions are required.

The common practice is to split the graph into disjoint training, validation, and testing sets. After the training or mining phase a model is evaluated by proposing answers to queries formed from the facts in the test set. For each of these evaluation facts a head query and a tail query are formed. For example, from $worksFor(anna, google)$ the queries $worksFor(anna, ?)$ and $worksFor(?, google)$ are formed, where $worksFor$ is a relation and $anna$ and $google$ are entities. A model has to propose candidate facts for the tail query, e.g., $worksFor(anna, e_1)$ and candidate facts for the head query $worksFor(e_2, google)$ for multiple $e_1, e_2 \in \mathcal{E}$. Each candidate fact is assigned with a score such that for each direction a ranking of answers can be formed.

The rankings are filtered, e.g., if $e_2 \neq anna$ but $worksFor(e_2, google)$ exists in one of the data splits, then it is removed from the ranking of the current query to not penalize the model when it correctly ranks true answers on top positions. Performance is measured by the ranking position of the respective true candidate $worksFor(anna, google)$ in both directions where the mean reciprocal

3.2 Rules and Application

The rules considered in this work can be best described as Datalog rules. In particular, we regard horn clauses as seen in the running example. We let a $c \in \tilde{\mathcal{C}}$ denote a rule, and $\tilde{\mathcal{C}}$ is a set of rules. The c will later be indexed and represented by separate random variables. Rules are composed of variables and relations and they additionally can contain entities from a KG:

$$speaks(X, english) \leftarrow livesIn(X, london)$$

We call $speaks(X, english)$ the head of the rule and $livesIn(X, london)$ the body of the rule. From a logic perspective, entities are constants, relations are predicates, and rules are clauses where all variables are implicitly universally quantified. We do not allow negation in the head of the rules. The facts of the KG are ground atoms. We will use the rule learner AnyBURL [15] in our experimental section and we refer to the respective work for further details.

A (ground) substitution is a mapping from variables to constants and in our case entities from $\mathcal{E}$. If we apply a substitution to a rule, we apply it separately to the body and the head of the rule. The result is one ground fact for the head (head grounding) and one or more facts for the body of the rule (body grounding). For instance, for the first rule from the running example with the substitution $\{X \mapsto anna, Y \mapsto google\}$, we obtain the head grounding $worksFor(anna, google)$ and the body grounding results in $internsAt(anna, google)$. Please note that substitutions are treated under object identity. We do not allow two distinct variables being mapped to the same entity. This has been shown to be beneficial for rule learning on KGs [14].

From an inference perspective, we exclusively regard the one-time application or, equivalently, the immediate consequences of the rules, given a KG. In general this procedure is termed *rule application*. Let $\tilde{\mathcal{C}}$ be a set of rules and $\mathcal{G}$ a KG.

Definition 1 (One-step entailment $\models_1$). *The fact t is **one-step entailed** by $\tilde{\mathcal{C}} \cup \mathcal{G}$, written as $\tilde{\mathcal{C}} \cup \mathcal{G} \models_1 t$, iff there is a rule in $\tilde{\mathcal{C}}$ for which a substitution exists such that the resulting body grounding is contained in $\mathcal{G}$ and the head grounding is equal to t.*

This is by no means a novel concept and it can likewise be formalized with the immediate consequence operator in Datalog (e.g., [33]). We use this particular definition as our viewpoint will always be from the perspective of a respective target fact. One-step entailment is weaker but more efficient than model theoretic entailment. Additionally, one-step-entailment implies entailment but not vice versa. In the context of KGC, the less formal notion of an individual rule predicting a candidate is often used, which we can now describe precisely.

Definition 2 (Prediction). *Let $\mathcal{G}$ be a KG. A rule $c \in \tilde{\mathcal{C}}$ **predicts** a fact t iff it individually one-step entails t, i.e., iff $\{c\} \cup \mathcal{G} \models_1 t$.*

For simplicity, we will write $c \models_1 t$ instead of $\{c\} \cup \mathcal{G} \models_1 t$, where from the context the reference to $\mathcal{G}$ will be clear. The section concludes with an example.

Example 2 (cont.) Let e_d, e_u, and e_g be entities in $\mathcal{E}$. Let $t = worksFor(e_d, e_g)$ and let us assume that

$$\mathcal{G} = \left\{ \begin{array}{l} cooperatesWith(e_g, e_u) \\ internAt(e_d, e_g) \\ studentAt(e_d, e_u) \end{array} \right\}.$$

Consider the three rules from the running example. Then the joint set of rules and every pairwise set of rules one-step entail t while only the first and the third rule predict t.

3.3 Rule Confidence Aggregation

For the remainder of the work, we assume that $\tilde{\mathcal{C}}$ is a given set of rules that has been learned from the training graph $\mathcal{G}$. Furthermore, for a target triple t, we let $\mathcal{C}_t(\mathcal{G})$ denote the set of rules that predicted t with respect to the KG $\mathcal{G}$. For performing ranking-based KGC, a model has to assign plausibility scores to candidate facts. For rule-based KGC, we need to introduce two additional concepts, rule confidences and confidence aggregation strategies.

Confidences. Rule confidences originate from the context of association rule mining. We henceforth assume that every rule is assigned with such a confidence. Let $c \in \tilde{\mathcal{C}}$ be a rule and $\mathcal{G}$ be a KG. The confidence of c can be calculated as follows.

$$\text{conf}(c) = \frac{|\{t' \mid c \models_1 t' \wedge t' \in \mathcal{G}\}|}{|\{t' \mid c \models_1 t'\}|} \tag{1}$$

where $c \models_1 t'$ is short for $\{c\} \cup \mathcal{G} \models_1 t'$ (see above). Equation (1) is used in many works and it is called the standard confidence by Galárraga et al., [8]. We made the assumption above that any fact $t \in \mathcal{G}$ is a true statement. Therefore, the confidence divides the number of all true predictions by the number of all predictions of the rule.

The confidence is a measure for the certainty of a rule prediction and larger confidence values are preferred over lower values. If a confidence is one, we can indeed not use it to make any new (unseen) predictions when applying the rule on the KG where the confidence was calculated. In practical scenarios and given the incompleteness assumption made above, this rarely occurs, however. Finally, we also use Laplace smoothing and always add five to the denominator.

Aggregation Strategies. In practical scenarios, most of the time a candidate fact is not predicted by only one rule. Frequently, many rules predict the same candidate, then it holds that $|\mathcal{C}_t(\mathcal{G})| > 1$. The confidence aggregation problem, also termed joint prediction [7], is concerned with defining a function that maps the confidences of the rules that predicted the candidate to a real valued score.

The number of rules that predict a candidate fact simultaneously can be large such that rules are to some extend redundant. For instance, if the second rule from the running example predicts *anna* to work for *google*, the question arises whether the third rule provides additional evidence for this prediction. The rules make the prediction for seemingly similar reasons, as it is more likely for a university and a company to cooperate when they are located in the same location. In the following the two most common aggregation strategies are defined.

Definition 3 (Max-Aggregation). *The Max-Aggregation score s^M is calculated according to the rule with the highest confidence from the rules that predicted the candidate, $s^M(t) = \max\{conf(c) \mid c \in \mathcal{C}_t(\mathcal{G})\}$.*

Max-aggregation was first used in the context of KGC by Galárraga et al. [7] and it was later adapted to *Max+ aggregation* [15] which allows for tie handling. When the two predicting rules with the highest confidences for two candidates are the same, the candidates are compared according to the rules with the second highest confidence which is continued until the candidates can be discriminated.

Definition 4 (Noisy-or aggregation). *The Noisy-or score s^{NO} is calculated as the noisy-or product over the predicting rules, $s^{NO}(t) = 1 - \prod_{c \in \mathcal{C}_t(\mathcal{G})}(1 - conf(c))$.*

The Noisy-or product originates from Bayesian networks where it is used to express independent causes [23] and it was proposed by Galárraga et al. [7] for KGC.

Example 3 (cont.) *Let us assume that Anna is predicted by all rules from the starting example to work for google, while Lisa is predicted by only the second and third rule to work for Google. The Max-aggregation and Noisy-or scores for Anna are 0.64 and 0.88, respectively. For Lisa they are 0.44 and 0.67.*

While the aggregation functions have the purpose of merging the various confidences into a final score, this value also should be meaningful in the sense that a higher value for one prediction should mean it is more likely than another prediction.

4 Probabilistic Confidence Aggregation

We start with presenting notation for the probabilistic representation in the following section. Subsequently, we introduce an inference model and show how the introduced aggregation functions can be recovered from the framework when making certain dependency assumptions. Finally, we will discuss the relationship to inference with model theoretic entailment and present an overlooked baseline. Our modelling approach starts similar to the modelling in ProbLog [4]. Our focus is on the differences that arise when only considering one-step entailment and when making varying assumptions about the joint distribution of a logic program, which in our terms will be a joint distribution over the rules.

4.1 Representation

We first enumerate the rules in $\tilde{\mathcal{C}}$ with an index set $\tilde{I} = \{1, ..., N\}$ such that $c_i \in \tilde{\mathcal{C}}$ for $i \in \tilde{I}$. The rules c_i are defined as symbolic objects, therefore we introduce new symbols for the random variables representing them. Specifically, each rule c_i is represented by a binary random variable $\tilde{R}_i$ which is likewise indexed by $\tilde{I}$. This random variable can take values $\tilde{r} \in \{0, 1\}$. We provide an explanation for the meaning of $\tilde{R}_i$ taking the value one in the next section.

We let $\tilde{\mathbf{R}}$ denote the random vector representing all N rules and likewise $\tilde{\mathbf{r}} = (\tilde{r}_i)_{i \in \tilde{I}} \in \{0, 1\}^N$ is the corresponding vector of values. For brevity, we write $p(\tilde{\mathbf{r}})$ for $p(\tilde{\mathbf{R}} = \tilde{\mathbf{r}})$, that is, the probability that $\tilde{\mathbf{R}}$ takes value $\tilde{\mathbf{r}}$.

For the confidence aggregation problem the set of rules $\mathcal{C}_t(\mathcal{G}) \subseteq \tilde{\mathcal{C}}$ that predict a target fact t based on $\mathcal{G}$ are of particular relevance. Therefore, similar as above $\mathcal{C}_t(\mathcal{G})$ is enumerated by $I = \{1, ..., k\}$ and the random vector $\mathbf{R}$ with value vector $\mathbf{r} = (r_j)_{j \in I} \in \{0, 1\}^k$ represents the rules that predict the target. Note that $\mathbf{R}, \mathbf{r}$, and I belong to a subset of all the rules which depends on target t and $\mathcal{G}$. As these are the main variables throughout the following derivations, and to not clutter notation, we do not write this explicitly and the reference to t and $\mathcal{G}$ will be clear from the context.

Moreover, we will also write $p_i = p(\tilde{R}_i = 1)$ and $p_j = p(R_j = 1)$ for the marginal probability that a rule takes value one. We assume that index sets are ordered according to the marginals, e.g., $p_m \geq p_n$ when $m \leq n$ with m, n being indices. Facts t are likewise represented as binary variables. Here we overload notation for brevity and write $p(t)$ for the probability of a query triple to be true. For an observed triple $t \in \mathcal{G}$ we set $p(t) = 1$.

4.2 Dealing with Uncertainty

We represent a symbolic rule c_i with a binary random variable $\tilde{R}_i$ for $i \in \tilde{I}$. Hence, we can write down an expression such as $p(\tilde{R}_i = 1)$ with $i \in \tilde{I}$, which represents the probability that the rule is true. Intuitively, a rule being true means that the expressed conditional statement is a correct statement. Therefore, we assume that, if the rule is true, everything that is derived from the rule must be true as well. Formally, we express this with a conditional distribution. For a KG $\mathcal{G}$ and a fact t, we write $p(t|\tilde{r}_i, \mathcal{G})$ for the conditional probability that the fact is true, given $\mathcal{G}$ and the value of $\tilde{R}_i$. We set this probability to one, if two conditions are fulfilled: First, the rule must be true, i.e., the value of $\tilde{R}_i$ must be one. Second, the underlying symbolic rule must predict the fact. However, we do not only have one rule but a learned set of rules. Therefore, for the random vector representing all learned rules $\tilde{\mathbf{R}}$ with values $\tilde{\mathbf{r}}$, we define the conditional probability as:

$$p(t|\tilde{\mathbf{r}}, \mathcal{G}) = \begin{cases} 1, & \text{if } L(\tilde{\mathbf{r}}) \models_1 t \\ 0, & \text{else} \end{cases} \quad (2)$$

Here, L is a simple mapping that first collects all rule objects in $\tilde{\mathcal{C}}$ whose corresponding values are one in $\tilde{\mathbf{r}}$. That is, it collects only the rules that are described to be true by the current $\tilde{\mathbf{r}}$. Subsequently, the union is taken with $\mathcal{G}$:

$$L_{\tilde{I}}^{\mathcal{G}} : \tilde{\mathbf{r}} \mapsto L_{\tilde{I}}^{\mathcal{G}}(\tilde{\mathbf{r}}) := \{c_i \mid \tilde{r}_i = 1 \text{ and } i \in \hat{I}\} \cup \mathcal{G} \quad (3)$$

We drop, as shown in Eq. (2), the reference to the index set $\tilde{I}$ and $\mathcal{G}$ from L for readability. Equation (2) has a simple interpretation. The conditional probability that the target triple is true is set to one, if there exists at least one rule in $\tilde{\mathbf{r}}$ which is true and additionally predicts the target. Otherwise it is set to zero. If the rules would not be associated with uncertainty, evaluating the equation would boil down to performing rule application as described in Sect. 3.2. However, the truth values of the rules cannot be directly observed from the data as we can not directly sample from these variables.

We have, on the other hand, an estimate that statistically quantifies the uncertainty of rule predictions, the defined rule confidences. The definition of the confidence aligns to a large extend with the understanding of the rule variables $\tilde{R}_i$. If $\tilde{R}_i$ is one, a prediction made by the rule is true. We can therefore use as an approximation for the rule marginals their respective confidences. However, we will need the joint distribution over the rules not only the marginals. In Sect. 4.4, we will indeed show how to construct the joint from the marginal distributions.

4.3 Inference for Target Facts

We want to calculate the query probability that an unknown target fact $t \notin \mathcal{G}$ is true, given the known triples, i.e., we seek to compute $p(t|\mathcal{G})$. However, we cannot observe the truth values $\tilde{\mathbf{r}}$ of the rules from the data and we therefore choose a standard approach regarding such settings. In fact, we marginalize over all possible values that the vector $\tilde{\mathbf{r}}$ can take:

$$p(t|\mathcal{G}) = \sum_{\tilde{\mathbf{r}} \in \{0,1\}^N} p(t|\tilde{\mathbf{r}}, \mathcal{G}) p(\tilde{\mathbf{r}}|\mathcal{G}) \quad (4)$$

where we set $p(t|\tilde{\mathbf{r}}, \mathcal{G})$ to Eq. (2). We can simply calculate $p(t|\tilde{\mathbf{r}}, \mathcal{G})$ by collecting all rules that are one in $\tilde{\mathbf{r}}$ and subsequently evaluate if one of these rules predicts the target. The distribution $p(\tilde{\mathbf{r}}|\mathcal{G})$ seems to be more problematic. It defines the joint distribution over all N rules, given the data, including the rules that did not predict t. The confidence aggregation, however, was defined with only the k rules that predicted a candidate. We will argue in the following proposition that under one-step entailment, for calculating $p(t|\mathcal{G})$, it is indeed sufficient also under the probabilistic model to exclusively take into account the rule variables $\mathbf{R}$ that represent the rules which actually predict t.

Proposition 1. *Under a one-step entailment regime, i.e., using Eq. (2) for $p(t|\tilde{\mathbf{r}},\mathcal{G})$, and a global distribution $p(\tilde{\mathbf{r}}|\mathcal{G})$ we have that*

$$p(t|\mathcal{G}) = \sum_{\mathbf{r}\in\{0,1\}^k} p(t|\mathbf{r},\mathcal{G})p(\mathbf{r}|\mathcal{G}). \tag{5}$$

The proof is in the additional report. Instead of using the global distribution we can focus directly on performing marginal inference $p(\mathbf{r}|\mathcal{G})$ with respect to the rules that predicted t. Although marginal inference can equally be expensive, the complexity can be reduced if the joint distribution is specified accordingly and if some parameters of the joint are known such as the individual rule marginals. Additionally, it might even be beneficial to model $p(\mathbf{r}|\mathcal{G})$ directly. Proposition (1) would not hold if we would consider general model theoretic entailment. Finally, from Eq. (2) and the definition of one-step entailment, we obtain the following proposition.

Proposition 2. *The query probability $p(t|\mathcal{G})$ is equal to the probability that at least one of the rules that predict target t is true, i.e., it holds that*

$$p(t|\mathcal{G}) = p\big(\sum_{j\in I} R_j \geq 1 \mid \mathcal{G}\big). \tag{6}$$

Proof. We write out $p(t|\mathbf{r},\mathcal{G})$ in Eq. (5). As we only regard the predicting rules, there is only one term of the sum that gets zero (where $\mathbf{r}$ is equal to the zero vector $\mathbf{0}$). In every remaining term, at least one component of $\mathbf{r}$ is one. That means, the probabilities of all configurations where at least one rule takes value one (is true) are summed up, which is equivalent to the statement in the proposition. □

We will henceforth refer to calculating $p(t|\mathcal{G})$ under the previous derivations when mentioning the inference model and we conclude the section with an example.

Example 4 (cont.) *Lisa is predicted by the two rules c_2 and c_3 to work for Google. Assuming that we know the joint distribution over all rules, we can calculate the probability that Lisa works for Google by querying the joint distribution for the probability that at least one of c_2 and c_3 is true.*

4.4 Recovering Aggregation Functions

We will demonstrate in this section that the inference model leads to the different aggregation strategies depending on the assumed joint distribution when marginals are approximated with the rule confidences. Therefore, we assume for the following derivations $p(\tilde{R}_i=1) = \mathit{conf}(c_i)$ for $i \in \tilde{I}$.

Probabilistic Max-Aggregation. Max-aggregation was introduced in the literature as a computational heuristic [7]. It was further described as accounting for strong rule dependencies without providing a detailed treatment [15], and it was even described with assuming fact independence [32]. We will now introduce the Fréchet-Hoeffding bound which will help us to achieve a formal derivation. It defines the maximal achievable correlation of two random variables [10]. Let p_i and p_j be the marginal probabilities for two Bernoulli variables, then it holds for the correlation ρ_{ij} that $\rho_{ij} \leq U(i,j)$ with

$$U(i,j) = \min\left\{ \left(\frac{p_i(1-p_j)}{p_j(1-p_i)}\right)^{1/2}, \left(\frac{p_j(1-p_i)}{p_i(1-p_j)}\right)^{1/2} \right\}. \tag{7}$$

Example 5 (cont.) Let $p_1 = 0.64$ and $p_2 = 0.44$. The maximal achievable correlation is $U(1,2) \approx 0.66$. Whereas for $p_3 = 0.41$, we have that $U(2,3) \approx 0.94$.

While the configuration of the marginals in Example 5 allows for complex dependencies in regard to the joint distribution, they are not compatible with complete dependence as this would require unit correlation. Interestingly, Eq. (7) suffices to specify a joint distribution $p(\tilde{\mathbf{r}}|\mathcal{G})$ such that the inference model from Sect. 4.3 performs Max-aggregation. As before, let $\mathcal{G}$ be a KG, let $\tilde{\mathbf{R}}$ with values $\tilde{\mathbf{r}} \in \{1,0\}^N$ denote the random vector representing all rule objects, and let t be a target fact. The following theorem is made under the assumption that rule marginals p_i are estimated with confidences, as stated in the section beginning.

Theorem 1. Let $\Omega \in [-1,1]^{(N,N)}$ be the correlation matrix for the random variables representing all the learned rules. If, for every entry ρ_{ij} of Ω with $i,j \in \tilde{I}$, it holds that $\rho_{Ij} = U(i,j)$, then a unique distribution for $p(\tilde{\mathbf{r}}|\mathcal{G})$ is induced, such that the query probability is equal to the Max-aggregation score, i.e., $p(t|\mathcal{G}) = s^M(t)$.

In other words: if we assume that the correlation of every pair of rule variables is maximal, then probabilistic inference is equal to Max-aggregation. We will briefly show the proof for the case where $k = 2$ rules predicted the candidate and the general case can be found in the additional report. Let $p_{\bar{i}} = 1 - p_i$ and let, e.g., $p_{\bar{i}j} = p(R_i=0, R_j=1|\mathcal{G})$ and likewise for the remaining value assignments of the random variables. Further note for the correlation $\rho_{ij} = \frac{p_{ij} - p_i p_j}{\tilde{\sigma}_i \tilde{\sigma}_j}$ where $\tilde{\sigma}$ is the respective standard deviation.

Proof (k=2). Let us assume that of all the rules only two rules c_i and c_j predicted the target fact t. Following Propositions (1) and (2), $p(t|\mathcal{G})$ is equivalent to querying the joint distribution marginally for $p(r_i + r_j \geq 1)$, i.e., the probability that at least one of the rules is true. We can write this probability as $p_{\bar{i}j} + p_{i\bar{j}} + p_{ij}$. We here assume the global distribution $p(\tilde{\mathbf{r}}|\mathcal{G})$ exists and is unique. It therefore suffices to show that

$$\max\{p_i, p_j\} = p_{\bar{i}j} + p_{i\bar{j}} + p_{ij}.$$

Assume w.l.o.g. that $p_i \geq p_j$. Then after plugging in $U(i,j)$ into ρ_{ij} and solving for p_{ij}, we obtain $p_{ij} = p_j$. However, by definition of the marginal it holds that $p_j = p_{ij} + p_{\bar{i}j}$ and therefore $p_{\bar{i}j} = 0$. Then we have,

$$\begin{aligned}
\max\{p_i, p_j\} &= \max\{p_{i\bar{j}} + p_{ij},\ p_{\bar{i}j} + p_{ij}\} \\
&= \max\{p_{i\bar{j}} + p_{ij},\ p_{ij}\} \\
&= p_{i\bar{j}} + p_{ij} \\
&= p_{\bar{i}j} + p_{i\bar{j}} + p_{ij}.
\end{aligned}$$

$\square$

Example 6 (cont.) *We use $p_1 = 0.64$ and $p_2 = 0.44$ from the running example. We obtain $p_{12} = 0.44$, $p_{\bar{1}\bar{2}} = 0$, and $p_{1\bar{2}} = p_1 - p_2 = 0.2$. This leads to $p(t|\mathcal{G}) = 0 \cdot p_{\bar{1}\bar{2}} + 1 \cdot p_{12} + 1 \cdot p_{1\bar{2}} + 1 \cdot p_{\bar{1}2} = 0.64 = \max\{p_1, p_2\}$.*

We have specified a unique multivariate Bernoulli distribution $p(\tilde{\mathbf{r}}|\mathcal{G})$ by only defining a correlation matrix. In general, setting the N^2 values of the correlation matrix is not sufficient for defining a distribution that has 2^N parameters and also not every correlation matrix is admissible in the first place [9].

Noisy-or Aggregation. To derive Noisy-or aggregation we have to make an assumption about the joint distribution that goes beyond pairwise interactions, i.e., it is not enough to assume zero correlation between all rules.

Proposition 3. *If the N rules in $p(\tilde{\mathbf{R}}|\mathcal{G})$ are mutually independent then the query probability is equivalent to Noisy-or aggregation, i.e., $p(t|\mathcal{G}) = s^{NO}(t)$.*

It is straightforward to derive the Noisy-or product from the inference model under the independence assumption and the proof is shown in the additional report for completeness.

4.5 Full Reasoning and Aggregation

The independence assumption of Proposition 3 reveals the explicit connection of the aggregation problem and using model theoretic entailment and probability with ProbLog [4]. The probability for a logic program $\mathcal{L}$ given a ProbLog program T is defined as

$$p(\mathcal{L}|T) = \prod_{x_i \in \mathcal{L}} p(x_i) \prod_{x_j \notin \mathcal{L}} (1 - p(x_j)), \tag{8}$$

where T is a collection of definite clauses (horn clauses) with assigned probabilities. In the scope of this work, when using the notation from ProbLog [4], we can set $T^* = \{p_i : c_i \mid i \in \tilde{I}\} \cup \{1 : t' \mid t' \in \mathcal{G}\}$ to obtain the ProbLog program representing the rules $\tilde{\mathcal{C}}$ and the facts $\mathcal{G}$. As in the sections before, we assume here that p_i is set to $conf(c_i)$.

Then ProbLog calculates the query probability $p(t|T^*)$ by summing the probabilities of all logic programs (Eq. 8) that entail the target t. If we, for instance, would only allow one-step entailment as the reasoning mechanism in ProbLog, we obtain the following result.

Proposition 4. *Calculating the query probability $p(t|T^*)$ with ProbLog under a one-step entailment regime is equivalent to Noisy-or aggregation, i.e., $p(t|T^*) = s^{NO}(t)$.*

The proof is given in the additional report. The next result shows the difference between confidence aggregation with Noisy-or and the full ProbLog algorithm.

Theorem 2. *The query probability $p(t|T^*)$ calculated by ProbLog is larger or equal than Noisy-or aggregation, i.e., $p(t|T^*) \geq s^{NO}(t)$.*

Proof details are given in the additional report. Intuitively, the proof follows from the fact that ProbLog sums the probabilities of all programs that entail the target fact. This includes 1) the programs that entail and one-step entail the query and 2) the programs that entail but not one-step entail the query. This clearly is larger than only summing up 1), which is done for Noisy-or aggregation.

ProbLog excels for smaller problems with mostly independent clauses in a knowledge base. It derives query answers through full reasoning. This includes using facts for a proof that are unknown but derived in a respective sub proof, i.e., in one of the reasoning steps. Nevertheless, we mentioned already that full reasoning is not feasible in contexts where millions of rules are learned and have to be applied on a similar number of facts (see also in the experimental section).

However, Theorem 2 reveals another intricacy. The Noisy-or scores already are often problematic as they tend to get very close to 1.0 as the score simply increases with the number of predicting rules for a target. If 10 rules with a confidence of 0.5 predict a target, the aggregated score is already 0.999. Often hundreds of rules predict a single target leading to floating point considerations and the fact that candidate predictions can not be discriminated properly anymore. Naturally, this problem will be only stronger when the scores are equal or higher than the scores of Noisy-or aggregation.

4.6 Mixing Assumptions

Both of the aggregation approaches derived in Sect. 4.4 make strong assumptions in regard to the dependence structure of the joint distribution over the rules. Clearly, this can lead to an overestimation or underestimation of the final probability. This is also reflected empirically in the context of KGC. Max and Max+ aggregation often assign very low scores to target predictions such as 0.02. Noisy-or scores, on the other hand, are often returned as 1.0 due to floating point problems, as discussed in the previous section. We will now present a simple approach that is overlooked in the literature so far and operates in between Noisy-or and Max-aggregation.

Definition 5. *(Noisy-or top-h)* Let $NO_h I^* \subseteq I$ be the subset of indices for the h rules with the highest confidences that predict target t. The Noisy-or top-h aggregation strategy calculates the final score according to $s(t)^{NO_h} = 1 - \prod_{j \in I^*}(1 - conf(c_j))$.

While the baseline does not characterize a joint distribution over all rules, intuitively it operates between mutual independence and maximal correlation, which is shown by the next result.

Proposition 5. *The score calculated with Noisy-or top-h falls between Max and Noisy-or aggregation, i.e., $s^M(t) \leq s^{NO_h}(t) \leq s^{NO}(t)$. The equalities are attained for $h = 1$ and $h = k$, where k is the number of rules that predicted target fact t.*

The proposition immediately follows from the definitions of the approaches. It also shows that Noisy-or top-h calculates more realistic scores compared to Noisy-or and Max-aggregation. Moreover it is conceptually more efficient to compute compared to Max+ aggregation and Noisy-or. The restriction of only using h rules with the highest confidences allows for a stopping criterion during rule application for every target fact. Finally, instead of setting one value for h we can exploit the mixture property more finegrained and set the value independently for relations and query-directions, which will be discussed in the next section.

5 Experiments

In the following, we evaluate the discussed aggregation strategies on four datasets. For Noisy-or top-h, we investigate a setting in which we use one global $h = 5$ on all datasets and a setting in which we search for the best value of h for relations and query directions independently, according to the performance on a validation graph (denoted by NO top-h^*). We abstain from comparing against the general KGC literature which is not the focus of this work. We refer to the recent literature on a discussion of the competitiveness of rule-based approaches [14,27,29]. We use the common KGs FB15k-237, WNRR [5], Codex-M [30], and Yago3-10 [5] and their respective train, valid, and test splits. The set of rules $\tilde{C}$ are taken from Meilicke et al. [13] and are mined with AnyBURL. For WNRR, there are 100k rules learned. For all the other KGs, the ruleset sizes are larger than five million. Yago3-10 is the largest KG with more than one million facts and WNRR is the smallest with 86k facts. Finally, we use the standard evaluation protocol from the literature (e.g., [27]) which is described in Sect. 3.1.

5.1 Results

Table 1 shows performance results. We compare Max (MAX), Max+ (MAX+), Noisy-or (NO), and Noisy-or top-h aggregation (NO top-h). For Noisy-or top-5, we set $h = 5$ for all datasets. For NO top-h^*, we search based on the validation performance over the values $h \in \{1, 4 \ldots 10\}$ where for $h=1$ we use MAX+.

Table 1. Results for the joint filtered Mean Reciprocal Rank (MRR) and Hits@X.

Approach	FB15k-237			WNRR			Codex-M			Yago3-10		
	h@1	h@10	MRR	h@1	h@10	MRR	h@1	h@10	MRR	h@1	h@10	MRR
MAX	0.236	0.496	0.321	0.442	0.561	0.482	0.240	0.443	0.309	0.394	0.640	0.477
MAX+	0.246	0.506	0.331	0.457	0.574	0.497	0.248	0.452	0.317	0.498	0.691	0.566
NO	0.251	0.499	0.333	0.391	0.560	0.446	0.219	0.427	0.290	0.367	0.628	0.456
NO top-5	0.260	0.524	0.347	0.458	0.578	0.499	0.243	0.461	0.317	0.486	0.697	0.560
NO top-h^*	0.263	0.524	0.349	0.459	0.578	0.499	0.253	0.464	0.326	0.498	0.698	0.568

NO top-5 performs surprisingly well and it only falls short for the h@1 and MRR metrics for Yago3-10 compared to MAX+ while being faster on average and 1.6PP better on FB15k-237. Not surprisingly, searching for the best h on the validation set performs equal or better compared to the second best approach.

The default aggregation function currently used for rule-based KGC is MAX+ (see e.g., [14,27]). Although the performance improvements of Noisy-or top-5 are minor, it is superior overall given that it is also more efficient to compute and provides better calibrated scores (compare Sect. 4.6). There exist works, on the other hand, that propose learnable confidence aggregation functions which can achieve better results [2,21,22]. However, they are also considerably slower and have not shown to run on datasets of the size of Yago3-10 or larger. For instance, the best performing single model from Ott et al. [21] achieves an MRR of 0.365 while running for 5.5 h on a GPU without taking into consideration the hyperparameter search. Noisy-or top-5 needs less than 1.5 min when using 6 threads on an Intel(R) Xeon(R) Silver CPU.

We also tried to run ProbLog on the dasets by transforming the rules $\tilde{\mathcal{C}}$ and the graphs into a ProbLog program. Even on the smallest dataset, WNRR, with a size of 86k facts and 6k test queries, ProbLog did not terminate after two hours. After restricting the number of rules from 100k to 400 cyclical rules of maximum length two and the number of test queries from 6000 to 20, ProbLog did still not terminate after two hours.

6 Conclusion

We demonstrated in this work that the rule confidence aggregation problem can be expressed with performing marginal inference over a joint distribution of all rules. We could show that Max-aggregation has a proper probabilistic interpretation. We also discussed the explicit connection of confidence aggregation to using full reasoning with ProbLog [4]. Subsequently we proposed a slightly superior baseline that is a conceptual mixture between the common aggregation functions. Future work can build on the theoretical foundations by finding suitable ways of modelling the joint distribution over the rules. For instance, rules could be grouped according to syntactic similarity, distributions might be estimated from more advanced statistics such as pairwise confidences or marginals could be approximated more rigorously. For practical applications, it can be analysed how rule dependencies may vary between different datasets. For instance, in our experiments, Noisy-or performs poor on some dataset whereas it performs quite well on others. Lastly, the applicability of the theoretical results to other fields where some form of maximum aggregation is used, provides an interesting direction.

References

1. Muggleton et al., S.: Stochastic logic programs. Adv. Inductive Logic Program. **32**, 254–264 (1996)
2. Betz, P., Meilicke, C., Stuckenschmidt, H.: Supervised knowledge aggregation for knowledge graph completion. In: Groth, P., et al. (eds.) ESWC 2022. LNCS, vol. 13261, pp. 74–92. Springer, Cham (2022). https://doi.org/10.1007/978-3-031-06981-9_5
3. Chen, Y., Wang, D.Z., Goldberg, S.: Scalekb: scalable learning and inference over large knowledge bases. VLDB J. **25**(6), 893–918 (2016)
4. De Raedt, L., Kimmig, A., Toivonen, H.: Problog: a probabilistic prolog and its application in link discovery. In: Proceedings of the Twentieth International Joint Conference on Artificial Intelligence, pp. 2462–2467 (2007)
5. Dettmers, T., Minervini, P., Stenetorp, P., Riedel, S.: Convolutional 2D knowledge graph embeddings. In: Proceedings of the AAAI Conference on Artificial Intelligence, pp. 1811–1818 (2018)
6. Fan, W., Fu, W., Jin, R., Lu, P., Tian, C.: Discovering association rules from big graphs. Proc. VLDB Endowment **15**(7), 1479–1492 (2022)
7. Galárraga, L., Teflioudi, C., Hose, K., Suchanek, F.M.: Fast rule mining in ontological knowledge bases with AMIE+. VLDB J. **24**(6), 707–730 (2015)
8. Galárraga, L.A., Teflioudi, C., Hose, K., Suchanek, F.: Amie: association rule mining under incomplete evidence in ontological knowledge bases. In: Proceedings of the 22nd international conference on World Wide Web, pp. 413–422. ACM (2013)
9. Huber, M., Marić, N.: Admissible Bernoulli correlations. J. Stat. Distrib. Appl. **6**(1), 1–8 (2019)
10. Joe, H.: Multivariate Models and Multivariate Dependence Concepts. CRC Press, Boca Raton (1997)
11. Kersting, K., De Raedt, L.: Towards combining inductive logic programming with Bayesian networks. In: Rouveirol, C., Sebag, M. (eds.) ILP 2001. LNCS, vol. 2157, pp. 118–131. Springer, Heidelberg (2001). https://doi.org/10.1007/3-540-44797-0_10
12. Lajus, J., Galárraga, L., Suchanek, F.: Fast and exact rule mining with AMIE 3. In: Harth, A., et al. (eds.) ESWC 2020. LNCS, vol. 12123, pp. 36–52. Springer, Cham (2020). https://doi.org/10.1007/978-3-030-49461-2_3
13. Meilicke, C., Betz, P., Stuckenschmidt, H.: Why a naive way to combine symbolic and latent knowledge base completion works surprisingly well. In: 3rd Conference on Automated Knowledge Base Construction (2021)
14. Meilicke, C., Chekol, M.W., Betz, P., Fink, M., Stuckenschmidt, H.: Anytime bottom-up rule learning for large scale knowledge graph completion. VLDB J. Int. J. Very Large Data Bases (2023)

15. Meilicke, C., Chekol, M.W., Ruffinelli, D., Stuckenschmidt, H.: Anytime bottom-up rule learning for knowledge graph completion. In: Proceedings of the Twenty-Eighth International Joint Conference on Artificial Intelligence, pp. 3137–3143. International Joint Conferences on Artificial Intelligence Organization (2019)
16. Meilicke, C., Fink, M., Wang, Y., Ruffinelli, D., Gemulla, R., Stuckenschmidt, H.: Fine-grained evaluation of rule- and embedding-based systems for knowledge graph completion. In: Vrandečić, D., et al. (eds.) ISWC 2018. LNCS, vol. 11136, pp. 3–20. Springer, Cham (2018). https://doi.org/10.1007/978-3-030-00671-6_1
17. Minervini, P., Bošnjak, M., Rocktäschel, T., Riedel, S., Grefenstette, E.: Differentiable reasoning on large knowledge bases and natural language. In: Proceedings of the AAAI Conference on Artificial Intelligence, vol. 34, pp. 5182–5190 (2020)
18. Muggleton, S., De Raedt, L.: Inductive logic programming: theory and methods. J. Logic Program. **19**, 629–679 (1994)
19. Nickel, M., Murphy, K., Tresp, V., Gabrilovich, E.: A review of relational machine learning for knowledge graphs. Proc. IEEE **104**(1), 11–33 (2015)
20. Ortona, S., Meduri, V.V., Papotti, P.: Robust discovery of positive and negative rules in knowledge bases. In: 34th IEEE International Conference on Data Engineering, pp. 1168–1179. IEEE Computer Society (2018)
21. Ott, S., Betz, P., Stepanova, D., Gad-Elrab, M.H., Meilicke, C., Stuckenschmidt, H.: Rule-based knowledge graph completion with canonical models. In: Proceedings of the 32nd ACM International Conference on Information and Knowledge Management, pp. 1971–1981 (2023)
22. Ott, S., Meilicke, C., Samwald, M.: SAFRAN: an interpretable, rule-based link prediction method outperforming embedding models. In: 3rd Conference on Automated Knowledge Base Construction (2021)
23. Pearl, J.: Probabilistic Reasoning in Intelligent Systems: Networks of Plausible Inference. Morgan Kaufmann, Burlington (1988)
24. Pellissier Tanon, T., Stepanova, D., Razniewski, S., Mirza, P., Weikum, G.: Completeness-aware rule learning from knowledge graphs. In: d'Amato, C., et al. (eds.) ISWC 2017. LNCS, vol. 10587, pp. 507–525. Springer, Cham (2017). https://doi.org/10.1007/978-3-319-68288-4_30
25. Richardson, M., Domingos, P.: Markov logic networks. Mach. Learn. **62**, 107–136 (2006)
26. Rocktäschel, T., Riedel, S.: End-to-end differentiable proving. In: Advances in Neural Information Processing Systems 30: Annual Conference on Neural Information Processing Systems 2017, pp. 3788–3800 (2017)
27. Rossi, A., Barbosa, D., Firmani, D., Matinata, A., Merialdo, P.: Knowledge graph embedding for link prediction: a comparative analysis. ACM Trans. Knowl. Discov. Data (TKDD) **15**(2), 1–49 (2021)
28. Ruffinelli, D., Broscheit, S., Gemulla, R.: You CAN teach an old dog new tricks! on training knowledge graph embeddings. In: 8th International Conference on Learning Representations (2020)
29. Sadeghian, A., Armandpour, M., Ding, P., Wang, D.Z.: Drum: End-to-end differentiable rule mining on knowledge graphs. In: Advances in Neural Information Processing Systems, pp. 15321–15331 (2019)
30. Safavi, T., Koutra, D.: CoDEx: a comprehensive knowledge graph completion benchmark. In: Proceedings of the 2020 Conference on Empirical Methods in Natural Language Processing, pp. 8328–8350. Association for Computational Linguistics (2020)

31. Sato, T., Kameya, Y.: Prism: a language for symbolic-statistical modeling. In: Proceedings of the Fifteenth International Joint Conference on Artificial Intelligence, vol. 97, pp. 1330–1339 (1997)
32. Svatoš, M., Schockaert, S., Davis, J., Kuželka, O.: Strike: rule-driven relational learning using stratified k-entailment. In: Proceedings of the European Conference of Artificial Intelligence (2020)
33. Tena Cucala, D.J., Cuenca Grau, B., Motik, B.: Faithful approaches to rule learning. In: Proceedings of the 19th International Conference on Principles of Knowledge Representation and Reasoning, pp. 484–493 (2022)
34. Wu, L., Sallinger, E., Sherkhonov, E., Vahdati, S., Gottlob, G.: Rule learning over knowledge graphs with genetic logic programming. In: 38th International Conference on Data Engineering, pp. 3373–3385. IEEE (2022)

RIFF: Inducing Rules for Fraud Detection from Decision Trees

Lucas Martins[1]([✉]), João Bravo[1], Ana Sofia Gomes[1], Carlos Soares[2], and Pedro Bizarro[1]

[1] Feedzai, Coimbra, Portugal
lucas.martins@feedzai.com
[2] Faculdade de Engenharia da Universidade do Porto, Porto, Portugal

Abstract. Financial fraud is the cause of multi-billion dollar losses annually. Traditionally, fraud detection systems rely on rules due to their transparency and interpretability, key features in domains where decisions need to be explained. However, rule systems require significant input from domain experts to create and tune, an issue that rule induction algorithms attempt to mitigate by inferring rules directly from data. We explore the application of these algorithms to fraud detection, where rule systems are constrained to have a low false positive rate (FPR) or alert rate, by proposing RIFF, a rule induction algorithm that distills a low FPR rule set directly from decision trees. Our experiments show that the induced rules are often able to maintain or improve performance of the original models for low FPR tasks, while substantially reducing their complexity and outperforming rules hand-tuned by experts.

Keywords: Fraud Detection · Rule Induction · Decision Trees

1 Introduction

Despite the advent of modern machine learning (ML) algorithms, rule systems continue to be important in many domains [1, 21]. Their simplicity and interpretability, often requirements in high stake problems, as well as their longstanding presence has earned the trust of many financial institutions. Many continue to use rule systems as their only solution for fraud detection, while others use them alongside machine learning models.

However, building rule sets traditionally requires expert input and their predictive performance is typically worse than modern machine learning models. This could potentially be attributed, at least in part, to the fact that rules are not automatically inferred from data, but instead manually created and tuned.

While there are several induction algorithms that infer rules from data [4–6, 11, 14, 17, 18, 20, 21], applying them to fraud detection can be problematic due to the extreme class imbalance that is often present, and the requirement to have very low FPR values, typically under 2%. The latter is necessary as incorrectly flagging legitimate transactions can cause friction, eroding customer trust, leading to financial losses, and putting undue pressure on manual reviewers. For this reason, experts try to minimize false positives when considering the trade-off with false negatives. Another requirement is to induce rules that are easily understood by experts, for two reasons: firstly, experts often need to review the decision made by a rule, and, as such, they must understand the reason behind it; secondly, experts need to manually modify rules periodically to keep up with new fraud patterns. As such, a rule system ideally has as few rules as possible so that it can be better understood by humans.

Our main contribution is a rule induction algorithm, RIFF, that leverages decision trees to build low FPR rule sets for fraud detection. We benchmark RIFF against state-of-the-art decision trees algorithms, CART and FIGS, and against expert made rules. Our experiments use both publicly available and private real world transaction data, and we benchmark RIFF using trees generated by CART, FIGS, and by our own modified version of FIGS, FIGU, that aims to reduce overlap between rules induced from different trees.

2 Related Work

Prior work on rule set induction can be divided into two distinct approaches. *Separate-and-conquer algorithms*, also known as covering algorithms, form rule sets by adding rules one by one until a stopping criterion is met [5, 7, 10, 15, 16, 19]. They build or refine rules incrementally, typically relying on a heuristic to choose the best condition or rule to add. In each iteration, these algorithms remove examples covered by the rule set so that new rules can focus on data that is not covered by the current rule set.

On the other hand, *divide-and-conquer algorithms* such as ID3 [18], C4.5 [20] and CART [4], use decision trees to describe the data. These trees are grown in a greedy fashion, by iteratively splitting a current leaf node based on the value of one attribute to maximize a chosen criterion, such as *information gain*. FIGS [21] expands on these algorithms (namely CART) by introducing the option of adding a new tree by splitting on a new root node instead of an existing leaf node. Each tree independently contributes to the model with a score that is summed to produce the final prediction.

Our work leverages both of these approaches. RIFF employs *divide-and-conquer* methods to build decision trees, and it uses a *separate-and-conquer* heuristic to build a rule set with the best performing rules while enforcing a low FPR or alert rate constraint.

3 Rule Induction for Fraud Detection

Rule systems used in the context of fraud detection are typically composed of tens to hundreds of simple rules, each designed to capture a particular fraud pattern. These rules are usually a conjunction of a small set of logical conditions that can be understood by a human and evolve with time by tuning specific thresholds. Fraud detection systems are also usually constrained to operate with an overall low False Positive Rate (FPR) or Alert Rate (AR). This is to limit the friction caused to legitimate users or to limit the total number of alerts generated according to the capacity of a fraud analyst team.

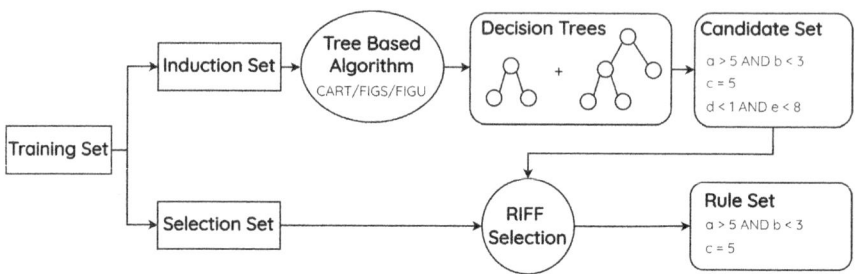

Fig. 1. RIFF Overview

Decision tree algorithms like CART have formed the basis of state-of-the-art algorithms for tabular data when used in ensembles such as Random Forests [3] or Gradient-Boosted Decision Trees [9]. However, even single decision trees can be hard to understand and interpret by humans and they can't be manually tuned by experts. We thus propose leveraging these algorithms to generate candidate rules with good discriminative performance. For this, our proposed algorithm, RIFF, is split into two steps (see Fig. 1):

1. We induce a set of candidate rules from the leaves of a tree-based model trained on an *induction set*. This candidate set would, ideally, contain different rules with high precision, corresponding to leaves with high purity of fraud examples.
2. We greedily select the rules with highest precision from the candidate set, based on their performance on an out of sample *selection set*.

Over the next sections we describe in detail these two steps.

3.1 Rule Induction from Decision Trees

In order to generate a low FPR rule set, we extract rules from decision trees. We base this decision on the fact that the typical splitting criterion tries to find the *purest* leaves, i.e., leaves with highest precision that in theory maximize the amount of gained recall per FPR. For this reason, we will assume that all rules in the extracted candidate set predict the *positive* class.

After creating a tree with suitable, high purity leaves, we form a candidate rule set by extracting one rule for each leaf. This is accomplished by traversing the path from the root node to each leaf, forming a new rule as a conjunction of the conditions in this path. Figure 2 shows an example where a tree model with 5 leaves was converted to a rule set.

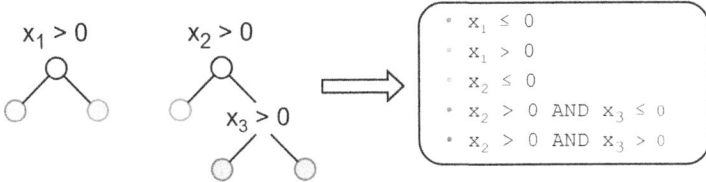

Fig. 2. Extracting rules from a FIGS model

This method does not extend well to additive tree models like FIGS, because it ignores tree scores when converting leaves to decision rules. To choose the best split on a tree $i \in \{1, 2, \ldots, T\}$, where T is the number of trees in the model, FIGS uses a mean squared error criterion with residuals calculated by subtracting from the label the predictions from all other trees j as targets. For a sample $(\mathbf{x}, y)$, the residual, r_i, for tree i is thus given by:

$$r_i(\mathbf{x}, y) = y - \sum_{\substack{j=1 \\ j \neq i}}^{T} \hat{y}_j(\mathbf{x}) , \qquad (1)$$

where $\hat{y}_j(\mathbf{x})$ is the prediction for tree j, given by the positive rate for the leaf node where the sample, $\mathbf{x}$, falls. This additive approach means that leaves generated by FIGS may not be pure enough to yield low FPR rules since they are meant to complement the predictions made by other trees.

For this reason, we modify FIGS by binarizing the residual computation, thus turning its Greedy Tree Sums into Greedy Tree Unions (FIGU). Concretely, when considering how to split a current leaf node in a tree i, we discard any samples that fall into the support of that node if they are already covered by a current leaf node of another tree j. I.e., we discard a sample $(\mathbf{x}, y)$ when evaluating the splitting criterion if:

$$\bigvee_{\substack{j=1 \\ j \neq i}}^{T} \hat{y}_j(\mathbf{x}) = \texttt{true} , \qquad (2)$$

where $\hat{y}_j(\mathbf{x})$ is now a binary prediction for tree j that evaluates to `true` if: 1) $\mathbf{x}$ falls into the support of a current leaf in tree j with high enough precision (as specified by a user provided threshold); 2) it falls into the support of the current best leaf of tree j as measured by precision.

3.2 Rule Selection

As mentioned in Sect. 3, the rule selection step aims to distill a potentially large set of candidate fraud rules into a smaller set, maximizing the number of fraud cases captured, i.e., the True Positive Rate (TPR) of the system, while keeping its FPR or Alert Rate below a given threshold. For concreteness, we will focus on the former constraint, FPR, in the exposition.

Writing as $\text{cov}(R; \mathcal{D})$ the example set covered by a rule set R on dataset $\mathcal{D}$, we have:

$$\text{TPR}(R) = \frac{|\text{cov}(R; \mathcal{D}^+)|}{|\mathcal{D}^+|}, \qquad \text{FPR}(R) = \frac{|\text{cov}(R; \mathcal{D}^-)|}{|\mathcal{D}^-|},$$

where we denote by $\mathcal{D}^+$ and $\mathcal{D}^-$ the subsets of positive and negative examples respectively. We can thus formalize the rule selection goal as choosing a subset of rules S from a given set of candidate rules $C = \{c_1, c_2, \ldots, c_n\}$ to solve:

$$\max_{S \in 2^C} \ \text{TPR}(S) \quad \text{s.t.} \quad \text{FPR}(S) \leq \text{FPR}_{\max}, \tag{3}$$

where $\text{FPR}_{\max}$ is the user-defined maximum desired FPR.

Both TPR and FPR are monotone non-decreasing submodular functions and this optimization problem is NP-hard [12]. We therefore propose a simple greedy method, described in Algorithm 1. It iteratively selects rules from C until a stopping criterion is met, which, in our case is when the FPR of the set of selected rules set surpasses $\text{FPR}_{\max}$. We assume that this always occurs over the runtime of the algorithm, i.e., that $\text{FPR}(C) \geq \text{FPR}_{\max}$. At each iteration, it selects the candidate rule with the highest precision in the set of samples that are not yet covered by any existing rules, where the precision of a rule, c, in a set of samples $\mathcal{D}$ is defined as:

$$\text{Precision}(c; \mathcal{D}) = \frac{|\text{cov}(c; \mathcal{D}^+)|}{|\text{cov}(c; \mathcal{D}^+)| + |\text{cov}(c; \mathcal{D}^-)|}. \tag{4}$$

Algorithm 1. Greedy Rule Selection Algorithm

Input: $(C = c_1, c_2, \ldots, c_n)$; $\text{FPR}_{\max}$; $\mathcal{D}$
$\mathcal{D}' \leftarrow \mathcal{D}$ ▷ $\mathcal{D}'$ corresponds to all samples not covered by rules in S
$S \leftarrow \{\}$ ▷ S is the selection set, containing all selected rules
$i \leftarrow 0$
while $\text{FPR}(S; \mathcal{D}) < \text{FPR}_{\max}$ **do**
  $i \leftarrow i + 1$
  $r_i \leftarrow \arg\max_{c \in C \setminus S} \text{Precision}(c; \mathcal{D}')$
  $\mathcal{D}' \leftarrow \mathcal{D}' \setminus \text{cov}(r_i; \mathcal{D}')$
  $S \leftarrow S \cup \{r_i\}$
end while
return $r_1, \ldots, r_i$

This algorithm returns a list of rules in the order they were selected. Defining $S_i := \{r_1, \ldots, r_i\}$ we have that S_{l-1} is guaranteed to satisfy the $\text{FPR}_{\max}$ constraint, whereas S_l may violate it, with l denoting the length of the returned list.

To compare rule sets with different FPR values generated from different candidate sets, we relax our solution set to include randomized rule sets. Instead of a fixed subset S of the candidate set, we output a probability, $\rho(c) \in [0,1]$ for every rule in $c \in C$ to be selected. For all but the last rule selected by Algorithm 1, i.e., $c \in S_{l-1}$, a probability of 1 is chosen. For the last rule selected, r_l, this probability is chosen in order to match the expected FPR with the desired FPR constraint. Formally, the probability $\rho(c)$ for a rule $c \in C$ is chosen as:

$$\rho(c) = \begin{cases} 1 & c \in S_{l-1} \\ \frac{\text{FPR}_{\max} - \text{FPR}(S_{l-1})}{\text{FPR}(S_l) - \text{FPR}(S_{l-1})} & c = r_l \\ 0 & c \notin S_l \end{cases},$$

With this in mind, we can interpret the TPR of this randomized rule system as a random variable with an expected value given by:

$$\text{TPR}(\rho) = (1 - \rho(r_l))\text{TPR}(S_{l-1}) + \rho(r_l)\text{TPR}(S_l).$$

4 Experiments

We evaluate RIFF on two public classification datasets: BAF [13], a synthetic bank account fraud dataset, and Taiwan credit [2], a credit card default dataset. We also use a private dataset, containing real transaction fraud data, which we cannot disclose due to privacy and contractual reasons. A baseline unique to this dataset is a set of rules manually tuned by data scientists allowing us to compare the rules generated by RIFF against rules handcrafted by experts. An overview of the used datasets can be seen in Table 1.

Table 1. Dataset Analysis Summary. The train/validation/test splits are time-based for the BAF and Industry datasets and random for Taiwan Credit.

	BAF	Industry	Taiwan Credit
Task	Account Fraud	Transaction Fraud	Credit Card Default
Positive rate	1%	7%	22%
#samples	1M	3.5M	30K
#features	32	113	25
Train split	75%	60%	60%
Validation and test split	12.5%	20%	20%

We sample the training set using a parameterized sample ratio into two smaller subsets, the induction and selection set. We use a sample ratio of 10% for the BAF and Industry datasets, and a sample ratio of 50% for the Taiwan credit dataset. In this step, we also parameterize the positive rate for the generated subsets, using a positive rate of 30% for all datasets. After using the induction set to train CART, FIGS and FIGU models, we extract candidate rules from the generated tree models, as described in Sect. 3.1. Then, the selection step of the algorithm extracts the best rules from each candidate set according to their performance on the selection set. In this step of the experiment we use a $\text{FPR}_{\max}$ of 1%. We use the validation set to tune the total number of splits used when training the decision-tree model, using a line search over the values [10, 20, 30, 40, 50] and we use the test set for the final evaluation of the generated rule set.

We use LightGBM as a strong baseline for predictive performance for two reasons: firstly, because gradient boosted decision trees are a state-of-the-art algorithm for tabular data; secondly, because of their popularity in fraud detection [8]. We also report the performance of the best CART and FIGS models trained in the induction step as divide-and-conquer baselines.

Table 2. Recall at 1% FPR in the test split for BAF, Credit and Industry Datasets

	BAF	Industry	Taiwan Credit
LightGBM	0.252	0.531	0.084
Expert Rules	–	0.158	–
CART	$0.160_{\pm 0.005}$	$0.315_{\pm 0.075}$	$0.063_{\pm 0.009}$
CART + RIFF	$\mathbf{0.184}_{\pm 0.006}$	$\mathbf{0.362}_{\pm 0.027}$	$\mathbf{0.139}_{\pm 0.018}$
FIGS	$\mathbf{0.210}_{\pm 0.006}$	$\mathbf{0.394}_{\pm 0.032}$	$0.067_{\pm 0.016}$
FIGS + RIFF	$0.158_{\pm 0.016}$	$0.311_{\pm 0.018}$	$\mathbf{0.136}_{\pm 0.019}$
FIGU + RIFF	$0.155_{\pm 0.010}$	$0.382_{\pm 0.039}$	$0.104_{\pm 0.007}$

Table 3. Generated Rule set length for BAF, Credit and Industry Datasets

	BAF	Industry	Taiwan Credit
Expert Rules	–	13.0	–
CART + RIFF	$10.4_{\pm 3.647}$	$17.8_{\pm 4.087}$	$5.2_{\pm 1.483}$
FIGS + RIFF	$8.0_{\pm 1.732}$	$9.2_{\pm 1.304}$	$7.6_{\pm 1.949}$
FIGU + RIFF	$\mathbf{3.6}_{\pm 0.548}$	$\mathbf{3.4}_{\pm 0.548}$	$\mathbf{1.0}_{\pm 0.000}$

We repeat our setup using 5 different seeds for the model training and the sampling of the induction and selection sets. In Tables 2 and 3 we report the average performance and average length of generated rule sets of all seeds respectively, as well as the associated standard deviations. Interestingly, using RIFF on CART always improved its performance, a possible indication that CART was overfitting and RIFF reduced this by selecting its best rules. For the dataset with fewer samples, Taiwan Credit, RIFF increased the performance of CART and FIGS significantly, surpassing even LightGBM's performance. FIGU appears to generate rule sets that have similar performance to FIGS with much fewer rules, an indication that FIGU is able to reduce the overlap between generated trees, leading to shorter and, in theory, simpler to understand rule sets.

5 Conclusion And Future Work

In this work we propose RIFF, a rule induction algorithm that builds low FPR rule sets for fraud detection by greedily extracting rules from a tree based model like CART or FIGS. We also propose a slight modification to FIGS, FIGU, that aims to lower decision tree complexity so that it can be used by the RIFF selection algorithm to generate shorter rulesets. We perform a study with real world transaction data that shows that RIFF is able to perform better than expert rules. Our experiments show that RIFF is able to maintain the predictive performance of the original models while reducing their complexity by turning them into rules. In addition, when paired with RIFF, FIGU is able to generate rule sets with fewer rules, with similar performance to rules generated by FIGS.

While RIFF effectively generates a more concise and shorter rule set, it might provide complex, lengthier rules. We could expand the candidate set to also consider all nodes, instead of only leaves. This methodology draws a parallel to pruning methods, as this ideally leads RIFF into choosing more general, lower depth nodes in favour of their more specific, children nodes, similar to pruning.

A possible way to generate a more varied and robust rule set could involve extracting rules from all the trained CART and FIGS models into an unique candidate set. Since our setup subsamples the training set into subsests, and uses them to train these models, this is equivalent to applying the RIFF selection algorithm to a Random Forest [3] or Bagging FIGS [21].

References

1. Aparício, D., Barata, R., Bravo, J., Ascensão, J.T., Bizarro, P.: ARMS: automated rules management system for fraud detection. CoRR **abs/2002.06075** (2020)
2. Bache, K., Lichman, M.: UCI machine learning repository (2013). http://archive.ics.uci.edu/ml
3. Breiman, L.: Random forests. Mach. Learn. **45**(1), 5–32 (2001). https://doi.org/10.1023/A:1010933404324
4. Breiman, L., Friedman, J.H., Olshen, R.A., Stone, C.J.: Classification and regression trees. Wadsworth (1984). http://lyle.smu.edu/~mhd/8331f06/cart.pdf
5. Cendrowska, J.: Prism: an algorithm for inducing modular rules. Int. J. Man Mach. Stud. **27**(4), 349–370 (1987). https://doi.org/10.1016/S0020-7373(87)80003-2
6. Clark, P., Niblett, T.: The cn2 induction algorithm. Mach. Learn. **3**, 261–283 (1989).https://doi.org/10.1023/A:1022641700528
7. Cohen, W.W.: Fast effective rule induction. In: Prieditis, A., Russell, S. (eds.) Machine Learning Proceedings 1995, pp. 115–123. Morgan Kaufmann, San Francisco (CA) (1995). https://doi.org/10.1016/B978-1-55860-377-6.50023-2
8. Cruz, A.F., Belém, C., Jesus, S., Bravo, J., Saleiro, P., Bizarro, P.: Fairgbm: gradient boosting with fairness constraints (2023). https://arxiv.org/abs/2209.07850
9. Friedman, J.H.: Greedy function approximation: a gradient boosting machine. Ann. Stat. 1189–1232 (2001). https://doi.org/10.1214/aos/1013203451
10. Fürnkranz, J., Widmer, G.: Incremental reduced error pruning. In: ICML, pp. 70–77 (1994). https://doi.org/10.1016/B978-1-55860-335-6.50017-9

11. Hong J., Mozetic I., M.R.S.: Aq15: incremental learning of attribute-based descriptions from examples, the method and user's guide. Reports of the Intelligent Systems Group, July 1986. https://hdl.handle.net/1920/1605
12. Iyer, R.K., Bilmes, J.A.: Submodular optimization with submodular cover and submodular knapsack constraints. CoRR **abs/1311.2106** (2013). http://arxiv.org/abs/1311.2106
13. Jesus, S., et al.: Turning the tables: biased, imbalanced, dynamic tabular datasets for ML evaluation. In: Advances in Neural Information Processing Systems (2022)
14. Kusters, R., Kim, Y., Collery, M., de Sainte Marie, C., Gupta, S.: Differentiable rule induction with learned relational features (2022). https://doi.org/10.48550/ARXIV.2201.06515
15. Michalski, R.S.: Pattern recognition as rule-guided inductive inference. IEEE Trans. Pattern Anal. Mach. Intell. **PAMI-2**, 349–361 (1980). https://api.semanticscholar.org/CorpusID:16719183
16. Michalski, R.S., Mozeti, I., Hong, J., Lavra, N.: The multi-purpose incremental learning system aq15 and its testing application to three medical domains. In: AAAI Conference on Artificial Intelligence (1986). https://api.semanticscholar.org/CorpusID:18018701
17. Qiao, L., Wang, W., Lin, B.: Learning accurate and interpretable decision rule sets from neural networks. CoRR **abs/2103.02826** (2021). https://arxiv.org/abs/2103.02826
18. Quinlan, J.R.: Induction of decision trees. Mach. Learn. **1**, 81–106 (1986). https://doi.org/10.1007/BF00116251
19. Quinlan, J.R.: Learning logical definitions from relations. Mach. Learn. **5**, 239–266 (1990). https://api.semanticscholar.org/CorpusID:6746439
20. Quinlan, J.R.: C4.5: Programs for Machine Learning. Morgan Kaufmann Publishers Inc., San Francisco, CA, USA (1993). https://doi.org/10.1007/BF00993309
21. Tan, Y.S., Singh, C., Nasseri, K., Agarwal, A., Yu, B.: Fast interpretable greedy-tree sums (FIGS). CoRR **abs/2201.11931** (2022)

Ontology-Based Update in Virtual Knowledge Graphs via Schema Mapping Recovery

Romuald Esdras Wandji[1] and Diego Calvanese[1,2]

[1] Department of Computing Science, Umeå Universitet, Umeå, Sweden
{romuald.esdras.wandji,diego.calvanese}@umu.se, diego.calvanese@unibz.it
[2] Faculty of Engineering, Free University of Bozen-Bolzano, Bolzano, Italy

Abstract. In Virtual Knowledge Graphs (VKGs), access to a relational data source is provided through an ontology, which is linked to the data source via declarative mappings. VKGs stand as a predominant paradigm for the access to (and integration of) heterogeneous data sources. However, little attention has been paid so far to the issue of updates in VKGs expressed over the ontology, which represents a crucial feature for fully managing data sources through the lens of an ontology. In this paper, we consider the problem of updating a VKG instance by specifying a set of insertions and deletions of ontology instances and propagating these updates to the underlying data source through the VKG mapping. We consider ontologies specified in the $DL\text{-}Lite_R$ lightweight ontology language and study the problem for the case where source queries in mappings are unions of conjunctive queries. We rely on the notion of maximum recovery of VKG mappings, borrowed from the data exchange setting, and propose methods to compute the set of source updates that translate an ontology update with a minimal side-effect, considering both insertions and deletions of multiple ABox assertions.

Keywords: Knowledge Representation · Virtual Knowledge Graph (VKG) · Ontology-based Data Access · View Updates

1 Introduction

Virtual Knowledge Graphs (VKGs) provide a powerful paradigm to address data integration, which has been studied extensively for the case of relational data sources. In VKGs, users interact with a high-level, conceptual representation of the domain of interest given in the form of an ontology that is linked to the data source via declarative mappings [6,23,25,26]. The ontology is typically expressed in the OWL 2 QL profile of the Web Ontology Language (OWL 2) [22]. Such language, which has been specifically designed to be used in this context, has its formal counterpart in $DL\text{-}Lite_R$, a Description Logic (DL) of the $DL\text{-}Lite$ family of lightweight DLs [7].

The primary focus of research on VKGs has been on query answering i.e., the problem of computing the answers to a user query posed over the ontology by exploiting the ontology axioms and the mapping layer to extract the relevant data from the underlying data source. In this paper, instead, we are concerned with the challenging problem of *updating* a VKG by operating on the ontology, which is a key task required in full-fledged ontology-based data management systems, where all operations that involve the data source should be carried out through the lens of the ontology. Notice that this problem requires on the one hand to deal with potential inconsistencies between the update and the axioms of the ontology TBox, and on the other hand to propagate the update via the mappings to the underlying data source. The first problem is rooted in the vast literature on knowledge base update and belief revision [15, 19, 20, 24], which includes work dealing specifically with lightweight DLs [27]. The latter problem, instead, is tightly connected to the problem of *view-update*, which has a long history in the database literature [4, 12, 18], but is still open in the general case. Instead, only very few works have dealt with how mappings impact updates in the context of VKGs. In [14], it is proposed to store ontology updates in additional tables, without affecting the original database, and by adjusting the mapping to reconstruct the updated VKG from the original one and the data in the additional tables. However, such approach cannot be applied in the very common case where the user has access to the data sources at the data level, but is not entitled to modify their schema or to add additional sources.

In this work, we are therefore interested in how to perform updates in VKGs by directly propagating them to the underlying data source via the mappings. For this, we have to address two key problems: *(i)* The update might not be *realizable*, since an insertion on the data source guaranteeing that the requested ABox facts are inserted from the VKG, might have as *side-effect* the insertion of additional ABox facts. Similarly for deletions. *(ii)* The mappings might lose information (e.g., due to the presence of disjunction or of existential variables in mapping queries), and therefore there might be multiple ways to update the source data corresponding to a VKG update.

As a motivating example, consider a data source with two relations: $RS(res, sup)$ that relates researchers to their supervisor(s), and $SG(sup, gr)$ that relates supervisors to the grants they have access to. The information in this source has to be integrated into a VKG whose ontology contains a role *access*, relating researchers to grants, and a class *Active* containing active supervisors. We consider a mapping $\mathcal{M}$ between this source schema and the ontology consisting of the following assertion:

$$\exists y. RS(x,y) \wedge SG(y,z) \rightsquigarrow access(x,z). \tag{1}$$

Let us assume a user wants to update the extensional content of the system by inserting a new grant access with the ABox fact $access(\text{john}, \text{grant1})$. Due to the existential variable in the mapping source query, there are (infinitely) many distinct translations of the given ABox insertion, e.g., the insertions in the data source of $\{RS(\text{john}, \text{sup1}), SG(\text{sup1}, \text{grant1})\}$, or of $\{RS(\text{john}, \text{sup2}), SG(\text{sup2}, \text{grant1})\}$. But in reality, which supervisor to choose for the researcher being inserted has no importance in this context as this information is not visible to the user. So, it can be randomly created, or a default value can be assigned to every added access. However, if $SG(x,y) \rightsquigarrow Active(x)$ is added to $\mathcal{M}$, the choice of the supervisor for an inserted access becomes important, because it may lead to an unintended effect over the VKG. Depending on other facts in the source, inserting a new grant access might lead to a side-effect, thus making the update unrealizable.

In this paper, we address this problem by proposing a comprehensive framework for ABox updates in VKGs that builds on the work on *schema mapping recovery* introduced in the context of data exchange [2] (see Sect. 4), and on *data lineage* in databases [9, 10] (see Sect. 5). Specifically, we show that we can use a so-called *maximum recovery* to characterize the source updates corresponding to ABox updates, and moreover, such maximal recoveries can be computed from the mapping assertions using query rewriting techniques. Exploiting these notions, we provide algorithms for translating a set of ABox deletions and insertions into suitable deletions or insertions over the source with minimal side effects (see Sect. 6). Section 7 concludes the paper.

2 Preliminaries

We now introduce the notions on DLs, databases (DBs), and VKGs necessary to understand the technical development in the paper, assuming familiarity with the syntax and semantics of first-order logic (FOL). We consider distinct, countably infinite, and pairwise disjoint alphabets $\mathbf{N}_C$ of *concept names*, $\mathbf{N}_P$ of *role names*, and $\mathbf{N}_I$ of constants.

2.1 Description Logic Knowledge Bases

Description Logics (DLs) [3] allow for modeling a domain of interest in terms of *concepts* and *roles*, which correspond to unary and binary predicates, respectively. A DL *knowledge base* (KB) $\mathcal{K} = \langle \mathcal{T}, \mathcal{A} \rangle$ consists of a *TBox* $\mathcal{T}$, capturing intensional information, and an *ABox* $\mathcal{A}$, providing extensional information. We consider DLs of the *DL-Lite* family [7,23], and specifically *DL-Lite$_R$*, which is the formal counterpart of the tractable OWL 2 QL profile of the Web Ontology Language (OWL 2) [22].

A *DL-Lite$_R$* TBox is a finite set of assertions of the form $B_1 \sqsubseteq B_2$ (*concept inclusion*), $B_1 \sqsubseteq \neg B_2$ (*concept disjointness*), $R_1 \sqsubseteq R_2$ (*role inclusion*), or $R_1 \sqsubseteq \neg R_2$ (*role disjointness*). Here, R (possibly sub-scripted) denotes an atomic role $P \in \mathbf{N}_P$ or its inverse P^-, while B (possibly sub-scripted) denotes a *basic concept*, which is either an atomic concept $A \in \mathbf{N}_C$, or a concept of the form $\exists R$. For a TBox $\mathcal{T}$, we use $\mathcal{T}^+$ to denote the set of concept and role inclusions in $\mathcal{T}$, and $\mathcal{T}^-$ to denote the set of concept and role disjointness assertions in $\mathcal{T}$, hence $\mathcal{T} = \mathcal{T}^+ \cup \mathcal{T}^-$. A *DL-Lite$_R$* ABox is a finite set of assertions of the form $A(c)$ or $P(c,c')$, with $A \in \mathbf{N}_C$, $P \in \mathbf{N}_P$, and $c, c' \in \mathbf{N}_I$.

The semantics of a DL KB is given in terms of first-order interpretations [3], where an *interpretation* $\mathcal{I} = \langle \Delta^{\mathcal{I}}, \cdot^{\mathcal{I}} \rangle$ consists of an *interpretation domain* $\Delta^{\mathcal{I}}$ and an *interpretation function* $\cdot^{\mathcal{I}}$, which maps each $A \in \mathbf{N}_C$ to $A^{\mathcal{I}} \subseteq \Delta^{\mathcal{I}}$, each $P \in \mathbf{N}_P$ to $P^{\mathcal{I}} \subseteq \Delta^{\mathcal{I}} \times \Delta^{\mathcal{I}}$, and each $c \in \mathbf{N}_I$ to $c^{\mathcal{I}} \in \Delta^{\mathcal{I}}$. The interpretation functions is extended to arbitrary concepts and roles as follows: $(P^-)^{\mathcal{I}} = \{(o',o) \mid (o,o') \in P^{\mathcal{I}}\}$, $(\exists R)^{\mathcal{I}} = \{o \mid \text{there exists } o' \text{ s.t. } (o,o') \in R^{\mathcal{I}}\}$, $(\neg B)^{\mathcal{I}} = \Delta^{\mathcal{I}} \setminus B^{\mathcal{I}}$, and $(\neg R)^{\mathcal{I}} = (\Delta^{\mathcal{I}} \times \Delta^{\mathcal{I}}) \setminus R^{\mathcal{I}}$. An interpretation $\mathcal{I}$ is a *model* of (or *satisfies*) $A(c)$ if $c^{\mathcal{I}} \in A^{\mathcal{I}}$, $P(c,c')$ if $(c^{\mathcal{I}}, c'^{\mathcal{I}}) \in P^{\mathcal{I}}$), and $E_1 \sqsubseteq E_2$ if $E_1^{\mathcal{I}} \subseteq E_2^{\mathcal{I}}$. Also, $\mathcal{I}$ is a *model* of $\mathcal{T}$, $\mathcal{A}$, and $\mathcal{K} = \langle \mathcal{T}, \mathcal{A} \rangle$ if it is a model of all assertions in $\mathcal{T}$, $\mathcal{A}$, and $\mathcal{T} \cup \mathcal{A}$, respectively. We denote with $Mod(\mathcal{K})$ the set of all models of $\mathcal{K}$, and say that $\mathcal{K}$ is *consistent* if $Mod(\mathcal{K}) \neq \emptyset$. We say that $\mathcal{A}$ is $\mathcal{T}$-*consistent*, if $\langle \mathcal{T}, \mathcal{A} \rangle$ is consistent. A TBox or ABox assertion α is *logically implied* by $\mathcal{T}$ (resp., $\mathcal{K}$), denotes $\mathcal{T} \models \alpha$ (resp., $\mathcal{K} \models \alpha$) if each model of $\mathcal{T}$ (resp., $\mathcal{K}$) satisfies α. We denote by $cl_{\mathcal{T}}(\mathcal{A})$ the *closure of* $\mathcal{A}$ w.r.t. $\mathcal{T}$, that is, the set of ABox assertions over individuals in $\mathcal{A}$ that are logically implied by $\langle \mathcal{T}, \mathcal{A} \rangle$. Similarly, the *deductive closure* of a TBox $\mathcal{T}$, denoted $cl(\mathcal{T})$ is the set of inclusions assertions that are logically implied by $\mathcal{T}$. Finally, given two ABoxes $\mathcal{A}_1$ and $\mathcal{A}_2$, we say that $\mathcal{A}_1$ is *logically equivalent* to $\mathcal{A}_2$ w.r.t. $\mathcal{T}$, denoted $\mathcal{A}_1 \equiv_{\mathcal{T}} \mathcal{A}_2$, if $cl_{\mathcal{T}}(\mathcal{A}_1) = cl_{\mathcal{T}}(\mathcal{A}_2)$.

We adopt here the *standard name assumption*, i.e., for each interpretation $\mathcal{I}$ of a KB $\mathcal{K} = \langle \mathcal{T}, \mathcal{A} \rangle$, $\Delta^{\mathcal{I}}$ contains all individuals of $\mathcal{A}$, and for each such individual c, $c^{\mathcal{I}} = c$.

2.2 Relational Databases and Queries

A *database schema* is a finite set $\mathcal{S} = \{r_1/n_1, \ldots, r_k/n_k\}$ of relation schemas, where each r_i is a predicate name of arity n_i. A database instance D over $\mathcal{S}$ maps each predicate r/n in $\mathcal{S}$ to an n-ary relation, denoted r^D. An *atom* for r/n has the form $r(t_1, \ldots, t_n)$, or simply $r(\boldsymbol{t})$, where each t_j is a term, which can be a constant from $\mathbf{N}_I$ or a variable. If all t_j's are constants, the atom is called ground, or simply a *tuple*.

A (FOL) formula over a relational schema $\mathcal{S}$ is constructed by using the relation names in $\mathcal{S}$, the equality predicate $=$, and the constants in $\mathbf{N}_I$. A formula φ with free variables $\boldsymbol{x}$ is denoted $\varphi(\boldsymbol{x})$, and is also called a (relational) *query* with *answer variables* $\boldsymbol{x}$. The formula is *closed* when $\boldsymbol{x}$ is empty. The closed formula obtained from $\varphi(\boldsymbol{x})$ by replacing every variable in $\boldsymbol{x}$ by the corresponding constant in $\boldsymbol{c}$ is denoted $\varphi(\boldsymbol{c})$. For an instance D over $\mathcal{S}$, we use $D \models \varphi(\boldsymbol{c})$ to denote that $\varphi(\boldsymbol{c})$ holds in D. For a closed formula φ and a set Σ of closed formulae over $\mathcal{S}$, we use $\Sigma \models \varphi$ to indicate that φ *is implied by* Σ, i.e., φ holds in all instances in which all formulae of Σ hold.

A *conjunctive query* (CQ) $Q(\boldsymbol{x})$ over the schema $\mathcal{S}$ is a query defined by a formula of the form $\exists \boldsymbol{y}.\varphi(\boldsymbol{x}, \boldsymbol{y})$, where $\varphi = r_1(\boldsymbol{t}_1) \wedge \cdots \wedge r_n(\boldsymbol{t}_n)$ is a conjunction of atomic formulae whose variables belong to $\boldsymbol{x} \cup \boldsymbol{y}$. The variables $\boldsymbol{y}$ are called *existential variables*. We also express such CQ as a logical rule of the form $Q(\boldsymbol{x}) \leftarrow r_1(\boldsymbol{t}_1), \ldots, r_n(\boldsymbol{t}_n)$, where $Q(\boldsymbol{x})$ is called the *head* and $r_1(\boldsymbol{t}_1), \ldots, r_n(\boldsymbol{t}_n)$ the *body* of the rule. A *union of conjunctive queries* (UCQ) is a finite disjunction of CQs with the same answer variables, also represented as a finite set of rules with the same head.

2.3 Schema Mappings

In VKGs, mappings are used to (virtually) populate ontology concepts and roles with individuals and values derived from the data in the underlying data source. We consider mappings specified in the standard language R2RML [11], but adopt a simplified abstract notation [23], which is also close to the one of *plain second-order tuple-generating dependency* (plain SO-tgds) introduced in data exchange [1].

Formally, a *VKG mapping* $\mathcal{M}$ from a source schema $\mathcal{S}$ to an ontology (TBox) $\mathcal{T}$ consists of a set of *mapping assertions* of the form $Q(\boldsymbol{x}) \rightsquigarrow E(\boldsymbol{t}(\boldsymbol{x}))$, where $Q(\boldsymbol{x})$ is a CQ (called *source query*) over $\mathcal{S}$ of arity $n > 0$, and $E(\boldsymbol{t}(\boldsymbol{x}))$ is an atom (called *target atom*) over $\mathcal{T}$ with variables in $\boldsymbol{x}$. Such atom has the form $A(t_1(\boldsymbol{x}_1))$, with $A \in \mathbf{N}_C$, or $P(t_1(\boldsymbol{x}_1), t_2(\boldsymbol{x}_2))$, with $P \in \mathbf{N}_P$, where the terms $t_1(\boldsymbol{x}_1)$ and $t_2(\boldsymbol{x}_2)$ denote so-called *IRI-templates*, obtained by applying (skolem) functions to the answer variables of the source query. Such IRI-templates[1] are used to generate strings representing object *IRIs* (Internationalized Resource Identifiers) or (RDF) literals, starting

---

[1] IRI-templates correspond to the R2RML *string templates*.

from DB values retrieved by the source query in the mapping. Notice that in practice, it is desired that the union of all templates corresponds to an *injective* function, i.e., there is a unique way to reconstruct from a string s, the actual IRI-template $t(\boldsymbol{x})$ and the constituent values $\boldsymbol{v}$ used to generate $s = t(\boldsymbol{v})$. Moreover we assume that for each IRI-template $f(x_1, \ldots, x_n)$, we have also n *inverse templates*[2] $f^1, \ldots, f^n$ such that $f^i(f(v_1, \ldots, v_n)) = v_i$, for each $i \in [1..n]$ and for all possible values $v_1, \ldots, v_n$ instantiating the variables in $t(x_1, \ldots, x_n)$.

Such a VKG mapping $\mathcal{M}$ from $\mathcal{S}$ to $\mathcal{T}$, which we also call a *source-to-ontology mapping* (*so-mapping*), maps a DB instance D of $\mathcal{S}$ to the (*unique*) ABox

$$\mathcal{M}(D) = \{\mathsf{as}(E(t(\boldsymbol{x})), \boldsymbol{x} \mapsto \boldsymbol{o}) \mid (\boldsymbol{x} \mapsto \boldsymbol{o}) \in Q(\boldsymbol{x})^D, (Q(\boldsymbol{x}) \rightsquigarrow E(t(\boldsymbol{x}))) \in \mathcal{M}\}$$

where $\boldsymbol{x} \mapsto \boldsymbol{o}$ represents a solution mapping from the evaluation $Q(\boldsymbol{x})^D$ of the source query $Q(\boldsymbol{x})$ over the DB instance D, and the term $\mathsf{as}(E(t(\boldsymbol{x})), \boldsymbol{x} \mapsto \boldsymbol{o}))$ denotes the ABox assertion obtained by applying the solution mapping $\boldsymbol{x} \mapsto \boldsymbol{o}$ to $E(t(\boldsymbol{x}))$. This application typically involves replacing $\boldsymbol{x}$ with $\boldsymbol{o}$ in the templates in $t(\boldsymbol{x})$ (using appropriate string concatenation operations). It is also convenient to consider an so-mapping $\mathcal{M}$ as the set of pairs $\{(D, \mathcal{M}(D)) \mid D \text{ is a DB instance of } \mathcal{S}\}$, so that $(D, \mathcal{A}) \in \mathcal{M}$ is an alternative notation for $\mathcal{A} = \mathcal{M}(D)$. Notice that, since a concept name A (or role name P) might appear as target atom of multiple mapping assertions, the source query that generates the instances of A (or P) is in general a UCQ.

2.4 Virtual Knowledge Graphs

We recall the main elements of the VKG framework, also known as *Ontology-based Data Access* (OBDA) [23,25]. A *VKG specification* is a tuple $\mathcal{P} = \langle \mathcal{T}, \mathcal{M}, \mathcal{S} \rangle$, where $\mathcal{T}$ is a *DL-Lite$_R$* TBox (typically expressed in OWL 2 QL), $\mathcal{S}$ is a data source schema, and $\mathcal{M}$ is a set of so-mappings from $\mathcal{S}$ to $\mathcal{T}$. A *VKG instance* is a pair $\langle \mathcal{P}, D \rangle$ where D is a source instance of $\mathcal{S}$. Its semantics is defined in terms of FO interpretations over $\mathcal{T}$. An interpretation $\mathcal{I}$ is a *model* of $\langle \mathcal{P}, D \rangle$ if it is a model of the DL KB $\langle \mathcal{T}, \mathcal{M}(D) \rangle$.

We recall also the notion of *mapping saturation* [21], which allows one to compile into the mapping $\mathcal{M}$ the inclusion assertions of $\mathcal{T}$ that do *not* involve an existential quantification $\exists R$ in the right-hand side. Specifically, to compute the *mapping saturation* $sat_{\mathcal{T}}(\mathcal{M})$ *of* $\mathcal{M}$ *w.r.t.* $\mathcal{T}$, we start from $\mathcal{M}$, and repeatedly add implied mapping assertions. E.g., if $Q(\boldsymbol{x}) \rightsquigarrow A_1(t(\boldsymbol{x}))$ is in $sat_{\mathcal{T}}(\mathcal{M})$ and $A_1 \sqsubseteq A_2$ is in $\mathcal{T}$, we add to $sat_{\mathcal{T}}(\mathcal{M})$ also $Q(\boldsymbol{x}) \rightsquigarrow A_2(t(\boldsymbol{x}))$; similarly for inclusions $\exists R \sqsubseteq A$ and $R_1 \sqsubseteq R_2$.

3 Instance-Level Updates in VKGs

We consider instance-level updates that consist of basic operations of two types, namely deletions and insertions of ABox assertions, and the key problem we are interested in is the translation of ABox updates into suitable source updates. In this paper, we restrict our attention to the two cases of updates consisting either of a set $\mathcal{U}_A^-$ of *ABox deletions*, or of a set $\mathcal{U}_A^+$ of *ABox insertions*, each given as a set of ABox facts, and consider

---

[2] These correspond to the `rr:inverseExpression` of R2RML.

translations that are of the same type as the ABox updates, i.e., $\mathcal{U}_A^-$ translates to a set $\mathcal{U}_D^-$ of source deletions, and $\mathcal{U}_A^+$ to a set $\mathcal{U}_D^+$ of source insertions. We leave the case of combined deletions and insertions and of more general translations for future work.

We concentrate here on the problem of propagating updates to the data source via the mappings and do not deal explicitly with possible inconsistencies w.r.t. the TBox and (virtual) ABox that an update might cause. Hence, we take the simple approach of rejecting updates that would lead to an inconsistency. Since for *DL-Lite$_R$*, inconsistencies are due to the violation of disjointness assertions only and deletions of ABox facts cannot cause such violations, we need to pay attention to inconsistency only for ABox insertions. Formally, we reject an insertion update $\mathcal{U}_A^+$ if $\langle \mathcal{T}, \mathcal{A} \cup \mathcal{U}_A^+ \rangle$ is inconsistent. Instead of rejecting inconsistent updates, we could also rely on the many approaches that have been proposed for handling inconsistency in KB updates, which typically are based on computing some form of *ABox repair* that removes the inconsistencies from the KB [19,20,24]. We can then consider the original update combined with the ABox repair as the overall consistent VKG update to which we apply our techniques.

Apart from possible inconsistencies, the TBox has additional effects on updates that we need to take into account. Since *DL-Lite$_R$* is Horn [7], an entailed ABox fact is already entailed by the TBox $\mathcal{T}$ together with a *single ABox fact* [27]. For an ABox insertion $\mathcal{U}_A^+$, we can, therefore account for $\mathcal{T}$ by adding to $\mathcal{U}_A^+$ all facts in $cl_\mathcal{T}(\mathcal{U}_A^+)$. For an ABox deletion $\mathcal{U}_A^-$, instead, we can account for $\mathcal{T}$ by (repeatedly) adding to $\mathcal{U}_A^-$ all those facts from the ABox $\mathcal{A}$ that would entail a fact already in $\mathcal{U}_A^-$. We denote such set of facts by $invcl_\mathcal{T}^\mathcal{A}(\mathcal{U}_A^-)$. Notice that $cl_\mathcal{T}(\mathcal{U}_A^+)$ and $invcl_\mathcal{T}^\mathcal{A}(\mathcal{U}_A^-)$ can be computed in polynomial time in the combined size of $\mathcal{U}_A^+, \mathcal{U}_A^-, \mathcal{T}$, and $\mathcal{A}$ [7,27]. Based on this, we will assume in the following that $\mathcal{U}_A^+$ is already closed w.r.t. $\mathcal{T}$, i.e., that $\mathcal{U}_A^+ = cl_\mathcal{T}(\mathcal{U}_A^+)$, and that $\mathcal{U}_A^-$ is already "inverse-closed" w.r.t. $\mathcal{T}$ and $\mathcal{A}$, i.e., that $\mathcal{U}_A^- = invcl_\mathcal{T}^\mathcal{A}(\mathcal{U}_A^-)$.

Considering (inverse-)closed updates brings us nearer to the case where we can restrict the attention to VKG specifications where the TBox does not contain any inclusion assertion, but only disjointness assertions. However, we have to consider that propagating ABox updates to the data source might lead to source updates that have side-effects in the ABox. Since we are interested in minimizing such side-effects, we also have to take into account how they are affected by the TBox. In the case of insertions, the TBox axioms might amplify side-effects, while for deletions, they might amplify them but also reduce them, as illustrated in the following example.

Example 1. Let $\mathcal{P}_0 = \langle \mathcal{T}_0, \mathcal{M}_0, \mathcal{S}_0 \rangle$ be a VKG specification, where $\mathcal{T}_0 = \{A_1 \sqsubseteq B_1, A_1 \sqsubseteq B_2\}$, $\mathcal{S}_0 = \{r_1/1, r_2/1, r_3/1\}$, and $\mathcal{M}_0 = \{r_1(x) \rightsquigarrow A_1(x), r_2(x) \rightsquigarrow B_1(x), r_3(x) \rightsquigarrow A_2(x)\}$, and let $\mathcal{J}_0 = \langle \mathcal{P}_0, D_0 \rangle$ be a corresponding VKG instance, where $D_0 = \{r_1(\mathsf{c}), r_2(\mathsf{c}), r_3(\mathsf{c})\}$. We obtain $\mathcal{M}_0(D_0) = \{A_1(\mathsf{c}), B_1(\mathsf{c}), A_2(\mathsf{c})\}$, and $cl_{\mathcal{T}_0}(\mathcal{M}_0(D_0)) = \mathcal{M}_0(D_0) \cup \{B_2(\mathsf{c})\}$. Suppose we want to delete the ABox fact $B_1(\mathsf{c})$. We express this as the (inverse-closed) deletion request $\mathcal{U}_A^- = \{B_1(\mathsf{c}), A_1(\mathsf{c})\}$. It is easy to see that a source deletion translating $\mathcal{U}_A^-$ is $\mathcal{U}_D^- = \{r_1(\mathsf{c}), r_2(\mathsf{c})\}$, which has as side-effect also the deletion of $B_2(\mathsf{c})$ from $cl_{\mathcal{T}_0}(\mathcal{M}_0(D_0))$. However, if $\mathcal{T}_0$ contained also the inclusion assertion $A_2 \sqsubseteq B_2$, then $\mathcal{U}_D^-$ would have no side-effect. ◁

In *DL-Lite$_R$*, disjointness assertions might lead to inconsistency, but do not contribute to the implication of ABox assertions [7]. Moreover, inclusion assertions of the form $B \sqsubseteq \exists R$ directly[3] imply only facts that involve an existentially quantified object, hence they do not directly contribute to the closure of an ABox. Therefore, to account for implied insertions and deletions of ABox facts, we can compute (in polynomial time) the deductive closure $cl(\mathcal{T})$ of the TBox $\mathcal{T}$, and use only the set of inclusion assertions in $cl(\mathcal{T})$ of the form $A' \sqsubseteq A$ or $\exists R \sqsubseteq A$ (i.e., with an atomic concept on the right-hand side), or $R_1 \sqsubseteq R_2$, which we denote $red(\mathcal{T})$. Considering then that in VKGs we want to account for the side-effects caused by $red(\mathcal{T})$ on the (virtual) ABox generated from a source instance via a mapping $\mathcal{M}$, we can do so while compiling away $red(\mathcal{T})$, and using instead of $\mathcal{M}$ the *saturated mapping* $sat_{red(\mathcal{T})}(\mathcal{M})$ [21]. Based on these considerations, we assume from now on that mappings are already saturated, and w.l.o.g. we restrict the attention to the case where the TBox contains only disjointness assertions, i.e., $\mathcal{T} = \mathcal{T}^-$.

We now characterize the translation of ABox deletions and insertions. For deletions, we can rely on the fact that they do not cause violations of disjointness assertions.

Definition 1 (Deletion translation). *Given a VKG instance $\mathcal{J} = \langle \langle \mathcal{T}, \mathcal{M}, \mathcal{S} \rangle, D \rangle$ and a set $\mathcal{U}_A^-$ of ABox deletions, a source update $\mathcal{U}_D^-$ is a translation of $\mathcal{U}_A^-$ in $\mathcal{J}$ if $\mathcal{U}_A^- \cap \mathcal{M}(D \setminus \mathcal{U}_D^-) = \emptyset$. $\mathcal{U}_D^-$ is an exact translation if $\mathcal{M}(D) \setminus \mathcal{U}_A^- = \mathcal{M}(D \setminus \mathcal{U}_D^-)$.* ◁

Hence, an exact translation of $\mathcal{U}_A^-$ in $\mathcal{J}$ ensures that exactly all assertions of $\mathcal{U}_A^-$ are deleted from the (virtual) ABox generated by the mapping from the data sourcex, while a non-exact translation might also cause the deletion of additional assertions not in $\mathcal{U}_A^-$.

Example 2. Consider the VKG specification $\mathcal{P}_1 = \langle \emptyset, \mathcal{M}_1, \mathcal{S}_1 \rangle$, where $\mathcal{S}_1 = \{RS/2, SG/2, RG/2\}$, and $\mathcal{M}_1$ consists of the mapping assertion in Eq. (1) and the assertion $RG(x, z) \rightsquigarrow access(x, z)$. Let $\mathcal{J}_1 = \langle \mathcal{P}_1, D_1 \rangle$ be a VKG instance, where D_1 consist of the following source tables (we have used names of components for clarity):

$RS:$

researcher	supervisor
r1	s1
r1	s2
r2	s2

$SG:$

supervisor	grant
s1	g1
s2	g1
s1	g2

$RG:$

researcher	grant
r1	g1

We obtain the ABox $\mathcal{M}_1(D_1) = \{access(\text{s1}, \text{g1}), access(\text{r2}, \text{g1}), access(\text{r1}, \text{g2})\}$. Consider now the ABox deletion $\mathcal{U}_A^- = \{access(\text{r1}, \text{g1})\}$. Then, $\mathcal{U}_D^- = \{RS(\text{r1}, \text{s2}), SG(\text{s1}, \text{g1}), RG(\text{r1}, \text{g1})\}$ is an exact translation of $\mathcal{U}_A^-$ in $\mathcal{J}_1$. Instead, $\mathcal{U}_D^- = \{RS(\text{r1}, \text{s1}), SG(\text{s1}, \text{g1}), RS(\text{r1}, \text{s2}), SG(\text{s2}, \text{g1}), RG(\text{r1}, \text{g1})\}$ is a translation of $\mathcal{U}_A^-$ in $\mathcal{J}_1$ but not an exact one, because it deletes from the ABox also $access(\text{r1}, \text{g2})$. ◁

For insertions, we have ruled out a priori insertions of ABox facts that are inconsistent with $\mathcal{T}$ (hence with $\mathcal{T}^-$), but we still have to consider that side effects might cause an inconsistency.

Definition 2 (Insertion translation). *Given a VKG instance $\mathcal{J} = \langle \langle \mathcal{T}^-, \mathcal{M}, \mathcal{S} \rangle, D \rangle$ and a set $\mathcal{U}_A^+$ of ABox insertions, a source update $\mathcal{U}_D^+$ is a translation of $\mathcal{U}_A^+$ in $\mathcal{J}$ if $\mathcal{M}(D) \cup \mathcal{U}_A^+ \subseteq \mathcal{M}(D \cup \mathcal{U}_D^+)$ and $\langle \mathcal{T}^-, \mathcal{M}(D \cup \mathcal{U}_D^+) \rangle$ is consistent. $\mathcal{U}_D^+$ is an exact translation of $\mathcal{U}_A^+$ if $\mathcal{M}(D) \cup \mathcal{U}_A^+ = \mathcal{M}(D \cup \mathcal{U}_D^+)$.* ◁

---

[3] $B \sqsubseteq \exists R$ might indirectly imply a proper ABox fact, e.g., for $\mathcal{T} = \{A_1 \sqsubseteq \exists R, \exists R \sqsubseteq A_2\}$ and $\mathcal{A} = \{A_1(c)\}$, we have that $A_2(c) \in cl_\mathcal{T}(\mathcal{A})$.

Hence, an exact translation of $\mathcal{U}_A^+$ in $\mathcal{J}$ ensures that exactly all assertions of $\mathcal{U}_A^+$ are inserted in the (virtual) ABox generated by the mapping from the data source, while a translation $\mathcal{U}_D^+$ that is non-exact might also cause the insertion of additional assertions not in $\mathcal{U}_A^+$. If the additional assertions cause an inconsistency w.r.t. $\mathcal{T}^-$, we rule out $\mathcal{U}_D^+$.

Example 3. Consider $\mathcal{J}_2 = \langle\langle\emptyset, \mathcal{M}_2, \mathcal{S}_1\rangle, D_2\rangle$, where $\mathcal{M}_2$ consists of the mapping assertion of Eq. (1) and D_2 contains the single tuple $RS(\texttt{r1}, \texttt{s1})$, and the ABox insertion $\mathcal{U}_A^+ = \{access(\texttt{r2}, \texttt{g2})\}$. Then $\mathcal{U}_D^+ = \{RS(\texttt{r2}, \texttt{s2}), SG(\texttt{s2}, \texttt{g2})\}$ is an exact translation of $\mathcal{U}_A^+$ in $\mathcal{J}_2$. Instead, $\mathcal{U}_D^+ = \{RS(\texttt{r2}, \texttt{s1}), SG(\texttt{s1}, \texttt{g2})\}$ is a translation of $\mathcal{U}_A^+$, but not an exact one, because it also leads to the insertion of $access(\texttt{r1}, \texttt{g2})$ in the ABox. ◁

ABox insertions and deletions can have more than one translation over the data source, which is mainly due to the *information loss* caused by VKG mappings. Moreover, the application of a translation over the source may lead to a side-effect due to unwanted deletions or insertions in the ABox. Our aim is to find the translations that minimize the side-effects, ideally exact translations without side effects.

4 Schema Mapping Recovery in VKGs

In our approach to VKG update, we propose to rely on a reverse mapping that maps the TBox back to the source schema. To define such reverse mapping, we make use of the notion of mapping recovery introduced in [2], but suitably adapted to our setting.

For an so-mapping $\mathcal{M}$, from a source schema $\mathcal{S}$ to a TBox $\mathcal{T}$, a *reverse mapping* describes a novel mapping now going from $\mathcal{T}$ back to $\mathcal{S}$, which we call *ontology-to-source mapping* (*os-mapping*). We consider such a mapping $\widehat{\mathcal{M}}$ as a set of pairs $(\mathcal{A}, D)$, with $\mathcal{A}$ an ABox for $\mathcal{T}$ and D a DB instance of $\mathcal{S}$, called *solution* of $\mathcal{A}$ under $\widehat{\mathcal{M}}$. Moreover, we define $\widehat{\mathcal{M}}(\mathcal{A}) = \{D \mid (\mathcal{A}, D) \in \widehat{\mathcal{M}}\}$. Notice that, while an so-mapping $\mathcal{M}$ generates from a DB instance D a unique ABox $\mathcal{M}(D)$ (hence, $\mathcal{M}$ is a function by definition), a reverse mapping $\widehat{\mathcal{M}}$, in general, is not a function but a relation that associates to an ABox a set of DB instances. This is because an so-mapping is in general not injective, i.e., it might map two different instances of $\mathcal{S}$ to the same ABox.

We are interested in os-mappings that maintain semantic consistency with the relationship established by $\mathcal{M}$, and which intuitively represent the inverse of such relationship, in line with the notion of *inverse mapping* for the relational setting [16].

Definition 3 (Recovery of a mapping [2]). *Let $\mathcal{P} = \langle\mathcal{T}, \mathcal{M}, \mathcal{S}\rangle$ be a VKG specification and $\widehat{\mathcal{M}}$ an os-mapping. We say $\widehat{\mathcal{M}}$ is a recovery of $\mathcal{M}$, if $D \in \widehat{\mathcal{M}}(\mathcal{M}(D))$ for every source instance D of $\mathcal{S}$.* ◁

For a source instance D, if $\widehat{\mathcal{M}}$ is a recovery of a mapping $\mathcal{M}$, then the smaller the set of DB instances provided by $\widehat{\mathcal{M}}(\mathcal{M}(D))$, the more informative is $\widehat{\mathcal{M}}$ about D. This leads to the definition of *maximum recovery*, which intuitively is among the best options to bring the exchanged data back.

Definition 4 (Maximum recovery of a mapping [2]). *Let $\mathcal{P} = \langle\mathcal{T}, \mathcal{M}, \mathcal{S}\rangle$ be a VKG specification. A recovery $\widehat{\mathcal{M}}$ of $\mathcal{M}$ is a maximum recovery, if for every recovery $\widehat{\mathcal{M}}'$ of $\mathcal{M}$, we have that $\widehat{\mathcal{M}}(\mathcal{M}(D)) \subseteq \widehat{\mathcal{M}}'(\mathcal{M}(D))$.* ◁

Although VKG mappings do not allow for existential variables in the target, IRI-templates (which account for *skolem terms*) give VKG mappings the expressive power to simulate st-tgds that contain existential variables in the target [13,17]. In fact, IRI-templates can also capture plain SO-tgds, which are a form of mappings that always admit a maximum recovery [1]. In [1], an algorithm called POLYSOINVERSE is proposed that, given a schema mapping $\mathcal{M}$ specified as plain SO-tgds, computes a SO-tgd mapping $\widehat{\mathcal{M}}$ that represents the maximum recovery of $\mathcal{M}$, by rewriting each atom in the target part of the SO-tgds as a query over the source. We make use of an adaptation of that algorithm to our setting, which we describe next. To do so, we make the simplifying assumption[4] that all mapping assertions for a concept or role E (including those introduced with mapping saturation) make use of the *same IRI-template*.

Given an n-ary tuple $t(x) = (t_1(x), \ldots, t_n(x))$ of terms over variables x, $u_{t(x)}$ is an n-tuple $(u_1, \ldots, u_n)$ of variables such that if $t_i(x) = t_j(x)$, then $u_i = u_j$, otherwise $u_i \neq u_j$. We then define $V_{t(x)} = V^1 \wedge \cdots \wedge V^n$, where each V^i is obtained as follows: (a) if $t_i(x)$ is a variable y in x, then V^i is the equality $y = u_i$, (b) otherwise, if $t_i(x)$ is an IRI-template $f(y_1, \ldots, y_k)$, where each y_j is a variable in x, then V^i is $(y_1 = f^1(u_i)) \wedge \cdots \wedge (y_k = f^k(u_i))$, where each f^j is the j-th inverse template of f. We are now ready to define, given an so-mapping $\mathcal{M}$, a specific os-mapping $\widehat{\mathcal{M}}^{mr}$.

Definition 5 (MR-os-mapping). *Let $\mathcal{M} = \bigcup_{E \text{ in } \mathcal{T}} \mathcal{M}_E$ be an so-mapping, where $\mathcal{M}_E = \bigcup_{\ell=1}^k \{\exists w_\ell . \varphi_\ell(x, w_\ell) \rightsquigarrow E(t(x))\}$ are all mapping assertions with concept or role E in the target (where $t(x)$ is the tuple of IRI-templates specific for E). Then, the set of os-mappings $\widehat{\mathcal{M}}^{mr} = \bigcup_{E \text{ in } \mathcal{T}} \left\{ E(u_{t(x)}) \rightsquigarrow \bigvee_{\ell=1}^k \exists x . \exists w_\ell . \varphi_\ell(x, w_\ell) \wedge V_{t(x)} \right\}$ is called the* MR-os-mapping *of $\mathcal{M}$.* ◁

Example 4. Consider the VKG mapping $\mathcal{M} = \{\exists z . r(x, y, z) \rightsquigarrow P(f(x, y), x)\}$. Then we have $t(x, y, z) = (f(x, y), x)$, and we obtain $u_{t(x,y,z)} = (u_1, u_2)$. Hence $\widehat{\mathcal{M}}^{mr}$ consists of the os-mapping assertion $P(u_1, u_2) \rightsquigarrow \exists x . \exists y . \exists z . r(x, y, z) \wedge x = f^1(u_1) \wedge y = f^2(u_1) \wedge x = u_2$. Notice that we can simplify this os-mapping assertion into the equivalent form $P(u_1, u_2) \rightsquigarrow \exists z . r(f^1(u_1), f^2(u_1), w) \wedge f^1(u_1) = u_2$. ◁

The following result can be shown by following the same line of proof as the analogous result for plain SO-tgds in [1].

Theorem 6. *Let $\mathcal{P} = \langle \mathcal{T}, \mathcal{M}, \mathcal{S} \rangle$ be a VKG specification. The os-mapping $\widehat{\mathcal{M}}^{mr}$ is a maximum recovery of $\mathcal{M}$.*

In the following, we restrict the attention to the maximum recovery of a VKG mapping $\mathcal{M}$ constructed as the MR-os-mapping $\widehat{\mathcal{M}}^{mr}$ of $\mathcal{M}$. In fact, we exploit the construction in the proof of the following result.

Theorem 7. *Let $\mathcal{P} = \langle \mathcal{T}, \mathcal{M}, \mathcal{S} \rangle$ be a VKG specification, $\widehat{\mathcal{M}}^{mr}$ the MR-os-mapping of $\mathcal{M}$, and D an instance of $\mathcal{S}$. Then, for every $f \in \mathcal{M}(D)$, we have $f \in \mathcal{M}(\widehat{\mathcal{M}}^{mr}(\{f\}))$.*

---

[4] Such assumption is quite restrictive in practice, but it can be lifted by resorting to the original version of the POLYSOINVERSE algorithm in [1]. We will address this in future work.

5 Data Lineage in VKGs

Data lineage (a.k.a. *provenance*) is concerned with identifying and managing the origin of data in a data management system, and has been studied extensively in the relational setting [9,12]. We now adapt the notions of lineage and *exclusive lineage* to virtual ABox assertions in the VKG setting. Specifically, we are interested in the subsets of the data source tuples that generate a fact in the virtual ABox.

Definition 8 (Lineage). *Let $\mathcal{P} = \langle \mathcal{T}, \mathcal{M}, \mathcal{S} \rangle$ be a VKG specification, $\langle \mathcal{P}, D \rangle$ a VKG instance, and $f \in \mathcal{M}(D)$ an ABox assertion. A subset $B \subseteq D$ is a lineage branch of f if $f \in \mathcal{M}(B)$, and for every $B' \subsetneq B$, $f \notin \mathcal{M}(B')$. The lineage of f, denoted $\mathsf{lineage}(f, \mathcal{P}, D)$, is the set of all lineage branches of f.* ◁

Example 5 (Continued from Example 2). For $f = access(\texttt{r1},\texttt{g1})$, $\mathsf{lineage}(f, \mathcal{P}, D) = \{\{RS(\texttt{r1},\texttt{s1}), SG(\texttt{s1},\texttt{g1})\}, \{RS(\texttt{r1},\texttt{s2}), SG(\texttt{s2},\texttt{g1})\}, \{RG(\texttt{r1},\texttt{g1})\}\}$ ◁

We are also interested in the subsets of the data source tuples that contribute to generating an ABox fact f but do not contribute to any ABox fact other than f.

Definition 9 (Exclusive lineage). *Let $\mathcal{P} = \langle \mathcal{T}, \mathcal{M}, \mathcal{S} \rangle$ be a VKG specification, $\langle \mathcal{P}, D \rangle$ a VKG instance, and $f \in \mathcal{M}(D)$ an ABox assertion. A subset B^* of a lineage branch of f is an exclusive lineage branch of f if for every $f' \in \mathcal{M}(D) \setminus \{f\}$ and every $B \in \mathsf{lineage}(f', \mathcal{P}, D)$, we have that $B^* \cap B = \emptyset$. The exclusive lineage of f, denoted $\mathsf{elineage}(f, \mathcal{P}, D)$, is the set of all exclusive lineage branches of f.* ◁

Example 6 (Continued from Example 5). The exclusive lineage of the assertion f is $\mathsf{elineage}(f, \mathcal{P}, D) = \{\{SG(\texttt{s1},\texttt{g1})\}, \{RS(\texttt{r1},\texttt{s2})\}, \{RG(\texttt{r1},\texttt{g1})\}\}$. Tuples $RS(\texttt{r1},\texttt{s1})$ and $SG(\texttt{s2},\texttt{g1})$ from f's lineage are not in f's exclusive lineage because $RS(\texttt{r1},\texttt{s1})$ is also in a lineage branch of $access(\texttt{r1},\texttt{g2})$ and $SG(\texttt{s2},\texttt{g1})$ in one of $access(\texttt{r2},\texttt{g1})$. ◁

Note that an exclusive lineage branch of an ABox fact f is in general *not* a lineage branch of f, i.e., its facts might not generate f via the mapping. Finding minimal subsets of the source instance D that generate via the VKG mapping $\mathcal{M}$ an ABox fact f is in general challenging. We now show that we can use a maximum recovery of $\mathcal{M}$ to guide that search.

Definition 10 ($\widehat{\mathcal{M}}$-instance recovery). *Let $\mathcal{J} = \langle \langle \mathcal{T}, \mathcal{M}, \mathcal{S} \rangle, D \rangle$ be a VKG instance and $\widehat{\mathcal{M}}$ a maximum recovery of $\mathcal{M}$. The $\widehat{\mathcal{M}}$-instance recovery for D is the function $\widehat{\mathcal{M}}_D$ from $\mathcal{M}(D)$ to 2^{2^D} such that*

$$\widehat{\mathcal{M}}_D(f) = \{B \mid B \subseteq D, B \in \widehat{\mathcal{M}}(\{f\}), \text{ and for every } B' \subsetneq B, B' \notin \widehat{\mathcal{M}}(\{f\})\}.$$

◁

Notice that, based on the definition and properties of maximum recovery as shown in Sect. 4, for two distinct maximum recoveries $\widehat{\mathcal{M}}^1$ and $\widehat{\mathcal{M}}^2$ and a source instance D, it holds that $\widehat{\mathcal{M}}_D^1 = \widehat{\mathcal{M}}_D^2$. This actually follows from the next result.

Proposition 11. Let $\mathcal{P} = \langle \mathcal{T}, \mathcal{M}, \mathcal{S} \rangle$ be a VKG specification, $\langle \mathcal{P}, D \rangle$ a VKG instance, $\widehat{\mathcal{M}}^{mr}$ the MR-os-mapping of $\mathcal{M}$, and $\widehat{\mathcal{M}}^{mr}_D$ the $\widehat{\mathcal{M}}^{mr}$-instance recovery for D. Then, for every ABox assertions $f \in \mathcal{M}(D)$, we have that $\widehat{\mathcal{M}}^{mr}_D(f) = \mathsf{lineage}(f, \mathcal{P}, D)$.

Proof. Let $f = E(\boldsymbol{a})$ for some concept or role E and some tuple $\boldsymbol{a}$ of ground terms. We recall that, by Theorem 6, $\widehat{\mathcal{M}}^{mr}$ is a maximum recovery of $\mathcal{M}$.

($\subseteq$) Let $B \in \widehat{\mathcal{M}}^{mr}_D(f)$, we need to show that $B \in \mathsf{lineage}(f, \mathcal{P}, D)$. By definition of $\widehat{\mathcal{M}}^{mr}_D(f)$, we have that $B \subseteq D$. Let $E(\boldsymbol{u}_{t(\boldsymbol{x})}) \rightsquigarrow \alpha(\boldsymbol{u}_{t(\boldsymbol{x})})$ be the (unique) os-mapping assertion in $\widehat{\mathcal{M}}^{mr}$ for concept/role E, where $\alpha(\boldsymbol{u}_{t(\boldsymbol{x})}) = \bigvee_{\ell=1}^{k} \exists \boldsymbol{x}. \exists \boldsymbol{w}_\ell. \varphi_\ell(\boldsymbol{x}, \boldsymbol{w}_\ell) \wedge V_{t(\boldsymbol{x})}$ is a UCQ over $\mathcal{S}$ by construction. Since $f = E(\boldsymbol{a})$ and $B \in \widehat{\mathcal{M}}^{mr}(\{f\})$, we have that $B \models \alpha(\boldsymbol{a})$, which means that there is an $\ell \in [1..k]$ such that $B \models \beta(\boldsymbol{a})$, where $\beta(\boldsymbol{a}) = \exists \boldsymbol{x}. \exists \boldsymbol{w}_\ell. \varphi_\ell(\boldsymbol{x}, \boldsymbol{w}_\ell) \wedge (V_{t(\boldsymbol{x})}[\boldsymbol{u}_{t(\boldsymbol{x})}/\boldsymbol{a}])$ and $V_{t(\boldsymbol{x})}[\boldsymbol{u}_{t(\boldsymbol{x})}/\boldsymbol{a}]$ is the formula obtained from $V_{t(\boldsymbol{x})}$ by instantiating $\boldsymbol{u}_{t(\boldsymbol{x})}$ with $\boldsymbol{a}$. By the form of $\beta(\boldsymbol{a})$, there exists a tuple $\boldsymbol{b}$ of constants such that $\boldsymbol{b} = \hat{\boldsymbol{t}}(\boldsymbol{a})$, where $\hat{\boldsymbol{t}}$ is the sequence of inverse templates corresponding to the IRI-templates $\boldsymbol{t}(\boldsymbol{x})$, such that $B \models \exists \boldsymbol{w}_\ell. \varphi_\ell(\boldsymbol{b}, \boldsymbol{w}_\ell)$. From the construction of $\widehat{\mathcal{M}}^{mr}$, we have that $\mathcal{M}$ contains the mapping assertion $\exists \boldsymbol{w}_\ell. \varphi_\ell(\boldsymbol{x}, \boldsymbol{w}_\ell) \rightsquigarrow E(\boldsymbol{t}(\boldsymbol{x}))$, and since $B \models \exists \boldsymbol{w}_\ell. \varphi_\ell(\boldsymbol{a}, \boldsymbol{w}_\ell)$, we have that $f \in \mathcal{M}(B)$. Moreover, by the definition of $\widehat{\mathcal{M}}$-instance recovery, there is no $B' \subsetneq B$ such that $B' \models \exists \boldsymbol{w}_\ell. \varphi_\ell(\boldsymbol{a}, \boldsymbol{w}_\ell)$. Hence, $B \in \mathsf{lineage}(f, \mathcal{P}, D)$.

($\supseteq$) Let $B \in \mathsf{lineage}(f, \mathcal{P}, D)$, we need to show that $B \in \widehat{\mathcal{M}}^{mr}_D(f)$. From Definition 8 we know that $f \in \mathcal{M}(B)$. Hence there is a mapping assertion $\exists \boldsymbol{w}. \beta(\boldsymbol{x}, \boldsymbol{w}) \rightsquigarrow E(\boldsymbol{t}(\boldsymbol{x})) \in \mathcal{M}$ and a tuple $\boldsymbol{b}$ of constants such that $\boldsymbol{b} = \hat{\boldsymbol{t}}(\boldsymbol{a})$, where $\hat{\boldsymbol{t}}$ is the sequence of inverse templates corresponding to the IRI-templates $\boldsymbol{t}(\boldsymbol{x})$, such that $B \models \exists \boldsymbol{w}. \beta(\boldsymbol{b}, \boldsymbol{w})$. Moreover, for every $B' \subsetneq B$, since by the definition of lineage $f \notin \mathcal{M}(B')$, we have that $B' \not\models \exists \boldsymbol{w}. \beta(\boldsymbol{b}, \boldsymbol{w})$. From the definition and construction of $\widehat{\mathcal{M}}^{mr}$, we have that $E(\boldsymbol{u}_{t(\boldsymbol{x})}) \rightsquigarrow \bigvee_{\ell=1}^{k} \exists \boldsymbol{x}. \exists \boldsymbol{w}_\ell. \varphi_\ell(\boldsymbol{x}, \boldsymbol{w}_\ell) \wedge V_{t(\boldsymbol{x})} \in \widehat{\mathcal{M}}^{mr}$, where for some $\ell \in [1..k]$, $\varphi_\ell(\boldsymbol{x}, \boldsymbol{w}_\ell) = \beta(\boldsymbol{x}, \boldsymbol{w})$. Hence, we have $B \models \exists \boldsymbol{w}_\ell. \varphi_\ell(\boldsymbol{b}, \boldsymbol{w}_\ell)$, which entails that $B \in \widehat{\mathcal{M}}^{mr}(\{f\})$ and $B' \notin \widehat{\mathcal{M}}^{mr}(\{f\})$. Since by the definition of lineage, $B \subseteq D$, we conclude that $B \in \widehat{\mathcal{M}}^{mr}_D(f)$. □

6 Update Framework in VKGs

When the translated ABox updates are propagated back through the mappings they might produce side effects, and we are interested in minimizing them, where we consider as measure the set difference between the desired and the obtained ABoxes. We use the function $\mathit{flatten}(X) = \bigcup_{S \in X} S$, which flattens a set X of sets into a set.

6.1 ABox Deletions

We first consider ABox deletions. We formalize the relationship between data lineage and translation of ABox deletions, and based on that, we provide an algorithm that translates ABox deletions into suitable source deletions.

Example 7 (Continued from Example 2). The set $\mathcal{U}_D^- = \mathit{flatten}(\mathsf{lineage}(f, \mathcal{P}, D))$ of source tuples is a translation of $\mathcal{U}_A^- = \{f\}$ but is not an exact translation. Instead, $\mathcal{U}_D^- = \mathit{flatten}(\mathsf{elineage}(f, \mathcal{P}, D))$ is an exact translation of $\mathcal{U}_A^-$. ◁

Algorithm 1: TRANSLATEDELETION

input : A VKG instance $\mathcal{J} = \langle \mathcal{P}, D \rangle$ with $\mathcal{P} = \langle \mathcal{T}, \mathcal{M}, \mathcal{S} \rangle$.
A set $\mathcal{U}_A^-$ of ABox deletions.
output: A set $\mathbf{U}_D^-$ of translations over the source of the set $\mathcal{U}_A^-$.

1 $B^* \leftarrow \mathit{flatten}(\bigcup_{f \in \mathcal{U}_A^-} \mathsf{elineage}(f, \mathcal{P}, D))$; // Compute flattening of elineage
2 $D' \leftarrow D \setminus B^*$; // Remove from D tuples in the exclusive lineage
3 **if** $\mathcal{M}(D) \setminus \mathcal{U}_A^- = \mathcal{M}(D')$ **then return** $\mathbf{U}_D^- = B^*$;
   $\mathbf{B} = \{B_1, \ldots, B_n\} \leftarrow \bigcup_{f \in \mathcal{U}_A^-} \mathsf{lineage}(f, \mathcal{P}, D')$; // Compute lineage branches in D'
4 $\mathbf{S} \leftarrow \{\{t_1, \ldots, t_n\} \mid t_i \in B_i, \text{for } i \in [1..n]\}$;
5 $\mathbf{U}_D^- \leftarrow \{\}$;
6 **for each** translation $T^* \in \mathbf{S}$ **do**
7 $\quad$ $add \leftarrow true$;
8 $\quad$ **for each** translation $T \in \mathbf{U}_D^-$ **do**
9 $\quad\quad$ **if** $\mathrm{COMPARE}_{\mathcal{J}}^-(T \cup B^*, T^* \cup B^*) = \,$'<' **then** $add \leftarrow false$
10 $\quad\quad$ **else if** $\mathrm{COMPARE}_{\mathcal{J}}^-(T^* \cup B^*, T \cup B^*) = \,$'<' **then** $\mathbf{U}_D^- \leftarrow \mathbf{U}_D^- \setminus \{T\}$
11 $\quad$ **if** add **then** $\mathbf{U}_D^- \leftarrow \mathbf{U}_D^- \cup \{T^*\}$
12 **return** $\{T \cup B^* \mid T \in \mathbf{U}_D^-\}$

We observe that, in principle, since no proper subset of a lineage branch of an assertion f generates f under the VKG mapping, we can delete f from the ABox by simply removing one tuple from each lineage branch of f, and we should do so while ensuring a minimal side-effect. E.g., in Example 7, by deleting one tuple per lineage branch of f, we can obtain the set $T = \{RS(\mathtt{r1}, \mathtt{s2}), SG(\mathtt{s1}, \mathtt{g1})\, RG(\mathtt{r1}, \mathtt{g1})\}$, which is a translation of $\mathcal{U}_A^- = \{f\}$ over the source data (which in this case has no side effect).

Proposition 12. *Let $\mathcal{P} = \langle \mathcal{T}, \mathcal{M}, \mathcal{S} \rangle$ be a VKG specification, $\langle \mathcal{P}, D \rangle$ a VKG instance, $f \in \mathcal{M}(D)$ such that $\mathsf{lineage}(f, \mathcal{P}, D) = \{B_1, \ldots, B_n\}$, and $\mathbf{T} = \{\{t_1, \ldots, t_n\} \mid t_i \in B_i\}$. Then for every $T \in \mathbf{T}$, we have that $f \notin \mathcal{M}(D \setminus T)$.*

Proof. Let $T = \{t_1, \ldots, t_n\} \in \mathbf{T}$. We have to show that $f \notin \mathcal{M}(D \setminus T)$. From the definition of lineage for an ABox assertion f, it follows that, for every $i \in [1..n]$ and $B_i' = B_i \setminus \{t_i\}$, we have that $f \notin \mathcal{M}(B_i')$. This means that, by removing t_i from D, the branch B_i will not be anymore in $\mathsf{lineage}(f, \mathcal{P}, D \setminus \{t_i\})$. Therefore, by removing T from D, $\mathsf{lineage}(f, \mathcal{P}, D \setminus T)$ will be empty, hence $f \notin \mathcal{M}(D \setminus T)$. □

From Definition 6, we can see that none of the source tuples contained in the exclusive lineage of an ABox assertion contribute to generating via the mapping any other assertion in the ABox, which means that their deletion is guaranteed to be side-effect free. Unfortunately, as observed also in [8], deleting from the source the exclusive lineage of a given ABox assertion will not always lead to its deletion in the ABox.

We propose the algorithm TRANSLATEDELETION, which takes as input a VKG instance $\mathcal{J}$ and a set $\mathcal{U}_A^-$ of ABox deletions. It first computes the exclusive lineage branch list $\mathbf{B}^*$ of every assertion in $\mathcal{U}_A^-$ and checks whether deleting the tuples in $\mathbf{B}^*$ will delete $\mathcal{U}_A^-$ from the ABox. If so, it returns the tuples in $\mathbf{B}^*$ as an exact translation. Instead, if some assertions of $\mathcal{U}_A^-$ still persist in the ABox, the algorithm searches for translations of $\mathcal{U}_A^-$ with minimum side effects by considering one tuple per branch in the remaining lineage list. However, the notion of *right* translation is not unique, as it depends on the metric used to evaluate the distance between the updated ABox and the desired one. In this regard, we use an abstract function called $\textsc{Compare}_{\mathcal{J}}^-$ that compares two translations T_1 and T_2 in terms of their side-effect and returns either '=' or '<', if T_1 has equal, resp., less side-effect than T_2 based on the metric under consideration. Our algorithm returns the set of translations with a minimum side effect.

The number of iterations in the search loop is bounded by $k^{|\mathbf{B}|}$ where $\mathbf{B} = \bigcup_{f \in \mathcal{U}_A^-} \text{lineage}(f, \mathcal{P}, D')$ and $\mathcal{U}_A^-$ in $D' = D \setminus \text{flatten}(\bigcup_{f \in \mathcal{U}_A^-} \text{elineage}(f, \mathcal{P}, D))$ (i.e., D after removing the exclusive lineage of all tuples in $\mathcal{U}_A^-$) and k is the size of the largest branch of $\mathbf{B}$. Note that, in general, we expect k and $|\mathbf{B}|$ to be small.

6.2 ABox Insertions

Inserting new ABox assertions is more challenging than deletions because, for these new assertions, we do not yet have a lineage in the database that we can manipulate. Also, the existential variables in source queries of mappings can result in infinitely many possible source insertions. Similar to the translation of ABox deletions, we want to minimize side effects in the ABox.

Example 8 (Continued from Example 3). From $\mathcal{M}$, we get the MR-os-mapping $\widehat{\mathcal{M}}^{mr} = \{access(\mathbf{r}, \mathbf{g}) \to \exists w. RS(\mathbf{r}, w) \wedge SG(w, \mathbf{g})\}$, which is a maximum recovery of $\mathcal{M}$. Then, for $\mathcal{U}_A^+ = \{access(\mathbf{r2}, \mathbf{g2})\}$, we have that $\widehat{\mathcal{M}}^{mr}(\mathcal{U}_A^+) = \{\exists w. RS(\mathbf{r2}, w) \wedge SG(w, \mathbf{g2})\}$. However, the source update is incompletely specified because of the existential variable w. By analyzing our data source D, we see that if we assign to w the value $\mathbf{s2}$, we obtain the source insertion $\{RS(\mathbf{r2}, \mathbf{s2}), SG(\mathbf{s2}, \mathbf{g2})\}$, which is an exact translation of $\mathcal{U}_A^+$. If we assign to w any value other than $\mathbf{s2}$, we still get a translation (but not an exact translation). ◁

This example shows that the choice of the assignment to the existential variables in the translated insertion request plays a crucial role in minimizing the side effects in the ABox. Also, since an ABox insertion can have several translations over the source, one has to find the one that, with a proper assignment, leads to a minimal side effect.

Towards computing an optimal translation of an ABox insertion request, let us first provide the definition of insertion branch and insertion tree of a set of ABox insertions. For convenience, we make use of γ, defined as $\gamma(\bigwedge_{i=1}^{n} r_i(\mathbf{a}_i)) = \bigcup_{i=1}^{n} \{r_i(\mathbf{a}_i)\}$, to transform a conjunction of facts into a set of tuples.

Definition 13 (Insertion tree). *Let $\mathcal{P} = \langle \mathcal{T}, \mathcal{M}, \mathcal{S} \rangle$ be a VKG specification, $\langle \mathcal{P}, D \rangle$ a VKG instance, $\widehat{\mathcal{M}}^{mr}$ the MR-os-mapping of $\mathcal{M}$, and $\mathcal{U}_A^+ = \{f_1, \ldots, f_n\}$ an ABox insertion. Then $B = \bigcup_{i=1}^{n} \{\exists \mathbf{w}_i . \varphi_i(\mathbf{a}_i, \mathbf{w}_i)\}$ is an insertion branch of $\mathcal{U}_A^+$ for $\widehat{\mathcal{M}}^{mr}$ if for $i \in [1..n]$ we have that $\gamma(\varphi_i(\mathbf{a}_i, \eta_i(\mathbf{w}_i))) \in \widehat{\mathcal{M}}^{mr}(\{f_i\})$, where $\mathbf{w}_i$ is the set of existential variables in $\exists \mathbf{w}_i . \varphi_i(\mathbf{x}_i, \mathbf{w}_i)$, $\mathbf{a}_i$ is a tuple of ground terms instantiating all free variables in $\exists \mathbf{w}_i . \varphi_i(\mathbf{x}_i, \mathbf{w}_i)$, and η_i is an arbitrary assignment of constants in $\mathbf{N}_I$ to $\mathbf{w}_i$. The insertion tree of $\mathcal{U}_A^+$ for $\widehat{\mathcal{M}}^{mr}$ is the set of its insertion branches.* ◁

Algorithm 2: TRANSLATEINSERTION

input: A VKG instance $\mathcal{J} = \langle\langle \mathcal{T}, \mathcal{M}, \mathcal{S}\rangle, D\rangle$.
A set $\mathcal{U}_A^+$ of ABox insertions.
output: A set $\mathbf{U}_D^+$ of translations over the source of the set $\mathcal{U}_A^+$.

1. Compute the MR-os-mapping $\widehat{\mathcal{M}}^{mr}$ of $\mathcal{M}$;
2. Compute the insertion tree $\mathbf{B} = \{B_1, \ldots, B_n\}$ of $\mathcal{U}_A^+$ for $\widehat{\mathcal{M}}^{mr}$;
3. $\mathbf{U}_D^+ \leftarrow \{\}$;
4. **for each** branch $B_i \in \mathbf{B}$ of the form $\bigcup_{i=1}^n \{\exists \boldsymbol{w}_i.\varphi_i(\boldsymbol{a}_i, \boldsymbol{w}_i)\}$ **do**
5. $\quad \Delta_{\boldsymbol{w}_i} \leftarrow \{b_1, \ldots, b_{|\boldsymbol{w}_i|}\} \cup \Delta_A \cup \Delta_D$, where Δ_A and Δ_D are the constants in $\mathcal{U}_A^+$ and D respectively, and each b_i is a fresh value from $\mathbf{N}_I$ not in $\Delta_A \cup \Delta_D$;
6. $\quad$ **for each** assignment $\eta(\boldsymbol{w}_i) \subseteq \Delta_{\boldsymbol{w}_i}$ **do**
7. $\quad\quad T^* \leftarrow \bigcup_{i=1}^n \gamma(\varphi_i(\boldsymbol{a}_i, \eta(\boldsymbol{w}_i)))$;
8. $\quad\quad$ $add \leftarrow true$;
9. $\quad\quad$ **for each** translation $T \in \mathbf{U}_D^+$ **do**
10. $\quad\quad\quad$ **if** COMPARE$_{\mathcal{J}}^+(T, T^*) = $ '<' **then** $add \leftarrow false$
11. $\quad\quad\quad$ **else if** COMPARE$_{\mathcal{J}}^+(T^*, T) = $ '<' **then** $\mathbf{U}_D^+ \leftarrow \mathbf{U}_D^+ \setminus \{T\}$
12. $\quad\quad$ **if** add **then** $\mathbf{U}_D^+ \leftarrow \mathbf{U}_D^+ \cup \{T^*\}$
13. **return** $\mathbf{U}_D^+$

Example 9 (Continued from Example 8). The insertion tree of the ABox insertion $\mathcal{U}_A^+ = \{access(\texttt{r2}, \texttt{g2})\}$ is $\mathbf{B} = \{\{\exists w. RS(\texttt{r2}, w) \wedge SG(w, \texttt{g2})\}\}$. ◁

We now show that, for every instantiation of its existential variables with constants in $\mathbf{N}_I$, an insertion branch provides a set of source tuples that generates through the mapping a set of ABox assertions that includes $\mathcal{U}_A^+$.

Theorem 14. *Let $\mathcal{P} = \langle \mathcal{T}, \mathcal{M}, \mathcal{S}\rangle$ be a VKG specification, $\langle \mathcal{P}, D\rangle$ a VKG instance, $\widehat{\mathcal{M}}^{mr}$ the MR-os-mapping of $\mathcal{M}$, $\mathcal{U}_A^+ = \{f_1, \ldots, f_n\}$, $\bigcup_{i=1}^n \{\exists \boldsymbol{w}_i.\varphi_i(\boldsymbol{a}_i, \boldsymbol{w}_i)\}$ an insertion branch of $\mathcal{U}_A^+$ for $\widehat{\mathcal{M}}^{mr}$, and η_i an assignment to $\boldsymbol{w}_i$, for $i \in [1..n]$. Then, the source update $\mathcal{U}_D^+ = \bigcup_{i=1}^n \gamma(\varphi_i(\boldsymbol{a}_i, \eta_i(\boldsymbol{w}_i)))$ is a translation of $\mathcal{U}_A^+$.*

Proof. By Theorem 7, we know that $f_i \in \mathcal{M}(\widehat{\mathcal{M}}^{mr}(\{f_i\}))$, and since we have $\gamma(\varphi_i(\boldsymbol{a}_i, \eta_i(\boldsymbol{w}_i)))) \in \widehat{\mathcal{M}}^{mr}(\{f_i\})$, we obtain $f_i \in \mathcal{M}(\gamma(\varphi_i(\boldsymbol{a}_i, \eta_i(\boldsymbol{w}_i))))$. By combining all the assertions f_i in $\mathcal{U}_A^+$, we obtain $\mathcal{U}_A^+ \subseteq \bigcup_{i=1}^n \mathcal{M}(\varphi_i(\boldsymbol{a}_i, \eta_i(\boldsymbol{w}_i)))$, hence $\mathcal{U}_A^+ \subseteq \mathcal{M}(\bigcup_{i=1}^n \varphi_i(\boldsymbol{a}_i, \eta_i(\boldsymbol{w}_i)))$, since $\mathcal{M}$ is specified as UCQs over the source and UCQs are monotone queries. Again, by the monotonicity of UCQs, we finally obtain $\mathcal{U}_A^+ \cup \mathcal{M}(D) \subseteq \mathcal{M}(\bigcup_{i=1}^n \varphi_i(\boldsymbol{a}_i, \eta_i(\boldsymbol{w}_i)) \cup D)$. □

This result shows that applying $\widehat{\mathcal{M}}^{mr}$ to an ABox insertion request always leads to a translation in the source data. Hence, we need to compute an insertion branch and an assignment to its existential variables that leads to a minimal side-effect. We propose the algorithm TRANSLATEINSERTION, which takes as input a VKG instance $\mathcal{J}$ and a set $\mathcal{U}_A^+$ of ABox insertions, computes the insertion tree of $\mathcal{U}_A^+$, and for every branch B in the tree, assigns to each of its existential variables (if it has any) a constant that might be from the source instance, from the insertion request, or fresh. In some situations, assigning arbitrary values to these variables, known as "do not care" variables, may be viable, allowing the translation process to fill in any value to maintain semantic consistency [12]. Similar to the deletion algorithm, we use $\text{COMPARE}_{\mathcal{J}}^{+}$ to compare insertion translations (resulting from the instantiation of existential variables) in terms of side effects in the ABox, and we keep the ones with minimal side effects. The algorithm needs to compute the insertion tree, and to do so it uses the MR-os-mapping $\widehat{\mathcal{M}}^{mr}$. The size of the insertion tree is $|\mathcal{U}_A^+|^k$, where $k = \max_{f_i \in \mathcal{U}_A^+}(|\widehat{\mathcal{M}}^{mr}(\{f_i\})|)$.

7 Conclusions and Discussion

We have studied an instance-level approach for updates in the context of VKGs through the lens of an ontology, where an update is specified through either a set of ABox deletions or a set of ABox insertions over the ontology. Based on the notion of maximum recovery of a VKG mapping, we have proposed algorithms that compute the set of changes in the source that realize a given ontology-based update with the minimum side effect. The computation is, in the worst case, exponential in the size of the update. For ABox deletions, the translation is computed at run-time, but our algorithm can compute at compile-time the maximum recovery and the lineage of all assertions in the ABox.

We are currently working on a technique to combine ABox deletions and insertions. We are also interested in studying optimization techniques when searching for possible translations, and in particular in understanding how constraints in the data source can be used to reduce the space of possible translations of ABox updates. We are also planning to implement our techniques in state-of-the-art VKG tools such as Ontop [5].

Acknowledgments. This research has been partially supported by the Province of Bolzano and DFG through the project D2G2 (DFG grant n. 500249124), by the HEU project CyclOps (grant agreement n. 101135513), and by the Wallenberg AI, Autonomous Systems and Software Program (WASP), funded by the Knut and Alice Wallenberg Foundation.

References

1. Arenas, M., Pérez, J., Reutter, J., Riveros, C.: The language of plain SO-tgds: composition, inversion and structural properties. JCSS **79**(6), 763–784 (2013). https://doi.org/10.1016/j.jcss.2013.01.002
2. Arenas, M., Pérez, J., Riveros, C.: The recovery of a schema mapping: Bringing exchanged data back. ACM TODS **34**(4), 1–48 (2009). https://doi.org/10.1145/1620585.1620589
3. Baader, F., Calvanese, D., McGuinness, D., Nardi, D., Patel-Schneider, P.F. (eds.): The Description Logic Handbook: Theory, Implementation and Applications. Cambridge University Press (2003). https://doi.org/10.1017/CBO9780511711787
4. Bancilhon, F., Spyratos, N.: Update semantics of relational views. ACM TODS **6**(4), 557–575 (1981). https://doi.org/10.1145/319628.319634
5. Calvanese, D., et al.: Ontop: answering SPARQL queries over relational databases. Semantic Web J. **8**(3), 471–487 (2017). https://doi.org/10.3233/SW-160217
6. Calvanese, D., et al.: Ontologies and databases: the DL-Lite approach. In: Tessaris, S., et al. (eds.) Reasoning Web 2009. LNCS, vol. 5689, pp. 255–356. Springer, Heidelberg (2009). https://doi.org/10.1007/978-3-642-03754-2_7

7. Calvanese, D., De Giacomo, G., Lembo, D., Lenzerini, M., Rosati, R.: Tractable reasoning and efficient query answering in description logics: the DL-Lite family. JAR **39**, 385–429 (2007). https://doi.org/10.1007/s10817-007-9078-x
8. Cui, Y., Widom, J.: Run-time translation of view tuple deletions using data lineage. Tech. rep., Stanford University (2001). http://ilpubs.stanford.edu:8090/496/1/2001-24.pdf
9. Cui, Y., Widom, J.: Lineage tracing for general data warehouse transformations. VLDBJ **12**(1), 41–58 (2003). https://doi.org/10.1007/s00778-002-0083-8
10. Cui, Y., Widom, J., Wiener, J.L.: Tracing the lineage of view data in a warehousing environment. ACM TODS **25**(2), 179–227 (2000). https://doi.org/10.1145/357775.357777
11. Das, S., Sundara, S., Cyganiak, R.: R2RML: RDB to RDF mapping language. W3C Recommendation, W3C (2012). http://www.w3.org/TR/r2rml/
12. Dayal, U., Bernstein, P.A.: On the correct translation of update operations on relational views. ACM TODS **7**(3), 381–416 (1982). https://doi.org/10.1145/319732.319740
13. De Giacomo, G., Lembo, D., Lenzerini, M., Poggi, A., Rosati, R.: Using ontologies for semantic data integration. In: Flesca, S., Greco, S., Masciari, E., Saccà, D. (eds.) A Comprehensive Guide Through the Italian Database Research Over the Last 25 Years. SBD, vol. 31, pp. 187–202. Springer, Cham (2018). https://doi.org/10.1007/978-3-319-61893-7_11
14. De Giacomo, G., Lembo, D., Oriol, X., Savo, D.F., Teniente, E.: Practical update management in ontology-based data access. In: d'Amato, C., Fernandez, M., Tamma, V., Lecue, F., Cudré-Mauroux, P., Sequeda, J., Lange, C., Heflin, J. (eds.) ISWC 2017. LNCS, vol. 10587, pp. 225–242. Springer, Cham (2017). https://doi.org/10.1007/978-3-319-68288-4_14
15. De Giacomo, G., Oriol, X., Rosati, R., Savo, D.F.: Instance-level update in DL-Lite ontologies through first-order rewriting. JAIR (2021). https://doi.org/10.1613/jair.1.12414
16. Fagin, R.: Inverting schema mappings. ACM TODS **32**(4), 2–53 (2007). https://doi.org/10.1145/1292609.1292615
17. Fagin, R., Kolaitis, P.G., Popa, L., Tan, W.C.: Composing schema mappings: second-order dependencies to the rescue. ACM TODS **30**(4), 994–1055 (2005). https://doi.org/10.1145/1114244.1114249
18. Fagin, R., Ullman, J.D., Vardi, M.Y.: On the semantics of updates in databases. In: Proceedings of the PODS, pp. 352–365 (1983). https://doi.org/10.1145/588058.588100
19. Flouris, G.: On belief change in ontology evolution. AI Commun. **19**(4), 395–397 (2006)
20. Katsuno, H., Mendelzon, A.: On the difference between updating a knowledge base and revising it. In: Proceedings of the KR, pp. 387–394 (1991)
21. Kontchakov, R., Rezk, M., Rodríguez-Muro, M., Xiao, G., Zakharyaschev, M.: Answering SPARQL queries over databases under OWL 2 QL entailment regime. In: Mika, P., et al. (eds.) ISWC 2014. LNCS, vol. 8796, pp. 552–567. Springer, Cham (2014). https://doi.org/10.1007/978-3-319-11964-9_35
22. Motik, B., Cuenca Grau, B., Horrocks, I., Wu, Z., Fokoue, A., Lutz, C.: OWL 2 Web Ontology Language profiles (second edition). W3C Recommendation, W3C (2012). http://www.w3.org/TR/owl2-profiles/
23. Poggi, A., Lembo, D., Calvanese, D., De Giacomo, G., Lenzerini, M., Rosati, R.: Linking data to ontologies. J. on Data Semantics **10**, 133–173 (2008). https://doi.org/10.1007/978-3-540-77688-8_5
24. Winslett, M.: Updating Logical Databases. Cambridge University Press (1990)
25. Xiao, G., et al.: Ontology-based data access: a survey. In: Proceedings of the IJCAI, pp. 5511–5519. IJCAI Org (2018).https://doi.org/10.24963/ijcai.2018/777
26. Xiao, G., Ding, L., Cogrel, B., Calvanese, D.: Virtual knowledge graphs: an overview of systems and use cases. Data Intell. (2019). https://doi.org/10.1162/dint_a_00011
27. Zheleznyakov, D., Kharlamov, E., Nutt, W., Calvanese, D.: On expansion and contraction of DL-Lite knowledge bases. J. Web Semantics **57**, 100484 (2019). https://doi.org/10.1016/j.websem.2018.12.002

Reevaluation of Inductive Link Prediction

Simon Ott[1,2(✉)], Christian Meilicke[2], and Heiner Stuckenschmidt[2]

[1] AIT Austrian Institute of Technology GmbH, Vienna, Austria
simon.ott@ait.ac.at
[2] University of Mannheim, Mannheim, Germany

Abstract. Within this paper, we show that the evaluation protocol currently used for inductive link prediction is heavily flawed as it relies on ranking the true entity in a small set of randomly sampled negative entities. Due to the limited size of the set of negatives, a simple rule-based baseline can achieve state-of-the-art results, which simply ranks entities higher based on the validity of their type. As a consequence of these insights, we reevaluate current approaches for inductive link prediction on several benchmarks using the link prediction protocol usually applied to the transductive setting. As some inductive methods suffer from scalability issues when evaluated in this setting, we propose and apply additionally an improved sampling protocol, which does not suffer from the problem mentioned above. The results of our evaluation differ drastically from the results reported in so far.

Keywords: Inductive link prediction · Evaluation · Rule-based baseline

1 Introduction

Knowledge graphs are commonly used to store knowledge in a structured format. However, even well-maintained, large-scale knowledge graphs such as Freebase [2], DBPedia [1] or the Google Knowledge Graph [12] are notoriously incomplete [5], which limits their usefulness. Given the knowledge already encoded in the graph, some of the missing facts can be entailed or are rather likely due to the probabilistic regularities inherent in the graph. The automated task of predicting missing facts in a knowledge graph without using external knowledge is known as link prediction or knowledge graph completion.

Over time many different approaches were proposed to address this task. Some of the most prominent ones, such as TransE [3], Complex [18], ConvE [4], and RotatE [15] are based on embedding entities (constants) and relations (predicates) in a vector space. These embeddings are learned as a solution to an optimization problem which is defined by the triples in the graph and a specific scoring function which determines the likelihood of a triple being correct. Learnt vectors are then applied to the scoring function to entail missing triples. While these models have proven to perform well in some established evaluation datasets [13], they can only make predictions about entities that were already seen during training. If no embedding for an entity has been learned, it is impossible to compute a score for this entity. Nevertheless, these models have been dominating knowledge base completion for a long time. This is related to the fact that the entities of the evaluation test sets of the most prominent benchmark datasets, such as FB15k-237 [17] and WN18RR [4], are subsets of the entities appearing in the training set. Such a scenario is referred to as **transductive** link prediction. However, there might be link prediction applications where it is not realistic to assume that a transductive setting is given.

A scenario, where the training and test set does not overlap is referred to as **inductive** link prediction [16,23]. The inductive setting has received lots of attention and many different approaches have been proposed [6–9,16,21,24–26]. Within this work we are concerned with a flaw of the data sets and evaluation principles that are usually applied in the context of inductive link prediction. Both transductive and inductive link prediction evaluation are based on computing rankings of candidates for a given completion query, such as *married(john, ?)*. The positions of the correct candidates in the rankings determine the evaluation result. Surprisingly, there is a major difference in the evaluation protocol not related to the difference between the inductive and the transductive setting: In the transductive setting usually the correct entity is ranked within all entities of the dataset. Contrary to this, in the inductive setting the correct entity is ranked only within a relatively small randomly drawn subset of all candidates.

We argue that the results obtained by the random sampling evaluation do not measure predictive accuracy but the capability to distinguish between a potentially meaningful candidate and a nonsensical. Suppose we create a random sample of 50 entities from a knowledge graph such as DBpedia or Freebase. This sample will contain entities of widely varying types, such as organisations, locations, languages, persons, currencies or other. How many entities are persons that might be married to someone? The answer is probably a relatively small number. Thus, it is obviously easy to rank the correct candidate at a top position for our example query given a set of 50 randomly chosen candidates.

Within this paper we analyse the problems of the random sampling evaluation protocol, which has become the de-facto standard for the inductive setting. We propose a simple rule-based baseline which is designed to solve the task to distinguish between a potentially meaningful candidate, that has an appropriate type, and nonsensical candidates. We show in a rich set of experiments that this baseline outperforms many other approaches when applying the random sampling evaluation protocol. This shows that this evaluation protocol is not really measuring predictive accuracy.

We propose, instead, to rank the correct entity within all possible candidates. If this is not possible due to scalability issues, we release a collection of type-matched negatives (TMN) for each benchmark dataset to rank the candidate within a set of entities that have at least an appropriate type. We perform experiments using both approaches with 13 current state-of-the-art methods. Our experiments prove that the random sampling evaluation yields misleading results and that results obtained by a reasonable evaluation protocol differ significantly. We release code, evaluation datasets, and additional results at https://github.com/nomisto/inductiveeval.

2 Preliminaries

2.1 Link Prediction

A knowledge graph (KG) $\mathcal{G} = (\mathcal{E}, \mathcal{R}, \mathcal{T})$ is a heterogeneous directed multigraph consisting of triples $\mathcal{T}$, a set of entities $\mathcal{E}$ and a set of relations $\mathcal{R}$. A triple $p(s, o) \in \mathcal{T}$ is a fact consisting of subject s, relation p and object o where $s \in \mathcal{E}$, $p \in \mathcal{R}$, $o \in \mathcal{E}$. From a logical point of view, a relation is a binary predicate and the entities in $\mathcal{E}$ are constants. Figure 1 shows a small example of a knowledge graph. The entities $\mathcal{E}$ described in this graph are cities, counties, countries and currencies. Some of these entities are linked with each other via one of the three relations in $\mathcal{R}$.

The term *link prediction* originates from calling a relation between two entities a link. In a realistic link prediction application, we have an incomplete knowledge graph $\mathcal{T}$ and we use a link prediction model to create new triples $\mathcal{T}'$ with $\mathcal{T}' \cap \mathcal{T} = \emptyset$. If the approach works well, most of the triples in $\mathcal{T}'$ are correct even though they have been missing in $\mathcal{T}$. Within an evaluation context we split a given knowledge graph $\mathcal{T}$ into train set $\mathcal{T}_{train}$, test set $\mathcal{T}_{test}$ and a validation set $\mathcal{T}_{valid}$. This split is jointly exhaustive and pairwise disjoint. $\mathcal{T}_{train}$ is usually used to train a model, $\mathcal{T}_{valid}$ can be used to optimize the hyperparameters and $\mathcal{T}_{test}$ to evaluate the model performance. Link prediction, often interchangeably called knowledge graph completion, is the task of predicting a target entity given a source entity and a relation. We call such a task a completion task. Each test triple $t_{test} \in \mathcal{T}_{test}$ results in two completion tasks $p(s, ?)$ and $p(?, o)$. The task of link prediction is to predict the correct candidate that acts as a substitution for the ? in the query.

In **transductive** link prediction the test set $\mathcal{T}_{test}$ only contains test triples where subject and object appear in the training set $\mathcal{T}_{train}$. Given a triple $p(s, o) \in \mathcal{T}_{test}$, we have at least one triple in train where s appears in subject or object position and at least one triple where o appears in subject or object position. The information encoded in the training set serves two purposes. It is used to

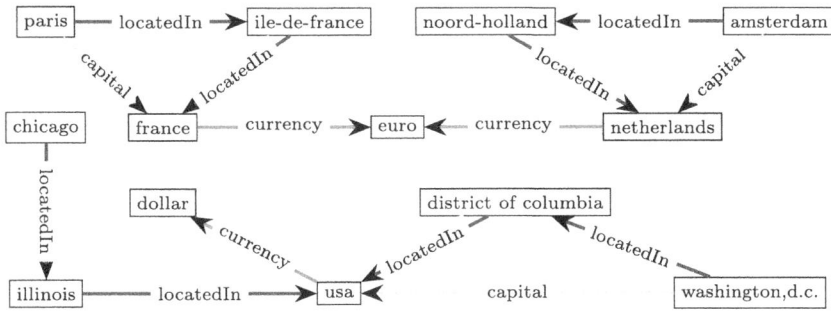

Fig. 1. Example KG of cities, counties, countries and currencies. Different colors represent different relations.

train the model and it contains also the information that describes the relevant features.

We illustrated this setting on the left side of Fig. 2. The area in the pie-chart colored with a violet/teal grid refers to $\mathcal{T}_{train}$, the blue area to $\mathcal{T}_{valid}$ and the red area to $\mathcal{T}_{test}$. Below the pie chart, we depicted an example graph. We used the same coloring scheme for the edges of the triples that belong to the respective sets. The important aspect of the transductive setting is related to the fact that each of the entities involved in a test triple is described also via one or several triples in the train graph. The fact that we have this type of overlap between $\mathcal{T}_{train}$ and $\mathcal{T}_{test}$ is a characteristic feature of the transductive setting, which allows, for example, to use embeddings of entities learned in the training phase to score candidates in the test phase.

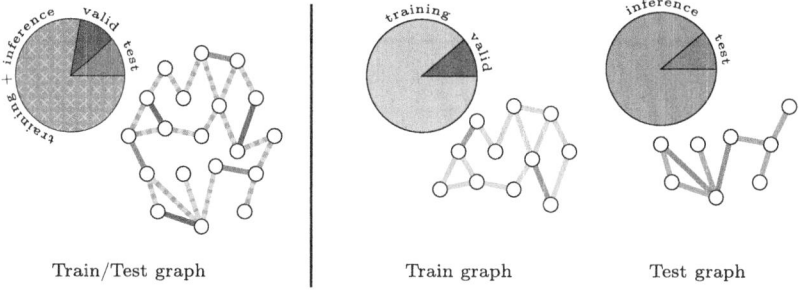

Fig. 2. Difference between transductive (on the left) and inductive link prediction (on the right).

On the right side of Fig. 2 we depicted the **inductive** setting. Here we have a strict separation of entities that appear in the graph used to train the model, and entities that appear in the triples of the test set. Note that the test graph contains not not only the test triples (red), but also triples (purple) that describe the entities that appear in the test triples. In the context of inductive link predictions this set of triples is sometimes called inference set, as it is required to infer the missing triples of the test set. The entities described in the training graph are not overlapping with the entities used in the test graph.

It is, nevertheless, possible to learn a model on a set of entities that are disjoint from the entities to which the model is applied. This is the case because both sets of entities are described by the same set of relations. If we would learn a rule-based model, we might for example learn the rule $genre(X, Y) \leftarrow prequel(X, Z), genre(Z, Y)$. This rule says that a movie has the same genre (with a certain probability) as its prequel (if there is a prequel of that movie). It is obviously applicable in the transductive and inductive setting. However, a rule containing constants such as $nationality(X, dutch) \leftarrow bornIn(X, amsterdam)$ (a person born in Amsterdam has nationality Dutch) can only be applied to the transductive setting.

2.2 Evaluation Protocol

The most prominent metrics for measuring the quality of link prediction methods are ranking-based metrics. They are calculated based on the position of the correct candidate within a ranking of candidate entities. These candidates are elements of a set of possible entities $\mathcal{E}^*$. The target candidate itself is always an element of $\mathcal{E}^*$. In the transductive setting, we have usually $\mathcal{E}^* = \mathcal{E}$. This means that all known entities have to be ranked. In the inductive setting, $\mathcal{E}^*$ is usually a sample from $\mathcal{E}$ with $|\mathcal{E}^*| \ll |\mathcal{E}|$. We call an evaluation protocol which asks to rank all possible candidates a **non-sampling evaluation protocol** contrary to a protocol that asks to rank the candidates from a restrictive set, which we call a **random sampling evaluation protocol**.

Furthermore, according to the filtering protocol of [3], already known triples in the knowledge graph are ignored when calculating the ranking. This filtered setting is the quasi standard and unfiltered scores are rarely reported. We follow this approach and report always filtered scores in our experiments.

The most prominent metrics are the hits@k and the mean reciprocal rank (MRR). Let $\mathcal{I}$ be the set of ranks of the correct candidates for the completion tasks $p(s,?)$ and $p(?,o)$ derived from all test triples $p(s,o)$ in a given datasets.

Hits@k is then the ratio of test queries where the rank i of the correct candidate is less than or equal to k and MRR is the arithmetic mean over individual reciprocal ranks. Let $\mathcal{I}$ be the set of ranks i of the correct candidates for the completion tasks $p(s,?)$ and $p(?,o)$ derived from all test triples $p(s,o)$ in a given datasets. Then we have:

$$hits@k = \frac{1}{|\mathcal{I}|} \sum_{i \in \mathcal{I}} 1 \text{ if } i \leq k \qquad MRR = \frac{1}{|\mathcal{I}|} \sum_{i \in \mathcal{I}} \frac{1}{i}$$

We argue in the following that a small and, in particular, randomly chosen $\mathcal{E}^*$ makes its easy to achieve high hits@10 and MRR scores. This is especially the case if the completion methods under discussion is tailored to such a setting, while such a method will perform poor in any realistic setting.

Sometimes classification metrics as AUC-PR are reported [8,16]. To calculate the AUC-PR, a single negative triple is constructed for each test triple $p(s,o)$ by randomly corrupting the head or the tail with a random entity. Since we want to compare our results with those of the transductive setting where primarily ranking-based metrics are used, we will only focus on them in the following. Nevertheless, our findings are also applicable to the AUC-PR metric and similar metrics.

3 The Random Sampling Evaluation Protocol

In [16] the authors proposed inductive link prediction as research problem and introduced a pioneering approach called GraIL. In this paper the authors also introduced the most commonly used benchmarks. These benchmarks would support also a non-sampling based evaluation protocol. However, the authors decided to use a random sampling-based variant of the evaluation protocol due to performance issues of GraIL. Instead of ranking $\mathcal{E}$ for each completion task they used a randomly chosen sample $\mathcal{E}^*$ of 50 candidates (one of them is the correct target candidate). Unfortunately most succeeding work [6–9,21,26] adapted this evaluation protocol. Thus, the random sampling approach has become the defacto standard for evaluating inductive link prediction.

Using the random sampling evaluation protocol the set of sampled negative entities contains a variety of entities of different types. Due to this variety, the type of the sampled negative often does not make sense. For example, for the completion task $genre(StarWars,?)$ the set of negatives could contain entities such as countries, artists or professions. Due to the lack of type-matched negatives it is sufficient for an approach to simply make predictions about the type of an entity rather than the entity itself to achieve high scores.

Furthermore, all approaches evaluated using this evaluation protocol report hits@10. This high choice of k further limits the ability to evaluate the models real inductive link prediction performance, as a model which randomly assigns scores to entities on average already achieves a hits@10 score of 0.2 as the probability of assigning a top-10 score to the correct entity by chance is $10/50 = 0.2$.

3.1 Baseline

We propose a simple baseline in which candidates are simply ranked higher if they are valid answers to a prediction task depending on the entity type of the candidate. For each relation p we learn rules that determine whether entities are valid candidates for the subject position and for the object position of p. We iterate over all possible pairs of relations h and b ($h \neq b$). If the set of subject entities of relation b has a high overlap with the set of subject entities of h, the presence of an outgoing relation b of an entity can be used to predict the outgoing relation h. We thus learn rules adhering to the following language bias

$$r_{ss} : h(X, A) \leftarrow b(X, B) \qquad r_{so} : h(X, A) \leftarrow b(B, X)$$
$$r_{os} : h(A, X) \leftarrow b(X, B) \qquad r_{oo} : h(A, X) \leftarrow b(B, X)$$

where h is the head relation and b is the relation of the body atom. Uppercase letters represent variables. A and B are unbound variables. Note that we learn rules for any combination of subject and object positions of relations h and b.

These rules are an indirect way to implicitly infer the type of an entity. Here a type expresses the validity of entities for the subject/object position of a relation. For each rule we calculate a confidence which can be used as how well a rule predicts an entity X for being a valid type for the subject or object position of h depending on whether the bound variable X is on the subject or object position of the rule. This confidence is the relative proportion of correctly predicted subject/object positions of all predicted entities $conf(r) = |\{x : x \in X_b \wedge x \in X_h\}|/|\{x : x \in X_b\}|$ where X_b is the set of subjects/objects (depending on the position of the bound variable X) of triples in the training set having body relation b, while X_h is the set of subjects/objects of triples in the training set having head relation h.

Given a list of entities to be ranked as predictions for a prediction task $p(s, ?)$, we then rank those entities higher that based on the confidence of the rule have a more suitable type for ?. For each head $p(?, o)$ and tail $p(s, ?)$ query in the test set of the test graph we apply the rules learned by our baseline. Since the same entity can be proposed by multiple rules, we order the entities via the confidence of the rule with the highest confidence.

For example, from Fig. 1 we might learn a rule r_1 that says that an entity might be a good candidate for the subject of the relation *currency* if it is the object of a triple with the relation *capital*. As both require entities of type *country* this rule makes sense. Furthermore, subjects of relation *locatedIn* can take on a mixture of entities of type *county* and *city*. A rule such as r_2 makes sense, however it can only predict a subset of types. Due to the mixture of types of subjects of relation *locatedIn*, its ability to determine entities of type *city* based on its presence is rather limited. Thus the confidence of r_3 is rather low.

$$r_1 : currency(X, A) \leftarrow capital(B, X) \qquad 1.0[3/3]$$
$$r_2 : locatedIn(X, A) \leftarrow capital(X, B) \qquad 1.0[3/3]$$
$$r_3 : capital(X, A) \leftarrow locatedIn(X, B) \qquad 0.3[3/10]$$

This baseline should result in low inductive link prediction performance as it is simply predicting linked entities based on correct types. For example a rule $marriedTo(X, A) \leftarrow bornIn(B, X)$ could be learned, which would have almost a perfect confidence as every person that was married was also born somewhere. In the context of link prediction this does not make sense as this would mean that e.g. the link prediction query $marriedTo(?, paul)$ would be answered with every person born. However, as we will show in later experiments, when evaluated using the flawed random sampling evaluation protocol this baseline appears to perform very well in inductive link prediction.

3.2 Type-Matched Sampling Protocol

Approaches which require repeated sampling of subgraphs such as GraIL [16] and its variants [7,9,21] are very slow to evaluate. In fact the flawed sampling evaluation protocol was introduced to help overcome this limitation. In order to be able to evaluate approaches where it is infeasible to score and rank all entities we release a collection of type-matched negatives (TMN) for each benchmark dataset. For each test query we provide 50 negatives that adhere to the type of the searched answer and thus create a more challenging set of negatives. For example for the test triple <Indie rock, /music/genre/artists, Oasis> of FB15k-237 v3 the set of type-matched head negatives contains genre entities like Pop rock, Hip hop music or Death metal while the set of tail negatives contains artist entities like Katy Perry, The Smashing Pumpkins, Miley Cyrus or AC/DC.

We created these sets by applying the rules learned by our baseline for each head $p(?, o)$ and tail $p(s, ?)$ query in the test set as described above. Since we aggregate the confidences of an entity predicted by multiple rules using the maximum it could be possible that one rule dominates the creation of the 50 negatives. For example if the rule with the highest confidence would be $city(X, A) \leftarrow capital(X, B)$ and would predict more than 50 entities the resulting set of negatives would only contain capitals. To circumvent this and provide a good mixture of high confident entities we bin the predictions in three buckets: entities with a confidence $c \geq 0.75$, entities with a confidence $0.75 > c \geq 0.25$ and entities with a confidence $0.25 > c$. First we try to randomly sample 50 negative entities from the bucket of entities with the highest confidence. If this bucket contains less than 50 entities, we try to sample missing entities from the bucket with the next highest confidence and so on until the a set of negatives reaches a size of 50 entities. If the baseline does not generate enough entities we fill missing entities with randomly sampled entities. Furthermore in each step we keep only true negative entities, which means that the resulting negative triples only contain triples that do not appear in the knowledge graph. This is true for all benchmarks and versions except NELL-995 v1 where due to the limited size of entities it was not possible to create 50 non-positive candidates for all queries. As mentioned in the introduction, we publicly release sets of type-matched negatives for all the benchmarks used in this paper, and code to generate such sets for other datasets.

4 Experimental Evaluation

4.1 Datasets, Approaches and Metrics

For the evaluation of different approaches we use the commonly used inductive link prediction benchmarks created by [16]. They were created by sampling two disjunct subgraphs from the transductive benchmark datasets FB15k-237 [17], WN18RR [4] and NELL-995 [20]. Each benchmark was released as 4 size-increasing different versions denoted v1, v2, v3 and v4. Table 1 shows the statistics of the benchmarks. It should be noted that the relation counts differ for unknown reasons from the original statistics in [16].

Table 1. Number of relations (#R), entities (#E) and training, validation and test triples of the training and test graph for each benchmark dataset.

	Graph	FB15k-237					WN18RR					NELL-995				
		#R	#E	Train	Valid	Test	#R	#E	Train	Valid	Test	#R	#E	Train	Valid	Test
v1	train	180	1594	4245	489	492	9	2746	5410	630	638	14	3103	4687	414	439
	test		1093	1993	206	205		922	1618	185	188		225	833	101	100
v2	train	200	2608	9739	1166	1180	10	6954	15262	1838	1868	88	2564	8219	922	968
	test		1660	4145	469	478		2757	4011	411	441		2086	4586	459	476
v3	train	215	3668	17986	2194	2214	11	12078	25901	3097	3152	142	4647	16393	1851	1873
	test		2501	7406	866	865		5084	6327	538	605		3566	8048	811	809
v4	train	219	4707	27203	3352	3361	9	3861	7940	934	968	76	2092	7546	876	867
	test		3051	11714	1416	1424		7084	12334	1394	1429		2795	7073	716	731

We perform experiments using different approaches for inductive link prediction, which can be categorized in rule-based (Neural-LP [22], DRUM [14], RuleN [11], AnyBURL [10]) and graph neural network (GNN) based (GraIL [16], ConGLR [7], COMPILE [9], SNRI [21], INDIGO [8], NBFNet [26], AStarNet [25], RED-GNN [24]). An exception to this classification is NodePiece [6] which can be used without a GNN in theory. However, due to its low performance otherwise, it is used in combination with a GNN in the context of inductive link prediction. We will now give a short overview of the different approaches. Approaches described within the same bullet point belong to the same family of approaches.

- RuleN [11] and AnyBURL [10] are both symbolic rule-based approaches, which extract first-order logic rules in the form of horn clauses directly from knowledge graphs. Both calculate an approximated rule confidence which is used to score predictions.
- NeuralLP [22] and DRUM [14] are end-to-end differentiable approaches for rule learning. NeuralLP uses TensorLog operations to learn first-order logic rules, while DRUM uses bidirectional RNNs.
- NBFNet [26], RED-GNN [24] and AStarNet [25] are both approaches that progressively propagate from a node to its neighborhood in a breadth-first-searching (BFS) manner. RED-GNN is utilizing dynamic programming for efficient subgraph encoding, while NBFNet is based on the Bellman-Ford algorithm for shortest path problems. AStarNet enhances scalability by learning to preselect important nodes and edges.
- Usually entities are encoded using shallow encoding which means there is one embedding for each entity. NodePiece [6] is an approach to reduce the number of embeddings needed by embedding-based approaches. The embedding of a node is retrieved using its relational context and the distance of it to selected anchor nodes. In the inductive setting only the relational context is used in combination with a relational message passing GNN based on CompGCN [19].
- INDIGO [8] is another GNN-based approach, which encodes the triples of the knowledge graph pair-wise, i.e. nodes in the graph correspond to pairs of entities. It is trained as a denoising autoencoder.
- GraIL [16] is a GCN-based approach adapted to the inductive link prediction setting. It scores triples consisting of unseen entities by performing message passing on extracted enclosing subgraphs between the target nodes using k-hop neighbourhood. Nodes in extracted subgraphs are labelled with respect to the target nodes using a double radius vertex labeling scheme. GraIL and all its extensions require to extract a subgraph for each link which is not scalable to large graphs. This was the main reason for using a random sampling evaluation protocol.
- CoMPILE, ConGLR and SNRI extend GraIL by adding additional processing steps. CoMPILE [9] introduces the ability to naturally handle asymmetric/antisymmetric relations. ConGLR [7] can be seen as a hybrid approach between GCN-based and rule-based approaches. It extends GraIL by the additional extraction of a context graph from the k-hop neighbourhood subgraph. SNRI [21] extends GraIL by not only considering the enclosing subgraph

between the target node, but also partial neighbouring relations by applying mutual information (MI) maximization.

We train each approach using the settings from their respective papers. We refer to https://github.com/nomisto/inductiveeval for details. Due to the amount of different versions of benchmark datasets we will mainly discuss averages over the four versions for each dataset. For better comparability with the random sampling protocol, for which hits@10 results have often been reported, we will also base most of our discussion on hits@10. Tables containing the results using both hits@10 and MRR can be found at the URL above.

4.2 Results

Random Sampling Evaluation Protocol. The upper part of Table 2 labeled *Random Sampling* shows the hits@10 results using the random sampling evaluation protocol. If available, we report the numbers presented in the original paper. If not available, we report results based on our own experiments with these approaches. As a cross-check, we compare all our models with models for which numbers are available. We observed only insignificant differences from the numbers of the original papers.

Our simple baseline outperforms current state-of-the-art approaches on FB15k-237. It achieves an average hits@10 of about 0.938 over the different versions by simply distinguishing the correct entity based on its type. The baseline also outperforms or rivals the performance of state-of-the-art approaches on NELL-995, especially on the bigger versions V3 and V4. Since WN18RR is a knowledge graph of word senses and general relations such as *hypernym*, it does not contain strongly typed entities. As a result, the baseline fails to achieve competitive results with the exception of the V3 version. The reason for that are different distributions of relations of the test sets. V3 is dominated by relations for which the tail entity is always an entity from a small set of entities (for example countries or regions), which can be learned by the baseline.

These results illustrate already clearly that the random sampling evaluation protocol together with the hits@10 metric is not an appropriate protocol to evaluate and rank approaches for inductive link prediction. With respect to the average hits@10 score our baseline ranks at position #1, #13 and #3 out of 14 approaches (including the baseline) on the three evaluation datasets. We also measured the MRR results, to check if we can observe a similar behaviour. For the MRR it is more important to rank the correct candidate at the top position, thus, the MRR has a stronger focus on a high precision. Here our baselines occupies the positions #7, #13 and #13. While the MRR solves some issues of the random sampling protocol, the baseline still achieves a midfield position for FB15k-237 and there are 7 approaches that perform worse.

Non-Sampling Evaluation Protocol. The middle part of Table 2 labeled *Non-Sampling* shows the hits@10 results for the non-sampling evaluation protocol, i.e. ranking the correct candidate within all entities of the knowledge graph. Since the evaluation of GraIL and its extensions is very inefficient, we decided to only evaluate benchmarks where the evaluation does not take significantly longer than 12 h. For example the evaluation of GraIL on FB15k-237 V3 takes 10 h, while the evaluation of CoMPILE/ConGLR/SNRI on FB15k-237 V2 already takes 9/10.75/11.5 h.

The non-sampling evaluation approach draws a completely different picture. Similar to the random sampling evaluation protocol, NBFNet still can be considered as the best performing approach by achieving the highest average hits@10 on FB15k-237 and NELL-995, while achieving the second highest average hits@10 on WN18RR. NodePiece, which showed one of the best performances when evaluated using the random sampling evaluation protocol, loses over-proportionally as it now only scores 0.450 average hits@10, scoring 0.476% points lower compared to the random sampling evaluation protocol, while NBFNet only scores 0.257% points lower. NodePiece, which was the best performing approach given the results of the random sampling protocol, has been overtaken by five other approaches in the realistic non-sampling protocol. One reason for its good performance on the random sampling evaluation could be, that as NodePiece primarily uses 1-hop incoming and outgoing relations of a node, it could be prone to leverage typing information of a node. AStarNet and RED-GNN appear to behave similarly to NBFNet, with a difference in scores of about 0.221% points for AStarNet and 0.207% points for RED-GNN compared to the random sampling evaluation protocol.

The predictive performances of rule-based approaches, such as the symbolic rule-based approach AnyBURL, seem to be actually better than assessed using the random sampling evaluation protocol. AnyBURL has an average hits@10 of 0.584 on FB15k-237, only 0.169% points less than the average sampled hits@10, achieving competitive results comparable to NBFNet. On WN18RR AnyBURL scores an average hits@10 of about 0.687, where the best performing approaches NBFNet achieve 0.664 and AStarNet 0.623. The difference of sampling and non-sampling average hits@10 for DRUM also only amount to 0.134% points and for NeuralLP 0.173.

Type-Matched Sampling Evaluation Protocol. Using sampled negatives that have an appropriate type draws a similar picture than using the non-sampling protocol. However, this protocol has the advantage that it is also applicable to less efficient models. The bottom part of Table 2 labeled *Type-matched Sampling* shows the hits@10 using the type-matched sampling evaluation protocol. This evaluation protocol still shows that NBFNet is one of the top-performing approaches as it achieves the best average hits@10 on all datasets. However approaches, such as NodePiece, that performed well on the random sampling evaluation approach as they might learn types of entities, do not perform well in this setting. It is still evident that rule-based approaches produce competitive results. Thus, the type-matched sampling protocol can be used as substitute for the non-sampling protocol in case of scalability issues.

Table 2. Hits@10 results using the **random sampling** (upper part), **non-sampling** (middle part) and **type-matched sampling** evaluation protocol (bottom part). † results were generated by us, * results are from [16], other results for **random sampling** evaluation protocol are from the original papers. All results using the **non-sampling** (middle part) and **type-matched sampling** evaluation protocol were generated by us. To compensate the variance of the random sampling protocol, we report the average of 100 evaluation runs. RED-GNN [24] and AStarNet [25] also report results using the non-sampling evaluation protocol in their respective papers. However, for reasons unknown, they do not only evaluate on the test set of the test graph, but rather a combination of the test set of the test graph and a further hold-out set of the test graph. The usage of this hold-out set, sometimes referred to as validation set of the test graph, is not really clear and is neither used for training, validation or testing in the original paper [16]. Numbers reported by us were created using solely the test set however.

	Approach	FB15k-237					WN18RR					NELL-995				
		V1	V2	V3	V4	avg	V1	V2	V3	V4	avg	V1	V2	V3	V4	avg
Random Sampling	Neural LP*	.529	.589	.529	.559	.552	.744	.689	.462	.671	.642	.408	.787	.827	.806	.707
	DRUM*	.529	.587	.529	.559	.551	.744	.689	.462	.671	.642	.194	.786	.827	.806	.653
	RuleN*	.498	.778	.877	.856	.752	.809	.782	.534	.716	.710	.535	.818	.773	.614	.685
	AnyBURL†	.517	.784	.845	.865	.753	.814	.776	.544	.719	.713	.795	.824	.775	.605	.750
	GraIL*	.642	.818	.828	.893	.795	.825	.787	.584	.734	.733	.595	.933	.914	.732	.794
	ConGLR [7]	.683	.860	.886	.893	.831	.856	.929	.707	.929	.855	.811	.949	.944	.816	.880
	COMPILE [9]	.676	.830	.847	.874	.807	.836	.798	.607	.755	.749	.584	.939	.928	.752	.801
	SNRI [21]	.718	.865	.896	.894	.843	.872	.831	.673	.883	.815	.643†	.900†	.918†	.191†	.663†
	INDIGO†	.451	.480	.483	.480	.473	.166	.156	.316	.203	.210	.520	.552	.510	.497	.520
	NodePiece [6]	.873	.939	.944	.949	.926	.830	.886	.785	.807	.827	.890	.901	.936	.893	.905
	NBFNet [26]	.834	.949	.951	.960	.924	.948	.905	.893	.890	.909	.908†	.956†	.968†	.939†	.943†
	AStarNet†	.687	.867	.904	.916	.844	.877	.836	.715	.799	.807	.940	.899	.860	.828	.882
	RED-GNN†	.516	.771	.829	.903	.755	.856	.824	.684	.777	.785	.853	.925	.954	.806	.884
	Baseline†	.887	.963	.954	.949	.938	.087	.145	.590	.138	.240	.761	.912	.945	.914	.883
Non-Sampling	NeuralLP	.351	.437	.388	.341	.379	.713	.684	.312	.636	.586	.750	.598	.544	.585	.619
	DRUM	.385	.468	.410	.403	.417	.715	.680	.310	.635	.585	.755	.554	.585	.591	.621
	AnyBURL	.461	.640	.620	.614	.584	.803	.772	.467	.705	.687	.830	.610	.486	.530	.614
	GraIL	.376	.415	.423	t/o	.404	.729	.744	.406	.675	.638	.685	.310	.336	.219	.387
	ConGLR	.373	.423	t/o	t/o	.398	.566	.688	t/o	t/o	.627	.810	.512	t/o	t/o	.661
	COMPILE	.417	.498	t/o	t/o	.457	.689	.656	t/o	.673	.673	.760	.606	t/o	t/o	.683
	SNRI	.246	.416	t/o	t/o	.331	.319	.465	t/o	t/o	.392	.800	.407	t/o	t/o	.603
	INDIGO	.198	.247	.246	.198	.222	.040	.011	.056	.005	.028	.615	.230	.193	.182	.305
	NodePiece	.429	.500	.451	.419	.450	.540	.661	.262	.506	.492	.895	.294	.306	.178	.418
	NBFNet	.617	.719	.659	.661	.664	.830	.787	.554	.700	.718	.925	.694	.688	.640	.737
	AStarNet	.534	.673	.647	.637	.623	.819	.804	.541	.736	.725	.960	.690	.646	.440	.684
	RED-GNN	.420	.590	.582	.600	.548	.774	.776	.532	.696	.694	.840	.582	.553	.301	.569
	Baseline	.351	.384	.253	.211	.300	.005	.002	.022	.000	.007	.835	.124	.129	.049	.284
Type-matched Sampling	NeuralLP	.441	.550	.499	.531	.505	.729	.689	.336	.652	.601	.750	.731	.734	.748	.741
	DRUM	.446	.556	.497	.533	.508	.729	.689	.336	.652	.602	.755	.752	.752	.758	.752
	AnyBURL	.495	.712	.717	.746	.668	.814	.776	.540	.719	.712	.830	.759	.645	.586	.705
	GraIL	.566	.690	.688	.546	.622	.840	.810	.596	.762	.752	.720	.798	.719	.613	.713
	ConGLR	.685	.659	.694	.699	.684	.785	.804	.501	.753	.711	.865	.889	.853	.769	.844
	COMPILE	.622	.759	.735	.724	.710	.835	.800	.591	.746	.743	.765	.888	.838	.574	.766
	SNRI	.554	.697	.679	.696	.656	.878	.815	.595	.773	.765	.805	.776	.663	.371	.654
	INDIGO	.344	.383	.388	.391	.376	.136	.091	.183	.131	.135	.615	.478	.420	.418	.483
	NodePiece	.532	.615	.625	.600	.593	.798	.842	.599	.765	.751	.905	.555	.575	.470	.626
	NBFNet	.688	.794	.776	.784	.760	.941	.910	.863	.899	.903	.970	.861	.868	.819	.880
	AStarNet	.651	.753	.754	.761	.730	.875	.832	.702	.797	.802	.975	.828	.794	.775	.843
	RED-GNN	.483	.700	.718	.754	.664	.854	.823	.665	.777	.780	.895	.842	.807	.540	.771

Comparing Different Protocols. Figure 3 shows trajectories that illustrate how the performance of the different approaches changes on the FB15k-237 benchmark, when evaluated using the random, type-matched and non-sampling evaluation protocols. As the different protocols get increasingly difficult we normalize the performance of each approach by showing the absolute difference to the performance of AnyBURL. As can be seen by the green trajectories, robust approaches such as NBFNet, AStarNet and RED-GNN can maintain a steady advantage compared to AnyBURL. NodePiece, however, which scored 0.173 better on hits@10 than AnyBURL evaluated using the random sampling protocol, scores about 0.068 lower on hits@10 than AnyBURL when evaluated under type-matched sampling protocol and substantially lower (0.134) when evaluated under non-sampling protocol. This might be a hint that this approach learns types very well instead of learning the likelihood of links between entities. GraIL and its extensions show similar behaviour using hits@10, where the lead of these approaches is diminishing when evaluated under type-matched sampling protocol and lose lead by a margin when evaluated under non-sampling protocol. On MRR AnyBURL already performs better than GraIL and its extensions using the random sampling protocol. Using the type-matched sampling protocol, they could make up leeway and perform similar or only a little worse than AnyBURL. Using the non-sampling protocol, MRR behaves similar to hits@10 again.

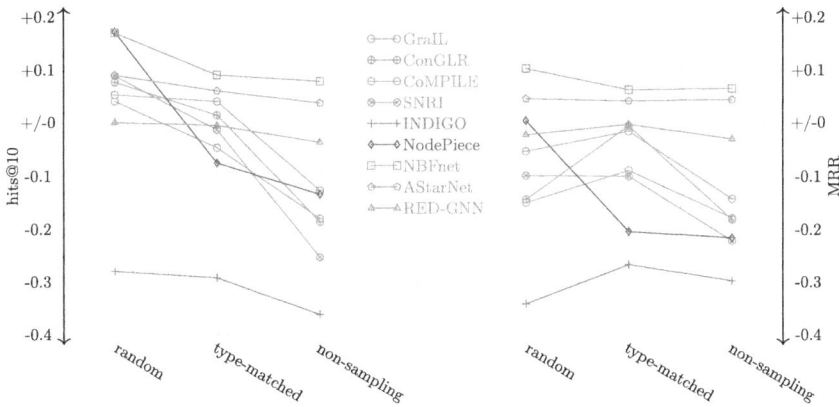

Fig. 3. Absolute changes in performance of different approaches compared to AnyBURL under different evaluation protocols (random sampling, type-matched and non-sampling) using average hits@10 (left) and average MRR (right) on FB15k-237.

5 Conclusion

Current inductive link prediction approaches are evaluated by comparing a prediction only against a small set of randomly selected negatives. Due to the limited size of the set of negatives, errors are introduced that prevent the assessment of the model's true inductive link prediction ability. We show that current state-of-the-art results for inductive link prediction can be achieved using a simple rule-based baseline. Furthermore, we re-evaluate approaches to inductive link prediction, where the order of the state-of-the-art changes drastically. Our corrected results indicate that GNN-based approaches such as NBNnet, AStarNet and RED-GNN are clearly ahead compared to the other approaches. The rule-based approach AnyBURL is an efficient and fully explainable alternative that performs only slightly worse. At the same time we observed that approaches as NodePiece and GraIL as well as its successors lag behind if we evaluate them under a realistic protocol.

We advocate that further research should be evaluated using an evaluation protocol where all entities of the knowledge graph are used as negatives. If it is not possible to evaluate an approach on all entities, we publish datasets of type-matched head and tail negatives and encourage inductive link prediction researchers to use them instead of randomly sampling negatives.

Acknowledgments. This work was funded by the Austrian security research program KIRAS of the Federal Ministry of Finance (BMF) through the DAGMAR project (grant No. 52224305).

Disclosure of Interests. The authors have no competing interests to declare that are relevant to the content of this article.

References

1. Auer, S., Bizer, C., Kobilarov, G., Lehmann, J., Cyganiak, R., Ives, Z.: DBpedia: a nucleus for a web of open data. In: Aberer, K., et al. (eds.) ASWC/ISWC -2007. LNCS, vol. 4825, pp. 722–735. Springer, Heidelberg (2007). https://doi.org/10.1007/978-3-540-76298-0_52
2. Bollacker, K., Evans, C., Paritosh, P., Sturge, T., Taylor, J.: Freebase: a collaboratively created graph database for structuring human knowledge. In: Proceedings of the 2008 ACM SIGMOD International Conference on Management of Data, pp. 1247–1250. ACM (2008)
3. Bordes, A., Usunier, N., Garcia-Duran, A., Weston, J., Yakhnenko, O.: Translating embeddings for modeling multi-relational data. In: Advances in Neural Information Processing Systems, vol. 26 (2013)
4. Dettmers, T., Minervini, P., Stenetorp, P., Riedel, S.: Convolutional 2D knowledge graph embeddings. In: Proceedings of the AAAI Conference on Artificial Intelligence, vol. 32 (2018)
5. Dong, X., et al.: Knowledge vault: a web-scale approach to probabilistic knowledge fusion. In: Proceedings of the 20th ACM SIGKDD International Conference on Knowledge Discovery and Data Mining, pp. 601–610 (2014)
6. Galkin, M., Denis, E., Wu, J., Hamilton, W.L.: Nodepiece: compositional and parameter-efficient representations of large knowledge graphs. In: International Conference on Learning Representations (2022). https://openreview.net/forum?id=xMJWUKJnFSw

7. Lin, Q., et al.: Incorporating context graph with logical reasoning for inductive relation prediction. In: SIGIR 2022: Proceedings of the 45th International ACM SIGIR Conference on Research and Development in Information Retrieval, pp. 893–903. Association for Computing Machinery, New York, NY, USA (2022). https://doi.org/10.1145/3477495.3531996
8. Liu, S., Grau, B.C., Horrocks, I., Kostylev, E.V.: Indigo: GNN-based inductive knowledge graph completion using pair-wise encoding. In: NeurIPS (2021)
9. Mai, S., Zheng, S., Yang, Y., Hu, H.: Communicative message passing for inductive relation reasoning. In: Proceedings of the AAAI Conference on Artificial Intelligence, vol. 35, pp. 4294–4302 (2021)
10. Meilicke, C., Chekol, M.W., Ruffinelli, D., Stuckenschmidt, H.: Anytime bottom-up rule learning for knowledge graph completion. In: Proceedings of the Twenty-Eighth International Joint Conference on Artificial Intelligence, pp. 3137–3143. Ijcai.org (2019)
11. Meilicke, C., Fink, M., Wang, Y., Ruffinelli, D., Gemulla, R., Stuckenschmidt, H.: Fine-grained evaluation of rule- and embedding-based systems for knowledge graph completion. In: Vrandečić, D., et al. (eds.) ISWC 2018. LNCS, vol. 11136, pp. 3–20. Springer, Cham (2018). https://doi.org/10.1007/978-3-030-00671-6_1
12. Noy, N., Gao, Y., Jain, A., Narayanan, A., Patterson, A., Taylor, J.: Industry-scale knowledge graphs: lessons and challenges: five diverse technology companies show how it's done. Queue **17**(2), 48–75 (2019)
13. Rossi, A., Barbosa, D., Firmani, D., Matinata, A., Merialdo, P.: Knowledge graph embedding for link prediction: a comparative analysis. ACM Trans. Knowl. Disc. Data (TKDD) **15**(2), 1–49 (2021)
14. Sadeghian, A., Armandpour, M., Ding, P., Wang, D.Z.: Drum: end-to-end differentiable rule mining on knowledge graphs. In: Advances in Neural Information Processing Systems, vol. 32. Curran Associates, Inc. (2019). https://proceedings.neurips.cc/paper/2019/file/0c72cb7ee1512f800abe27823a792d03-Paper.pdf
15. Sun, Z., Deng, Z.H., Nie, J.Y., Tang, J.: Rotate: knowledge graph embedding by relational rotation in complex space. arXiv preprint arXiv:1902.10197 (2019)
16. Teru, K.K., Denis, E.G., Hamilton, W.L.: Inductive relation prediction by subgraph reasoning. In: ICML 2020: Proceedings of the 37th International Conference on Machine Learning. JMLR.org (2020)
17. Toutanova, K., Chen, D.: Observed versus latent features for knowledge base and text inference. In: Proceedings of the 3rd Workshop on Continuous Vector Space Models and Their Compositionality, pp. 57–66 (2015)
18. Trouillon, T., Welbl, J., Riedel, S., Gaussier, É., Bouchard, G.: Complex embeddings for simple link prediction. In: International Conference on Machine Learning, pp. 2071–2080. PMLR (2016)
19. Vashishth, S., Sanyal, S., Nitin, V., Talukdar, P.: Composition-based multi-relational graph convolutional networks. In: International Conference on Learning Representations (2020). https://openreview.net/forum?id=BylA_C4tPr
20. Xiong, W., Hoang, T., Wang, W.Y.: DeepPath: a reinforcement learning method for knowledge graph reasoning. In: Palmer, M., Hwa, R., Riedel, S. (eds.) Proceedings of the 2017 Conference on Empirical Methods in Natural Language Processing, pp. 564–573. Association for Computational Linguistics, Copenhagen, Denmark (2017). https://doi.org/10.18653/v1/D17-1060
21. Xu, X., Zhang, P., He, Y., Chao, C., Yan, C.: Subgraph neighboring relations infomax for inductive link prediction on knowledge graphs. In: Raedt, L.D. (ed.) Proceedings of the Thirty-First International Joint Conference on Artificial Intelligence, pp. 2341–2347. IJCAI-22 (2022).https://doi.org/10.24963/ijcai.2022/325

22. Yang, F., Yang, Z., Cohen, W.W.: Differentiable learning of logical rules for knowledge base reasoning. In: NIPS, pp. 2319–2328 (2017)
23. Yang, Z., Cohen, W.W., Salakhutdinov, R.: Revisiting semi-supervised learning with graph embeddings. In: ICML 2016: Proceedings of the 33rd International Conference on International Conference on Machine Learning, vol. 48, pp. 40–48. JMLR.org (2016)
24. Zhang, Y., Yao, Q.: Knowledge graph reasoning with relational digraph. In: Proceedings of the ACM Web Conference 2022, pp. 912–924 (2022)
25. Zhu, Z., et al.: A*net: a scalable path-based reasoning approach for knowledge graphs. arXiv preprint arXiv:2206.04798 (2022)
26. Zhu, Z., Zhang, Z., Xhonneux, L.P., Tang, J.: Neural bellman-ford networks: a general graph neural network framework for link prediction. In: Advances in Neural Information Processing Systems, vol. 34 (2021)

Judicial Explanations

Cecilia Di Florio[ID] and Antonino Rotolo[✉][ID]

ALMA AI and Department of Legal Studies, University of Bologna, Bologna, Italy
{cecilia.diflorio2,antonino.rotolo}@unibo.it

Abstract. The use of machine and deep learning techniques to predict outcomes in legal proceedings is a highly debated topic among legal scholars and policymakers. These technologies have the potential to support judicial decision-making, assist litigants, and analyze biases within the legal process. However, challenges remain, notably in the reluctance of judges to adopt such tools due to concerns over judicial independence, the normative correctness, accuracy, and robustness of algorithmic decisions, and the transparency of AI systems. It is claimed that methods are needed to validate AI-based judicial predication mechanisms. This paper contributes to addressing these challenges by developing a general framework for judicial case-based reasoning (CBR) grounded in Defeasible Logic and Argumentation Semantics. We explore legal CBR, focusing on inconsistencies and incomplete knowledge within case bases, and emphasize the importance of normative explanations to ensure transparency and justification in legal decision-making. By reconstructing CBR and normative explanations within an argumentation framework, we provide a formal mechanism for validating AI-based judicial predictions.

1 Introduction

The growing interest in leveraging *machine learning* and *deep learning* to predict legal outcomes is evident in both academic literature and discussions among policymakers [5,8,16,30]. These advanced AI techniques are seen as potential tools for various applications in the legal field. For instance, they can serve as algorithmic decision predictors that:

1. **Support Judges:** These tools can assist judges by providing data-driven insights and predictions for individual cases, potentially improving the consistency and efficiency of judicial decision-making.
2. **Assist Litigants:** Litigants can use these AI tools to estimate their likelihood of winning a case, helping them make informed decisions about whether to pursue legal action or seek settlements.
3. **Examine Biases:** AI can analyze and identify biases in legal decision-making processes, shedding light on disparities related to ethnicity, gender, socioeconomic status, and other factors [8].

A. Rotolo was partially supported by the projects CN1 "National Centre for HPC, Big Data and Quantum Computing" (CUP: J33C22001170001) and PE01 "Future Artificial Intelligence Research" FAIR (CUP: J33C22002830006).

Despite the potential benefits, the integration of AI in judicial contexts faces significant challenges. Judges show reluctance towards adopting AI tools due to several reasons:

1. **Judicial Independence:** There is a concern that AI could undermine the independent exercise of judicial power, potentially influencing decisions unduly.
2. **Normative Issues and Accuracy:** Judges and legal scholars question whether the outcomes generated by AI predictors are normatively correct, accurate, and robust. The alignment of AI decisions with legal and ethical standards is not always clear.
3. **Transparency and Explainability:** As is well-known, AI algorithms often lack transparency. This "black box" nature makes it difficult for users to understand how predictions are made, which is problematic in a field that requires explainable and accountable decision-making.

Given these challenges, it is crucial to develop robust methods for validating AI-based judicial prediction mechanisms. Validation ensures that these AI systems are reliable, accurate, and ethical in their predictions [31].

In response to this need, our paper proposes a general framework for *judicial case-based reasoning* (CBR). CBR has played an important role in AI & law research. While different models have been adopted, factor-based representations have been most popular, where *factors are features of cases that support possible judicial outcomes* (i.e., *plaintiff wins*, *defendant wins*). This line of research started with HYPO [4,38], in whose framework a factor-based representation enables various patterns of analogical reasoning: citing a precedent, distinguishing it, and reasoning *a fortiori*.

John Horty has studied the logical properties of legal CBR, developing a method for determining whether a certain decision is consistent or inconsistent with a case base [21]. Applying the idea of *a fortiori* reasoning, he has argued that any decision in a new case would be inconsistent with a precedent if that decision is different from the precedent's, even though the new case has a more (or equally) inclusive set of facts favoring the precedent's conclusion and a less (or equally) inclusive set of factors against that conclusion. Further developments include the so-called *reason model*, wherein the reason distinguished in a case is the specified set of elements that the judge considers to provide sufficient support to the case decision, outweighing the factors to the contrary.

Recent research, such as in [10,13,14,40], has argued that some of the usual assumptions in legal CBR can be relaxed or weakened in order to deal with more realistic scenarios. In particular, in the context of the reason model:

- **Inconsistent case bases -** The concept of consistency assumes that the initial background case base is consistent, which is not a realistic assumption; Horty [22] outlined a broader interpretation of the reason model's constraint concept, extending it to also encompassing inconsistent case bases; recent investigations have been accordingly developed (such as [10,35]);

- **Incomplete knowledge** - The idea of complete knowledge in the context of legal CBR means that any case base is such that all situations have been decided in favor of the defendant or the plaintiff and, for example, that all features in the base have a direction (i.e., if they are pro or con factors, i.e., they support the plaintiff or the defendant). This assumption can also be unrealistic [13,33].

1.1 Our Contribution

Our framework work with incomplete and potentially inconsistent case bases leveraging:

- **Defeasible Logic (DL):** A logic that accommodates reasoning with incomplete and potentially conflicting information, which is common in legal contexts.
- **Argumentation Semantics:** This aspect focuses on the formal representation and analysis of arguments and counterarguments, providing a structured approach to legal reasoning.

By integrating these components, our framework aims to develop AI systems that are not only predictive but also transparent and normatively aligned with judicial standards. We somehow continue the research effort of [14], where we have proposed an inference mechanism with incomplete knowledge for the identification of factors, among the features that are present in a case base, and the determination of their direction [6], i.e., if they are in favor of the plaintiff or the defendant. Our approach was based on the logical framework described in [27,28] and adopted the view that a legal case-based reasoner is nothing but a binary classifier [13,29].

The limit of the above-mentioned lines of research is that it flattens the reasoning mechanism by simply connecting, as done in HYPO, features and outcomes: a case is a rule linking the facts of the case and its outcome, being it a decision in favor either of the plaintiff or of the defendant. Here, we enrich the view by using DL and by concatenating rules supporting the different judicial outcomes. This way, rules in argumentation capture the idea of *ratio decidendi*, which is a possibly complex set of legal binding rules grounded of the specific facts of the case and which justifies the judicial decision [9] and can be used to predict possible undecided cases.

To do so, *we devise two reasoning layers, one capturing the reasoning procedures internal to each judicial case, and a second layer on top of the first one, which is meant to reconstruct how different judicial precedents interact and can be used to settle an undecided case.*

The layout of article is as follows. Section 2 presents a suitable variant of Defeasible Logic (DL) and its corresponding argumentation semantics, as proposed in [15,39], which offers the tools for first layer to model the reasoning mechanism internal to judicial cases. Section 3 reconstructs the reason-based standard model of CBR developed by Horty. Section 4 proposes proof theory and argumentation for the second layer (i.e., argumentation frameworks for CBR) and for inferring judicial decisions for undecided cases; the proof theory relaxes consistency and completeness assumptions of case bases. Section 5 offers a basic definition of judicial explanation in that context. Some conclusion ends the paper.

2 Layer 1: Logic and Argumentation

2.1 Logic

Our framework is Defeasible Logic (DL) [3]. The basic language consists of a set Lit of literals. The *complementary* of a literal ϕ is denoted by $\sim\phi$: if ϕ is positive then $\sim\phi$ is $\neg\phi$, if ϕ is negative then $\sim\phi$ is ϕ. Let Lab be a set of labels to represent names of rules. A rule r has the form $r\colon A(r) \Rightarrow C(r)$, where: (i) $r \in$ Lab is the unique name of the rule, (ii) $A(r) \subseteq$ Lit is r's (set of) antecedents, (iii) $C(r) = \phi \in$ Lit is its conclusion. Unlike standard DL, *we only use defeasible rules*, in which, if the premises are the case, then typically the conclusion holds unless we have contrary evidence.

We also use a special type of logical theory in DL:

Definition 1 (Argumentation theory). *An* argumentation theory D *is a tuple* $(F, R, >)$ *where (a)* $F \subseteq$ Lit *is a finite and consistent set of facts (indisputable statements), (b)* R *is a finite rule set, and (c) a binary superiority relation over* R *(which is used to solve rule conflicts). We state that* $\forall \phi \in F$, $R[\phi] \cup R[\sim\phi] = \emptyset$.

As a convention, $R[\phi]$ denotes the set of all rules in R whose conclusion is ϕ.

A *conclusion* of D is a *tagged literal* with the following form: $+\partial\phi$ (resp. $-\partial\phi$) means that ϕ is *defeasibly proved* (resp. *defeasibly refuted*) in D, i.e., there is a defeasible proof for ϕ in D (resp. a proof does not exist). A proof P of length n in D is a finite sequence $P(1), P(2), \ldots, P(n)$ of tagged literals for which specific proof conditions are defined [3]. $P(1..n)$ denotes the first n steps of P.

$+\partial\phi$: If $P(n+1) = +\partial\phi$ then either
    (1) $\phi \in F$, or
    (2.1) $\exists r \in R[\phi]$ s.t. $\forall \psi \in A(r)$. $+\partial\psi \in P(1..n)$ and
    (2.2) $\forall s \in R[\sim\phi]$ either
        (2.2.1) $\exists \psi \in A(s)$. $-\partial\psi \in P(1..n)$, or
        (2.2.2) $\exists t \in R[\phi]$ s.t. $\forall \psi \in A(t)$. $+\partial\psi \in P(1..n)$ and $t > s$.

$-\partial\phi$: If $P(n+1) = -\partial\phi$ then
    (1) $\phi \notin F$, and
    (2.1) $\forall r \in R[\phi] : \exists \psi \in A(r)$. $-\partial\psi \in P(1..n)$ or
    (2.2) $\exists s \in R[\sim\phi]$ such that
        (2.2.1) $\forall \psi \in A(s)$. $+\partial\psi \in P(1..n)$, and
        (2.2.2) $\forall t \in R[\phi] : \exists \psi \in A(t)$. $-\partial\psi \in P(1..n)$ or $t \not> s$.

Definition 2 (Extension). *Given an argumentation theory D, we define the set of positive and negative conclusions of D as its extension:*

$$E(D) = (+\partial, -\partial),$$

where $\pm\partial = \{\phi \mid \phi \text{ appears in } D \text{ and } D \vdash \pm\partial l\}$.

2.2 Argumentation

Argumentation frameworks for DL have been studied in [17]. Here, we present a variant of it, which is based on the above fragment of DL [18,19].

Definition 3 (Argument). *Let $D = (F, R, >)$ be an argumentation theory. An argument A constructed from D has either the the form $\Rightarrow_F \phi$ (factual argument), where $\phi \in F$, or the form $A_1, \ldots, A_n \Rightarrow_r \phi$ (plain argument), where $1 \leq k \leq n$, and*

- A_k *is an argument constructed from D, and*
- $r : \mathsf{Conc}(A_1), \ldots, \mathsf{Conc}(A_n) \Rightarrow \phi$ *is a rule in R.*

For a given argument A, Conc returns its conclusion, Sub returns all its sub-arguments, and $\mathsf{TopRule}$ returns the last rule in the argument.

Any argument A is a tree whose root is labelled by $\mathsf{Conc}(A)$, and for every node x labelled by any ϕ, its children $x_1, \ldots, x_n$ are labelled by $\phi_1, \ldots, \phi_n$ (except its leaves, which can be also labelled by $\emptyset$) and the arcs are labeled by a rule $r : \phi_1, \ldots, \phi_n \Rightarrow \phi$. Arguments of height 1 are called *atomic arguments*; for any argument A, the set of its atomic sub-arguments is denoted by $\mathsf{ASub}(A)$.

The notions of *attack*, *support*, and *undercut* are the standard ones for DL: we refer the reader to [17] for the details. We can now define the argumentation framework.

Definition 4 (Argumentation Framework). *Let D be an argumentation theory. The argumentation framework $\mathsf{AF}(D)$ determined by D is $(\mathcal{A}, \gg)$ where $\mathcal{A}$ is the set of all arguments constructed from D, and $\gg$ is the attack relation.*

The core of argumentation semantics are the notions of *acceptable* and *rejected argument*. An argument is acceptable with respect to a set of arguments that undercut any attacks. Then, we can define recursively the *extension of an argumentation theory D and of the corresponding framework $\mathsf{AF}(D)$*, which is the set of *justified arguments* w.r.t. $\mathsf{AF}(D)$. The definitions of the set $JArgs^D$ of justified arguments and of the set $RArgs^D$ of rejected arguments are a fix-point construction. For the details, we refer again the reader to [17].

Theorem 1. *Let D be an argumentation theory and A be an argument in $\mathsf{AF}(D)$ such that $\mathsf{Conc}(A) = \phi$. Then, (a) $A \in JArgs^D$ iff $D \vdash +\partial\phi$; (b) $A \in RArgs^D$ iff $D \vdash -\partial\phi$.*

3 Judicial Cases: Background

One of the most influential frameworks of judicial reasoning is the case-based reasoning/precedential constraint proposed by John Horty [20–22,25]. Horty has reconstructed factor-based representations of CBR [4,38] and developed such factor-based models into a theory of precedential constraints, i.e., of how a new case must be decided, in order to preserve consistency in the case law.

Horty takes into account the fact that judges may provide explicit reasons for their choice of a certain outcome. This leads to the distinction between the result and the reason model of precedents. In the first model, the message conveyed by the case is only that all factors supporting the case-outcome (pro-factors) outweigh all factors against that outcome (con-factors). In the second, the message is that the factors for the case outcome indicated by the judge outweigh all factors against that outcome. We say *result model* for "the factor-based result model of precedential constraint" and *reason model* for "the factor-based reason model of precedential constraint".

In standard Horty's model the language is based on the set of factors $Atm_0 = Plt \cup Dfd$ where Plt and Dfd are disjoint sets of factors favoring the plaintiff and defendant respectively. In addition, let $Val = \{1, 0, ?\}$ where elements stand for *plaintiff wins*, *defendant wins* and *indeterminacy* respectively. Let $Dec = \{\mathsf{t}(x) : x \in Val\}$ and read $\mathsf{t}(x)$ as "the actual decision/outcome (of the judge/classifier) takes value x". An outcome $\mathsf{t}(1)$ or $\mathsf{t}(0)$ means that, the judge is predicted to decide for the plaintiff or for the defendant. The outcome $\mathsf{t}(?)$ means either outcome would be consistent: the judge may develop the law in one direction or the other. The set Atm denotes $Atm_0 \cup Dec$.

A set $s \subseteq Atm_0$ is called a *fact situation*. A set of atoms X is called a *reason* for an outcome (decision) x if it a set of factors all favoring the same outcome: $X \subseteq Plt$ is a reason for 1 and $X \subseteq Dfd$ is a reason for 0. We can think of reasons X favoring an outcome x as a rule $X \Rightarrow x$. For readability, we make a convention that, for $x \in \{0, 1\}$, let $\overline{x} = 1 - x$ and $\overline{\overline{x}} = x$. Moreover, let $Atm_0^x = Plt$ if $x = 1$, and $Atm_0^x = Dfd$ if $x = 0$.

In the reason model, a *precedent case* (precedent) is a triple $c = (s, X, x)$, where $s \subseteq Atm_0$, $X \subseteq s \subseteq Atm_0^x, x \in \{0, 1\}$. In plain words, $s \cap Atm_0^x$ contains all *pro-factors* in s for x, while $s \cap Atm_0^{\overline{x}}$ all *con-factors* in s for x. X is the *reason of the case*, namely a subset of the pro-factors which the judge considers sufficient to support that outcome, relative to all con-factors in the case.

A *case base* CB (for reason model) is a set of precedential cases. When the reason contains all pro-factors within the situation (i.e., when $c = (s, s \cap Atm_0^x, x)$) all such factors are considered equally decisive. If a case base only contains cases of this type, we obtain what Horty calls "the result model", and note such a case base CB^{res}. The class of all CBs and $CB^{res}s$ are noted **CB** and **CB**^{res} respectively.

A case base can be inconsistent when two precedents map the same fact situation to different outcomes. Another scenario is that a consistent case base becomes inconsistent after *update*, namely after expanding it with some new case. Hence maintaining consistency is the crucial concern of legal case-based reasoning. The following definitions are based on [22,36].

Definition 5 (Preference relation derived from a case). *Let $c = (s, X, x)$ be a case. Then the preference relation $\prec_c$ derived from c is s.t. for any two reasons Y, Y' favoring x and $\bar{x}$ respectively, $Y' \prec_c Y$ iff $Y' \subseteq s \cap Atm_0^{\bar{x}}$ and $X \subseteq Y$.*

Definition 6 (Preference relation derived from a case base). *Let CB be a case base. Then the preference relation $\prec_{CB}$ derived from CB is s.t. for any two reasons Y, Y' favoring x and $\bar{x}$ respectively, $Y' \prec_{CB} Y$ iff $\exists c \in CB$ s.t. $Y' \prec_c Y$.*

Definition 7 ((In)consistency). *A case base CB is inconsistent, if there are two reasons Y, Y' s.t. $Y' \prec_{CB} Y$ and $Y \prec_{CB} Y'$. CB is consistent if it is not inconsistent.*

Definition 8 (Precedential constraint). *Let CB be a consistent case base, X is a reason for x in CB and applicable in a new fact situation s', i.e. $X \subseteq s'$. Updating CB with the new case (s', X, x) meets the precedential constraint, iff $CB \cup \{(s', X, x)\}$ is still consistent.*

There is more than one way to satisfy the precedential constraint, depending on how the precedents in CB interacts with the new case. The requirement of consistency dictates the outcome when the "a fortiori" constraint applies: if reason X for x outweighs (i.e., is stronger than) reason $s \cap Atm_0^{\bar{x}}$, a fortiori any superset of X outweighs any subset of $s \cap Atm_0^{\bar{x}}$, so that only by deciding for x rather than for $\bar{x}$ consistency is maintained.

Reconstructing Horty's intuition in DL requires some changes. A major difference with respect to that reason-based standard model is that it is not meaningful in DL to a priori differentiate factors which favor the plaintiff and factors which favor the defendant, so we simply state: DL is precisely meant to establish the direction of factors, so $Atm_0 \subseteq Lit$ is the set of *factors* of the case language and $Dec \subset Lit$.

Since DL is the logical engine for case-based reasoning, the reason model based on DL defines precedents as follows:

Definition 9 (Case, standard model). *A case is a triple $c = (D, X, x)$ where*

1. *D is an argumentation theory $(F, R, >)$ where $F \subseteq Atm_0$ is the fact situation of c;*
2. *$X \subseteq F$ and $x \in \{0, 1\}$ such that*
   (a) *$D \vdash +\partial x$;*
   (b) *for any $X' \subset X$, $D' \vdash -\partial x$ where $D' = (S', R, >)$.*

Notice that condition 2b states that the set X of reasons must be minimal [15].

This leads to reconstruct some well-known notions from Horty reason-based model. Since we use DL as an inferential engine, we do not a priori partition factors into those which favor the plaintiff and those which favor the defendant.

Definition 10 (Reason). *Let $F \subseteq Atm_0$ be a fact situation of the case $c = (D = (F, R, >), X, x)$. We say that that the set X is a reason for the outcome x.*

Definitions 5–8 can be simply adjusted on the basis of Definitions 9–10.

4 Layer 2: Judicial Cases, Beyond the Standard Model

In Sect. 3 we have recalled the basic intuitions of Horty's standard model and presented how to reconstruct at least some of them in DL.

In this section we take stock of the above analysis but we go beyond that model. Following [10, 13, 40], we argued in [14] that some of the usual assumptions in legal CBR can be relaxed in order to deal with more realistic scenarios. In particular, in the context of the reason model we can abandon the requirements that case bases be consistent and complete.

4.1 Logic

A first immediate consequence in our framework of the choice of abandoning consistency and completeness is a revision of Definition 9, thus admitting that, in any case $c = (D, X, x)$, $x \in \{0, 1, ?\}$ (in other words, we may explicitly consider undecided cases in CB). Another consequence is that we need to prioritize cases when we have to deal with inconsistencies in the case base: conceptually, the order can be built using, e.g., the ranking of courts involved in the previous cases (e.g., supreme courts prevail over courts of appeal, which prevail over courts of first instance) or the importance of values promoted [7].

Since we have to extend the machinery of DL and embed CBR in it, we adjust out notation by stating that, for $x \in \{0, 1, ?\}$, let $\overline{x} = y$ such that $y \in \{0, 1, ?\} - \{x\}$. In other words, $\forall y \in \{0, 1, ?\}$ we have that $\sim y = \{0, 1, ?\} - \{y\}$. We also state that $\sim(s, x) = (s, \overline{x})$.

Definition 11 (Case, general model). *A case is a triple $c = (D, X, x)$ where*

1. *D is an argumentation theory $(F, R, >)$ where $F \subseteq Atm_0$ is the fact situation of c;*
2. *$X \subseteq F$ and $x \in \{0, 1, ?\}$ such that*
   (a) if $x \in \{0, 1\}$, $D \vdash +\partial x$;
   (b) if $x =?$, $D \vdash +\partial ?$, or $D \vdash -\partial 1$ and $D \vdash -\partial 0$;
   (c) if $x \in \{0, 1\}$, for any $X' \subset X$, $D' \vdash -\partial x$ where $D' = (S', R, >)$;
   (d) if $x =?$, for any $X' \subset X$, $D' \vdash +\partial y$ where $D' = (S', R, >)$ and $y \in \{0, 1\}$.

Notice that conditions 2c–2d ensure minimality of reasons, i.e., that the set X must be minimal [15].

Definition 12 (Priority among cases). *Let CB the case base. For any two cases $c, c' \in CB$ we write $c \ll c'$ to denote that c prevails over c'. The relation $\ll$ is the priority relation for CB.*

As we have just said, the priority may depend on the ranking of courts involved in the previous cases or on the importance of values promoted. Here, for the sake of simplicity we assume that the priority is given, but nothing prevents to adopt Horty's approach and reframe in DL his procedure for defining a preference order.

As usual in legal CBR, analogical reasoning means that precedents can be cited to support the decision of new cases on the basis of the similarity between fact situations. We thus need first of all to establish the similarity between sets of factors[1].

Definition 13 (Similarity between sets of factors). *Let $D = (\emptyset, R, >)$ be an argumentation theory and $s, s' \subset Atm_0$. The degree of similarity between s and s' relative to D, noted $sim_D(s,s')$, is defined as follows:*

$$sim_D(s,s') = |\{\phi \in Atm_0 : (s, R, >) \vdash +\partial\phi \text{ iff } (s', R, >) \vdash +\partial\phi\}|.$$

We state that $sim_D(s,s') > 0$, otherwise $\neg sim_D(s,s')$.

The key notion of our model is the one of *decidable fact situation for an outcome x*, which consists in developing a defeasible reasoning mechanism working on many cases and exploiting the inferential power of DL to predict the decision of an undecided fact situation.

Definition 14 (Undecided Fact Situations). *Let s be a fact situation. We say that s is undecided in CB iff $\forall c = ((s, R, >), X, x) \in CB$ it is the case that $x \notin \{0, 1\}$.*

Definition 15 (Decidable Fact Situations). *We define that a fact situation s is decidable in CB in favor of x, i.e., $+\Delta_{CB}(s, x)$, as follows:*

$+\Delta_{CB}(s,x)$: If $+\Delta_{CB}(s,x)$ then either
    (1) $\exists c = ((s, R, >), X, x) \in CB$, or
    (2.1) $\exists c' = ((s', R', >'), X', x) \in CB$ s.t.
        $sim_{(\emptyset, R', >')}(s,s')$ is maximal and
    (2.2) $\forall c'' = ((s'', R'', >''), X'', \overline{x})$ either
        (2.2.1) $sim_{(\emptyset, R'', >'')}(s,s'')$ is not maximal, or
        (2.2.2) $\exists c''' = ((s''', R''', >'''), X''', x) \in CB$ s.t.
            $sim_{(\emptyset, R''', >''')}(s,s''')$ is maximal and $c''' \ll c''$.

$-\Delta_{CB}(s,x)$: If $-\Delta_{CB}(s,x)$ then
    (1) $\not\exists c = ((s, R, >), X, x) \in CB$, and

---

[1] The dual notion of distance can be defined. In accordance with [12], it is nothing but the Hamming distance, which counts the cardinality difference of features' values. [13] has shown that, in this context, building similarity between cases via Hamming distance coincides with building it via subset inclusion relation (i.e., via shared properties as done in HYPO). Of course, more refined notions of similarity can be developed, which e.g. contextualize this measure of similarity with respect to specific logical conclusions.

(2.1) $\not\exists c' = ((s', R', >'), X', x) \in CB$ s.t.
$sim_{(\emptyset, R', >')}(s,s')$ is maximal or
(2.2) $\exists c'' = ((s'', R'', >''), X'', \overline{x})$ s.t.
(2.2.1) $sim_{(\emptyset, R'', >'')}(s,s'')$ is maximal, and
(2.2.2) $\forall c''' = ((s''', R''', >'''), X''', x) \in CB$
either $sim_{(\emptyset, R''', >''')}(s,s''')$ is not maximal or
$c''' \not\ll c''$.

As a notational convention, we write $CB \vdash +\Delta(s,x)$ and $CB \vdash -\Delta(s,x)$ to denote, respectively, $+\Delta_{CB}(s,x)$ and $-\Delta_{CB}(s,x)$.

One may think of the inference of a decidable factual situation $+\Delta_{CB}(s,x)$ as a way to show that there is a set of argumentation theories, including $(s, R, >)$, supporting the conclusion of x.

The following is a trivial result.

Proposition 1 (Proving Undecidable Fact Situations). *Let CB be a case base.*

$+\Delta_{CB}(s,?)$: *If $+\Delta_{CB}(s,?)$ then $-\Delta_{CB}(s,1)$ and $-\Delta_{CB}(s,0)$.*

$-\Delta_{CB}(s,?)$: *If $-\Delta_{CB}(s,?)$ then either $+\Delta_{CB}(s,1)$ or $+\Delta_{CB}(s,0)$.*

The following result can also be easily proved.

Proposition 2. *Let CB be a case base. If $+\Delta_{CB}(s,x)$ and $+\Delta_{CB}(s,\overline{x})$, then $\exists c = ((s, R, >), X, x)$ and $\exists c' = ((s, R', >'), X', \overline{x}) \in CB$. Otherwise, the fact situation s is undecided in CB and, if $+\Delta_{CB}(s,x)$, then $-\Delta_{CB}(s,\overline{x})$.*

Definition 16 (Case Base Extension). *Given a case base CB, we define the set of positive and negative conclusions of CB as its case base extension:*

$$E(CB) = (+\Delta, -\Delta),$$

where $\pm\Delta = \{(s,x)|\ CB \vdash \pm\Delta_{CB}(s,x)\}$.

4.2 Argumentation

Given the inference rules of Definition 15, we can introduce a new layer of argumentation.

Definition 17 (Case Argument). *Let CB be a case base. A case argument for fact situation s being decidable in CB in favor of x, i.e., for (s,x), has either the form*

- $\Rightarrow_{CB} ((s, R, >), X, x)$ *(factual case argument), where $((s, R, >), X, x) \in CB$,*
  or
- $A_1, \ldots, A_n \Rightarrow_r (s', x)$ *(plain case argument), where $1 \leq k \leq n$, and $A_k \in JArgs^{D_k}$ for some case $c = (D_k = (s, R, >), X, x) \in CB$ such that $sim_{D_k}(s,s') > 0$, $r \in R$, and $D_k \vdash +\partial\mathsf{Conc}(A_k)$.*

Remark 1. The notions of *attack*, *support*, and *undercut* are structurally the standard ones for DL. For example, we must simply note that the proof theory of Definition 15 is based on the intuition that, when $+\Delta_{CB}(s,x)$, it means that there exists a suitable theory $(s', R', >')$ supporting the conclusion x, i.e., there is a defeasible rule $r : (s', R', >'), X' \Rightarrow x$. Under this view, it is easy to check the proof theory mimics the standard one of DL with rules having the form of r.

We can now define the notion of case-based argumentation framework.

Definition 18 (Case-based Argumentation Framework). *Let CB be a case base. The case-based argumentation framework $\mathsf{AF}(CB)$ determined by CB is $(\mathcal{A}_{CB}, \gg_{CB})$ where $\mathcal{A}_{CB}$ is the set of all case arguments constructed from CB, and $\gg_{CB}$ is the attack relation.*

As for DL, the core of case-based argumentation semantics are the notions of *acceptable* and *rejected case argument*. Since Definition 15 precisely mimics the standard proof conditions of DL, the argumentation machinery of this layer is the same. Then, we can define recursively the *extension of a case-based argumentation framework* $\mathsf{AF}(CB)$, which is the set of *justified case arguments* w.r.t. $\mathsf{AF}(CB)$. The definitions of the set $JArgs^{CB}$ of *justified case arguments* and of the set $RArgs^{CB}$ of *rejected case arguments* are a standard fix-point construction.

Theorem 2. *Let CB be a case base and A be an argument in $\mathsf{AF}(CB)$ such that $\mathsf{Conc}(A) = (s, x)$. Then*

1. *$A \in JArgs^{CB}$ iff $CB \vdash +\Delta(s, x)$;*
2. *$A \in RArgs^{CB}$ iff $CB \vdash -\Delta(s, x)$.*

The relation between the standard DL layer and the case layer is captured as follows:

Corollary 1. *Let CB be a case base and A be an argument in $\mathsf{AF}(CB)$ such that $\mathsf{Conc}(A) = (s, x)$. Then,*

1. *if $A \in JArgs^{CB}$ then there exists a case $c = ((s, R, >), X, x) \in CB$ such that $D \vdash +\partial x$;*
2. *if $A \in RArgs^D$ then either there exists no case $c = ((s, R, >), X, x) \in CB$ such that $D \vdash +\partial x$ or there exists a case $c = ((s, R, >), X, x) \in CB$ such that $D \vdash -\partial x$.*

5 Judicial Explanations

Definitions 9 and 11 identify the reasons for judicial outcomes as the *minimal set of factors* (i.e., facts in DL original terminology) needed for supporting the inference of x. This idea is imported also in Definition 15, which simply uses different argumentation theories as rules with respect to those that are usually employed in the standard proof theory of DL. This idea corresponds to a basic idea of *normative explanation* of a decision [18,19,29,39].

As recalled in [39], a normative explanation is an explanation where norms are crucial: in legal decision-making, this means to explain why a legal conclusion ought to be the case on the basis of certain norms and facts [1,19,26,29,34,37]. In this context, we have two ways for approaching this idea: by focusing on the facts that are used to draw certain normative conclusions, and by considering the arguments used for conclusions, which also use legal rules constituting the ratio decidendi. We adopt the second route and extend [39]'s definition to cover the analysis of Sect. 4. The idea of judicial explanation can be defined accordingly.

Definition 19 (Judicial explanation). *Let CB a case base and $\mathsf{AF}(CB) = (\mathcal{A}, \gg)$ be the case-based argumentation framework determined by CB. The set $\mathrm{arg} \subseteq \mathcal{A}$ is a judicial explanation $\mathsf{Expl}((s,x), \mathsf{AF}(CB))$ in $\mathsf{AF}(CB)$ for (s,x) iff*

- *$A \in \mathrm{arg}$ is case argument for (s,x) and A is justified w.r.t. $\mathsf{AF}(CB)$;*
- *arg is a minimal set in $\mathsf{AF}(CB)$ such that A is acceptable w.r.t to arg.*

Example 1. Consider the following very simple case base CB:

$$c_1 = (D_1 = (s_1, R_1, >_1), X_1, 0)$$
$$c_2 = (D_2 = (s_2, R_2, >_2), X_2, 1)$$
$$c_3 = (D_3 = (s_3, R_3, >_3), X_3, 0)$$

Assume D_1 is as follows:

$$F = \{\iota, \lambda\},$$
$$R = \{s_1 \colon \Rightarrow 0,\ s_2 \colon \lambda \Rightarrow 1,\ s_3 \colon \beta, \pi \Rightarrow 1,\ s_4 \colon \delta \Rightarrow 0,\ s_5 \colon \iota \Rightarrow \delta\}$$
$$>= \{\langle s_2, > s_1\rangle, \langle s_3 > s_1\rangle, \langle s_4 > s_3\rangle, \langle s_4 > s_2\rangle\}.$$

Then, $\mathsf{AF}(D_1) = (\mathcal{A}_1, \gg_1)$ is as follows:

$$\mathcal{A}_1 = \{A_1 \colon \Rightarrow_F \iota,\ A_2 \colon \Rightarrow_F \lambda,\ A_3 \colon A_1 \Rightarrow_{s_5} \delta,\ A_4 \colon A_3 \Rightarrow_{s_4} 0,\ A_5 \colon A_2 \Rightarrow_{s_2} 1\}$$
$$\gg = \{\langle A_4, A_5\rangle\}.$$

Assume D_2 is as follows:

$$F = \{\iota\},$$
$$R = \{s_1 \colon \Rightarrow 0,\ r_2 \colon \iota \Rightarrow 1\}$$
$$>= \{\langle s_2, > s_1\rangle\}.$$

Then, $\mathsf{AF}(D_2) = (\mathcal{A}_2, \gg_2)$ is as follows:

$$\mathcal{A} = \{A_1 \colon \Rightarrow_F \iota,\ A_6 \colon \Rightarrow_{r_1} 0,\ A_7 \colon A_1 \Rightarrow_{r_2} 1\}$$
$$\gg = \{\langle A_7, A_6\rangle\}.$$

Assume D_3 is as follows:

$$F = \{\lambda\},$$
$$R = \{r_3 \colon \lambda \Rightarrow 0\}$$
$$\gg = \emptyset.$$

Then, $\mathsf{AF}(D_3) = (\mathcal{A}_3, \gg_3)$ is as follows:

$$\mathcal{A} = \{A_2 \colon \Rightarrow_F \lambda,\ A_{11} \colon A_2 \Rightarrow_{r_3} 0\},$$
$$\gg = \emptyset.$$

Let us consider the undecided factual situation $s_3 = \{\iota, \lambda, \omega\}$ and assume $c_1 \ll c_2$ and $c_2 \ll c_3$.

The resulting cased-based argumentation framework $\mathsf{AF}(CB)$ is as follows:

$$\mathcal{A} = \{A_7 \colon \Rightarrow_{CB} (s_1, 0),\ A_8 \colon \Rightarrow_{CB} (s_2, 1),\ A_9 \colon A_4 \Rightarrow_{s_4} (s_3, 0),$$
$$A_{10} \colon A_1 \Rightarrow_{r_1} (s_3, 1),\ A_{11} \colon A_2 \Rightarrow_{r_3} (s_3, 0),\ A_{12} \colon \Rightarrow_{CB} (s_3, 0)\}$$
$$\gg = \{\langle A_9, A_{10}\rangle, \langle A_{10}, A_{11}\rangle\}.$$

It is easy to see that $\{A_1, A_4\} \in JArgs^{D_1}$, $\{A_1, A_7\} \in JArgs^{D_2}$, and $\{A_2, A_{11}\} \in JArgs^{D_3}$. Accordingly, it is also easy to check that

$$CB \vdash +\Delta(s_3, 0)$$

and that $\mathsf{Expl}((s_3, 0), \mathsf{AF}(CB)) = \{A_9\}$.

6 Conclusion

Following the extensive AI & Law literature springing from the study of HYPO and CATO, in the last decade a significant effort has been put in investigating axioms as well as formal properties of factor-based case-based reasoning, and in providing the logical foundations for such a type of reasoning (see, among others, [2,6,10,11,22–24,29,36,37]). Also due to development of explainable AI [5,32], the quest for logical foundations of factor-based CBR has been recently focused, e.g., on formal models of argumentative explanation [37] or on logics for classifier systems [13,14,29].

In [13,14] we proposed a novel approach to address this issue, starting from the intuition, introduced in [29], that a case base can be represented through a binary classifier. One limit of that approach was to flatten knowledge bases by simply connecting fact situations and judicial outcomes.

In this paper, we solved the problem and developed a novel framework for judicial case-based reasoning grounded in Defeasible Logic and Argumentation Semantics. The motivation behind this research stems from the increasing interest and debate around the use of AI techniques, such as machine learning and deep learning, in predicting judicial outcomes. Despite the potential benefits of these technologies in supporting judicial decision-making, assisting litigants, and analyzing biases within the legal process, there remain considerable challenges. These challenges include concerns over judicial independence, the normative correctness of algorithmic decisions, transparency, and robustness.

Our framework addresses these challenges by formalizing judicial CBR to handle inconsistencies and incomplete knowledge within case bases using Defeasible Logic and Argumentation Semantics. The framework enriches the traditional view by incorporating a method to generate and validate explanations of judicial decisions through logical and argumentation-based structures. This approach provides a structured way to ensure that AI-based judicial predictions are not only accurate but also transparent and aligned with normative standards.

Key contributions include:

- A general model for judicial case-based reasoning that can deal with inconsistent and incomplete case bases, extending traditional models to more realistic judicial scenarios.
- The formal definition and construction of argumentation frameworks derived from case bases, integrating the logical strength of Defeasible Logic with the argumentative structure essential for legal reasoning.
- A mechanism for determining decidable fact situations in new cases, enhancing the ability of the system to predict outcomes by leveraging established precedents.
- The introduction of normative explanations within this framework, providing a clear, structured way to validate and understand AI-based predictions in judicial contexts.

By reconstructing judicial reasoning within this logical and argumentative framework, we have taken a step towards building more reliable, ethical, and explainable AI systems for judicial decision-making. Future work will focus on empirical validation of the framework using real-world legal datasets and exploring how different prioritization strategies among cases affect the robustness of judicial explanations.

References

1. Alexy, R.: A Theory of Legal Argumentation: The Theory of Rational Discourse as Theory of Legal Justification. Clarendon (1989)
2. Amgoud, L., Beuselinck, V.: Towards a principle-based approach for case-based reasoning. In: Dupin de Saint-Cyr, F., Öztürk-Escoffier, M., Potyka, N. (eds.) Scalable Uncertainty Management, SUM 2022. Lecture Notes in Computer Science, vol. 13562, pp. 37–46. Springer, Cham (2022). https://doi.org/10.1007/978-3-031-18843-5_3
3. Antoniou, G., Billington, D., Governatori, G., Maher, M.: Representation results for defeasible logic. ACM Trans. Comput. Log. **2**(2), 255–287 (2001). https://doi.org/10.1145/371316.371517
4. Ashley, K.D.: Modeling Legal Argument: Reasoning with Cases and Hypotheticals. MIT, Cambridge (1990)

5. Atkinson, K., Bench-Capon, T., Bollegala, D.: Explanation in AI and law: past, present and future. Artif. Intell. **289**, 103387 (2020). https://doi.org/10.1016/j.artint.2020.103387, https://www.sciencedirect.com/science/article/pii/S0004370220301375
6. Bench-Capon, T.J.M., Atkinson, K.: Precedential constraint: the role of issues. In: ICAIL 2021. ACM (2021)
7. Bench-Capon, T.J.M., Sartor, G.: A model of legal reasoning with cases incorporating theories and values. Artif. Intell. **150**(1-2), 97–143 (2003). https://doi.org/10.1016/S0004-3702(03)00108-5
8. Bex, F., Prakken, H.: On the relevance of algorithmic decision predictors for judicial decision making. In: Maranhão, J., Wyner, A.Z. (eds.) ICAIL '21: Eighteenth International Conference for Artificial Intelligence and Law, São Paulo Brazil, 21–25 June 2021, pp. 175–179. ACM (2021). https://doi.org/10.1145/3462757.3466069
9. Branting, L.K.: A computational model of ratio decidendi. Artif. Intell. Law **2**, 1–31 (1993). https://doi.org/10.1007/BF00871744
10. Canavotto, I.: Precedential constraint derived from inconsistent case bases. In: JURIX 2022. IOS Press (2022)
11. Canavotto, I., Horty, J.: Piecemeal knowledge acquisition for computational normative reasoning. In: AIES 2022. ACM (2022)
12. Dalal, M.: Investigations into a theory of knowledge base revision: preliminary report. In: Proceedings of the Seventh National Conference on Artificial Intelligence, pp. 475—479 (1988)
13. Di Florio, C., Liu, X., Lorini, E., Rotolo, A., Sartor, G.: Finding factors in legal case-based reasoning. In: Logics for AI and Law (LAIL-23). College Publications (2023)
14. Di Florio, C., Liu, X., Lorini, E., Rotolo, A., Sartor, G.: Inferring new classifications in legal case-based reasoning. In: Proceedings of JURIX 2023, IOS Press (2023)
15. Di Florio, C., Rotolo, A., Governatori, G., Sartor, G.: Stable normative explanations: From argumentation to deontic logic. In: Gaggl, S.A., Martinez, M.V., Ortiz, M. (eds.) Logics in Artificial Intelligence - 18th European Conference, JELIA 2023, Dresden, Germany, 20–22 September 2023, Proceedings. Lecture Notes in Computer Science, vol. 14281, pp. 123–131. Springer, Cham (2023). https://doi.org/10.1007/978-3-031-43619-2_9
16. Gan, L., Kuang, K., Yang, Y., Wu, F.: Judgment prediction via injecting legal knowledge into neural networks. Proc. AAAI Conf. Artif. Intell. **35**(14), 12866–12874 (2021). https://doi.org/10.1609/aaai.v35i14.17522, https://ojs.aaai.org/index.php/AAAI/article/view/17522
17. Governatori, G., Maher, M.J., Antoniou, G., Billington, D.: Argumentation semantics for defeasible logic. J. Log. Comput. **14**(5), 675–702 (2004)
18. Governatori, G., Olivieri, F., Rotolo, A., Cristani, M.: Inference to the stable explanations. In: Gottlob, G., Inclezan, D., Maratea, M. (eds.) Logic Programming and Nonmonotonic Reasoning, LPNMR 2022, LNCS, vol. 13416, pp. 245–258. Springer, Cham (2022). https://doi.org/10.1007/978-3-031-15707-3_19
19. Governatori, G., Olivieri, F., Rotolo, A., Cristani, M.: Stable normative explanations. In: Francesconi, E., Borges, G., Sorge, C. (eds.) Legal Knowledge and Information Systems - JURIX 2022: The Thirty-fifth Annual Conference, Saarbrücken, Germany, 14-16 December 2022. Frontiers in Artificial Intelligence and Applications, vol. 362, pp. 43–52. IOS Press (2022). https://doi.org/10.3233/FAIA220447
20. Horty, J.: Reasoning with dimensions and magnitudes. In: International Conference on Artificial Intelligence and Law, ICAIL2017, ACM (2017)

21. Horty, J.F.: The result model of precedent. Leg. Theory **10**, 19–31 (2004)
22. Horty, J.F.: Rules and reasons in the theory of precedent. Leg. Theory **17**, 1–33 (2011)
23. Horty, J.F.: Reasoning with dimensions and magnitudes. Artif. Intell. Law **27**(3), 309–345 (2019). https://doi.org/10.1007/s10506-019-09245-0
24. Horty, J.F.: Modifying the reason model. Artif. Intell. Law **29**(2), 271–285 (2021). https://doi.org/10.1007/s10506-020-09275-z
25. Horty, J.F., Bench-Capon, T.J.M.: A factor-based definition of precedential constraint. Artif. Intell. Law **20**, 181–214 (2012)
26. Liao, B., van der Torre, L.: Explanation semantics for abstract argumentation. In: Prakken, H., Bistarelli, S., Santini, F., Taticchi, C. (eds.) Computational Models of Argument - Proceedings of COMMA 2020, Perugia, Italy, 4–11 September 2020. Frontiers in Artificial Intelligence and Applications, vol. 326, pp. 271–282. IOS Press (2020).https://doi.org/10.3233/FAIA200511
27. Liu, X., Lorini, E.: A logic for binary classifiers and their explanation. In: Baroni, P., Benzmüller, C., Wáng, Y.N. (eds.) CLAR 2021. LNCS (LNAI), vol. 13040, pp. 302–321. Springer, Cham (2021). https://doi.org/10.1007/978-3-030-89391-0_17
28. Liu, X., Lorini, E.: A unified logical framework for explanations in classifier systems. J. Log. Comput. **33**(2), 485–515 (2023)
29. Liu, X., Lorini, E., Rotolo, A., Sartor, G.: Modelling and explaining legal case-based reasoners through classifiers. In: Francesconi, E., Borges, G., Sorge, C. (eds.) Legal Knowledge and Information Systems - JURIX 2022: The Thirty-fifth Annual Conference, Saarbrücken, Germany, 14-16 December 2022. Frontiers in Artificial Intelligence and Applications, vol. 362, pp. 83–92. IOS Press (2022). https://doi.org/10.3233/FAIA220451
30. Medvedeva, M., Vols, M., Wieling, M.: Using machine learning to predict decisions of the European court of human rights. Artif. Intell. Law **28**(2), 237–266 (2020). https://doi.org/10.1007/s10506-019-09255-y
31. Jacob de Menezes-Neto, E., Clementino, M.B.M.: Using deep learning to predict outcomes of legal appeals better than human experts: a study with data from brazilian federal courts. PLOS ONE **17**(7), 1–20 (2022). https://doi.org/10.1371/journal.pone.0272287
32. Miller, T., Hoffman, R., Amir, O., Holzinger, A. (eds.): Artificial Intelligence journal: Special issue on explainable artificial intelligence (XAI) (2022)
33. Odekerken, D., Bex, F., Prakken, H.: Justification, stability and relevance for case-based reasoning with incomplete focus cases. In: Proceedings of ICAIL 2023, pp. 177–186. ACM (2023)
34. Peczenik, A.: On Law and Reason. Kluwer, Dordrecht (1989)
35. Peters, J.G.T., Bex, F.J., Prakken, H.: Model- and data-agnostic justifications with a fortiori case-based argumentation. In: Proceedings of ICAIL 2023, pp. 207–216. ACM (2023)
36. Prakken, H.: A formal analysis of some factor- and precedent-based accounts of precedential constraint. Artif. Intell. Law **29**(4), 559–585 (2021). https://doi.org/10.1007/s10506-021-09284-6
37. Prakken, H., Ratsma, R.: A top-level model of case-based argumentation for explanation: Formalisation and experiments. Argument Comput. **13**(2), 159–194 (2022). https://doi.org/10.3233/AAC-210009
38. Rissland, E.L., Ashley, K.D.: A case-based system for trade secrets law. In: Proceedings of the First International Conference on Artificial Intelligence and Law (ICAIL), pp. 60–66. ACM (1987)

39. Rotolo, A., Sartor, G.: Argumentation and explanation in the law. Frontiers Artif. Intell. **6** (2023). https://doi.org/10.3389/FRAI.2023.1130559
40. van Woerkom, W.K., Grossi, D., Prakken, H., Verheij, B.: Hierarchical precedential constraint. In: ICAIL 2023, ACM (2023)

OntoRaster: Extending VKGs with Raster Data

Arka Ghosh[1(✉)], Albulen Pano[2], Guohui Xiao[3], and Diego Calvanese[1,2]

[1] Department of Computing Science, Umeå Universitet, Umeå, Sweden
{arka.ghosh,diego.calvanese}@umu.se
[2] Faculty of Engineering, Free University of Bozen-Bolzano, Bolzano, Italy
{albulen.pano,diego.calvanese}@unibz.it
[3] Department of Information Science and Media Studies, University of Bergen, Bergen, Norway
guohui.xiao@uib.no

Abstract. The Virtual Knowledge Graph (VKG) paradigm facilitates access to large heterogeneous data sources by leveraging an OWL 2 QL ontology representing the domain knowledge and a set of declarative R2RML mapping assertions. We are interested in heterogeneous data sources consisting of relational data together with spatial geometrical data (a.k.a. *vector data*) and large multidimensional *raster data*. The latter forms of data pose a significant challenge for traditional DBMSs to manage effectively and are instead efficiently processed by tailored array database management systems (*ArrayDBMS*s). To query such data within the VKG paradigm, we propose a novel framework, called ONTORASTER, that allows for integrated query processing of relational, raster, and vector data, by keeping each type of data in the system tailored for their efficient processing, while minimising costly data-transfer operations. In OntoRaster, we devised custom raster functions extending SPARQL to query raster data efficiently and developed mechanisms for delegating their computation to the ArrayDBMS. We have implemented the whole framework as an extension of the state-of-the-art VKG system *Ontop* and have demonstrated its effectiveness and efficiency through a curated case study.

Keywords: Virtual Knowledge Graphs · Spatial-Temporal Reasoning · Raster Data · Vector Data · Multidimensional Arrays · Query Answering

1 Introduction

Scientific and business applications produce data in different representations at a massive scale, leading to bottlenecks in data management and processing and giving rise to the notorious issue of data heterogeneity [27,28]. Resolution of data heterogeneity allows for multiple databases (DBs) to be integrated and their contents to be uniformly queried. In our study, we are considering two different types of data: traditional relational data and large-scale raster data represented as multidimensional arrays [19,25]. We are particularly interested in spatial data in the Geographic Information System (GIS) field, which are classified into two types: vector data and raster data. *Vector data* are a special kind of relational data that represent geometries (e.g., points, lines, and polygons) of real-world discrete features such as static locations (points), road networks (lines), and country boundaries (polygons), with additional attributes. Geospatial *raster data* are a notable example of generic raster data, which have become a prime source of modern-day big data, e.g., due to advancements in air-borne and space-borne remote sensing [23]. Geospatial raster data are characterised by differences in spatial, temporal, and spectral resolutions, varying conditions in observations (e.g., different atmospheric conditions), and diverse spatial data structures [18]. Tailored array DB systems (Array DBMSs) are used to store and manage multidimensional arrays due to their outstanding scalability, adaptability, and in-place data processing capacity [6,29]. In our work, we decided to exploit the capabilities of *rasdaman*[1] (for "raster data manager") [3,4], a domain-agnostic Array DBMS that supports a variety of array operations, such as aggregation, filtering, scaling, and extraction of sub-spaces.

The support for raster data has also been attempted in classical relational DB management systems (RDBMSs) using spatial extensions. To do so, large raster data must undergo a conversion (e.g., using *raster2pgsql*[2] for PostgreSQL extended with PostGIS) from their native format of multidimensional arrays to a suitable relational form (e.g., *postgis raster*) that can be queried using SQL. This conversion leads in general to a massive increment in the data volume, which might be difficult to manage in a relational table. Therefore, we take an alternative approach that does not rely on the RDBMS's internal materialisation of raster data.

To address data heterogeneity resulting from the combination of the different forms of data, we rely on the paradigm of *Virtual Knowledge Graphs* (VKGs) also known as *Ontology-Based Data Access* (OBDA) [22,33]. In VKGs, domain knowledge is conceptually represented as an *ontology*, typically expressed in the lightweight ontology language OWL 2 QL [21], while actual data are maintained in a relational *data source*, but are *not* materialised at the conceptual level (which justifies the term "virtual"). To establish the relationship between the ontology and the data at the source, VKGs rely on a declarative specification, provided in terms of a set of *mapping assertions*.

In the traditional VKG setting, date sources are restricted to RDBMSs, but such systems are inefficient at querying raster data in their native multidimensional array format [7,20], and at combining them with relational data, including vector data. Various recent proposals aim at addressing these challenges, as also discussed in [15]. Notably, a semantic data cube system, named *Plato* [9,10], has been proposed within the EU H2020 project DeepCube[3]. The system relies on a geospatial extension of the VKG system ONTOP [8] and uses PostgreSQL Foreign Data Wrappers. It has been deployed in a case study on fire risk-management [11]. Similarly, another study [16] proposed an architecture to query raster data stored in an RDBMS using the VKG paradigm and extending the GeoSPARQL ontology[4] with a semantic representation model for raster data cubes. Our work differs from these works as we rely on rasdaman's array management abilities to query multidimensional raster data without any conversion.

In this paper, we present our ongoing work on the ONTORASTER framework, which allows for integrated querying of both relational data and raster data by extending the

---

[1] http://www.rasdaman.org/.
[2] https://postgis.net/docs/using_raster_dataman.html#RT_Loading_Rasters.
[3] https://deepcube-h2020.eu/.
[4] https://www.ogc.org/standard/geosparql/.

VKG paradigm to handle also array-based sources. In ONTORASTER, we still use a relational DBMS, namely PostgreSQL, as the main data source to which the VKG system connects, and we provide within this DBMS novel functionalities for virtual access to an Array DBMS, namely rasdaman. Specifically, we have extended the SPARQL query language with special raster functions (e.g., to compute multi-dimensional aggregations), and we have devised a set of stored procedures for PostgreSQL that translate such raster functions into array operations supported by rasdaman. These are executed directly on the Array DBMS, hence avoiding costly transfers and transformations into relational data of large arrays (unless such arrays need to be returned as an answer to a query, in which case the data transfer is unavoidable).

2 Preliminaries

In the standard VKG paradigm [22,33], existing heterogeneous data sources (e.g., relational) are accessed via a domain ontology that is linked to the source through semantic mappings, and exposes the underlying data as a (virtual) knowledge graph represented in RDF [26]. Formally, a *VKG specification* $\mathcal{P} = (\mathcal{O}, \mathcal{M}, \mathcal{S})$ consists of *(i)* an *ontology* $\mathcal{O}$ that represents intensional knowledge about the domain of interest and is expressed as a TBox in the lightweight ontology language OWL 2 QL [21], *(ii)* a relational *data source schema* $\mathcal{S}$, and *(iii)* a declarative mapping $\mathcal{M}$ that associates to each element (i.e., class or property) in $\mathcal{O}$ a (SQL) query over $\mathcal{S}$, specifying how to (virtually) populate that element through the data retrieved from the source.

In traditional VKGs, the mapping $\mathcal{M}$ consists of a set of R2RML [13] *mapping assertions* of the form $\texttt{sql}(\boldsymbol{x}) \rightsquigarrow E(\boldsymbol{f}(\boldsymbol{x}))$, where $\texttt{sql}(\boldsymbol{x})$ is a (SQL) query over $\mathcal{S}$ with answer variables $\boldsymbol{x}$, E is a class or property of $\mathcal{O}$, and $\boldsymbol{f}(\boldsymbol{x})$ denotes a set of so-called *IRI templates* applied to the variables in $\boldsymbol{x}$. Each IRI template is a function that constructs an ontology literal or an IRI identifying an ontology object, from the values in each answer to $\texttt{sql}(\boldsymbol{x})$ instantiating $\boldsymbol{x}$. Then, a *VKG instance* is a pair $(\mathcal{P}, \mathcal{D}^{rel})$, where $\mathcal{D}^{rel}$ is a relational database instance conforming to $\mathcal{S}$. Thus, by applying the mapping assertions in $\mathcal{M}$ to $\mathcal{D}^{rel}$, one obtains a knowledge graph $\mathcal{M}(\mathcal{D}^{rel})$ (which is actually kept virtual).

Semantic queries formulated in SPARQL [17] are posed over $\mathcal{O}$ and are answered by accessing the data in $\mathcal{D}^{rel}$ through the mapping $\mathcal{M}$. Specifically, given a SPARQL query q over a VKG instance $\mathcal{J} = (\mathcal{P}, \mathcal{D}^{rel})$, we are interested in the *certain answers* to q over $\mathcal{J}$, denoted $\text{cert}(q, \mathcal{J})$, which are the answers obtained by evaluating q over the knowledge base $(\mathcal{O}, \mathcal{M}(\mathcal{D}^{rel}))$ under the OWL 2 QL entailment regime [21]. Actual VKG systems such as ONTOP [12,34] avoid costly materialization of the KG $\mathcal{M}(\mathcal{D}^{rel})$ and its storage in a triple store, and rather translate the SPARQL query into a relational SQL query that is directly evaluated by the underlying DBMS (e.g., PostgreSQL), thus ensuring also freshness of query answers concerning source updates.

2.1 Vector Data

Vector data are used to describe the spatial characteristics of discrete real-world phenomena, each conceived as a feature according to the *ISO 19123 Geographic Inf. Part 1*

OGC Geometry Type	Region Geometry Illustration	Exterior & interior boundaries	OGC WKT Literal Representation (i.e. regionWkt)	Description
Point	•	NA	POINT (x, y)	A WKT point (e.g. pin location)
LineString		NA	LINESTRING(POINT$_{01}$,POINT$_{02}$,......,POINT$_m$)	A LineString with at least two or more points (e.g., road network)
LinearRing		exterior = 1 interior = 0	LINEARRING (POINT$_{01}$,POINT$_{02}$,......,POINT$_n$, POINT$_{01}$)	An enclosed LineString where start point = end point with zero measurable area
Polygon		exterior = 1 interior = 2	POLYGON ((LINEARRING$_{01}$), [(LINEARRING)]*)	A LinearRing with a valid measurable area with zero or more holes or interiors (e.g., countries, lake within forest)
Multi-Polygon		exterior = 3 interior = 3	MULTIPOLYGON (((POLYGON$_{01}$), [(POLYGON)]*))	Collection of two or more Polygons with zero or more interiors or holes (e.g., scattered islands, enclaves)
Geometry-Collection		exterior = 4 interior = 2	GEOMETRYCOLLECTION([POINT*], [LINEARSTRING*], [POLYGON*], [MULTIPOLYGON*])	Heterogeneous collection of every OGC standard geometries

Fig. 1. Primary components of vector data in their respective OGC WKT forms

Standard[5]. Typical examples of such discrete features are rivers, lakes, and administrative regions. These are represented by a set of one or more geometric primitives, such as points, curves, and surfaces with their positional parameters either in Cartesian coordinates (X and Y) in a topological planar surface or geographic coordinates (longitude a.k.a. geoX and latitude a.k.a. geoY). Other characteristics of the discrete phenomenon are recorded as feature attributes. Vector data are represented in popular file formats like CSV, shapefiles, and GeoJSON or relational tables in a RDBMS with a spatial extension.

We consider geometries that conform to the *OGC ISO 19125 OpenGIS* Standard[6], which foresees *Well-Known Text* (WKT) literals[7] as the most common representation of geometries. According to this standard, a *Point* is a pair of longitude and latitude (which in the WKT representation are separated by blanks), while a *LineString* is a sequence of points separated by ','. A valid *Polygon* is a topologically closed planar surface defined by one exterior boundary and zero or more interior boundaries (where each interior boundary defines a hole in the polygon). Each boundary is a *LinearRing*, which is a LineString in which the last point must coincide with the first point. A *MultiPolygon* is a collection of one or more valid Polygons, separated by ','. Finally, a *GeometryCollection* is a sequence of one or more of the previously introduced elements. Figure 1 illustrates some of the basic geometry elements of vector data (i.e., regionGeometry) with their representation as OGC WKT literals (i.e., regionWkt) with examples. All geometries in OGC ISO 19125 are a combination of these primary geometries.

---

[5] https://www.iso.org/obp/ui/en/#iso:std:iso:19123:-1:ed-1:v1:en.
[6] https://www.ogc.org/standard/sfa/.
[7] https://docs.ogc.org/is/18-010r7/18-010r7.html.

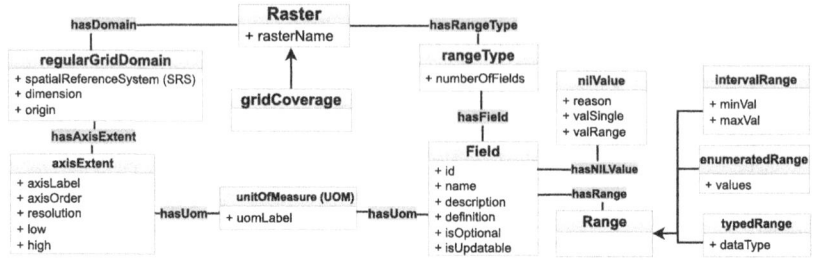

Fig. 2. Ontology for generic raster data, including grid coverage

2.2 Raster Data

Raster data, also referred to as *gridded data* [7], or *multidimensional discrete data* (MDD), represent real-world phenomena that vary continuously over space, time, and maybe even more dimensions, depending on the particular *domain of interest* (DOI) or field such as medical, astronomy, geospatial, etc. In this paper, we focus on raster data in the geospatial domain, also referred to as *datacube* [2] or gridded *coverage* as per *OGC Coverage Implementation Schema* (CIS) v1.1 Standard [5] adopted by ISO 19123 Geographic information - Schema for coverage geometry and functions. According to Part 2 of this ISO standard[8] the concept of *coverage* represents multidimensional grids of both regular and irregular type as the natural representation of various space-time-varying phenomena predominantly in the geospatial domain. Common examples include 1-D time series, 2-D imagery, 3-D x/y/t image time-series and x/y/z geophysical data, as well as 4-D x/y/z/t atmospheric climate and ocean data.

Inspired by [1], we have defined the *Raster Ontology* shown in Fig. 2, which describes n-dimensional generic raster data or coverage based on the OGC CIS v1.1 Standard. The ontology describes so far only regular gridded coverage or geospatial raster data. The RegularGridDomain and RangeType classes capture all the information about the domains and ranges of a grid coverage. For measurement units, we use the UnitOfMeasure class defined by the *Quantities, Units, Dimensions, and Types* (QUDT) ontology [24].

Coverages can be encoded in a suitable raster file format such as GML, NetCDF, GeoTIFF, HDF, etc., which greatly benefits for use case specific small datasets that can be accessed ad hoc via Python, R, Matlab scripts, etc. However, problems begin to emerge when data become very large in volume (e.g. terabytes) and it becomes challenging to query the required information [30]. Moreover, to deal with gridded coverage data, or raster data, one must also include metadata such as domain, range, and provenance information. In contrast to arrays, the structure of this metadata is substantially less regular, and it may be incomplete or vary between arrays.

In our research, we rely on rasdaman (for "raster data manager"), a domain-agnostic array DBMS that implements the OGC standards for gridded coverages, and manages such large data with its substantially rich array algebra. Rasdaman offers a SQL-like

---
[8] https://www.iso.org/obp/ui/en/#iso:std:70948:en.

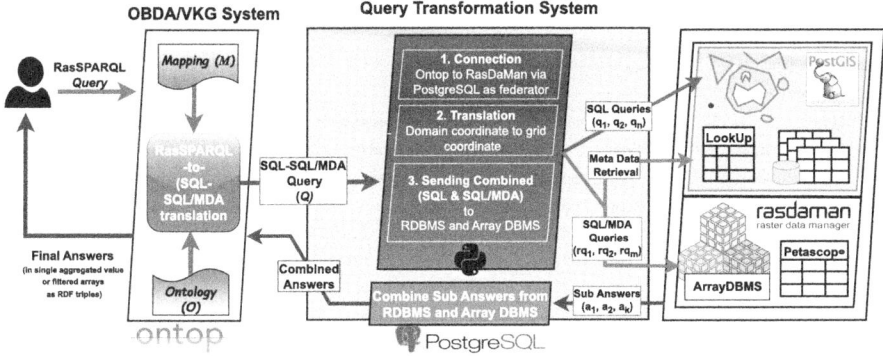

Fig. 3. The ONTORASTER framework extending the VKG framework

query language known as *RaSQL*[9] to query any kind of raster data of arbitrary dimensions [4] following *ISO 9075 SQL Part 15: Multi-Dimensional Arrays* (SQL/MDA)[10]. It features a geo service front-end component called *petascope*[11], which adds geo semantics on top of arrays, thereby enabling regular and irregular grids based on the OGC CIS v1.1. To implement the geo-semantics, petascope uses a relational database such as PostgreSQL to store related metadata for each raster dataset. This metadata is distributed across 62 relational tables in a separate database called *petascopedb* within PostgreSQL. Rasdaman also includes *rasdapy*[12], a client API that allows building and executing rasql queries using Python.

3 The OntoRaster Framework

We present the ONTORASTER framework, which extends the capabilities of a VKG engine to handle also multidimensional raster datasets. The architecture of ONTORASTER is shown in Fig. 3, and discussed below.

3.1 RasSPARQL: An Extension of SPARQL with Raster Functions

We introduce now RasSPARQL, which extends SPARQL and the OGC GeoSPARQL functions used to manage vector data [34], with the support for raster data and the corresponding functions. To provide such an extension, we have first devised and added to SPARQL, custom raster-based functions and corresponding SQL DB functions, to be handed over for execution to an Array DBMS. The currently supported RasSPARQL raster-based functions with their input arguments and output type are listed in Table 1.

Notice that the RasSPARQL functions `rasClipRaster()`, and `rasClipRaster AnyGeom()` return a portion of raster data as an array of values (e.g., pixels) by relying on rasdaman's embedded 'clip' function[13], which extracts a raster array based on

---
[9] https://doc.rasdaman.org/04_ql-guide.html.
[10] https://www.iso.org/obp/ui#iso:std:iso-iec:9075:-15:ed-2:v1:en.
[11] https://doc.rasdaman.org/02_inst-guide.html?highlight=petascope#petascope.
[12] https://pypi.org/project/rasdapy3/.
[13] https://doc.rasdaman.org/04_ql-guide.html#clipping-operations.

Table 1. RasSPARQL raster functions and respective PL/Python stored procedures

RasSPARQL function	Input arguments	Output type	PL/Python stored proc.
rasDimension()	rasterName	xsd:string	query2string()
rasCellOp()	timeStamp, operator, operand, rasterName	xsd:string	query2array()
rasSpatialAverage()	timeStamp, regionGeometry, rasterName	xsd:double	query2numeric()
rasSpatialMinimum()	timeStamp, regionGeometry, rasterName	xsd:double	query2numeric()
rasSpatialMaximum()	timeStamp, regionGeometry, rasterName	xsd:double	query2numeric()
rasTemporalAverage()	startTime, endTime, regionGeometry, rasterName	xsd:double	query2numeric()
rasTemporalMinimum()	startTime, endTime, regionGeometry, rasterName	xsd:double	query2numeric()
rasTemporalMaximum()	startTime, endTime, regionGeometry, rasterName	xsd:double	query2numeric()
rasClipRaster()	timeStamp, regionGeometry, rasterName	xsd:string	query2array()
rasClipRasterAnyGeom()	timeStamp, regionGeometry, rasterName	xsd:string	query2array()

the geometry (or shape) of a region: all pixels outside of the given region are set to null or 'NaN', while pixels on and within the region are preserved. We represent the returned array as a string since RDF does not support arrays yet.

3.2 Extending Ontop to Translate RasSPARQL to SQL-SQL/MDA

To properly deal with RasSPARQL functions within Ontop, we have implemented an extension of the system that, as a part of query reformulation, translates each such function into a corresponding SQL function and embeds it into the generated SQL/MDA query as indicated in Fig. 3. Notice that the RasSPARQL query is in general a SPARQL query that might contain both GeoSPARQL functions and raster functions. This query is translated to a plain SQL query containing corresponding PostGIS functions and PL/Python stored procedures that connect to rasdaman, as specified in the last column of Table 1. As an example, when Ontop parses a RasSPARQL query that embeds the raster function rasSpatialAverage, it translates it to a call to query2numeric which in turn executes the SQL/MDA standard rasql query over rasdaman.

3.3 Query Transformation System

We now describe how the generated SQL-SQL/MDA query produced by Ontop is processed as shown in Fig. 3. The PostGIS functions embedded in the SQL part can be directly processed by PostgreSQL through its PostGIS extension. Instead, we rely on PL/Python and PL/pgSQL stored procedures to ensure smooth retrieval of the metadata corresponding to the relevant raster data, and the ability to call suitable rasql queries that are directly executed by rasdaman.

PL/Python Stored Procedures. The stored procedures are specified in the PL/Python procedural language[14], which also supports all PostgreSQL and PostGIS functions, and *rasdapy* to connect to rasdaman. The procedures are stored in the VectorTablesDB database inside PostgreSQL (in a schema called rasdaman_op). We elaborate now on the stored procedures shown in Table 2.

---
[14] https://www.postgresql.org/docs/current/plpython.html.

Table 2. Selected PL/Python stored procedures to connect Ontop and rasdaman federated by PostgreSQL via rasdapy

Stored procedure	Input arguments	Output
geo2grid_coords()	GEOMETRY regionGeometry, DOUBLE minLon, DOUBLE minLat, DOUBLE resLon, DOUBLE resLat	GEOMETRY regionGrid
query2numeric()	STRING rasqlQuery	DOUBLE value
query2array()	STRING rasqlQuery	DOUBLE[] array

- geo2grid_coords(): Being a domain-agnostic array DBMS, rasdaman (rasql precisely) only supports array indices (i and j) or grid coordinates (gridX and gridY) and does not consider any domain-specific coordinates such as geo-coordinates (i.e., longitude and latitude) natively. Therefore, we devised this mapping function inspired by a generic affine transformation model [32], which translates the geo-coordinates to corresponding grid coordinates, taking into account the respective geographical coordinate reference system (CRS). Our current implementation assumes that both the vector and the raster data use the same CRS, which we require to be WGS84[15]. We will provide support for different CRSs in the future. In practice, this function takes five input arguments, namely the geometry of the chosen *region of interest* (ROI), and minLon, minLat, resLon, resLat of the selected raster data. It returns a translated grid geometry of the region (regionGrid) as output. This enables the user to send the geometry (polygon or multi-polygon) of any ROI to rasdaman as a part of the rasql query. The embedded geometry will be translated into grid coordinates to be used as an input to rasql's array operations to extract data from raster data. As an example, rasql's 'clip'operation can crop out a portion of raster data based on the translated geometry of a user's region.
- query2numeric(): Takes a rasql query as a string input and executes it over raster data stored inside rasdaman using rasdaman's supported array condenser operations[16], such as avg_cells, max_cells, etc. and retrieve aggregated numeric results back to PostgreSQL.
- query2array(): Evaluates rasql queries over raster arrays using rasdaman supported array operations[17] such as clip, concatenation, scaling and retrieve filtered arrays back to PostgreSQL.

PL/pgSQL Stored Procedures. - timestamp2grid(): This PL/pgSQL function translates timestamp from 'DateTime' format to integer format (e.g., gridTime) that is comprehended by rasdaman since rasdaman treats the timestamp as an integer instead of the actual 'DateTime' format.

These are just selected necessary stored procedures that make PostgreSQL a *federator* between rasdaman and Ontop. In the future, more stored procedures can be added based on the user's demands. Based on these stored procedures (both PL/Python and

---
[15] https://epsg.io/4326.
[16] https://doc.rasdaman.org/04_ql-guide.html#condensers.
[17] https://doc.rasdaman.org/04_ql-guide.html#array-operations.

PL/pgSQL), Ontop-generated SQL/MDA queries can be executed on any geospatial raster data using the array manipulation capabilities of rasdaman.

Raster LookUp Table Creation. As previously stated, the essential metadata stored in petascopedb must accompany the corresponding raster in order to interact with it. Every time a user queries specific raster data, the relevant metadata needs to be searched among 62 separate tables in petascopedb and attached with the corresponding raster data automatically for subsequent processing. If the user selects another raster dataset to query, the automatic search and combine procedure is repeated, resulting in overhead. To address this issue, we created a *Raster Lookup*, a single table that stores all necessary metadata in one place for every raster data stored in rasdaman. We have built this table inside the VectorTablesDB database from the petascopedb database using *dblink*[18] where petascopedb serves as a remote database. Whenever a new raster data is uploaded to rasdaman, we defined a PostgreSQL trigger to automatically update the *LookUp* table with the metadata of newly added raster data.

4 Case Study for the OntoRaster System

We demonstrate the proposed ONTORASTER framework on a case study where we integrate vector data (i.e., regions) with geospatial raster data and return their spatiotemporal patterns and correlations as a knowledge graph, for possible further processing. We build the mappings using the Protégé ontology editor [14] with the Ontop plugin [12] and set up a SPARQL endpoint available on GitHub[19] including the complete implementation as docker with the required data.

4.1 VKG Specification for OntoRaster

Ontology ($\mathcal{O}$). We rely on the GeoSPARQL ontology, representing the geometries of a vector region (See footnote 4).

Data Sources ($\mathcal{D}^{rel}$, $\mathcal{D}^{arr}$). Table 3 displays all the vector and raster datasets considered for the ONTORASTER framework demonstration. In our work, we represent vector data with their corresponding geometries (e.g., regionGeometry) and attributes (e.g., regionId, regionName), using one or more relational tables for every *area of interest* (AOI), stored in a DB named *VectorTablesDB* within PostgreSQL, as shown in Fig. 4. For the case study, we consider Sweden, Bavaria (Germany), and South Tyrol (Italy) as our AOIs with their corresponding municipalities as ROIs (resulting in ~500 unique ROIs in total).

Related vector data are downloaded as shapefiles from GADM[20]. Then utilizing the shp2pgsql[21] data loader we import each shapefile as a suitable default SQL binary object format (with regionGeometry in hex format, i.e., regionHex) into separate

---
[18] https://www.postgresql.org/docs/current/contrib-dblink-function.html.
[19] https://github.com/aghoshpro/OntoRaster.git.
[20] https://gadm.org/index.html.
[21] https://postgis.net/docs/using_postgis_dbmanagement.html#shp2pgsql_usage.

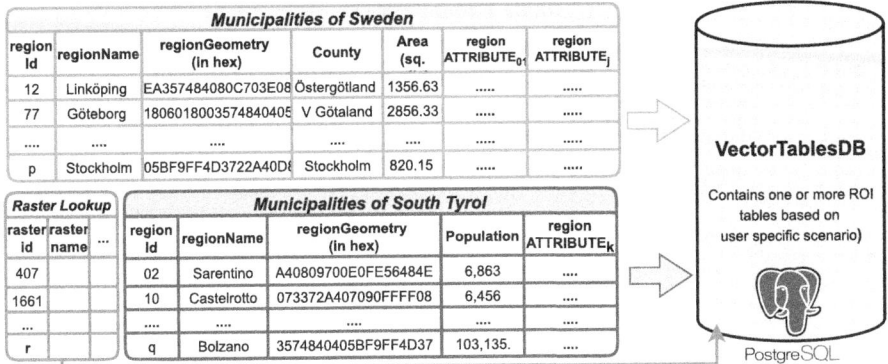

Fig. 4. VectorTablesDB containing tables for Areas of Interest and Raster Lookup

tables into VectorTablesDB, as shown in Fig. 4. Notice that we have used convenient names for the tables and their columns in VectorTablesDB, However, any other choice would have been possible, as long as such names are used in a coherent way in the source queries of the VKG mappings that provide the link between vector and raster data (see, e.g., Fig. 5).

As for raster data, we use the MODIS land surface temperature dataset [31] from NASA's *Earth Science Data Systems* (ESDS) covering the respective AOIs, i.e., Sweden, Bavaria, and South Tyrol. This is 3-D raster data with a spatial dimension (2-D) and a temporal dimension (1-D) with temperature as a field (or band). ONTORASTER also supports an arbitrary number of fields, such as precipitation, elevation, etc., sharing the same axis extents (cf. the ontology in Fig. 2). The *Raster Lookup* table, of which we show in Table 4 only five out of seventeen columns, maintains the necessary metadata of the raster datasets and is stored in VectorTablesDB, as shown in Fig. 4.

Mappings ($\mathcal{M}$). We show in Fig. 5 only one example mapping, in which the class Region is mapped with its respective data properties such as id, name, and geometry in OGC WKT geometry serialization, i.e., regionWkt, for all regions of Sweden. Based on this mapping, at query execution time, the geometry is retrieved using the input region name. The SQL source query of the mapping contains a CASE statement that

Table 3. Heterogeneous datasets used for the case study

Areas of Interest (AOI)	Sweden		Bavaria (Germany)		South Tyrol (Italy)	
Datasets	Vector	Raster	Vector	Raster	Vector	Raster
Type	Municipalities	Temperature	Municipalities	Temperature	Municipalities	Temperature
Native Format	.shp	NetCDF	.shp	NetCDF	.shp	NetCDF
Logical Format	relational	MDA	relational	MDA	relational	MDA
Array Dim (t x lon x lat)	–	217 × 1586 × 1648	–	305 × 584 × 396	–	305 × 252 × 106
Spatial Resolution	None	1 km × 1 km	None	1 km × 1 km	None	1 km × 1 km
Temporal Resolution	None	daily	None	daily	None	daily
Temporal Coverage	None	1 year	None	1 year	None	1 year
Features	290	1,001,057,824	96	70,006,640	116	8,038,275

Table 4. Raster Lookup

raster_id	raster_name	min_lon	max_lon	res_lon	...
407	Surface_Temperature_Sweden	10.9583	24.1749	0.00833	...
1661	Bavaria_Temperature_MODIS_1km	8.9749	13.8416	0.008333332653	...
800	South_Tyrol_Temperature_MODIS_1km	10.3833	12.4833	0.0083332586793	...

```
Target (Triples Template):
:vector/{regionId} a :Region ; rdfs:label {regionName}^^xsd:string ; geo:asWKT {regionWkt}^^geo:wktLiteral
▲▼
Source (SQL Query):
SELECT gid as regionId, name_2 AS regionName,
       CASE
           WHEN ST_NumGeometries(geom) = 1 THEN ST_AsText(ST_GeometryN(geom, 1))
           ELSE ST_AsText(geom)
       END AS regionWkt
FROM region_sweden
▲▼
SQL Query results:
regionid  regionname
6         Linköping    POLYGON((15.283931732177848 58.128513336181754,15.2924165725708 58.12883377075201,15.30...
117       Gnesta       POLYGON((17.3850154876709 58.97632980346691,17.38535308837902 58.9718437194248,17.3940...
8         Motala       POLYGON((15.311992645263615 58.43120193481457,15.303435325622672 58.43088150024414,15.2...
9         Norrköping   MULTIPOLYGON(((16.427499771118278 58.608196258545036,16.427499771118278 58.608749389648...
10        Söderköping  MULTIPOLYGON(((16.758054733276367 58.33069610595709,16.756389617920036 58.3306961059570...
11        Vadstena     POLYGON((14.834283828735408 58.34504699707037,14.825750350952205 58.34469604492199,14.8...
```

Fig. 5. Example mapping to retrieve region id, name and geometry

checks whether the geometry of the input region is a polygon or a multi-polygon, as they need to be treated differently in the `geo2grid_coords` function. This is necessary to transform any single polygon represented as a multi-polygon (technically possible but a bad representation) into its actual polygonal format. Similar types of mapping apply for all other vector regions, including the regions of Bavaria and South Tyrol.

In our framework, we have set up a number of mappings to connect the data attributes of the `Region` and `Raster` classes, for which we refer the reader to the GitHub repository (See footnote 19). We will further extend this set of mappings in the future.

4.2 Queries (Q)

To demonstrate our results, and the capability of ONTORASTER for query answering over virtually integrated vector data and raster data under the VKG paradigm, we provide RasSPARQL queries of four types: simple, with spatial aggregation, with temporal aggregation, and with spatial raster filtering. All queries can be found on GitHub (See footnote 19). Here we show only a few of them. The used prefixes are listed in Table 5 and refer to the base namespaces of the ONTORASTER and auxiliary vocabularies, such as RDFS and GeoSPARQL.

Q1 is a simple raster query that retrieves dimension information of the input raster data. Query *Q2* conducts element-wise operations on raster arrays.

Queries *Q3–Q5* perform spatial aggregations and return a single aggregated value from a chosen raster dataset over a vector region at a specific timestamp.

Table 5. List of prefixes used for RasSPARQL queries

Prefix	IRI Namespace
:	https://github.com/aghoshpro/OntoRaster/
geo	http://www.opengis.net/ont/geosparql#
rdfs	http://www.w3.org/2000/01/rdf-schema#
rasdb	https://github.com/aghoshpro/RasterDataCube/

- *Q3*: Find the spatial average temperature over München on 24 July 2023, using the available temperature raster data over Bavaria.

```
SELECT ?answer {
    ?region a :Region ; rdfs:label ?regionName ; geo:asWKT ?regionWkt .
    ?gridCoverage a :Raster ; rasdb:rasterName ?rasterName .
    FILTER (?regionName = 'München')
    FILTER (CONTAINS(?rasterName, 'Bavaria'))
    BIND ('2023-07-24T00:00:00+00:00'^^xsd:dateTime AS ?timeStamp)
    BIND (rasdb:rasSpatialAverage(?timeStamp, ?regionWkt, ?rasterName)
        AS ?answer)
}
```

Similarly, *Q4* and *Q5* enable the user to find the maximum and minimum temperature values by using the respective RasSPAQRL spatial functions `rasSpatialMaximum` and `rasSpatialMinimum` over 'München', or any other region from VectorTablesDB, combined with the corresponding raster datasets (i.e., Bavaria, Sweden, or South-Tyrol).

Queries *Q6–Q8* perform temporal aggregations and return a single aggregated value by integrating a user-specific vector region and a raster dataset over a time interval between the given start and end times.

- *Q7*: Find the maximum temperature over Göteborg between 5 April 2022 and 19 June 2022, using the available temperature raster data over Sweden.

```
SELECT ?answer {
    ?region a :Region ; rdfs:label ?regionName ; geo:asWKT ?regionWkt .
    ?gridCoverage a :Raster ; rasdb:rasterName ?rasterName .
    FILTER (?regionName = 'Göteborg')
    FILTER (CONTAINS(?rasterName, 'Sweden'))
    BIND ('2022-04-05T00:00:00+00:00'^^xsd:dateTime AS ?startTimeStamp)
    BIND ('2022-06-19T00:00:00+00:00'^^xsd:dateTime AS ?endTimeStamp)
    BIND (rasdb:rasTemporalMaximum(?startTimeStamp, ?endTimeStamp,
            ?regionWkt, ?rasterName) AS ?answer)
}
```

Queries *Q9* and *Q10* perform a 'clipping' operation by cropping a portion of the actual raster data based on the geometrical extent of the specified region at a given time, and return a filtered array that covers the input region.

- **Q9**: Clip an available temperature raster data for South Tyrol with region Bolzano on 24 September 2023 at time 00:00:00, and return filtered arrays.

```
SELECT ?answer {
  ?region a :Region ; rdfs:label ?regionName ; geo:asWKT ?regionWkt .
  ?gridCoverage a :Raster ; rasdb:rasterName ?rasterName .
  FILTER (?regionName = 'Bolzano')
  FILTER (CONTAINS(?rasterName, 'Tyrol'))
  BIND ('2023-09-24T00:00:00+00:00'^^xsd:dateTime AS ?timeStamp)
  BIND (rasdb:rasClipRaster(?timeStamp, ?regionWkt, ?rasterName)
      AS ?answer)
}
```

- **Q10**: Clip a portion of user-specific raster data based on a custom vector region on 24 July 2024 at time 00:00:00, and return filtered arrays.

```
SELECT ?answer {
  ?gridCoverage a :Raster ; rasdb:rasterName ?rasterName .
  FILTER (CONTAINS(?rasterName, 'Bavaria'))
  BIND ('POLYGON((11.324157714843748 48.29050321714061,
        11.911926269531248 48.279537342260085,
        11.88995361328125 48.01932418480118,
        11.340637207031248 48.01564978668938,
        11.324157714843748 48.29050321714061))' AS ?customRegionWkt)
  BIND ('2023-07-24T00:00:00+00:00'^^xsd:dateTime AS ?timeStamp)
  BIND (rasdb:rasClipRasterAnyGeom(?timeStamp, ?customRegionWkt,
        ?rasterName) AS ?answer)
}
```

4.3 Issues

Currently, the ONTORASTER system provides support for the types of RasSPARQL queries shown in Sect. 4.2. However, the system is still under development and we intend to extend it to support more general forms of RasSPARQL queries, so as to accommodate arbitrary multivariate raster data of n-dimensions. We are also working to make our solution more robust by addressing the following issues:

- Multi-polygons with holes and multi-polygons with small polygons (sometimes the area is smaller than the pixel size of the corresponding raster arrays) still have limited support. Hence, the `geo2grid_coords` function needs to be improved to translate the aforementioned types of multi-polygonal geometry to an equivalent grid geometry.
- Multiple raster data sets with the same name have to be taken into account. A possible solution is to include a second filter argument in addition to the raster name, to distinguish different fields of the raster.
- Missing timestamps between the start time and end time of the raster data are not taken into account in the `timestamp2grid` function.
- RDF does not yet support array datatype, leading to optimisation issues when raster arrays that are retrieved as RDF strings require further processing.

– The inclusion of post-processing operations for raster data is crucial in converting the raw data values to a format that is convenient for the end user. But their usage differs for every raster dataset, may not always be included in the metadata, and whether to use them or not, depends on the end user's objective with the data. All these aspects need to be taken into account.

5 Conclusions

We have presented a novel extended VKG framework, ONTORASTER to query for the first time multidimensional raster data combined with relational data, including vector data, on the fly by connecting the array DBMS rasdaman to the VKG system Ontop. To achieve this, we defined the RasSPARQL language, by extending SPARQL with custom raster functions to query over VKGs. Then we developed a query transformation system that includes several stored procedures defined in PL/Python and PL/pgsql that make PostgreSQL a federator between VKG engine Ontop and heterogeneous data sources (e.g., raster and relational). It guides the translated SQL-SQL/MDA query coming from Ontop to the respective data sources stored in RDBMS & array DBMS as mentioned in the RasSPARQL query by the user and executes them separately. After execution, the retrieved sub-answers (containing relational and raster arrays) are joined and then guided back to the Ontop to generate a virtual knowledge graph (VKG) that answers the user's semantic query. The most notable contribution of this article lies in its utilisation of the array handling capabilities of an array DBMS to perform queries on large raster data in their original data structure, i.e., multidimensional arrays, without any conversion. This eliminates the need for costly data transfer and transformation of raster data into relational databases. ONTORASTER supports a wide range of potential queries, only limited to the data processing and functional capabilities of PostgreSQL (RDBMS) and rasdaman (array DBMS) for managing relational data and raster data, respectively.

We plan to continue the work on ONTORASTER along the following lines:

– It is of interest to incorporate SPARQL endpoints of public knowledge graphs (e.g., DBPedia, LinkedGeoData, and Wikidata) into the ONTORASTER framework, to enable the building of a coherent (partially virtual and partially materialized0 knowledge graph that can be queried holistically.
– The possibility to delegate further procession of the query results to BI Tools such as MS Power BI and Tableau.
– Publishing and displaying query results as an interactive visualisation on the web, using the OGC CoverageJSON[22].
– Translating natural language queries into RasSPARQL queries to explore VKG using NLP and LLMs.

Acknowledgments. This research has been partially supported by the Province of Bolzano and DFG through the project D2G2 (DFG grant n. 500249124), by the HEU project CyclOps (grant agreement n. 101135513), and by the Wallenberg AI, Autonomous Systems and Software Program (WASP), funded by the Knut and Alice Wallenberg Foundation.

---

[22] https://covjson.org/.

References

1. Andrejev, A., Misev, D., Baumann, P., Risch, T.: Spatio-temporal gridded data processing on the semantic web. In: Proceedings of IEEE International Conference on Data Science and Data Intensive Systems (DSDIS) (2015). https://doi.org/10.1109/DSDIS.2015.109
2. Baumann, P.: The datacube manifesto. Technical Report, EU EarthServer (2017). https://earthserver.eu/tech/datacube-manifesto/The-Datacube-Manifesto.pdf
3. Baumann, P.: RasDaMan - Raster data manager. Technical Report, 9.5.0, Zenodo (2018). https://doi.org/10.5281/zenodo.1163021
4. Baumann, P., Furtado, P., Ritsch, R., Widmann, N.: The rasdaman approach to multidimensional database management. In: Proceedings of the 12th ACM Symposium on Applied Computing (SAC), pp. 166–173 (1997). https://doi.org/10.1145/331697.331732
5. Baumann, P., Hirschorn, P.E., Masó, J.: OGC coverage implementation schema (CIS), v1.1. Technical Report, Open Geospatial Consortium (2017). http://docs.opengeospatial.org/is/09-146r8/09-146r8.html
6. Baumann, P., Holsten, S.: A comparative analysis of array models for databases. In: Kim, T., et al. (eds.) FGIT 2011. CCIS, vol. 258, pp. 80–89. Springer, Heidelberg (2011). https://doi.org/10.1007/978-3-642-27157-1_9
7. Baumann, P., Misev, D., Merticariu, V., Huu, B.P.: Array databases: concepts, standards, implementations. J. Big Data **8**(28) (2021). https://doi.org/10.1186/s40537-020-00399-2
8. Bereta, K., Xiao, G., Koubarakis, M.: Ontop-spatial: ontop of geospatial databases. J. Web Semantics **58** (2019). https://doi.org/10.1016/j.websem.2019.100514
9. Bilidas, D., Mantas, A., Yfantis, F., Stamoulis, G., Koubarakis, M.: Plato: a semantic data cube implementation using ontology-based data access technologies. In: Proceedings of the Conference on Big Data from Space (BiDS) (2023). https://cgi.di.uoa.gr/~koubarak/publications/2023/Plato-BiDS2023.pdf
10. Bilidas, D., Mantas, A., Yfantis, F., Stamoulis, G., Koubarakis, M.: The Semantic Data Cube System Plato and Its Applications. In: Proceedings of the IEEE International Geoscience and Remote Sensing Symposium (IGARSS) (2024). https://cgi.di.uoa.gr/~koubarak/publications/2024/plato_igrass.pdf
11. Bilidas, D., et al.: Fire risk management using data cubes, machine learning and OBDA systems. In: Proceedings of SIGSPATIAL, pp. 1–4. ACM (2023). https://doi.org/10.1145/3589132.3625615
12. Calvanese, D., et al.: Ontop: answering SPARQL queries over relational databases. Semantic Web J. (2017). https://doi.org/10.3233/SW-160217
13. Das, S., Sundara, S., Cyganiak, R.: R2RML: RDB to RDF mapping language. W3C Recommendation, World Wide Web Consortium (2012). http://www.w3.org/TR/r2rml/
14. Gennari, J.H., et al.: The evolution of Protégé: an environment for knowledge-based systems development. Int. J. Hum.-Comput. Stud. (2003). https://doi.org/10.1016/S1071-5819(02)00127-1
15. Ghosh, A., Simkus, M., Calvanese, D.: Semantic querying of integrated raster and relational data: a virtual knowledge graph approach. In: Proceedings of the 17th International Rule Challenge and 7th Doctoral Consortium at RuleML+RR. CEUR Workshop Proceedings, vol. 3485. CEUR-WS.org (2023). https://ceur-ws.org/Vol-3485/paper8240.pdf
16. Hamdani, Y., Xiao, G., Ding, L., Calvanese, D.: An ontology-based framework for geospatial integration and querying of raster data cube using virtual knowledge graphs. ISPRS Int. J. Geo-Inf. **12**(9), 375 (2023). https://doi.org/10.3390/ijgi12090375
17. Harris, S., Seaborne, A.: SPARQL 1.1 query language. W3C Recommendation, World Wide Web Consortium (2013). http://www.w3.org/TR/sparql11-query

18. Lewis, A., et al.: Rapid, high-resolution detection of environmental change over continental scales from satellite data - the earth observation data cube. Int. J. Digit. Earth (2016). https://doi.org/10.1080/17538947.2015.1111952
19. Lu, M., Appel, M., Pebesma, E.: Multidimensional arrays for analysing geoscientific data. ISPRS Int. J. Geo-Inf. **78**(8), 313 (2018). https://doi.org/10.3390/ijgi7080313
20. Marathe, A.P., Salem, K.: Query processing techniques for arrays. Very Large Database J. 68–91 (2002). https://doi.org/10.1007/s007780200062
21. Motik, B., Cuenca Grau, B., Horrocks, I., Wu, Z., Fokoue, A., Lutz, C.: OWL 2 Web Ontology Language Profiles (Second Edition). W3C Recommendation, World Wide Web Consortium, December 2012. http://www.w3.org/TR/owl2-profiles/
22. Poggi, A., Lembo, D., Calvanese, D., De Giacomo, G., Lenzerini, M., Rosati, R.: Linking data to ontologies. J. Data Semantics **10**, 133–173 (2008). https://doi.org/10.1007/978-3-540-77688-8_5
23. Quartulli, M., Olaizola, I.G.: A review of EO image information mining. ISPRS J. Photogrammetry Remote Sens. **75**, 11–28 (2013). https://doi.org/10.1016/j.isprsjprs.2012.09.010
24. Ray, S.: Quantities, Units, Dimensions and Types (QUDT). Technical Report, Fairsharing.org (2011). https://doi.org/10.25504/FAIRsharing.d3pqw7
25. Rusu, F.: Multidimensional array data management. Foundations Trends Databases **12**(1–3), 69–220 (2023). https://doi.org/10.1561/1900000069
26. Schreiber, G., Raimond, Y.: RDF 1.1 Primer. W3C Working Group Note, World Wide Web Consortium, June 2014. http://www.w3.org/TR/rdf11-primer/
27. Sheth, A.P., Larson, J.A.: Federated database systems for managing distributed, heterogeneous, and autonomous databases. ACM Comput. Surv. **22**(3), 183–236 (1990). https://doi.org/10.1145/96602.96604
28. Spanos, D.E., Stavrou, P., Mitrou, N.: Bringing relational databases into the semantic web: a survey. Semantic Web J. **3**(2), 169–209 (2012). https://doi.org/10.3233/SW-2011-0055
29. Stonebraker, M., Brown, P., Poliakov, A., Raman, S.: The architecture of SciDB. In: Proceedings of SSDBM (2011). https://doi.org/10.1007/978-3-642-22351-8_1
30. Tan, Z., Yue, P., Gong, J.: An array database approach for earth observation data management and processing. ISPRS Int. J. Geo-Inf. **6**(7) (2017). https://doi.org/10.3390/ijgi6070220
31. Wan, Z., Hook, S., Hulley, G.: MODIS/terra land surface temperature daily L3 global 1km grid V061 (2021). https://doi.org/10.5067/MODIS/MOD11A1.061
32. Warmerdam, F.: The geospatial data abstraction library. In: Hall, G.B., Leahy, M.G. (eds.) Open Source Approaches in Spatial Data Handling. Advances in Geographic Information Science, vol. 2, pp. 87–104. Springer, Berlin (2008). https://doi.org/10.1007/978-3-540-74831-1_5
33. Xiao, G., et al.: Ontology-based data access: a survey. In: Proceedings of the 27th International Joint Conference on Artificial Intelligence (IJCAI) (2018). https://doi.org/10.24963/ijcai.2018/777
34. Xiao, G., et al.: The virtual knowledge graph system ontop. In: Pan, J.Z., et al. (eds.) ISWC 2020. LNCS, vol. 12507, pp. 259–277. Springer, Cham (2020). https://doi.org/10.1007/978-3-030-62466-8_17

Complete Approximations of Incomplete Queries

Julien Corman, Werner Nutt[✉][iD], and Ognjen Savković[iD]

Faculty of Engineering, Free University of Bozen-Bolzano, Bolzano, Italy
{JulienLouisMichel.Corman,Werner.Nutt,Ognjen.Savkovic}@unibz.it

Abstract. This paper studies the completeness of conjunctive queries over a partially complete database and the approximation of incomplete queries. Given a query and a set of completeness rules (a special kind of tuple generating dependencies) that specify which parts of the database are complete, we investigate whether the query can be fully answered, as if all data were available. If not, we explore reformulating the query into either Maximal Complete Specializations (MCSs) or the (unique up to equivalence) Minimal Complete Generalization (MCG) that can be fully answered, that is, the best complete approximations of the query from below or above in the sense of query containment. We show that the MSG can be characterized as the least fixed-point of a monotonic operator in a preorder. Then, we show that an MCS can be computed by recursive backward application of completeness rules. We study the complexity of both problems and discuss implementation techniques that rely on an ASP and Prolog engines, respectively.

1 Introduction

Completeness is one of the classical dimensions of data quality, well studied both in the context of relational data [1,4,5,7] and more recently in the context of knowledge graphs [6,11]. An information system may be incomplete because some data has not yet been inserted, or simply because some information is unavailable for certain records. As a consequence, a query Q that retrieves data may itself be incomplete, in the sense that when Q is evaluated over the actual (incomplete) database, some answers to Q over the ideal (complete) database are missing. Similarly, if Q produces statistics (e.g., count answers), then these statistics may be incorrect.

On the other hand, part of the data is often *known* to be complete. This information may be sufficient to confirm that Q is complete, or, if this is not the case, to produce a query that is complete and *approximates* Q. The latter task is the one investigated in this paper. More precisely, we consider two natural strategies to approximate Q. The first strategy consists in producing a complete query Q' that is more *general* than Q, in the sense that the answers to Q over the ideal (complete) database are a subset of the answers to Q'. In a scenario where one is searching for a specific piece of information, this strategy ensures that it will be retrieved. Instead, the second strategy consists in producing a complete query that is more *specific* than Q. This can be useful for statistics: the answers to Q may not be complete yet (e.g., for a whole country), but one may already publish partial statistics (e.g., for a given region) that are guaranteed to be correct.

As a (toy) running example, we will consider a database instance D of a hypothetical school information system in the Italian province of Bolzano. Following the approach of [8,10,12], one can express which (parts of which) tables in D are known to be complete, using so-called *table-completeness statements* (TCSs). For example, one may write three TCSs that say that D contains *(i)* "all primary schools," *(ii)* "all pupils attending a school in the district of Merano," and *(iii)* "all English learners that are pupils at a primary school," respectively. Conceptually, the TCS *(ii)* for instance asserts that for every pupil enrolled in a school in the district of Merano, there exists a corresponding record in D's "pupils" table.

Now consider the query Q that retrieves all language learners enrolled in a primary school in the district of Merano. The three TCSs above are not sufficient to infer that Q is complete. However, one can approximate Q by either generalizing or specializing it. For instance, the query Q^+ that retrieves all pupils enrolled in a primary school in the district of Merano generalizes Q, and is complete, from TCSs *(i)* and *(ii)*. If the purpose of Q was to retrieve a specific pupil (among the ideal answers to Q), then the answers to Q' are guaranteed to contain this pupil. Conversely, the query Q^- that retrieves all English learners enrolled in a primary school in the district of Merano specializes Q, and is also complete, from TCSs *(i)*, *(ii)* and *(iii)*. If the purpose of Q was to publish statistics (e.g., its number of answers), then partial statistics (e.g., the number of answers to Q restricted to English learners, a.k.a. Q^-) can already be published.

Previous work studied the problem of checking whether a conjunctive query (CQ) is complete wrt to a set of TCSs. In particular, it was shown in [12] that this problem can be reduced to the classical problem of query containment [2]. Then in [10], this same problem was reduced to reasoning in Datalog programs under answer-set semantics, extending the setting by considering the presence of keys, foreign keys, and finite domain constraints. We pursue this work by studying the two types of complete approximations (generalization and specialization) sketched above, still focusing on CQs.

Contributions. Among the complete CQs that generalize a CQ Q, we identify the most specific ones, which we call *Minimal Complete Generalizations* (MCGs). And we define the *Maximal Complete Specializations* (MCSs) of Q analogously. Our main contributions can be summarized as follows:

– We show that if Q admits an MCG, then it is unique up to query equivalence. To this end, we introduce a generalization operator that maps incomplete queries to "less" incomplete ones, and show that a fixed-point of this operator (modulo query equivalence) is a complete generalization. This yields an algorithm to compute an MCG. We also study the computational complexity of the corresponding decision problem.

– We show that there can be multiple MCSs, or (infinitely many) complete specializations but no maximal one. As a consequence, we restrict our search space for an MCS to queries of a given bounded size. For this latter problem, we first propose an algorithm that finds MCSs (if any) that can be obtained without adding any atom to Q, leveraging unification between the query under construction and atoms in TCSs. We then extend this idea to identify MCSs that may contain more atoms.
– We discuss implementation techniques for finding MSG and MCSs using forward rule application in Datalog and backward rule application in Prolog, respectively.

Due to space limitations, the paper contains only selected proofs and intuitions for theorems. A complete version can be found at: http://arxiv.org/abs/2407.20932.

Organization. In Sect. 2, we recall basic definitions from database theory and formally introduce the problem of query completeness and relevant characterization theorems. In Sects. 3 and 4, we discuss the generalization and specialization problems, respectively. Section 5 discusses corresponding implementation techniques.

2 Query Completeness

Preliminaries. We adopt standard notation from databases. We assume an infinite set each of relation symbols, constants, and variables. The constants make up the set dom (the *domain*). Terms are constants or variables. For variables, we use upper-case, for constants lower-case letters, tuples are indicated by an overline, like $\bar{c}$. For a relation symbol R with arity n, an *atom* is an expression $R(t_1, \ldots, t_n)$, where $t_1, \ldots, t_n$ are terms. A database *instance* D is a finite set of ground atoms (facts), that is, atoms that contain only constants. A *conjunctive query* (CQ) is written as $Q(\bar{u}) \leftarrow B$, where $Q(\bar{u})$ is an atom and B a conjunction of atoms. We call B the *body* of Q and $\bar{u}$ the *head terms*. A CQ is *safe* if all variables of $\bar{u}$ occur in B. Given a CQ $Q(\bar{u}) \leftarrow B$ and an instance D, a tuple $\alpha\bar{u}$ is an *answer* of Q over D, written $Q(D)$, if α is an assignment of variables from Q to dom such that $\alpha B \subseteq D$. A query Q is *contained* in a query Q', written $Q \sqsubseteq Q'$, if for every database instance D it holds that $Q(D) \subseteq Q'(D)$. We say that Q and Q' are *equivalent* if $Q \sqsubseteq Q'$ and $Q' \sqsubseteq Q$. The query Q is *strictly contained* in Q' if Q is contained in Q' and Q' is not equivalent to Q. If Q is contained in Q', then Q' is *more general* than Q, and Q is *more special* than Q'.

Completeness Theory. When stating that data is potentially incomplete, one must have a conceptual complete reference. We model an *incomplete database* in the style of [9] as a pair of database instances $\mathcal{D} = (D^i, D^a)$, where $D^a \subseteq D^i$. Here, D^i is called the *ideal* state and D^a the *available* state. In an application, the state stored in a DBMS is the available state, which often represents only a part of the facts that hold in reality. The facts holding in reality constitute the ideal state, which however is unknown.

Given a query Q and an incomplete database $\mathcal{D} = (D^i, D^a)$, we say that Q is *complete over* D if $Q(D^i) = Q(D^a)$ and we write $\mathcal{D} \models Compl(Q)$.

To specify that parts of a relation instance are complete, we introduce a kind of metadata, which we call *table completeness* (TC) statements (or TCS for short). A TCS, written $Compl(R(\bar{s}); G)$, has two components, a relational atom $R(\bar{s})$, where $\bar{s}$ is a tuple of terms, and (a possibly empty) conjunction of atoms G, called *condition*. Intuitively, a TC statement $Compl(R(\bar{s}); G)$ asserts that table R is complete for all tuples that match $\bar{s}$ and can be joined with G. We denote a TC statement generically as C.

To define the semantics of a TCS C, we associate to it a query $Q_C(\bar{s}) \leftarrow R(\bar{s}), G$. Then C is satisfied by $\mathcal{D} = (D^i, D^a)$, written $\mathcal{D} \models Compl(R(\bar{s}); G)$, if $Q_C(D^i) \subseteq R(D^a)$. This means that the ideal instance D^i is used to determine the tuples in the ideal instance $R(D^i)$ of R that match $\bar{s}$ and satisfy G, and that the statement C is satisfied if these tuples are present in the available version $R(D^a)$. If no TC statement is associated with a relation then we do not know anything about the completeness of that relation.

Let **C** be a set of TC statements. We say that **C** entails the completeness of Q, written $\mathbf{C} \models Compl(Q)$, if for every $\mathcal{D}$ it holds that $\mathcal{D} \models \mathbf{C}$ implies $\mathcal{D} \models Compl(Q)$.

Example 1. We consider a simplified database "schoolBolzano", modeling schools in the province of Bolzano. It consists of the three tables below:

$pupil(pname, code, sname)$, $school(sname, type, district)$, $learns(pname, lang)$.

The table *pupil* contains for each pupil the name, the class and the school the pupil attends. The table *school* records for each school the name, the type (e.g., primary or middle school), and its school district. Finally, the table *learns* records which pupil learns which language. Next, we assume the following completeness statements:

C_{sp}: $Compl(school(S, primary, D); true)$,
C_{pb}: $Compl(pupil(N, C, S); school(S, T, merano))$,
C_{enp}: $Compl(learns(N, english); pupil(N, C, S), school(S, primary, D))$.

The statements say that the database contains all primary schools (C_{sp}), all pupils attending a school in the district of Merano (C_{pb}), and all English learners that are pupils attending a primary school (C_{enp}).

For instance, let $D^a = \{school(goethe, primary, merano)\})$ and $D^i = D^a \cup \{pupil(john, 1, goethe)\}$. Then, $(D^i, D^a) \models C_{sp}$, but $(D^i, D^a) \not\models C_{pb}$.

Now consider the query for the "names of all pupils that attend a primary school in the district of Merano":

$$Q_{ppb}(N) \leftarrow pupil(N, C, S), school(S, primary, merano). \qquad (1)$$

Intuitively, the query is complete because our database contains all records of pupils from primary schools in the district of Merano (C_{pb}) and it contains all such schools (C_{sp}).

Alternatively, let us consider the query for "the names of all pupils that attend a primary school in the district of Merano and that learn some language":

$$Q_{pbl}(N) \leftarrow pupil(N,C,S), school(S, primary, merano), learns(N,L). \qquad (2)$$

This query is not complete since some language learners (of a language other than English) may be missing from the database. △

Reasoning about Query Completeness. To reason about completeness, we define for every set **C** of TC statements the operator $T_\mathbf{C}$ that maps database instances to database instances. If C is a TC statement about R, then we define

$$T_C(D) := \{R(\bar{t}) \mid \bar{t} \in Q_C(D)\} \quad \text{and} \quad T_\mathbf{C}(D) := \bigcup_{C \in \mathbf{C}} T_C(D). \qquad (3)$$

Since all queries Q_C are monotonic, the operator $T_\mathbf{C}$ is monotonic in that for any $D \subseteq D'$ it holds that $T_\mathbf{C}(D) \subseteq T_\mathbf{C}(D')$. Moreover, for every instance D, the pair $(D, T_\mathbf{C}(D))$ is an incomplete database that satisfies **C**, and $T_\mathbf{C}(D)$ is the smallest set (wrt set inclusion) for which this holds. Below we cite a proposition that summarizes the connection between the $T_\mathbf{C}$ operator and the satisfaction of the set **C** by a in incomplete database:

Proposition 2 ($T_\mathbf{C}$**Operator** [10, **Proposition 1**]). *Let **C** be a set of TC statements. Then*

- $T_\mathbf{C}(D) \subseteq D$, *for all database instances D;*
- $(D^i, D^a) \models \mathbf{C}$ *iff* $T_\mathbf{C}(D^i) \subseteq D^a$, *for all $D^a \subseteq D^i$.*

In [10] it has been shown that, similar to containment checking [2], completeness checking can be reduced to the question whether a test query returns a specific result over a test database. Below, we summarize that approach.

In what follows, we always consider a set of TC statements **C** and a conjunctive query Q defined by the rule $Q(\bar{u}) \leftarrow R_1(\bar{t}_1),\ldots,R_n(\bar{t}_n)$. We define the set of facts D_Q, which we call the *canonical database* of Q, obtained by freezing the atoms in the body of Q.[1] Thus,

$$D_Q = \{R_1(\theta\bar{t}_1),\ldots,R_n(\theta\bar{t}_n)\},$$

where θ is the substitution that maps each variable X to the "frozen version" θX of X.

To check whether Q is complete one applies $T_\mathbf{C}$ to D_Q and verifies whether Q can retrieve the frozen tuple of distinguished variables.

Theorem 3 (Characterization of Completeness [10, **Theorem 2**]**).** *Let **C** be a set of TC statements, and $Q(\bar{u}) \leftarrow B$ be a conjunctive query. Then*

$$\mathbf{C} \models Compl(Q) \quad \Longleftrightarrow \quad \theta\bar{u} \in Q(T_\mathbf{C}(D_Q)).$$

---

[1] "Freezing" variables is a well-known concept in logic programming and database theory, which allows one to treat a variable like a constant.

Example 4. We illustrate this theorem with our running example. Suppose $\mathcal{D} = (D^i, D^a)$ satisfies $\{C_{sp}, C_{pb}\}$. Consider an answer, say n', returned by Q_{ppb} over the ideal instance D^i. Then D^i contains two atoms of the form $pupil(n', c', s')$ and $school(s', primary, merano)$. Now, due to C_{sp}, also D^a contains $school(s', primary, merano)$, and due to C_{pb}, the atom $pupil(s', c', goethe)$ is in D^a, too. Consequently, Q_{ppb} returns n' also over D^a. Since D^i and D^a were arbitrary, this shows that $\{C_{sp}, C_{pb}\} \models Compl(Q_{ppb})$. △

Example 5 (Complete Generalizations and Specializations). We recall query $Q_{pbl}(N)$ that was incomplete given the assumptions. One way to obtain a more general query is to drop some of the query atoms (that is, to relax the query conditions). For instance, if we drop the *learns* atom we obtain the query

$$Q_{pbl}^{gen}(N) \leftarrow pupil(N, C, S), school(S, primary, merano),$$

which is identical to the query Q_{ppb} in (1), which we know is complete.

To obtain query specializations one can turn variables into constants or add new atoms to the body (or both). For instance, we observe that if in the query $Q_{pbl}(N)$ in (2) we replace $learns(N, L)$ with $learns(N, english)$ we obtain the query

$$Q_{pbl}^{spec}(N) \leftarrow pupil(N, C, S), school(S, primary, merano), learns(N, english),$$

which is complete, since C_{enp} guarantees completeness of the *learns*-atom. △

3 Query Generalization

In this section, we study the problem of finding a complete generalization of a (possibly incomplete) query. We restrict our scope to the case where all queries (input query and generalizations) are CQs.

First, we rephrase in our formalism the well-known characterization of containment among conjunctive queries due to Chandra and Merlin [2].

Proposition 6 (Characterization of Containment). *Let* $Q(\bar{u}) \leftarrow B$ *and* $Q'(\bar{u}') \leftarrow B'$ *be conjunctive queries. Then*

$$Q \sqsubseteq Q' \iff \theta\bar{u} \in Q'(D_Q).$$

The proposition holds because Q is contained in Q' iff there exists a homomorphism δ from Q' to Q. Such a δ can be seen as an assignment of constants and variables in D_Q to the variables in Q' that satisfies Q' and returns the tuple of head terms $\theta\bar{u}$ of Q.

We say that a query Q' is a *complete generalization* of Q wrt a set of TC statements **C** if Q' is more general than Q and Q' is complete wrt **C**.

Definition 7 (Minimal Complete Generalization). *A query* Q' *is a minimal complete generalization (MCG) of Q wrt a set of TC statements **C** if:*

– Q' is a complete generalization of Q wrt $\mathbf{C}$, and
– it is a minimal one, that is, there exists no query Q'' such that Q'' is a complete generalization of Q and Q'' is strictly contained in Q'.

Computing Minimal Complete Generalizations. In the following we investigate properties of MCGs. We first show that in our search for MCGs of Q it is sufficient to concentrate on *subqueries* of Q, that is, (safe) queries obtained by dropping some atoms from the body of Q. Note that if Q_0 is a subquery of Q, then Q is contained in Q_0. More specifically, we will show the following proposition.

Proposition 8 (MCGs are Subqueries). *Let $\mathbf{C}$ be a set of TC statements, Q a conjunctive query, and Q' a complete generalization of Q wrt $\mathbf{C}$. Then there exists a subquery Q_0 of Q such that $Q_0 \sqsubseteq Q'$ and Q_0 is a complete generalization of Q.*

For our proof we rely on the properties of minimal conjunctive queries. We remind the reader that Q is *minimal* if all its subqueries are strictly more general that Q, or, in other words, if Q does not have redundant atoms. This means that for any subquery Q_0 obtained from Q by dropping some of the atoms in Q it holds that $Q_0 \not\sqsubseteq Q$. Every conjunctive query is equivalent to a minimal query [2].

If $Q(\bar{u}) \leftarrow B$ is a query, and α a substitution, then with αQ we denote the query $\tilde{Q}(\alpha \bar{u}) \leftarrow \alpha B$. We call αQ an *instantiation* of Q.

Next we identify properties of minimal queries that we use later in the proofs. In particular, we show that a minimal query Q is complete iff the image of the frozen query D_Q under $T_\mathbf{C}$ comprises all of D_Q. Moreover we show that any instantiation of a complete minimal query is again complete.

Lemma 9 (Completeness of Minimal Queries). *Let $\mathbf{C}$ be a set of TC statements, $Q(\bar{u}) \leftarrow B$ a minimal conjunctive query, and α a substitution. Then*

1. $\mathbf{C} \models Compl(Q) \iff D_Q \subseteq T_\mathbf{C}(D_Q)$;
2. $\mathbf{C} \models Compl(Q) \implies \mathbf{C} \models Compl(\alpha Q)$.

Proof. Claim 1. ($\Leftarrow$) This direction holds for all conjunctive queries: if $D_Q \subseteq T_\mathbf{C}(D_Q)$, then the freezing mapping θ trivially satisfies $\theta B \subseteq D_Q$, hence, θ is an assignment that satisfies B over D_Q and returns $\theta \bar{u}$ as an answer. Thus, $\theta \bar{u} \in Q(D_Q) \subseteq Q(T_\mathbf{C}(D_Q))$, so that Q is complete wrt $\mathbf{C}$ according to Theorem 3.

($\Rightarrow$) Let $\tilde{B}$ be the set of atoms obtained by unfreezing $T_\mathbf{C}(D_Q)$, that is, $\tilde{B} = \theta^{-1} T_\mathbf{C}(D_Q)$, and define $\tilde{Q}$ by the rule $\tilde{Q}(\bar{u}) \leftarrow \tilde{B}$. Note that $\tilde{Q}$ is a subquery of Q. Since Q is complete, Theorem 3 implies that $\theta \bar{u} \in Q(T_\mathbf{C}(D_Q))$. It follows that all variables in $\bar{u}$ occur in $\tilde{B}$ so that the query $\tilde{Q}(\bar{u}) \leftarrow \tilde{B}$ is safe. It also follows that $\theta \bar{u} \in Q(\theta \tilde{B}) = Q(D_{\tilde{Q}})$, which by Proposition 6 entails that $\tilde{Q} \sqsubseteq Q$. However, as Q is minimal, this is only possible if $B = \tilde{B}$, so that $D_Q = \theta B = \theta \tilde{B} = T_\mathbf{C}(D_Q)$.

Claim 2. Since the "$\Leftarrow$" direction of Claim 1 holds for all CQs, it suffices to show that $D_{\alpha Q} \subseteq T_\mathbf{C}(D_{\alpha Q})$, which amounts to showing $\theta \alpha B \subseteq T_\mathbf{C}(\theta \alpha B)$. To this end, let $R(\bar{t})$ be an atom of B. Then $R(\theta \bar{t}) = \theta R(\bar{t}) \in T_\mathbf{C}(\theta B)$ by Claim 1.

This is only possible if there exists a TC statement $C = \mathrm{Compl}(R(\bar{s}); G)$ that is applicable to $\theta R(\bar{t})$. Applicability implies there is an assignment β such that $R(\beta\bar{s}) = R(\theta\bar{t})$ and $\beta G \subseteq \theta B$.

We can use C also to map $\theta\alpha R(\bar{t}) = R(\theta\alpha\bar{t})$ from $\theta\alpha B$, using instead of β the assignment $\theta\alpha\theta^{-1}\beta$. This new assignment essentially instantiates β by α, but also unfreezes the frozen variables introduced by β and finally freezes again all variables.

With this assignment we have $R(\theta\alpha\theta^{-1}\beta\bar{s}) = R(\theta\alpha\theta^{-1}\theta\bar{t}) = R(\theta\alpha\bar{t}) \in \theta\alpha B$. Moreover, since $\beta G \subseteq \theta B$, we also have $\theta\alpha\theta^{-1}\beta G \subseteq \theta\alpha\theta^{-1}\theta B = \theta\alpha B$. Consequentely, C is applicable to $\theta\alpha R(\bar{t})$ in $\theta\alpha B$ and $\theta\alpha R(\bar{t}) \in \theta\alpha B = D_\alpha Q$. □

Note that Claim 2 does not hold for non-minimal queries. For example, for the non-minimal query $Q(X) \leftarrow R(X,a), R(X,Y)$, the TCS $C = \mathrm{Compl}(R(X,a); true)$, and the substitution $\alpha = \{Y \mapsto c\}$ we have that $\{C\} \models \mathrm{Compl}(Q)$, but $\{C\} \not\models \mathrm{Compl}(\alpha Q)$.

Now, we are ready to prove that it suffices to concentrate on subqueries when looking for MCGs.

Proof of Proposition 8. Consider a conjunctive query $Q(\bar{u}) \leftarrow B$ and a complete generalisation $Q'(\bar{u}') \leftarrow B'$ of Q. Since every conjunctive query is equivalent to a minimal one and a query equivalent to a complete one is also complete, we assume without loss of generality that Q' is minimal.

Since $Q \sqsubseteq Q'$, there exists a query homomorphism δ from Q' to Q. Let $B_0 = \delta B$ and define Q_0 as $Q_0(\bar{X}) \leftarrow B_0$. Then $Q_0 = \delta Q'$ and using Claim 2 of Lemma 9 we conclude that Q_0 is complete.

Since Q_0 is a subquery of Q, we have $Q \sqsubseteq Q_0$. Moreover, since Q' is minimal and δ is a substitution with $Q_0 = \delta Q'$, we have $Q_0 \sqsubseteq Q'$. □

While Proposition 8 leaves us with all subqueries of Q as candidates for MCGs, we can still do better. We will modify the monotonic $T_\mathbf{C}$ operator on database instances to a monotonic operator $G_\mathbf{C}$ on queries. This will allow us to characterize completeness in terms of fixed points. We will then conclude that MCGs are least fixed points, are unique up to equivalence, and can be computed by fixed point iteration.

First we define the *generalization operator* $G_\mathbf{C}$. To make the mathematics in this section work, we consider *generalized conjunctive queries* $Q(\bar{u}) \leftarrow B$, where we give up the safety condition that every head variable (that is, every variable occurring in $\bar{u}$) also occurs in B. As for conjunctive queries, the set of answers of a generalized conjunctive query Q over an instance D is defined as $Q(D) = \{\alpha\bar{u} \mid \alpha B \subseteq D\}$, where α ranges over all assignments of domain values to variables of Q. Note that if Q is unsafe, that is, Q has a head variable not occurring in B, D is an instance, and α satisfies Q over D, then for every domain value c the modified assignment $\alpha[x/c]$ also satisfies Q over D. Consequently, an unsafe query can have an infinite answer set. Clearly, unsafe queries are not of practical interest, but are needed for the mathematical development.

For a set of TC statements **C** we define the operator $G_\mathbf{C}$ as follows. If $Q(\bar u) \leftarrow B$ is a generalized conjunctive query, then the query $G_\mathbf{C}(Q)$ is computed in four steps:

1. freeze B to obtain the database instance D_Q,
2. compute $D'_Q := T_\mathbf{C}(D_Q)$,
3. unfreeze D'_Q to obtain a set of atoms $B' \subseteq B$,
4. finally, set $G_\mathbf{C}(Q) := Q'$ where $Q'(\bar u) \leftarrow B'$.

Since $D'_Q = T_\mathbf{C}(D_Q) \subseteq D_Q$, it follows that $B' \subseteq B$. Thus, $G_\mathbf{C}(Q)$ is a subquery of Q. Intuitively, $G_\mathbf{C}$ keeps only those atoms of a query body that are "complete" wrt **C**. Note that even if Q is safe, $G_\mathbf{C}(Q)$ may be unsafe.

Now we point out properties of the $G_\mathbf{C}$ operator that will help us answer the questions about MCGs posed above. We first observe that the completeness characterization in Theorem 3 can be reformulated in terms of fixed points (modulo equivalence) of $G_\mathbf{C}$.

Proposition 10 (Complete Queries are Fixed Points of $G_C(Q)$). *Let* **C** *be a set of TC statements and Q, Q' be generalized conjunctive queries. Then,*

1. $Q \sqsubseteq Q' \implies G_\mathbf{C}(Q) \sqsubseteq G_\mathbf{C}(Q')$;
2. $\mathbf{C} \models \mathrm{Compl}(Q) \iff Q \equiv G_\mathbf{C}(Q)$.

Proof Idea. Claim 1 can be shown using the fact that the containment "$Q \sqsubseteq Q'$" implies the existence of a homomorphism δ from Q' to Q such that $\delta Q' \subseteq Q$ [2]. For each atom $A \in Q'$, if $A \in T_\mathbf{C}(D_{Q'})$ then $\theta \delta A \in T_\mathbf{C}(D_Q)$. Thus, δ is also a homomorphism from $G_\mathbf{C}(Q')$ to $G_\mathbf{C}(Q)$.

To see Claim 2, note that the characterizing condition for completeness in Theorem 3, "$\theta \bar u \in Q(T_\mathbf{C}(D_Q))$," is equivalent to the existence of a query homomorphism from Q to $G_\mathbf{C}(Q)$ and thus to the containment $G_\mathbf{C}(Q) \sqsubseteq Q$. Since, according to Claim 1, the converse containment $Q \sqsubseteq G_\mathbf{C}(Q)$ holds anyway, this yields Claim 2. □

We are now in a position to prove that there is at most one MCG. As the proof solely applies simple principles of order theory, we first fix a suitable vocabulary. We remind the reader that a *preorder* is a reflexive and transitive binary relation $\preceq$ on some set S. A *least element* of S is an $l \in S$ such that $l \preceq s$ for all $s \in S$ (note that S may admit several least elements). The *equivalence relation* $\approx$ *induced by* $\preceq$ is defined over S by $s \approx s'$ iff $s \preceq s'$ and $s' \preceq s$. A function $f: S \to S$ is *monotonic* if $f(s) \preceq f(s')$ whenever $s \preceq s'$. An element $s \in S$ is a *fixed point of f modulo* $\approx$ if $f(s) \approx s$. With f^0 we denote the identity function on S while f^i, where $i > 0$, denotes the $(i-1)$-fold composition of f with itself. The following lemma is folklore, but is usually expressed for orders (that is, antisymmetric preorders), so we write it up explicitly for the sake of self-containment:

Lemma 11 (Least Fixed Points). *Let S be a finite set with preorder $\preceq$ and a least element $\bot$, and let $f: S \to S$ be a monotonic function. Then*

1. f has a least fixed point p_0 modulo $\approx$, and
2. $p_0 = f^k(\bot)$, where $k = \min\{i \mid f^{i+1}(\bot) \preceq f^i(\bot)\}$.

Proof. Since $\bot$ is a least element, $\bot \preceq f(\bot)$. Because f is monotonic, this implies $f(\bot) \preceq f(f(\bot))$. Inductively, we conclude that $f^i(\bot) \preceq f^{i+1}(\bot)$ for all $i \geq 0$. Next, because S is finite, the sequence $f^i(\bot)$ must enter a loop. So there exists a least $k \geq 0$ such that $f^{k+1}(\bot) \preceq f^k(\bot)$. Together with the fact that $f^k(\bot) \preceq f^{k+1}(\bot)$, this implies that $f^k(\bot) \approx f^{k+1}(\bot)$, therefore $p_0 = f^k(\bot)$ is a fixed point modulo $\approx$.

Let p be another fixed point modulo $\approx$. Then $\bot \preceq p$, and consequently (since f is monotonic), $p_0 = f^k(\bot) \preceq f^k(p) \approx p$. So p_0 is a least fixed point modulo $\approx$. □

We can use Lemma 11 to rephrase Proposition 10, using the operator $G_\mathbf{C}$ as the function f, and leveraging the fact that containment is a preorder on CQs. Precisely, for a given Q, we denote the set of subqueries of Q, including those that are not safe, as Sub_Q. Clearly, Sub_Q is finite, containment is a preorder on Sub_Q (whose induced equivalence relation is query equivalence), Q is a least element of Sub_Q, and $G_\mathbf{C}$ is a monotonic function on Sub_Q. Thus, all prerequisites of Lemma 11 are satisfied and we conclude the following proposition.

Proposition 12. *Let Q be a conjunctive query and $\mathbf{C}$ be a set of TC statements. Then*

(a) $G_\mathbf{C}$ *has a least fixed point (modulo $\equiv$) $\tilde{Q}$ in Sub_Q ;*
(b) $\tilde{Q}$ *is complete;*
(c) $\tilde{Q} = G_\mathbf{C}^n(Q)$ *where n is less or equal than the number of atoms in Q;*
(d) *if Q' is any complete generalization of Q, then $\tilde{Q} \sqsubseteq Q'$;*
(e) *if $\tilde{Q}$ is safe, then $\tilde{Q}$ is the MCG of Q wrt $\mathbf{C}$,
    otherwise no complete generalisation of Q wrt $\mathbf{C}$ exists.*

Proof. Claim (a) immediately follows from Lemma 11, while Claim (b) holds because fixed points of $G_\mathbf{C}$ are complete (by Proposition 10). Claim (c) holds because the application of $G_\mathbf{C}$ to an incomplete query causes the removal of at least one atom. Claim (d) holds, since by Proposition 8, every complete generalization of Q has some complete query $Q_0 \in Sub_Q$ as a subquery, and by Proposition 10, $\tilde{Q}$ is contained in every complete query $Q_0 \in Sub_Q$. Finally, if $\tilde{Q}$ is not safe, then there is no safe subquery of Q that is complete, and therefore no complete generalisation of Q. Hence, Claim (e) holds. □

A possible algorithm suggested by Proposition 12 would repeatedly apply the $G_\mathbf{C}$ operator to Q, producing a sequence of subqueries $Q_i = G_\mathbf{C}^i(Q)$, and stop when $Q_{i+1} \sqsubseteq Q_i$. Alternatively, the termination condition could be a check that Q_i is complete. A third possibility (used below in Algorithm 1) is to stop when $Q_{i+1} = Q_i$, that is, when $G_\mathbf{C}$ does not remove any atom from Q_i. The following result shows that this is correct.

Proposition 13. *Let Q be a CQ, $\mathbf{C}$ be a set of TC statements, and $Q_i = G_{\mathbf{C}}{}^i(Q)$ for $i \geq 0$. If $Q_{i+1} \equiv Q_i$, then Q_i is a least fixed point of $G_{\mathbf{C}}$ modulo $\equiv$ in Sub_Q.*

Proof. By Proposition 12, repeatedly applying $G_{\mathbf{C}}$ to Q leads to a first Q_k that is a fixed point modulo $\equiv$, this query Q_k is a least fixed point modulo $\equiv$, and $Q_j \equiv Q_k$ for each $j \geq k$. If $Q_i \equiv Q_{i+1}$, then $i \geq k$, so $Q_i \equiv Q_k$, therefore Q_i is also a least fixed point modulo $\equiv$. □

Generalization Algorithm. Following Proposition 12, we construct Algorithm 1, which computes an MCG for a query Q and TCSs C.

Algorithm 1: Computes an MCG if one exists

Input : query $Q(\bar{u}) \leftarrow B$, set of TCSs $\mathbf{C}$
Output: MCG of Q if one exists; otherwise null
$Q_{old} := Q$, $Q_{new} = G_{\mathbf{C}}(Q)$;
while Q_{new} is safe and $Q_{new} \not\equiv Q_{old}$ **do**
  | $Q_{old} := Q_{new}$
  | $Q_{new} := G_{\mathbf{C}}(Q_{old})$
if Q_{new} is not safe **then**
  | **return** null
else
  | **return** Q_{new}

Computational Complexity. We study two decision problems related to generalizing a (possibly) incomplete CQ. The first problem estimates the cost of the $G_{\mathbf{C}}$ operator. We show that this problem is complete for the complexity class DP, which intuitively consists of all problems that can be decided by an algorithm that performs two calls to an NP-oracle: the algorithm responds "yes" if the first oracle call returns "yes" and the second one returns "no".

Proposition 14. *For a set $\mathbf{C}$ of TC statements and two CQs Q and Q', deciding whether $Q' \equiv G_{\mathbf{C}}(Q)$ is DP-complete.*

Our second decision problem estimates the cost of computing an MCG. We show that this problem is in P^{NP}, which is the class of problems that can be decided in polynomial time by a Turing machine that uses an NP-oracle. We do not know whether the problem is also P^{NP}-hard.

Proposition 15. *For a set $\mathbf{C}$ of TC statements and two CQs Q and Q', deciding whether Q' is an MCG of Q wrt $\mathbf{C}$ is in P^{NP}.*

Proof sketch. In order to decide whether Q' is an MCG of Q, it is sufficient to execute Algorithm 1, check whether the output query Q_{new} is null, and if it is not, determine whether $Q_{new} \equiv Q'$. The latter can be done with a call to an NP oracle, since equivalence of CQs is known to be in NP (and the size of Q_{new} is bounded by the size of Q).

Next, we observe that Algorithm 1 performs a number of iterations that is linear in the size of Q (because the $G_\mathbf{C}$ operator intuitively discards atoms from the body of its input query). So to complete the proof, it is sufficient to observe that each of these iterations can be executed in linear time, assuming an NP oracle. More precisely, for any query Q_{old}, the query $G_\mathbf{C}(Q_{old})$ can be computed by retaining certain atoms in the body B of Q_{old}: retain an atom A' iff there is a TCS $Compl(A; G)$ in $\mathbf{C}$ and a substitution α such that $\alpha A = A'$ and $\alpha G \subseteq B$. Deciding the existence of such a substitution is in NP, because *(i)* the size of α is bounded by the size of G (so it can be encoded as a certificate with polynomial length), and *(ii)* "$\alpha A = A'$" and "$\alpha G \subseteq B$" can be trivially verified in polynomial time. □

4 Query Specialization

As discussed in the introduction, another common way to approximate a query is to make it more specific. Analogously to the previous section, we study the existence and computation of CQs that specialize Q and are complete wrt a set of TCSs. As in the preceding section, all queries mentioned are assumed to be conjunctive queries.

We say that Q' is a *complete specialization* (CS) of Q wrt a set $\mathbf{C}$ of TCSs if $Q' \sqsubseteq Q$ and $\mathbf{C} \models Compl(Q')$. Among those queries, the preferred ones are the *maximal* ones:

Definition 16 (Maximal Complete Specialization). *A query Q' is a maximal complete specialization (MCS) of Q wrt a set $\mathbf{C}$ of TCSs if:*

- *Q' is a CS of Q wrt $\mathbf{C}$, and*
- *it is a maximal one, that is, there exists no query Q'' such that Q'' is a CS of Q, and Q' is strictly contained in Q''.*

Even though the definition of an MCS is symmetric to the one of an MCG, it turns out that there are important differences between these two settings, requiring different approaches. First, a query may have several non-equivalent MCSs (whereas it admits at most one MCG up to equivalence). Second, a query may admit CSs but no MCS:

Theorem 17 (MCGs May not Exist). *There are a set $\mathbf{C}$ of TCSs and an incomplete query Q, such that Q admits infinitely many CSs, none of which is maximal.*

Proof. Consider a schema with a binary relation *edge*, and let C be the TCS $Compl(edge(X,Y); edge(Y,Z))$. The boolean query $Q() \leftarrow edge(X,Y)$, which intuitively checks for the existence of an edge, is not complete wrt $\{C\}$. To see this, consider for instance the incomplete database $\mathcal{D} = (D^i, D^a)$ where $D^i = \{edge(b,c)\}$ and $D^a = \emptyset$. The database $\mathcal{D}$ trivially satisfies C, because

$Q_C(D^i) = \emptyset$. However, $Q(D^i) = \{()\}$, whereas $Q(D^a) = \emptyset$, therefore $Q(D^i) \not\sqsubseteq Q(D^a)$. Observe also that Q admits CSs wrt $\{C\}$, for instance the query $Q_2() \leftarrow edge(X,Y), edge(Y,X)$.

Now let Q' be any complete specialization of Q wrt $\{C\}$. Because Q' is complete, its body must contain a set $\mathcal{A}_k$ of atoms that form a cycle of length k for some $k \geq 1$, having the form $\mathcal{A}_k = \{edge(X_0, X_1), edge(X_1, X_2), \ldots, edge(X_{k-1}, X_0)\}$. Let k' be the largest k for which this holds (that is, k' is the size of the largest cycle in Q'), and consider the query $Q_{2k'}() \leftarrow \mathcal{A}_{2k'}$. This query is also a complete specialization of Q. Moreover, the function $\delta_{k'}$ that maps each X_i to $X_{i \bmod k'}$ is a homomorphism from $Q_{2k'}$ to Q', which implies $Q' \sqsubseteq Q_{2k'}$. However, $\mathcal{A}_{k'}$ cannot be mapped to $\mathcal{A}_{2k'}$, therefore there is no homomorphism from Q' to $Q_{2k'}$, which implies $Q_{2k'} \not\sqsubseteq Q'$. So Q' is not an MCS. □

These observations lead us to investigate restrictions on a set $\mathbf{C}$ of TCSs that guarantee finiteness of the set of MCSs of a query wrt $\mathbf{C}$. We define the *dependency graph* of $\mathbf{C}$ as the graph whose nodes are the relation names appearing in $\mathbf{C}$, and with an edge from R to R' iff R' appears in G for some statement of the form $Compl(A; G)$, where the atom A is over R. We say that $\mathbf{C}$ is *acyclic* if its dependency graph is acyclic. The following result provides an upper bound on the size of an MCS for such a $\mathbf{C}$.

Theorem 18. *Let Q be a CQ, $\mathbf{C}$ an acyclic set of TCSs and s the number of relation names that appear in $\mathbf{C}$. Then the number of atoms in a MCS of Q wrt $\mathbf{C}$ is in $\mathcal{O}(|Q| \times |\mathbf{C}|^{s+1})$.*[2]

In the rest of this section, we show how to compute the CSs of Q that are maximal (wrt $\sqsubseteq$) within the space of queries with at most $|Q| + k$ atoms, for some $k \in \mathbb{N}$. We call such a query a k-MCS. Theorem 18 implies that, if $\mathbf{C}$ is acyclic, then MCSs and k-MCSs coincide for a large enough k. We also restrict our investigations to the case where Q is a minimal query in the sense of Lemma 9, that is Q has no redundant atoms.

We first analyze how to compute MCSs without adding atoms to the body of Q (we call such MCSs maximal complete instantiations, defined below), and we then extend this approach to finding k-MCSs.

4.1 Maximal Complete Instantiations

Definition 19 (Maximal Complete Instantiation). *If $\mathbf{C}$ is a set of TCSs, then a maximal complete instantiation (MCI) of Q wrt $\mathbf{C}$ is an instantiation of Q that is complete wrt $\mathbf{C}$ and maximal wrt containent among these instantiations.*

As an illustration, in the proof sketch of Theorem 17, the query $Q'(X) \leftarrow edge(X,X)$ is the only MCI for Q wrt $\mathbf{C}$.

Our approach to compute MCIs revolves around a specific type of substitution that we call a *complete unifier*, defined as follows:

---

[2] This acyclicity requirement on $\mathbf{C}$ can be relaxed, while guaranteeing a bound on the size of an MCS. In particular, it is sufficient to require that $\mathbf{C}$ is *weakly acyclic*, as defined in [3].

Definition 20 (Complete Unifier). *Let Q be a CQ and $\mathbf{C}$ a set of TCSs. A complete unifier for Q and $\mathbf{C}$ is a substitution γ such that, for each atom A in the body of Q, there is a TCS $C = Compl(A'; G) \in \mathbf{C}$ that satisfies*

$$\gamma A = \gamma A' \quad \text{and} \quad \gamma G \subseteq \gamma B.$$

Applying a complete unifier to Q yields a complete query:

Proposition 21. *If γ is a complete unifier for a query Q and a set $\mathbf{C}$ of TCSs, then $\mathbf{C} \models Compl(\gamma Q)$.*

Example 22. In Example 1, the substitution $\gamma = \{L \mapsto english\}$ is a complete unifier for Q_{pbl} and the set of TCSs, and $\gamma Q_{pbl} = Q_{pbl}^{spec}$ is indeed complete. △

Theorem 23. *Let $\mathbf{C}$ be a set of TCSs, let Q be a query, and Q' be a complete instantiation of Q wrt $\mathbf{C}$. Then there is a complete unifier γ for Q and $\mathbf{C}$ such that $Q' \sqsubseteq \gamma Q$.*

Example 22 (continued). Let $Q'(N) \leftarrow pupil(N, 1, S), school(S, primary, merano), learns(N, english)$. Then Q' is a complete instantiation of Q_{pbl} and $Q' \sqsubseteq \gamma Q_{pbl}$. △

Observe that if γ is a complete unifier for Q and $\mathbf{C}$, then there must be a subset $\mathbf{C}'$ of $\mathbf{C}$ such that γ is a complete unifier for Q and every atom A in Q is unified with the head of exactly one TCS from $\mathbf{C}'$. We call such a $\mathbf{C}'$ a *matching subset* of $\mathbf{C}$ for Q. Since Q and $\mathbf{C}'$ admit a complete unifier, they admit a (unique) most general one. Let $mgu(Q, \mathbf{C}')$ denote this unifier, and let $mgu(Q, 2^{\mathbf{C}}) = \{mgu(Q, \mathbf{C}') \mid \mathbf{C}'$ is a matching subset of $\mathbf{C}$ for Q, Q and $\mathbf{C}'$ admit a complete unifier$\}$. Since $\mathbf{C}$ is finite, $mgu(Q, 2^{\mathbf{C}})$ is finite, too. As an immediate consequence of Theorem 23 and Proposition 21, each MCI of Q wrt $\mathbf{C}$ is equivalent to γQ for some $\gamma \in mgu(Q, 2^{\mathbf{C}})$. This is the rationale behind our procedure to compute all MCIs of Q wrt $\mathbf{C}$ described in Algorithm 2. The first loop computes $\{\gamma Q \mid \gamma \in mgu(Q, 2^{\mathbf{C}})\}$, relying on a function MGU that returns $mgu(Q, \mathbf{C}')$ if it exists, and null otherwise. The second loop discards non-maximal instantiations within these.

Computational Complexity of the MCI Decision Problem. We study the problem that consists in deciding whether a query is an MCI.

Theorem 24. *Given a query Q, a candidate query Q' and a set $\mathbf{C}$ of TCSs, deciding whether Q' is an MCI of Q wrt $\mathbf{C}$ is in Π_2^P.*

Proof sketch. We show that a non-deterministic Turing machine can verify in polynomial time that Q' is *not* an MCI, assuming an oracle for NP, as follows:

Algorithm 2: Computes Maximal Complete Instantiations

Input : a query $Q(\bar{u}) \leftarrow A_1, \ldots, A_n$, a set $\mathbf{C}$ of TCSs
Output: the set S of all MCIs of Q wrt $\mathbf{C}$

1   $S := \emptyset$, $\gamma := \texttt{null}$
2   **foreach** *matching subset $\mathbf{C}'$ of $\mathbf{C}$ for Q* **do**
3 | $\gamma := \texttt{MGU}(Q, \mathbf{C}')$
4 | **if** $\gamma \neq \texttt{null}$ **then**
5 | | $S := S \cup \{\gamma Q\}$
6   **foreach** Q' *in* S **do**
7 | **if** *there exists* $Q'' \in S$ *such that* $Q' \sqsubseteq \{Q\}''$ **then** $S := S \setminus \{Q'\}$
8   **return** S

(I) determine whether Q' is complete,
(II) if it is, then determine whether it is also an instantiation of Q,
(III) if it is, then verify that there is a more general complete instantiation of Q.

For Step (I), it was show in [12] that deciding whether a CQ is complete wrt to a set of TCSs is NP-complete. Therefore one can determine whether Q' is complete with one call to an NP oracle.

For Step (II), similarly, we show that deciding whether Q' is an instantiation of Q is in NP. Observe that Q' is an instantiation of Q iff there is a substitution α such that $Q' = \alpha Q$. If such a substitution exists, then it is a function from the variables that appear in Q to the variables and constants that appear in Q'. So α can be encoded as a certificate with length polynomial in the size of Q and Q'. And given α, one can (trivially) verify in polynomial time that $Q' = \alpha Q$.

For Step (III), it is sufficient to verify that there exists a substitution β such that *(i)* βQ is complete, *(ii)* $Q' \sqsubseteq \beta Q$ and *(iii)* $\beta Q \not\sqsubseteq Q'$. Again, such a substitution can be encoded as a certificate with polynomial length. Next, as we explained above for Step (I), whether *(i)* holds can be determined (therefore also verified) with one call to an NP oracle. And it is well-known that containment of CQs is in NP, therefore *(ii)* and *(iii)* can also be verified by calling such an oracle (note that a quantifier alternation is only needed here for *(iii)*, which is in co-NP, whereas *(i)* and *(ii)* are in NP). □

It is not hard to show (using a similar technique as for Proposition 14) that deciding the MCI problem is DP-hard. Whether it is Π_2^P-complete is an open question.

4.2 Adding Atoms

We now extend our approach to computing all k-MCSs of a query $Q(\bar{u}) \leftarrow B$ of size n wrt a set $\mathbf{C}$ of TCSs. The key idea is to proceed in three steps: first, we create candidate queries that are as general as possible; second, we apply Algorithm 2 to compute all maximal complete instantiations of the candidate queries; finally, we discard all queries that are not maximal.

Let $\Sigma_{\mathbf{C}}$ be the set of all relation names appearing in $\mathbf{C}$. The candidate queries are *extensions* of Q obtained by adding a "fresh" set of atoms with relation symbols from $\Sigma_{\mathbf{C}}$ to the body of Q. A set of atoms is *fresh* if the arguments of each atom are pairwise distinct variables that do not appear in Q and no two atoms share common variables.

The question is how big a fresh set we have to add to guarantee that we capture all MCSs of Q with up to $n+k$ atoms. Suppose $Q'(\bar{v}) \leftarrow B'$ is such a MCS of Q. Our goal is to create an extension Q^+ of Q so that Q' is a MCI of Q^+.

Because Q' is a specialisation of Q, there is a homomorphism δ from Q to Q'. Let $B^- := B' \setminus \delta B$ be the set atoms in B' that have no preimage under δ. Thus, Q' can be written as $Q'(\bar{v}) \leftarrow \delta B, B^-$. In the most extreme case, δ maps all atoms of B to the same atom of B', so that the size of B^- is between k and $k+n-1$.

From B^- we construct $\tilde{B}$ as a fresh set of atoms that we obtain by keeping the relation symbols and replacing the arguments with new variables. Then $B^- = \eta \tilde{B}$ for a suitable substitution η. Next, we define $Q^+(\bar{u}) \leftarrow B, \tilde{B}$ as a query whose body consists of the body of Q and a fresh version of B^-. By this construction, Q' is an instantiation of Q^+, since δB is an instance of B via δ and B^- is an instance of $\tilde{B}$ via η.

This shows that we capture all k-MCSs of Q if we follow these three steps and test all extensions of Q by fresh sets of up to $k+n-1$ atoms. Algorithm 3 implements this idea. The first loop combines the two initial steps and the function $\mathtt{MCI}_{\leq n+k}(Q^+, \mathbf{C})$ returns the MCIs of Q^+ wrt $\mathbf{C}$ of size $\leq n+k$. Then the second loop performs the third step by discarding the non-maximal instantiations.

Algorithm 3: Computes k-MCSs

Input : a query $Q(\bar{u}) \leftarrow B$, a set $\mathbf{C}$ of TCSs , $k \in \mathbb{N}_0$
Output: the set $\mathcal{S}$ of all k-MCSs of Q wrt $\mathbf{C}$

1 $\mathcal{S} := \emptyset$
2 **foreach** *fresh set $\tilde{B}$ of atoms of size $n+k-1$ over $\Sigma_{\mathbf{C}}$* **do**
3 $\quad$ construct $Q^+(\bar{u}) \leftarrow B, \tilde{B}$
4 $\quad$ $\mathcal{S} := \mathcal{S} \cup \mathtt{MCI}_{\leq n+k}(Q^+, \mathbf{C})$
5 **foreach** Q' *in* $\mathcal{S}$ **do**
6 $\quad$ **if** *exists* $Q'' \in \mathcal{S}$ *such that* $Q' \sqsubseteq Q''$ **then** $\mathcal{S} := \mathcal{S} \setminus \{Q'\}$
7 **return** $\mathcal{S}$

---

5 Implementation

We now briefly discuss how we chose platforms to implement our algorithms in the demo tool MAGIK [13].

Implementing Generalization. At its core the generalization algorithm repeatedly applies the $G_{\mathbf{C}}$ operator to the database instance D_Q until it has reached a fixed point. In each round, starting from an instance of the size of the query, a new instance is produced by applying TC statements in a forward fashion, until original and new instance are identical. We implemented this via a datalog engine, namely the ASP solver dlv. The instance D_Q is represented by facts, initially obtained by freezing the query, and the TC statements are translated into TC rules.

For example, the query $Q_{ppb}(N)$ would be translated into the facts $pupil^i(n', c', s')$, and $school^i(s', primary, merano)$, while the statement C_{pb} would be translated into the rule $pupil^a(N, C, S) \leftarrow pupil^i(N, C, S), school^i(S, T, merano))$. To distinguish original and new atoms, the relation symbols are either labeled with the superscript ^{i}, standing for "ideal", or ^{a}, standing for "available". A fixed point is reached if each "ideal" fact is translated into an "available" fact.

While the ASP functionality is not used here, it becomes beneficial when taking account of disjunctive constraints such as finite domain constraints.

Implementing Specialization. The core operation of the specialization algorithm in Sect. 4 is unification, which makes ASP systems unsuitable as a platform while it is offered as a functionality by Prolog. We implemented it in SWI-Prolog. The problem is inherently hard, due to the doubly exponential search space.

For instance, let us consider the query $Q_l \leftarrow learns(N, L)$, and the set of TCSs from our running example, minus the TCS C_{pb}, and extended with $Compl(pupil(N, C, S); class(C, S, L, halfDay))$ and $Compl(pupil(N, C, S); class(C, S, L, fullDay))$. The search for all 3-MCSs would run out of memory.[3]

To avoid this we implemented several optimizations.[4] Briefly, to compute k-MCSs, we consider extensions of size 0, then $1, 2, \ldots, k$. For $j > i$, the i-MCSs are likely to be identical to the j-MCSs. By keeping in memory the list of maximal specializations collected so far, we can compare them for containment with the currently analyzed extensions. This step reduces the search space at line 2 of Algorithm 3. This way, we reduce the number of specializations that we store, and this reduces memory consumption. Further optimizations can be implemented in the presence of integrity constraints (e.g., foreign keys) which we do not present in this paper.

We performed preliminary tests of our optimized code, and reached size $|Q_l|+$ 7 after around more than 2 h. The average running times (over multiple runs) are reported in Table 1. We observe that the running time grows exponentially with the number of atom added to the query.

This small experiment shows two things. First that the optimizations improves the initially proposed specialization algorithm (especially, concerning the memory). Second that such optimization may still not be enough for sufficiently large queries.

---

[3] Using an Intel Core i7 with 8 GB of RAM, and 2 GB allocated to SWI-Prolog.
[4] The code is available at: https://github.com/osavkovic/QuerySpecProlog/.

Table 1. Time required for the specialization algorithm to compute k-MCS of query Q_l.

k-MCS	0	1	2	3	4	5	6	7
CPU time (sec)	0	0	0	0	0	8	725	9083

6 Conclusion

In this work, we studied the completeness of conjunctive queries over partially complete databases where completeness is determined via so-called completeness statements. For queries that cannot be answered completely, we study ways to approximate such queries with more general or more special queries that are complete. In particular, we established characterizations and algorithms for finding maximal complete specializations (MCSs) or the (unique) minimal complete generalization (MCG). The MCG can be characterized as the least fixed-point of a monotonic operator in a preorder. An MCS can be computed through unification between the query and completeness statements. The complexity of both problems is studied, and implementation techniques using ASP and Prolog engines are discussed.

References

1. Arenas, M., Bertossi, L., Chomicki, J., He, X., Raghavan, V., Spinrad, J.: Scalar aggregation in inconsistent databases. Theor. Comput. Sci. **296**(3), 405–434 2003
2. Chandra, A.K., Merlin, P.M.: Optimal implementation of conjunctive queries in relational data bases, STOC 1977, pp. 77-90. Association for Computing Machinery (1977)
3. Fagin, R., Kolaitis, P.G., Miller, R.J., Popa, L.: Data exchange: semantics and query answering. In: Proceedings ICDT, pp. 207–224 (2002)
4. Fan, W., Geerts, F.: Relative information completeness. In: PODS (2009)
5. Fan, W., Geerts, F.: Capturing missing tuples and missing values. In: PODS (2010)
6. Fensel, D., et al.: Knowledge Graphs: Methodology, Tools and Selected Use Cases, Springer, Cham (2020). https://doi.org/10.1007/978-3-030-37439-6
7. Guagliardo, P., Libkin, L.: Making SQL queries correct on incomplete databases: a feasibility study. In: PODS 2016 (2016)
8. Levy, A.Y.: Obtaining complete answers from incomplete databases. In: Proceedings of VLDB, pp. 402–412 (1996)
9. Motro, A.: Integrity = validity + completeness. ACM TODS **14**(4), 480–502 (1989)
10. Nutt, W., Paramonov, S., Savkovic, O.: Implementing query completeness reasoning. In: CIKM, pp. 733–742 (2015)
11. Razniewski, S., Arnaout, H., Ghosh, S., Suchanek, F.: Completeness, recall, and negation in open-world knowledge bases: a survey. ACM Comput. Surv. **56**(6), 1–42 (2024)
12. Razniewski, S., Nutt, W.: Completeness of queries over incomplete databases. PVLDB **4**(11), 749–760 (2011)
13. Savković, O., Mirza, P., Tomasi, A., Nutt, W.: Complete approximations of incomplete queries. VLDB Endowment **6**(12), 1378–1381 (2013)

Reasoning in Rough Description Logics with Multiple Indiscernibility Relations

Rafael Peñaloza[1] and Anni-Yasmin Turhan[2]

[1] University of Milano-Bicocca, Milano, Italy
rafael.penaloza@unimib.it
[2] Paderborn University, Paderborn, Germany
turhan@uni-paderborn.de

Abstract. Rough description logics (DLs) can express approximations of concepts by partitioning the interpretation domain into so-called granules by an indiscernibility relation. Admitting a family of indiscernibility relations yields multi-granular partitionings which can interact with each other. In this paper, we investigate reasoning in rough DLs with multiple indiscernibility relations. We focus on the extension of rough $\mathcal{EL}$ with linear multigranulation orders, where granulations are structured from finest to coarsest, and provide a polynomial-time procedure for deciding concept subsumption. If the indiscernibility relations are not linearly ordered, subsumption becomes ExpTime-hard. We also study reasoning in the rough DL $\mathcal{SHI}(\mathsf{Self})$ w.r.t. arbitrary multi-granular partitionings, and show that the complexity of reasoning remains exponential, just as in classical $\mathcal{ALC}$.

Keywords: Rough description logics · multigranularity · reasoning

1 Introduction

Rough description logics [20] extend classical description logics (DLs) [2] by new concept constructors that, through the use of rough sets, add a qualitative notion of vagueness. In the context of rough sets, the domain is partitioned by a so-called *indiscernibility relation* ρ—formally an equivalence relation—which groups indistinguishable elements into *granules*, i.e. the equivalence classes. Based on this granulation, each set M is associated with two additional sets: the *lower approximation* $\underline{M}$, which contains all elements whose granule is completely contained in M and the *upper approximation* $\overline{M}$, which contains all those elements that belong to a granule that overlap with M. As a concept constructor in rough DLs, the lower approximation $\underline{C}$ models the set of "prototypical" instances of a concept C, while the upper approximation $\overline{C}$ represents the set of elements that are at least "similar" to instances of C.

Several rough description logics, extending classical DLs ranging from $\mathcal{EL}$ to $\mathcal{ALC}$ (and beyond) have been defined, and their main reasoning tasks (deciding subsumption [11,12,16,20] and answering conjunctive queries [17]) investigated.

These rough DLs are well-behaved in the sense that reasoning in them is usually of the same complexity as in their classical counterparts. One limitation of the existing rough DL formalisms is that they admit only a single indiscernibility relation; and yet, whether objects are indiscernible or not may vary depending on the perspective taken. That is, concept members can be indiscernible or discernible w.r.t. different criteria. For example, patients can be indiscernible according to genetic factors or according to the symptoms they present. This can be represented by the use of two or more indiscernibility relations, say ρ_{genetic} and ρ_{symptoms}. This leads to multi-granular rough sets [13,18], which have been intensively investigated in the rough set community over the last decade. So far, the incorporation of several indiscernibility relations has not been considered for reasoning in rough DLs.

In this paper we introduce multigranular rough DLs, which admit upper and lower approximation constructors that use several different indiscernibility relations, and investigate the complexity of reasoning in them. As it turns out, multi-granular rough DLs have a rugged complexity landscape. Even for very inexpressive DLs, we show that allowing arbitrary sets of indiscernibility relations leads to an EXPTIME-hard subsumption problem. On the other hand, if the set of indiscernibility relations is linearly ordered (forming coarser and coarser partitions), then reasoning is as hard as in the corresponding classical DL. A linear order on the indiscernibility relations may seem like a strong restriction, but the resulting rough DLs still enable to vary the "degree" of indiscernibility. This, in turn, admits structuring the data into finer or coarser granules and thus considering the data on different levels of abstraction. There are methods to generate indiscernibility relations that give a hierarchy of granulations [7–9], that result in a linearly ordered set of indiscernibility relations.

In general, clustering algorithms structure data as these algorithms group data items according to their proximity or homogeneity into clusters. There are many such clustering methods and corresponding implementations readily available. A very common type of clustering methods are the hierarchical clustering methods like the classical COBWEB algorithm [5] and its variants. These clustering algorithms partition the data and effectively construct a dendrogram of the data. This means their result is a hierarchy of clusters. The corresponding partitions are then effectively a linearly ordered set of equivalence relations.

The hierarchy of partitions obtained from hierarchical clustering methods or from indiscernibility relations motivates the extension of rough DLs by a set of linearly ordered equivalence relations (being used as indiscernibility relations) $\rho_1, \ldots, \rho_n$. The results of clustering the data can, in principle, be incorporated in the knowledge base by augmenting the ABox with the role assertions for pairs from the same cluster, i.e., from pairs related by some ρ_i. Such an augmentation of the ABox could be realised by a mapping commonly used in ontology-based data access (OBDA). The idea to incorporate an indiscernibility relation in the ABox by an ODBA mapping was already described in [10].

After introducing basic notions and defining multigranular rough DLs, we present the following results. In Sect. 4, we show that for the DL that offers only

$$(r^-)^{\mathcal{I}} := \{(\delta, \eta) \mid (\eta, \delta) \in r^{\mathcal{I}}\}$$
$$(C \sqcap D)^{\mathcal{I}} := C^{\mathcal{I}} \cap D^{\mathcal{I}}$$
$$(C \sqcup D)^{\mathcal{I}} := C^{\mathcal{I}} \cup D^{\mathcal{I}}$$
$$(\neg C)^{\mathcal{I}} := \Delta^{\mathcal{I}} \setminus C^{\mathcal{I}}$$
$$(\exists s.C)^{\mathcal{I}} := \{\delta \in \Delta^{\mathcal{I}} \mid \exists \eta \in C^{\mathcal{I}}.(\delta, \eta) \in r^{\mathcal{I}}\}$$
$$(\forall s.C)^{\mathcal{I}} := \{\delta \in \Delta^{\mathcal{I}} \mid \forall \eta \in \Delta^{\mathcal{I}}.(\delta, \eta) \in r^{\mathcal{I}} \Rightarrow \eta \in C^{\mathcal{I}}\}$$
$$(\exists r.\mathsf{Self})^{\mathcal{I}} := \{\delta \in \Delta^{\mathcal{I}} \mid (\delta, \delta) \in r^{\mathcal{I}}\}$$

Fig. 1. Interpretation of complex concepts and roles in $\mathcal{SHI}$.

conjunction, reasoning in its multigranular extension with an arbitrary set of indiscernibility relations is already ExpTime-hard—which is a surprising result. Then we study linearly ordered sets of indiscernibility relations and show in Sect. 5 that deciding subsumption in multigranular $\mathcal{EL}_\bot$ remains polynomial by developing a subsumption algorithm and in Sect. 6 we show that reasoning in multigranular $\mathcal{SHI}(\mathsf{Self})$ remains in ExpTime.

2 Preliminaries

We start by introducing the main notions of description logics and rough sets needed to understand this work. Specifically, we introduce the expressive DL $\mathcal{SHI}$ and some of its sub-logics, followed by multigranular rough sets.

2.1 The Description Logic $\mathcal{SHI}$

$\mathcal{SHI}$ is a very expressive description logic which allows various constructors for concepts and roles. Syntactically, given mutually disjoint sets $\mathsf{N_C}$ of *concept names* and $\mathsf{N_R}$ of *role names*, a *role* is either a role name $r \in \mathsf{N_R}$ or an *inverse role* r^-, where $r \in \mathsf{N_R}$. The class of *concepts* is constructed via the syntactic rule

$$C ::= A \mid C \sqcap C \mid C \sqcup C \mid \neg C \mid \exists s.C \mid \forall s.C \mid \exists r.\mathsf{Self}$$

where $A \in \mathsf{N_C}$, s is a role, $r \in \mathsf{N_R}$, and Self is a designated symbol.

This logic uses an interpretation-based semantics. An *interpretation* is a pair $\mathcal{I} = (\Delta^{\mathcal{I}}, \cdot^{\mathcal{I}})$ where $\Delta^{\mathcal{I}}$ is a non-empty set called the *domain* and $\cdot^{\mathcal{I}}$ is the *interpretation function* which maps every $A \in \mathsf{N_C}$ to a set $A^{\mathcal{I}} \subseteq \Delta^{\mathcal{I}}$ and every $r \in \mathsf{N_R}$ to a binary relation $r^{\mathcal{I}} \subseteq \Delta^{\mathcal{I}} \times \Delta^{\mathcal{I}}$. This function is extended to arbitrary roles as concepts as shown in Fig. 1.

Knowledge in this logic—as in all description logics—is expressed through a set of restrictions over the "meaningful" interpretations of the symbols. A knowledge base (KB) is a set of *axioms*, which can be *general concept inclusions* (GCI) of the form $C \sqsubseteq D$ where C, D are concepts; *role inclusions* (RI) $s \sqsubseteq t$ where s and t are roles; or *transitivity axioms* of the form $\mathsf{tran}(r)$ where $r \in \mathsf{N_R}$.

The interpretation $\mathcal{I}$ *satisfies* the GCI $C \sqsubseteq D$ or the RI $s \sqsubseteq t$ iff $C^\mathcal{I} \subseteq D^\mathcal{I}$ or $s^\mathcal{I} \subseteq t^\mathcal{I}$, respectively; it *satisfies* the transitivity axiom $\mathsf{tran}(r)$ iff $r^\mathcal{I}$ is a transitive relation. $\mathcal{I}$ is a *model* of the KB $\mathcal{K}$ iff it satisfies all the axioms in $\mathcal{K}$.

The two main reasoning problems are *consistency*—that is, deciding whether there is at least one model for a given KB $\mathcal{K}$—and *concept subsumption*—deciding whether every model $\mathcal{I}$ of $\mathcal{K}$ also satisfies a given GCI $C \sqsubseteq D$. In this case, we denote it by $\mathcal{K} \models C \sqsubseteq D$.

We consider the following sublanguages of $\mathcal{SHI}$. $\mathcal{ALC}$ is the sub-logic obtained by removing inverse roles and Self from the concept constructors, and disallowing RIs and transitivity axioms from appearing in the KBs. $\mathcal{EL}_\bot$ further restricts the language to exclude concept negations ($\neg$) and value restrictions ($\forall$), but introducing two new concepts: $\top$ and $\bot$, which are interpreted by $\top^\mathcal{I} = \Delta^\mathcal{I}$ and $\bot^\mathcal{I} = \emptyset$. The DL $\mathcal{HL}_\bot$ removes from $\mathcal{EL}_\bot$ the existential quantification ($\exists$). $\mathcal{ELI}$ instead extends $\mathcal{EL}_\bot$ with inverse roles, but disallows $\bot$. It is well-known that concept subsumption w.r.t. a KB can be decided in polynomial time in $\mathcal{EL}_\bot$ [1] and $\mathcal{HL}_\bot$, and is ExpTime-complete in $\mathcal{ELI}$ [4], $\mathcal{ALC}$ [19], and $\mathcal{SHI}$ [3].

2.2 Rough Sets

Rough sets [14] allow for approximate descriptions of sets through an indiscernibility relation between elements of the universe U. Briefly, the elements of U are associated through an equivalence (i.e., transitive, symmetric, and reflexive) relation $\sim$. The equivalence classes of $\sim$ are often called *granules* in the context of rough sets. With the help of this relation $\sim$, we can define, for every $S \subseteq U$, its *lower* ($\underline{S}$) and *upper* ($\overline{S}$) approximations as the sets of elements that are: indiscernible only with elements of S; or indiscernible from at least one element of S, respectively. More formally, $s \in \underline{S}$ iff $[s]_\sim \subseteq S$ and $s \in \overline{S}$ iff $[s]_\sim \cap S \neq \emptyset$, where $[s]_\sim$ denotes the equivalence class of s w.r.t. $\sim$.

The idea is that elements in one equivalence class cannot be distinguished from a point of view that defines $\sim$. But they could still be distinguishable from a different perspective. This gives rise to the idea of multigranular rough sets, where multiple equivalence relations (and hence multiple upper and lower approximations) are considered [13,18]. As we see next, these notions can be used to approximate concepts (which semantically are sets of domain elements) by means of equivalence relations over the interpretation domain.

3 Multigranular Rough Description Logics

Let $\mathcal{L}$ be an arbitrary but fixed DL, and $n \in \mathbb{N}$. The multigranular rough extension of $\mathcal{L}$ (with n indiscernibility relations) $\mathcal{L}^{\rho,n}$ is obtained, syntactically, by allowing the new concept constructors $\underline{C}_i$ and $\overline{C}^i$, where $1 \leq i \leq n$. Concepts of the form $\underline{C}_i$ are called *lower approximation* of C w.r.t. $\sim_i$ and those of the form $\overline{C}^i$ are called *upper approximation* of C w.r.t. $\sim_i$. To interpret the new concepts, we extend the notion of an interpretation.

Definition 1. A rough interpretation *(with n indiscernibility relations)* is a tuple $\mathcal{I} = (\Delta^{\mathcal{I}}, \cdot^{\mathcal{I}}, \sim_1, \ldots, \sim_n)$ where $(\Delta^{\mathcal{I}}, \cdot^{\mathcal{I}})$ is a (classical) interpretation and each $\sim_i$ is an equivalence relation over $\Delta^{\mathcal{I}}$. Given an element $\delta \in \Delta^{\mathcal{I}}$, $[\delta]_i$ denotes the equivalence class of δ w.r.t. $\sim_i$. The interpretation function is extended to rough concepts by:

$$(\underline{C}_i)^{\mathcal{I}} := \{\delta \in \Delta^{\mathcal{I}} \mid [\delta]_i \subseteq C^{\mathcal{I}}\}$$
$$(\overline{C}^i)^{\mathcal{I}} := \{\delta \in \Delta^{\mathcal{I}} \mid [\delta]_i \cap C^{\mathcal{I}} \neq \emptyset\}.$$

We will sometimes index the indiscernibility relations with a finite set of names $\mathcal{N}$ and represent an interpretation as $(\Delta^{\mathcal{I}}, \cdot^{\mathcal{I}}, \{\sim_i \mid i \in \mathcal{N}\})$.

By construction, for every concept C, every $i, 1 \leq i \leq n$, and every interpretation $\mathcal{I}$ it holds that $(\underline{C}_i)^{\mathcal{I}} \subseteq C^{\mathcal{I}} \subseteq (\overline{C}^i)^{\mathcal{I}}$. Other important properties which combine the approximation concept constructors for each given indiscernibility relation are the following.

Proposition 2. *(from [16]).* Let $\mathcal{L}$ be a DL, $i, 1 \leq i \leq n$, $\mathcal{K}$ a KB, and C, D, E three rough $\mathcal{L}$ concepts. The following properties hold:

1. $\mathcal{K} \models \overline{C}^i \sqsubseteq D$ iff $\mathcal{K} \models C \sqsubseteq \underline{D}_i$; and
2. if $\mathcal{K} \models C \sqsubseteq \overline{D}^i$ and $\mathcal{K} \models D \sqsubseteq \underline{E}_i$, then $\mathcal{K} \models C \sqsubseteq \underline{E}_i$; and
3. if $\mathcal{K} \models C \sqsubseteq \overline{D}^i$ and $\mathcal{K} \models \underline{D}_i \sqsubseteq E$, then $\mathcal{K} \models C \sqsubseteq \underline{E}_i$.

These properties, which indicate how rough information is propagated within the same granulation, will be useful when we design a reasoning algorithm in Sect. 5.

Note that, as introduced in this section, the different equivalence relations do not have to preserve any relationship between them, which means that an analogue of Proposition 2 connecting different indiscernibility relations is impossible in this general setting. For instance, in general even $\overline{C}^i$ and $\overline{C}^j$ may be incomparable. As we see in the next section, this freedom leads to EXPTIME-hardness of reasoning, even in the inexpressive logic $\mathcal{HL}_\bot$.

4 Multigranular Rough $\mathcal{HL}_\bot$ Is Hard

We show that subsumption in $\mathcal{HL}_\bot^{\rho,n}$, which is a very inexpressive logic that does not use any roles, is EXPTIME-hard. The proof is based on a reduction from $\mathcal{ELI}$, whose subsumption problem is known to be EXPTIME-hard [1].

Let $\mathcal{K}$ be an $\mathcal{ELI}$ KB. Without loss of generality, we can assume that all its GCIs are in normal form; that is, all GCIs take one of the forms

$$A \sqcap B \sqsubseteq C, \quad A \sqsubseteq \exists s.B, \quad \exists s.B \sqsubseteq A,$$

where $A, B, C \in \mathsf{N_C} \cup \{\top\}$, and s is a role (i.e., a role name or the inverse of a role name). Following the ideas from [4,6], we construct an $\mathcal{HL}_\bot^{\rho,n}$ KB $\mathcal{K}_\rho$ that preserves the same subsumptions of atomic concepts as $\mathcal{K}$.

For each role name $r \in \mathsf{N_R}$ appearing in $\mathcal{K}$, we introduce two equivalence relations $\sim_{r1}, \sim_{r2}$, and three concept names N_r, M_r, and V_r that do not appear in $\mathcal{K}$. We define the function h that maps each $\mathcal{ELI}$ GCI in normal form to an $\mathcal{HL}_\bot^{\rho,n}$ KB depending on its shape as follows:

$h(A \sqcap B \sqsubseteq C) = \{A \sqcap B \sqsubseteq C\};$

$h(A \sqsubseteq \exists r.B) = \{A \sqsubseteq \overline{A \sqcap N_r}^{r1},\ A \sqsubseteq \overline{V_r}^{r1},\ V_r \sqcap \overline{A}^{r1} \sqsubseteq \overline{V_r \sqcap \overline{B \sqcap M_r}^{r2}}^{r1}\} \cup$
$\quad \{N_r \sqcap V_r \sqsubseteq \bot,\ M_r \sqcap V_r \sqsubseteq \bot\};$

$h(A \sqsubseteq \exists r^-.B) = \{A \sqsubseteq \overline{A \sqcap M_r}^{r2},\ A \sqsubseteq \overline{V_r}^{r2},\ V_r \sqcap \overline{A}^{r2} \sqsubseteq \overline{V_r \sqcap \overline{B \sqcap N_r}^{r1}}^{r2}\} \cup$
$\quad \{N_r \sqcap V_r \sqsubseteq \bot,\ M_r \sqcap V_r \sqsubseteq \bot\};$

$h(\exists r.B \sqsubseteq A) = \{N_r \sqcap \overline{B \sqcap M_r}^{r2}^{r1} \sqsubseteq A,\ \overline{N_r \sqcap A}^{r1} \sqsubseteq A\};$

$h(\exists r^-.B \sqsubseteq A) = \{M_r \sqcap \overline{B \sqcap N_r}^{r1}^{r2} \sqsubseteq A,\ \overline{M_r \sqcap A}^{r2} \sqsubseteq A\}.$

Given an $\mathcal{ELI}$ KB $\mathcal{K}$, we define $\mathcal{K}_\rho := \bigcup_{\alpha \in \mathcal{K}} h(\alpha)$, and denote by $\mathsf{N_C}(\mathcal{K})$ and $\mathsf{N_R}(\mathcal{K})$ the set of all concept names and all role names appearing in $\mathcal{K}$, respectively. We see that this transformation preserves atomic subsumptions. For a lack of space, the proof is available in the long version of this paper.[1]

Theorem 3. *Let $\mathcal{K}$ be an $\mathcal{ELI}$ TBox in normal form, $\mathcal{K}_\rho$ the $\mathcal{HL}_\bot^{\rho,n}$ TBox obtained from $\mathcal{K}$, and A, B two concept names appearing in $\mathcal{K}$. $\mathcal{K} \models A \sqsubseteq B$ iff $\mathcal{K}_\rho \models A \sqsubseteq B$.*

We explain the intuition behind this construction with an example.

Example 4. Consider the $\mathcal{ELI}$ KB

$$\mathcal{K} = \{A \sqsubseteq \exists r.B,\quad \exists r^-.A \sqsubseteq C,\quad \exists r.C \sqsubseteq D\},$$

which entails $A \sqsubseteq D$. We demonstrate how the $\mathcal{HL}_\bot^{\rho,n}$ KB $\mathcal{K}_\rho$ yields this result. Consider an object δ_0 belonging to A. The axioms in $h(A \sqsubseteq \exists r.B)$ enforce the existence of two (distinct) objects η_0 and γ_0 belonging to $A \sqcap N_r$ and to V_r, respectively, which are indiscernible through $\sim_{r1}$, and another object (δ_1) belonging to $B \sqcap M_r$ indiscernible from γ_0 through $\sim_{r2}$ (see Fig. 2 (a)). Intuitively, N_r and M_r represent the first and second element of an r-edge, respectively, and V_r is a "border" element, which connects $\sim_{r1}$ and $\sim_{r2}$ granules.

From $h(\exists r^-.A \sqsubseteq C)$, since δ_1 belongs to M_r and is connected through a $\sim_{r2} \circ \sim_{r1}$-path to an element in $A \sqcap N_r$, we conclude that δ_1 must also belong to C. Note that since $\sim_{r1}$ and $\sim_{r2}$ are reflexive, the concept names N_r, M_r are needed to avoid deducing (erroneously) that δ_0 and η_0 also belong to C (Fig. 2 (b)). An analogous analysis, over $h(\exists r.C \sqsubseteq D)$ allows us to conclude that η_0 must belong to D (Fig. 2 (c)). Yet, recall that we are trying to conclude that $A \sqsubseteq D$ which is not yet satisfied by δ_0. This is where the axiom $\overline{N_r \sqcap D}^{r1} \sqsubseteq D$

---

[1] https://rpenalozan.github.io/Toolbox/RR-long.pdf.

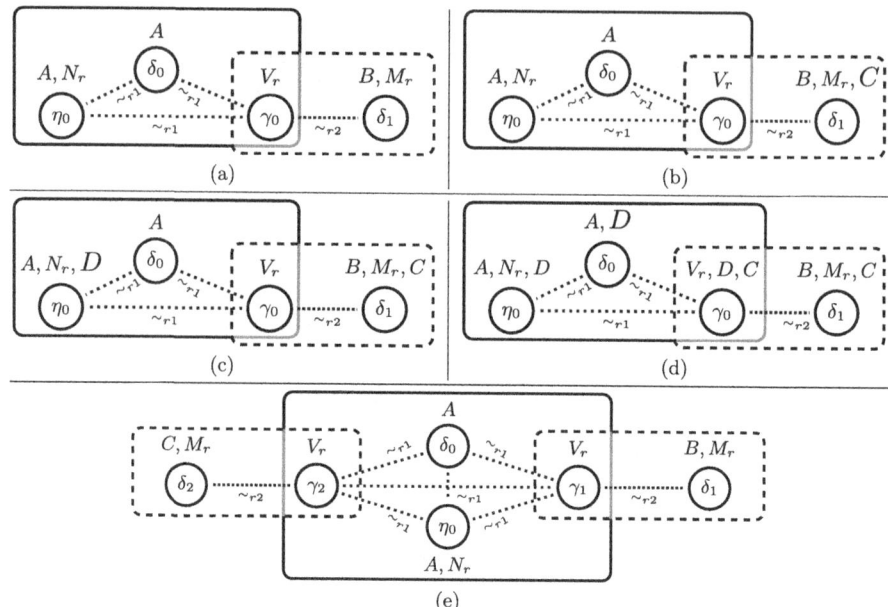

Fig. 2. Step-wise construction of a model for the $\mathcal{HL}_\bot^{\rho,n}$ reduction from the $\mathcal{ELI}$ KB in Example 4. Boxes represent equivalence classes: a continuous border refers to a class of $\sim_{r1}$, while dashed borders refer to $\sim_{r2}$.

introduced by $h(\exists r.C \sqsubseteq D)$ comes into play. Indeed, at this point, δ_0 belongs to $\overline{N_r \sqcap D}^{r1}$, which the axiom forces to be subsumed by D, thus concluding that δ_0 belongs to D. The result of this construction appears in Fig. 2 (d).

If we "zoom out" from this structure, we can think of each equivalence class as a domain element, and the border elements as bridges (edges) between these elements. Under this view, $[\delta_0]_{\sim_{r1}}$ belongs to A and D; $[\delta_1]_{\sim_{r2}}$ belongs to B and C; and there is an r-connection from $[\delta_0]_{\sim_{r1}}$ to $[\delta_1]_{\sim_{r2}}$. To emphasise this intuition, Fig. 2 (e) depicts the construction arising from the KB $\{A \sqsubseteq \exists r.B, A \sqsubseteq \exists r.C\}$. Note that while the figure represents only one object η_0 belonging to A and N_r, several such objects exist. The important aspect of this is that, at least one of them must exists in each model.

Since deciding subsumption in $\mathcal{ELI}$ is ExpTime-hard, Theorem 3 shows the same exponential lower bound for $\mathcal{HL}_\bot^{\rho,n}$. The matching upper bound is a consequence of the upper bound for rough $\mathcal{SHI}$ shown in Sect. 6.

Corollary 5. *Deciding subsumption in $\mathcal{HL}_\bot^{\rho,n}$ is ExpTime-complete.*

To regain tractability, we impose a restriction on the set of indiscernibility relations in the next section, requiring them to form a linear order.

5 The Multigranular Rough Description Logic $\mathcal{EL}_\bot^{\rho/\text{lin}}$

We now consider a variant of multigranular rough $\mathcal{EL}_\bot$, where the indiscernibility relations are totally ordered from the coarsest to the most finely-grained. More formally, given $n \geq 1$, we consider n equivalence relations $\sim_1, \ldots, \sim_n$ such that $\sim_i \subseteq \sim_{i+1}$ for all $1 \leq i < n$. That is, $\sim_1$ is the most fine-grained relation, while $\sim_n$ is the coarsest. Note that $\sim_i$ partitions each equivalence class of $\sim_{i+1}$ into (possibly) smaller classes.

The new logic, which we call $\mathcal{EL}_\bot^{\rho/\text{lin}}$, is $\mathcal{EL}_\bot^{\rho,n}$ exactly as defined in Sect. 3, with the only difference that models are *required* to interpret the n indiscernibility relations as linearly ordered. In particular, for every $\delta \in \Delta^\mathcal{I}$ and every i where $1 \leq i < n$, it holds that $[\delta]_i \subseteq [\delta]_{i+1}$, and hence also for all concepts C

$$(\underline{C}_{i+1})^\mathcal{I} \subseteq (\underline{C}_i)^\mathcal{I} \subseteq (\overline{C}^i)^\mathcal{I} \subseteq (\overline{C}^{i+1})^\mathcal{I}.$$

The following proposition is a consequence of these properties.

Proposition 6. *For all i, j with $1 \leq i \leq j \leq n$, all concepts C, and all interpretations $\mathcal{I}$ the following equivalences hold:*

1. (a) $\left(\underline{(\underline{C}_i)}_j\right)^\mathcal{I} = (\underline{C}_j)^\mathcal{I}$; (b) $\left(\underline{(\underline{C}_j)}_i\right)^\mathcal{I} = (\underline{C}_j)^\mathcal{I}$;
2. (a) $\overline{\left(\overline{C}^i\right)}^j{}^\mathcal{I} = (\overline{C}^j)^\mathcal{I}$; (b) $\overline{\left(\overline{C}^j\right)}^i{}^\mathcal{I} = (\overline{C}^j)^\mathcal{I}$;
3. $\overline{\left(\underline{(\underline{C}_j)}\right)}^i{}^\mathcal{I} = (\underline{C}_j)^\mathcal{I}$; and
4. $\underline{\left(\overline{(\overline{C}^j)}\right)}_i{}^\mathcal{I} = (\overline{C}^j)^\mathcal{I}$.

Proof. We prove only the Claims 1. and 3.; the other two can be shown analogously. For Claim 1.(a), $\delta \in \left(\underline{(\underline{C}_i)}_j\right)^\mathcal{I}$ iff $[\delta]_j \subseteq (\underline{C}_i)^\mathcal{I}$ iff (since $\sim_i \subseteq \sim_j$) $[\delta]_i \subseteq [\delta]_j \subseteq C^\mathcal{I}$ iff $\delta \in (\underline{C}_j)^\mathcal{I}$. Similarly for 1.(b), $\delta \in \left(\underline{(\underline{C}_j)}_i\right)^\mathcal{I}$ iff $[\delta]_i \subseteq (\underline{C}_j)^\mathcal{I}$ iff for every $\eta \in [\delta]_i$, it holds that $[\eta]_j \subseteq C^\mathcal{I}$ iff (since $\delta \sim_i \eta$ holds and implies that $\delta \sim_j \eta$ holds) $[\delta]_j \subseteq C^\mathcal{I}$ iff $\delta \in (\underline{C}_j)^\mathcal{I}$.

For Claim 3., $\delta \in \overline{\left(\underline{(\underline{C}_j)}\right)}^i{}^\mathcal{I}$ iff $[\delta]_i \cap (\underline{C}_j)^\mathcal{I} \neq \emptyset$ iff there exists $\eta \in [\delta]_i$ such that $\eta \in (\underline{C}_j)^\mathcal{I}$ iff there is $\eta \in [\delta]_i$ with $[\eta]_j \subseteq C^\mathcal{I}$ iff (because $\delta \sim_i \eta$ holds and implies that $\delta \sim_j \eta$ holds) $[\delta]_j \subseteq C^\mathcal{I}$ iff $\delta \in (\underline{C}_j)^\mathcal{I}$. □

If $i = j$ Claim 1 and Claim 2 from Proposition 6 cover idempotence of both kinds of approximations. This affects the decision algorithm for subsumption, which is based on extending the completion algorithm for $\mathcal{EL}_\bot$ [1] to propagate information w.r.t. a single relation $\sim_i$. Instead for relations at different levels of granularity ($i < j$) the equivalences from Proposition 6 indicate how information is to be propagated or absorbed between different levels of roughness.

The rough DL $\mathcal{EL}_\bot^\rho$ [16] is the special case of $\mathcal{EL}_\bot^{\rho/\text{lin}}$ where $n = 1$; that is, where only one indiscernibility relation is used. Since $\mathcal{EL}_\bot$ is a particular case of $\mathcal{EL}_\bot^\rho$, where the GCIs $A \sqsubseteq \underline{A}_1$ and $\overline{A}^1 \sqsubseteq A$ are satisfied for all $A \in \mathsf{N_C}$, $\mathcal{EL}_\bot^{\rho/\text{lin}}$ is obviously a generalisation of the classical DL $\mathcal{EL}_\bot$. We are mainly interested

Table 1. Normalisation rules. Where $A \in \mathsf{N_C} \cup \{\top\}$, C, D are complex concepts, and X is a new concept name (not previously appearing in the KB).

NF1	$F \sqcap C \sqsubseteq E$	$\{C \sqsubseteq X, F \sqcap X \sqsubseteq E\}$
NF2	$\exists r.C \sqsubseteq E$	$\{C \sqsubseteq X, \exists r.X \sqsubseteq E\}$
NF3	$\underline{C}_i \sqsubseteq E$	$\{C \sqsubseteq X, \underline{X}_i \sqsubseteq E\}$
NF4	$\overline{C}^i \sqsubseteq E$	$\{C \sqsubseteq E_i\}$
NF5	$C \sqsubseteq D$	$\{C \sqsubseteq X, X \sqsubseteq D\}$
NF6	$A \sqsubseteq E \sqcap F$	$\{A \sqsubseteq E, A \sqsubseteq F\}$
NF7	$A \sqsubseteq \exists r.C$	$\{A \sqsubseteq \exists r.X, X \sqsubseteq C\}$
NF8	$A \sqsubseteq \underline{C}_i$	$\{A \sqsubseteq \underline{X}_i, X \sqsubseteq C\}$
NF9	$A \sqsubseteq \overline{C}^i$	$\{A \sqsubseteq \overline{X}^i, X \sqsubseteq C\}$
NF10	$\bot \sqsubseteq E$	$\emptyset$

in deciding subsumption between two concept names. Recall that $A \in \mathsf{N_C}$ is *subsumed* by $B \in \mathsf{N_C}$ w.r.t. the KB $\mathcal{K}$ ($\mathcal{K} \models A \sqsubseteq B$) iff every model of $\mathcal{K}$ also satisfies the GCI $A \sqsubseteq B$.

We develop a reasoning algorithm for solving this problem in $\mathcal{EL}^{\rho/\mathsf{lin}}_\bot$. As this logic is an extension of $\mathcal{EL}^{\rho}_\bot$, we extend the known completion algorithm [16] to handle the new cases required by the multiple indiscernibility relations available. As a first step, we require the KB to be in $\mathcal{EL}^{\rho/\mathsf{lin}}_\bot$ *normal form*; i.e. all the axioms should be of one of the forms

$$A_1 \sqcap A_2 \sqsubseteq C, \quad A \sqsubseteq \exists r.B, \quad \exists r.A \sqsubseteq C, \quad \underline{A}_i \sqsubseteq C, \quad A \sqsubseteq \underline{B}_i, \quad A \sqsubseteq \overline{B}^i,$$

where $A, B \in \mathsf{N_C} \cup \{\top\}$, $C \in \mathsf{N_C} \cup \{\top, \bot\}$, and $1 \le i \le n$.[2]

Any KB $\mathcal{K}$ can be transformed into normal form applying the rules from Table 1—where **NF1** uses the commutativity of conjunction—until no rule can be applied anymore. The resulting KB is a conservative extension of $\mathcal{K}$ which, importantly, is only polynomially larger than $\mathcal{K}$ as it is found after only a polynomial number of rule applications.

Our completion algorithm extends the ideas introduced in [16] to handle lower and upper approximation concepts. Briefly, the completion algorithm for $\mathcal{EL}^{\rho}_\bot$ preserves, for each concept name A appearing in a normalised KB $\mathcal{K}$, a family of completion sets, which store the information of how the lower and upper approximations of other concept names relate to A. This information is needed for an adequate handling of the properties of these concept constructors. In the present case, we must extend this idea to differentiate between the available indiscernibility relations.

More formally, for each $A \in \mathsf{N_C} \cup \{\top\}$ appearing in the normalised KB $\mathcal{K}$, and for each $i, 1 \le i \le n$ we preserve two sets called $\overline{S}^i(A)$ and $\underline{S}_i(A)$. In addition, we keep track of a set $S(A)$ and for each role name $r \in \mathsf{N_R}$ appearing in $\mathcal{K}$ a

---

[2] For brevity, we consider axioms of the form $A \sqsubseteq B$ as $\top \sqcap A \sqsubseteq B$.

set $S(A,r)$. Hence, for each such A, we keep $2n + \ell + 1$ many such completion sets, where ℓ is the number of role names in $\mathcal{K}$. With polynomially many concept names in the normalised KB, the completion algorithm uses polynomially many completion sets.

The elements of each completion set all belong to $\mathsf{N_C} \cup \{\top, \bot\}$. The idea is that these sets represent subsumption relations among syntactically simple concepts that can be derived from subsumptions that were previously found, in a sound manner. Specifically, throughout the completion algorithm, the application of completion rules preserves the following invariants:

1. if $B \in \overline{S}^i(A)$ then $\mathcal{K} \models A \sqsubseteq \overline{B}^i$
2. if $B \in \underline{S}_i(A)$ then $\mathcal{K} \models A \sqsubseteq \underline{B}_i$
3. if $B \in S(A)$ then $\mathcal{K} \models A \sqsubseteq B$ and
4. if $B \in S(A,r)$ then $\mathcal{K} \models A \sqsubseteq \exists r.B$

for all $A \in \mathsf{N_C} \cup \{\top\}$, $B \in \mathsf{N_C} \cup \{\top, \bot\}$, $r \in \mathsf{N_R}$, and $1 \leq i \leq n$. These are essentially the same invariants that were used for $\mathcal{EL}^\rho_\bot$ in [16], but extended to consider the different indiscernibility relations.

The completion sets are initialized with obvious tautologies; that is, at the beginning of the algorithm the sets are defined as

$$S(A) = \overline{S}^i(A) := \{A, \top\}, \qquad \underline{S}_i(A) := \{\top\}, \qquad S(A,r) := \emptyset$$

for all $A \in \mathsf{N_C} \cup \{\top\}, r \in \mathsf{N_R}, 1 \leq i \leq n$. Clearly this initialization preserves the invariants mentioned above. These sets are extended through the application of the *completion rules* described in Table 2.

As usual for these kinds of algorithms, the rules are only applied if they add an element to one of the sets involved; that is, if the concept to be added is not already present in the set. The completion algorithm applies rules until no rule is applicable anymore; at that point, we say that the algorithm is *saturated*.

Interestingly, this completion algorithm becomes saturated after at most polynomially many rule applications (in n and the size of $\mathcal{K}$). Indeed, there are $(2n + \ell + 1)m$ many sets, where ℓ is the number of role names in $\mathcal{K}$ and m is the number of concept names in $\mathcal{K}$. Each of these sets contains at most $m + 2$ elements (the concept names in $\mathcal{K}$ plus $\top$ and $\bot$). Since each rule application adds one element to one of the sets, at most $(2n + \ell + 1)(m + 2)m$ many rule applications are needed before reaching saturation. In addition, the conditions for the application of a rule require only a lookup between the sets and the GCIs in $\mathcal{K}$, which can also be performed in polynomial time. Thus, overall the algorithm needs only polynomial time until it becomes saturated.

The result of the completion algorithm can be used to decide all the atomic subsumption relations entailed by the KB $\mathcal{K}$. That is, for every $A, B \in \mathsf{N_C}$ we get that $\mathcal{K} \models A \sqsubseteq B$ iff $B \in S(A)$. In what follows we prove this claim. First, soundness is a consequence of the invariants described above.

Lemma 7. *The completion algorithm preserves the four invariants, throughout all rule applications.*

Table 2. Completion rules for $\mathcal{EL}_\bot^{\rho/\text{lin}}$.

CR1	if $\{B_1, B_2\} \subseteq S(A)$ and $B_1 \sqcap B_2 \sqsubseteq C \in \mathcal{K}$, then add C to $S(A)$
CR2	if $B \in S(A)$ and $B \sqsubseteq \exists r.C \in \mathcal{K}$, then add C to $S(A,r)$
CR3	if $B \in S(A,r), C \in S(B)$ and $\exists r.C \sqsubseteq D \in \mathcal{K}$, then add D to $S(A)$
CR4	if $\{B_1, B_2\} \in \underline{S}_i(A)$ and $B_1 \sqcap B_2 \sqsubseteq C \in \mathcal{K}$, then add C to $\underline{S}_i(A)$
CR5	if $B_1 \in \underline{S}_i(A)$, $B_2 \in \overline{S}^i(A)$ and $B_1 \sqcap B_2 \sqsubseteq C \in \mathcal{K}$, then add C to $\overline{S}^i(A)$
CR6	if $B \in \underline{S}_i(A)$ and $\underline{B}_i \sqsubseteq C \in \mathcal{K}$, then add C to $\underline{S}_i(A)$
CR7	if $B \in \overline{S}^i(A)$ and $B \sqsubseteq \underline{C}_i \in \mathcal{K}$, then add C to $\underline{S}_i(A)$
CR8	if $B \in \overline{S}^i(A)$ and $B \sqsubseteq \overline{C}^i \in \mathcal{K}$, then add C to $\overline{S}^i(A)$
CR9	if $B \in \underline{S}_i(A)$, then add B to $S(A)$
CR10	if $B \in S(A)$, then add B to $\overline{S}^i(A)$
CR11	if $B \in \underline{S}_j(A)$ and $i < j$, then add B to $\underline{S}_i(A)$
CR12	if $B \in \overline{S}^i(A)$ and $i < j$, then add B to $\overline{S}^j(A)$
CR13	if $B \in \underline{S}_i(A)$ and $C \in S(B)$, then add C to $\underline{S}_i(A)$
CR14	if $B \in \overline{S}^i(A)$ and $C \in \overline{S}^i(B)$, then add C to $\overline{S}^i(A)$
CR15	if $B \in \underline{S}_i(A)$ and $C \in \underline{S}_i(B)$, then add C to $\underline{S}_i(A)$
CR16	if $B \in S(A,r)$ and $\bot \in S(B)$, then add $\bot$ to $S(A)$
CR17	if $B \in \overline{S}^i(A)$ and $\bot \in \overline{S}^i(B)$, then add $\bot$ to $\underline{S}_i(A)$
CR18	if $\bot \in \overline{S}^i(A)$, then add $\bot$ to $\underline{S}_i(A)$

Proof. The proof is by induction on rule applications. The induction base is satisfied by the initialization. For rules without rough constructors (CR1-CR3 and CR16) soundness was shown already in [1].

For rules CR6 to CR15, CR17, and CR18 soundness is a consequence of Propositions 2 and 6. Since the rules CR11 and CR12 treat the interaction of different indiscernibility relations, we give a detailed proof for these. For CR11, suppose $\mathcal{K} \models A \sqsubseteq \underline{B}_j$ and $i < j$. For every model $\mathcal{I}$ and every $\delta \in \Delta^\mathcal{I}$, if $\delta \in A^\mathcal{I}$, then $\delta \in \underline{B}_j^\mathcal{I}$ and thus $[\delta]_j \subseteq B^\mathcal{I}$. Since from $i < j$ follows that $[\delta]_i \subseteq [\delta]_j$, we obtain $[\delta]_i \subseteq B^\mathcal{I}$ holds and thus $\delta \in \underline{B}_i^\mathcal{I}$. This implies $\mathcal{K} \models A \sqsubseteq \underline{B}_i$. The proof for CR12 is analogous.

The only remaining rules are CR4 and CR5. For the rule CR4, suppose that $\mathcal{K} \models A \sqsubseteq \underline{B_1}_i$ and $\mathcal{K} \models A \sqsubseteq \underline{B_2}_i$. For every model $\mathcal{I}$ and every $\delta \in \Delta^\mathcal{I}$, if $\delta \in A^\mathcal{I}$ then $[\delta]_i \subseteq B_1^\mathcal{I} \cap B_2^\mathcal{I}$ and hence (as $\mathcal{I} \models B_1 \sqcap B_2 \sqsubseteq C$) $[\delta]_i \subseteq C^\mathcal{I}$, which implies $\mathcal{K} \models A \sqsubseteq \underline{C}_i$. Rule CR5 can be treated analogously. □

This shows that any atomic subsumption relation derived by the algorithm (in the form of $B \in S(A)$) is indeed a consequence of the KB.

For the converse direction—completeness—we follow the usual approach of building a sort of "canonical" model of $\mathcal{K}$ that serves as a counterexample for all the atomic subsumption relations which do *not* appear explicitly in the generated sets. In our case, the domain $\Delta^\mathcal{I}$ of the canonical model is composed of three

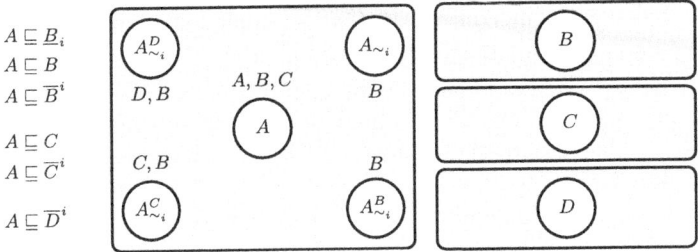

Fig. 3. The construction of the model for the proof of Lemma 8. Each grey box is an equivalence class for $\sim_i$. The details of $[A]_{\sim_i}$ are given, relative to the derived subsumptions depicted on the left.

kinds of elements. First, as usual for the $\mathcal{EL}$ family of DLs, it includes one domain element for each satisfiable concept name A appearing in $\mathcal{K}$, which stands for a standard instance representing that concept; i.e., it is a minimal representative of A. Hence, it will belong to each concept B that subsumes A w.r.t. $\mathcal{K}$. The two other kinds of domain elements handle the lower and upper approximations of named concepts in the interpretation domain. For the lower approximation, we include, for each $\sim_i$, with $1 \leq i \leq n$, an element $A_{\sim_i}$ that belongs to all concepts B such that $\mathcal{K} \models A \sqsubseteq \underline{B}_i$. In other words, $A_{\sim_i}$ keeps information about all the concept names B such that all objects indiscernible from instances of A are necessarily in B.

Dealing with the upper approximations requires a more nuanced construction, as a single element cannot fully witness the existence of indiscernible elements belonging to different concepts. Indeed, note that it could very well happen that $\mathcal{K} \models A \sqsubseteq \overline{B}^i$ and $\mathcal{K} \models A \sqsubseteq C$ while B and C are required to be disjoint concepts. Thus, we need different objects to handle different upper approximations. Specifically, for each concept name B such that $\mathcal{K} \models A \sqsubseteq \overline{B}^i$, we create an element $A^B_{\sim_i}$ which is a representative instance of B (i.e., belongs to B and all its subsumers), but exists only through its connection to the representative of A. To handle the indiscernibility relations, these elements A, $A_{\sim_i}$, and $A^B_{\sim_i}$ all belong to the same $\sim_i$-equivalence class. As this is not a trivial structure, we explain it in more detail here. Note that $\mathcal{K} \models A \sqsubseteq \overline{B}^i$ means that every element of A must be associated (via $\sim_i$) with some element of the concept B. In particular, the representative of A must have such an association as well. But we cannot connect A to the representative of B because the symmetry of $\sim_i$ would then entail that $B \sqsubseteq \overline{A}^i$, which is not necessarily a consequence of $\mathcal{K}$. We can also not choose only one representative, as we did for the lower approximations, because (again) we cannot guarantee that the representative belongs to other concepts that are not known subsumers of B. Figure 3 describes this intuition graphically. Each grey box is an equivalence class for $\sim_i$. There can be more elements than those shown in each class, but the figure zooms into some relevant elements of $[A]_{\sim_i}$, given by the derivations shown at the left of the figure. Since $A \sqsubseteq \underline{B}_i$, the object $A_{\sim_i}$ belongs to the concept B. On the other hand, since A is subsumed by $\overline{B}^i, \overline{C}^i$, and $\overline{D}^i$, we create the three objects $A^B_{\sim_i}, A^C_{\sim_i}$, and $A^D_{\sim_i}$, respectively. Importantly, these objects belong to the concepts B, C, and D (respectively), but not to $[B]_{\sim_i}, [C]_{\sim_i}$, or $[D]_{\sim_i}$, represented as the three boxes on the right. Also, since $A_{\sim_i}$ belongs to the concept B—which represents that $A \sqsubseteq \underline{B}_i$, all objects in $[A]_{\sim_i}$ belong to B as well.

Before formalising this construction, recall that $\bot$ requires a special treatment as a subsumer of a concept name. If $\mathcal{K} \models A \sqsubseteq \bot$, we know that every model makes A empty, and hence A is subsumed by all concepts. Rather than making all these relations explicit, we simply handle this special case separately.

Lemma 8. *Let A, B be two concept names appearing in the normalised $\mathcal{EL}^{\rho/lin}_{\bot}$ KB $\mathcal{K}$, and $S(A)$ the set obtained after saturation of the completion algorithm. If $\{B, \bot\} \cap S(A) = \emptyset$, then $\mathcal{K} \not\models A \sqsubseteq B$.*

Proof. We build a model $\mathcal{I}$ of $\mathcal{K}$ such that $A^{\mathcal{I}} \not\subseteq B^{\mathcal{I}}$. The domain of this interpretation is

$$\Delta^{\mathcal{I}} := \{C, C_{\sim_i}, C^D_{\sim_i} \mid 1 \leq i \leq n, \text{ and } C, D \text{ are concept names appearing in } \mathcal{K}\}.$$

For each i, with $1 \leq i \leq n$, the equivalence relation $\sim_i$ is the transitive, symmetric, and reflexive closure of the relation

$$\{(C, C_{\sim_i}), (C, C^D_{\sim_i}) \mid C, D \text{ are concept names appearing in } \mathcal{K}\}.$$

Note that all objects in $\Delta^{\mathcal{I}}$ are of the form C, $C_{\sim_i}$, or $C^D_{\sim_i}$. By the definition of the equivalence relations $\sim_i$, there exists for every $\delta \in \Delta^{\mathcal{I}}$ some concept name C such that $\delta \sim_i C$. In particular, this means that every equivalence class of $\sim_i$ contains at least one concept name or, in other terms, that for every $\delta \in \Delta^{\mathcal{I}}$ there exists some $E \in \mathsf{N_C}$ such that $[\delta]_i = [E]_i$.

To define the interpretation function $\cdot^{\mathcal{I}}$, we set for each concept name C appearing in $\mathcal{K}$

$$C^{\mathcal{I}} := \{D \mid C \in S(D)\} \cup \{D_{\sim_i} \mid C \in \underline{S}_i(D)\} \cup$$
$$\{D^E_{\sim_i} \mid C \in S(E), E \in \overline{S}^i(D)\} \cup \{D^E_{\sim_i} \mid C \in \underline{S}_i(D), E \in \mathsf{N_C}\}$$

and for each role name r

$$r^{\mathcal{I}} := \{(C, D) \mid D \in S(C, r)\} \cup \{(C_{\sim_i}, D) \mid D \in S(E, r), E \in \underline{S}_i(C)\} \cup$$
$$\{(C^E_{\sim_i}, D) \mid D \in S(E, r), E \in \overline{S}^i(C)\} \cup$$
$$\{(C^E_{\sim_i}, D) \mid D \in S(F, r), F \in \underline{S}_i(C), E \in \mathsf{N_C}\}.$$

By construction $A \in A^{\mathcal{I}}$ and since $B \notin S(A)$ we know that $A \notin B^{\mathcal{I}}$. It remains to show that this is indeed a model of $\mathcal{K}$. This is shown through a case distinction over the possible types of axioms admitted in the normal form. We show only the cases involving rough constructors.

[**Case** $\underline{C}_i \sqsubseteq D$] If $\delta \in (\underline{C}_i)^{\mathcal{I}}$, then by definition $[\delta]_i \subseteq C^{\mathcal{I}}$. Let $E \in \mathsf{N_C}$ be such that $[\delta]_i = [E]_i$. Then $E_{\sim_i} \in C^{\mathcal{I}}$ and hence $C \in \underline{S}_i(E)$. As the algorithm has finished, the rule CR6 is not applicable, this means that $D \in \underline{S}_i(E)$ and by CR9 $D \in S(E)$. Consider now an arbitrary $E^F_{\sim_i} \in [E]_i$. Since $D \in \underline{S}_i(E)$, by construction we know that $E^F_{\sim_i} \in D^{\mathcal{I}}$. Overall, this means that $\delta \in [E]_i \subseteq D^{\mathcal{I}}$, which proves the result.

[**Case** $C \sqsubseteq \underline{D}_i$] If $\delta \in C^{\mathcal{I}}$ and $[\delta]_i = [E]_{\sim_i}$ for some $E \in \mathsf{N_C}$, then by the rules CR9, CR10, and CR14 it follows that $C \in \overline{S}^i(E)$ which, by rule CR7 implies that $D \in \underline{S}_i(E) \subseteq S(E) \subseteq \overline{S}^i(E)$. Then, $[\delta]_i = [E]_i \subseteq D^{\mathcal{I}}$; that is, $\delta \in (\underline{D}_i)^{\mathcal{I}}$.

[**Case** $C \sqsubseteq \overline{D}^i$] As in the last case, if $\delta \in C^{\mathcal{I}}$ with $[\delta]_i = [E]_i$, then $C \in \overline{S}^i(E)$. Rule CR8 then implies that $D \in \overline{S}^i(E)$ and hence $E^D_{\sim_i} \in D^{\mathcal{I}}$. By construction, $E^D_{\sim_i} \in [\delta]_i$, which implies that $[\delta]_i \cap D^{\mathcal{I}} \neq \emptyset$, and hence $\delta \in (\overline{D}^i)^{\mathcal{I}}$. □

Thus we have a decision procedure for subsumption in $\mathcal{EL}^{\rho/\mathsf{lin}}_\bot$. Overall, we get tractability for reasoning in this logic.

Theorem 9. *Subsumption between concept names w.r.t. $\mathcal{EL}^{\rho/\mathsf{lin}}_\bot$ KBs can be decided in polynomial time.*

Note that the completion algorithm can be used also to check KB consistency and concept satisfiability. For the latter, we have from Lemma 8 that A is unsatisfiable w.r.t. $\mathcal{K}$ iff $\bot \in S(A)$. For the former, we can add the GCI $\top \sqsubseteq X$ and check whether X is unsatisfiable. The results presented in this section appear, in a compact manner, in [15].

6 Multigranular Rough $\mathcal{SHI}(\mathsf{Self})$

We have seen that for the rather inexpressive DL $\mathcal{EL}_\bot$, extending the language to include linearly ordered multigranular rough set semantics does not affect tractability of reasoning, by providing a polynomial-time decision algorithm for subsumption between concepts. Conversely, if the multiple indiscernibility relations can be freely interpreted, then this problem becomes ExpTime-hard, even if existential restrictions are not allowed. A remaining question is how the complexity is affected by adding rough constructors to expressive DLs.

As observed already in [20], the upper and lower approximation operators behave as an existential and universal restriction over the relation $\sim$ (seen as a role), if $\sim$ is interpreted as an equivalence relation. That is, $\overline{C}^i$ corresponds to $\exists\sim_i.C$ and $\underline{C}_i$ corresponds to $\forall\sim_i.C$. Hence, the authors of [20] show that any DL which can restrict roles to be transitive, reflexive, and symmetric can express rough concepts natively. In particular, in the DL $\mathcal{SHI}(\mathsf{Self})$ we can restrict a role $\sim_i$ to be

– transitive through the axiom $\mathsf{tran}(\sim_i)$;
– reflexive via the GCI $\top \sqsubseteq \exists\sim_i.\mathsf{Self}$; and

- symmetric through the RI $\sim_i \sqsubseteq \sim_i^-$.

In other words, $\mathcal{SHI}(\mathsf{Self})^{\rho,n}$ is exactly as expressive as $\mathcal{SHI}(\mathsf{Self})$, and transforming a $\mathcal{SHI}(\mathsf{Self})^{\rho,n}$ KB into a $\mathcal{SHI}(\mathsf{Self})$ one incurs in only a linear blow-up. As a consequence, reasoning (that is, deciding KB consistency, concept satisfiability, or concept subsumption) in this multigranular rough logic remains ExpTime-complete.

Theorem 10. *Reasoning in $\mathcal{SHI}(\mathsf{Self})^{\rho,n}$ is ExpTime-complete.*

Note that this reduction into classical DLs requires at least to express existential and value restrictions and symmetric roles. As even (i) $\mathcal{EL}$ extended with symmetric roles and (ii) the DL $\mathcal{FL}_0$ which allows value restrictions are known to be ExpTime-hard [1] for the reasoning problems considered, any logic that natively expresses the rough constructors requires at least exponential time for reasoning.

7 Conclusions and Future Work

In this paper we introduced multigranular rough DLs, which extend the class of rough DLs to multiple indiscernibility relations. These logics admit reasoning w.r.t. several granulations, which can be obtained in applications, for instance, by the use of different clusterings of the data. We investigated the complexity of reasoning regarding (i) the expressivity of the underlying DL and (ii) whether either arbitrary sets or linearly ordered sets of indiscernibility relations are admitted. We showed that for arbitrary sets of indiscernibility relations, reasoning is already ExpTime-hard even if only conjunction is admitted in the DL. This is a somewhat severe and unexpected result.

In contrast, the complexity remains as in the classical DL for $\mathcal{EL}_\bot^{\rho/\mathsf{lin}}$ where the set of indiscernibility relations is linearly ordered and also for multigranular $\mathcal{SHI}(\mathsf{Self})^{\rho,n}$ where arbitrary sets of indiscernibility relations are used. Specifically, we have shown that testing subsumption in $\mathcal{EL}_\bot^{\rho/\mathsf{lin}}$ is in P by developing a decision procedure for it and for the expressive Boolean-complete $\mathcal{SHI}(\mathsf{Self})^{\rho,n}$ we have shown ExpTime-completeness by employing the reduction from [20].

There are many open questions to address. With the investigated multigranular DL being either P- or ExpTime-complete, it is not clear whether there are multigranular DLs that admit PSpace-complete reasoning. Furthermore, since our reduction from Sect. 4 uses only the upper approximation constructor, it is uncertain whether admitting only lower approximations would lead to lower complexity. Finally, it would be interesting to extend reasoning in rough DLs in general and in multigranular DLs in particular to ABox reasoning.

Acknowledgements. This work was partially supported by the MUR for the Department of Excellence DISCo at the University of Milano-Bicocca and under the PRIN project PINPOINT Prot. 2020FNEB27, CUP H45E21000210001; and by the European Union–Next Generation EU within the project NRPP M4C2, Investment 1.,3 DD. 341 - 15 march 2022 – FAIR – Spoke 4 - PE00000013 - D53C22002380006

References

1. Baader, F., Brandt, S., Lutz, C.: Pushing the $\mathcal{EL}$ envelope. In: Proceedings of 18th International Joint Conference on Artificial Intelligence (IJCAI 2005) (2005)
2. Baader, F., Calvanese, D., McGuinness, D.L., Nardi, D., Patel-Schneider, P.F. (eds.): The Description Logic Handbook: Theory, Implementation, and Applications. Cambridge University Press, 2nd edn. (2007)
3. Baader, F., Hladik, J., Peñaloza, R.: Automata can show PSpace results for description logics. Inf. Comput. **206**(9–10), 1045–1056 (2008)
4. Baader, F., Lutz, C., Brandt, S.: Pushing the $\mathcal{EL}$ envelope further. In: Proceedings of 4th OWLED Workshop, CEUR, vol. 496. CEUR-WS.org (2008)
5. Fisher, D.H.: Knowledge acquisition via incremental conceptual clustering. Mach. Learn. **2**(2), 139–172 (1987). https://doi.org/10.1007/BF00114265
6. Halpern, J.Y., Moses, Y.: A guide to completeness and complexity for modal logics of knowledge and belief. Artif. Intell. **54**(3), 319–379 (1992)
7. Hirano, S., Tsumoto, S.: Hierarchical clustering of non-Euclidean relational data using indiscernibility-level. In: Wang, G., Li, T., Grzymala-Busse, J.W., Miao, D., Skowron, A., Yao, Y. (eds.) RSKT 2008. LNCS (LNAI), vol. 5009, pp. 332–339. Springer, Heidelberg (2008). https://doi.org/10.1007/978-3-540-79721-0_47
8. Keet, C.M.: Granulation with indistinguishability, equivalence, or similarity. In: 2007 IEEE International Conference on Granular Computing (GrC 2007), pp. 11–16. IEEE Computer Society (2007)
9. Keet, C.M.: From granulation hierarchy to granular perspective. In: The 2009 IEEE International Conference on Granular Computing (GrC), pp. 306–311. IEEE Computer Society (2009)
10. Keet, C.M.: Ontology engineering with rough concepts and instances. In: Cimiano, P., Pinto, H.S. (eds.) EKAW 2010. LNCS (LNAI), vol. 6317, pp. 503–513. Springer, Heidelberg (2010). https://doi.org/10.1007/978-3-642-16438-5_40
11. Keet, C.M.: Rough subsumption reasoning with rOWL. In: Proceedings of the 2011 Annual Conference of the South African Institute of Computer Scientists and Information Technologists, SAICSIT 2011. ACM (2011)
12. Liau, C.J.: On rough terminological logics. In: Proceedings of the 4th International Workshop on Rough Sets, Fuzzy Sets and machine Discovery (RSFD 1996), pp. 47–54 (1996)
13. Liu, C., Miao, D., Qian, J.: On multi-granulation covering rough sets. Int. J. Approximate Reas. **55**(6), 1404–1418 (2014)
14. Pawlak, Z.: Rough sets. Int. J. Comput. Inf. Sci. **11**, 341–356 (1982). https://doi.org/10.1007/BF01001956
15. Peñaloza, R., Turhan, A.Y.: Rough, rougher, roughest: extending $\mathcal{EL}$ with a Hierarchy of Indiscernibility Relations. In: Proceedings of the 37th international Workshop on Description Logics, CEUR (2024)
16. Peñaloza, R., Zou, T.: Roughening the $\mathcal{EL}$ envelope. In: Proceedings of of International Symposium on Frontiers of Combining Systems (FroCoS 2013). LNCS, Springer (2013)
17. Peñaloza, R., Thost, V., Turhan, A.Y.: Query answering for rough $\mathcal{EL}$ ontologies. In: Proceedings of the 16th International Conference on Principles of Knowledge Representation and Reasoning (KR 2018), AAAI Press (2018)
18. Qian, Y., Liang, J., Yao, Y., Dang, C.: MGRS: a multi-granulation rough set. Inf. Sci. **180**(6), 949–970 (2010)

19. Schild, K.: A correspondence theory for terminological logics: preliminary report. In: Proceedings of 12th International Joint Conference on Artificial Intelligence (IJCAI 1991) (1991)
20. Schlobach, S., Klein, M.C., Peelen, L.: Description logics with approximate definitions - precise modeling of vague concepts. In: Proceedings of 19th International Joint Conference on Artificial Intelligence (IJCAI 2007), pp. 557–562 (2007)

A Benchmark for Rule Induction in Automated Business Decisions

Hagen Völzer[1](✉)[iD], Daniel Horn[2], Yusik Kim[3][iD], and Greger Ottosson[4][iD]

[1] University of St. Gallen, St. Gallen, Switzerland
hagen.voelzer@unisg.ch
[2] IBM Germany, Stuttgart, Germany
[3] IBM Research - Europe, Orsay, France
[4] Cube5 AI, Nice, France

Abstract. We consider *rule induction* as a valuable tool in developing automated business decision services. For this use case, we present first results towards a comprehensive benchmark of rule induction pipelines. In this paper, we focus on typical binary business decision classification problems. The chosen pipelines include classical algorithms as well as promising recent approaches. The data sets vary substantially in terms of their characteristics such as imbalance, noise, size and label complexity. Our results suggest that out-of-the-box rule induction often generates short rule sets within acceptable training time that have a predictive performance close to the non-interpretable reference xgboost. Our results also show some shortcomings and open problems. We also present several synthetic experiments that differentiate the selected pipelines further.

1 Introduction

The increased use of machine-learning based predictions in high-stakes business decisions, e.g., loan approval, has increased the demand for transparent predictions. While several incidents of undesirable and unexplained business decisions have become public and have fueled the public discussion about the trustworthiness of AI, these incidents only constitute the tip of the iceberg since the models produced by many machine learning techniques are inherently non-transparent, i.e., their internal prediction logic is not clearly and fully understood, not just by the end user but neither by the data scientist who creates the model.

While there is substantial research into *explainable AI*, i.e., methods that gain insights into existing black-box models, there is also an increased interest in *interpretable* models, which are models that essentially have the same form as human-written code. Such code cannot only be inspected and understood but also debugged and enhanced by engineers or analysts. Examples of enhancements include adjusting the model for additional requirements such as fairness constraints or adding domain knowledge from a subject matter expert to the predictive model to increase predictive performance. Rudin [17] argues strongly in favor of interpretable models for use in high-stakes decisions, cf. also [11]. This is in line with the proposed European Artificial Intelligence Act [2], which requires a certified conformance assessment for high-stakes decision services including the traceability of decisions.

Decision rules are an appealing form for an interpretable decision model as they have been used traditionally in business automation. *Rule induction* [13] generates decision rules from tabular labeled data. For example, a loan application data set that is labeled with the information whether the applicant has paid back the loan in time can be used to generate a set of rules that can be used to decide whether a loan application should be granted or rejected. Once a set of rules has been created from data, it can be further enhanced, deployed and maintained as usual. While some specialized decisioning platforms, e.g., online transaction fraud detectors, have worked with rule induction for some time, some vendors for more generic tools are now experimenting with it [1].

There is a wealth of rule induction algorithms, cf. Section 2, but no comprehensive benchmark is currently available that helps with the selection of a particular algorithm for a given data set. New algorithms, some of which are very recent, are often proposed with an evaluation on a small suite of small to medium-sized cherry-picked data sets. Moreover, those evaluations typically focus on accuracy to measure predictive performance. Accuracy is not adequate for imbalanced classification problems which are however prevalent in various business use cases, cf. Section 3.1.

A technical report [18] presents a comparative performance analysis of various rule induction algorithms. That study however has not taken into account important characteristics of the data sets, such as imbalance, noise, size and others. Furthermore, new approaches to rule induction have recently emerged, e.g., based on column generation [9] and neural network based [15,16], which were not included in the earlier study.

In this paper, we contribute towards a comprehensive benchmarking by:

(i) Providing an extensible benchmark for community use [3]. To this end, we have also updated and re-packaged a set of rule induction algorithms as a Python package *rulelearn*[1].
(ii) Running the benchmarking, we see that rule induction can deliver a predictive performance for many data sets that is close to our non-interpretable reference model xgboost [7]. We identify some rules of thumb for selecting pipelines, in particular for imbalanced and noisy data sets and for trading-off predictive performance and model size. Furthermore, we point out performance gaps and open questions.

2 Rule Induction Pipelines

For this paper, we restrict the scope to *binary* classification on tabular data with numerical and categorical features. *Rule induction* [13] computes a set of *decision rules* from the input table. A *rule* consists of an *antecedent* (if-part) and a *consequent* (then-part). A rule describes how the target label depends on the input features. The antecedent of a rule is usually a conjunction of possibly negated predicates, the consequent refers to one of the two label values. A *rule set* is a set of rules that have the same consequent (referring to the *positive* value of the label). Therefore, the rules can be evaluated in

---

[1] https://github.com/IBM/rulelearn An earlier version of the rulelearn code is contained in the broader AIX360 package [4]. Some of the code is taken from earlier AIX360 contributions of other authors, some code was provided by some of the authors of this paper and integrated into AIX360 before forking.

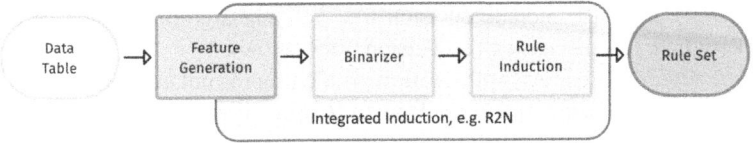

Fig. 1. The Basic Rule Induction Pipeline

any order to determine whether the positive value is returned. If none of the antecedents of the rule set evaluates to True, then the *negative value* of the label is returned. This *default rule* is sometimes displayed explicitly at the end of a rule set.

Figure 1 shows the main components of a rule induction pipeline. The readability and the predictive performance of the output rule set can sometimes benefit from additional features that are generated from the existing features of the input table. For example, the difference or the quotient of two existing numerical features can be added. Typically, this would be done manually or automated based on domain-specific knowledge, but there also exist rule induction approaches, e.g., R2N [15] that learn restricted forms of new interpretable features generically. Then, a *binarizer* transforms the data table into a *binarized data table*, i.e., a table where each feature is a binary, i.e., Boolean predicate. The main rule induction algorithm learns the rule set from the binarized data table.

Binarizers. A categorical feature x with values $\{a, b, \ldots\}$ is typically binarized into the set of predicates $(x = a), (x = b), \ldots$, often also with the negations $(x \neq a), (x \neq b), \ldots$. A numerical feature with values $V = \{r_1, \ldots, r_n\}$, where $r_1 = \min V$ and $r_n = \max V$ is binarized into a set of predicates of the form $\{(x \leq b_i) \mid i = 1, \ldots, k\}$ where the $b_i \in [r_1, r_2]$ are k thresholds chosen in different ways. Often, the corresponding negated predicates $\{(x > b_i) \mid i = 1, \ldots, k\}$ are added as well, or predicates of the form $(b_i < x \leq b_{i+1})$ are used. In all theses cases, conjunctions $\bigwedge_{j=1,\ldots n}(x_j \leq b_i)$ are n-dimensional hyper-rectangles. The following are different approaches for binarizing a numerical feature x with values V:

- *k-naive*: k equidistant threshold values $b_i, i = 1, \ldots, k$ are used, i.e., the set of predicates is $\{(x \leq b_i) \mid i = 1, \ldots, k\}$ where $b_i = r_1 + i \cdot w$ and $w = (r_n - r_1)/k$.
- *k-quantile*: Predicates are $\{(x \leq b_i) \mid i = 1, \ldots, k\}$ where b_i is the threshold of the i-th quantile of V.
- *Brute-force*: The predicates are $\{(x \leq r_l) \mid r_l \in V\}$.

Furthermore, the binarization can also be *supervised*, i.e., driven by the classification label. For example, we use in the benchmarking the TREES binarizer that trains one or more decision trees on the labeled data table (categorical and numerical features) and uses the split predicates in the nodes of the decision trees as output predicates.

Rule Induction. We distinguish the following families of rule induction algorithms:

- *Heuristic Search:* Rules are greedily grown to efficiently cover positive examples. Different metrics are used to prune rules, avoid overfitting and optimize the rule set as a whole. Algorithms include RIPPER [8] and its predecessor IREP [12] as well

as CN2. We can also include decision tree learning algorithms such as C4.5 and CART [6] here (cf. discussion on decision trees below).
- *Discrete Optimization:* An optimization problem is formulated that correlates with prediction performance and passed on to a discrete optimization algorithm, e.g. linear optimization, e.g., BRCG [9] or branch and bound, e.g., CORELS [10]. To decrease time, often a strong prior is used to prune the search space, e.g., the number of predicates in a rule does not exceed 2, or search heuristics such as beam search are employed, which may converge to a local optimum. Also other optimization algorithms have been used, e.g. ant-colony optimization and genetic algorithms, or a form of simulated annealing, e.g. in Bayesian Rule Sets [20].
- *Differentiable:* An artificial neural network that is homomorphic to the rule set being learned is trained with back-propagation, e.g. RuleNet [16], R2N [15].
- *Random Forest Extraction:* A random forest is trained and rules are extracted from certain paths of the trees in the forest, e.g., paths that frequently occur across different trees, e.g., SIRUS [5].

Different modes of coupling exist between the components in Fig. 1. Components are typically coupled loosely, e.g., the binarizer creates a full binarized data table in memory before the rule induction starts. This can quickly create a memory bottleneck when the binarizer produces many predicates, especially if the subsequent rule induction is an optimization algorithm that constructs large parts of the rule set search space explicitly. A limited number of predicates on the other hand, can also limit predictive performance. Our implementation of RIPPER has an integrated brute-force binarizer that binarizes only some part of the input table in each step. Moreover, in R2N [15], the three components are tightly coupled, i.e., in each round of learning, the error signal is back-propagated from the output of the rule induction not only through the rule induction, but also through the binarizer and the feature generator.

Rule Lists and Decision Trees. In contrast to a rule set, a *rule list* is an ordered set of rules, i.e., an if-then statement followed by a sequence of else-if statements where each else-if statement may have a different consequent, i.e., decision value. For example, an else-if statement that decides for the positive value maybe followed by an else-if statement deciding for the negative value, which in turn can be followed by an else-if statement deciding again for the positive value. This makes a rule list harder to understand as the effect of each rule must be understood in context of its preceding rules. Note that each rule of a rule set can be understood in isolation.

Like a rule list, a *decision tree* provides a structure for decision rules that has a different user experience compared to rule sets, for a deeper discussion see [11], hence we do not compare generated rule lists, decision trees and rule sets directly. However, all are similar interpretable methods that can be compared regarding their predictive performance and rule lists and decision trees can be easily transformed into rule sets (with some blowup in size) such that the resulting rule sets can be compared directly.

3 Benchmarking Setup

3.1 Goals and General Setup

Goals and Scope. The main goal of the benchmarking is to capture the state of the art within a *scope* and to identify technology gaps. The scope for this paper are rule-based predictions for binary business-relevant decisions. One special aspect for rule induction is to understand which pipeline compositions and configurations are best for which data set and purpose. Such knowledge can help a data scientist or an automated meta-learner to compose or select pipelines for a given data set.

Prediction Problem and Predictive Performance. Prominent use cases for automated business predictions include customer churn prediction, fraud detection, and loan default prediction, which are asymmetric in the sense that they aim at predicting an *exceptional* situation (customer churn, fraud, loan default). Therefore, we assume that one of the two target values of the binary classification is distinguished as the *positive value* that represents the exceptional situation. The exceptional situation is often infrequent, hence many data sets are imbalanced to some extent. To reflect this situation, we report f-score and balanced accuracy along with other metrics as predictive performance, where we set the f-score to 0 for the classifier that has no rule for the positive value.

To compare the predictive performance of rule induction with other state-of-the-art models, we select a non-interpretable reference model. Tree-based ensemble learners are often considered as a reference for tabular data, cf. [14], within this class boosted trees in particular. Hence we use xgboost [7] as the reference. We refer to the inverse of the reference performance as the *noise* level of a data set, i.e., a high reference performance represents a low noise level and vice versa.

Model Complexity and Trade-off with Predictive Performance. Besides the predictive performance, it is important within our problem scope that rule sets are easy to interpret. This clearly has domain-specific and subjective aspects that we cannot address in a generic automated benchmarking. However, we report two metrics of *model complexity* of a rule set to compare different rule induction pipelines: the number of rules and the sum of the number of conjuncts over all rules of a set.

Note that there is a theoretical trade-off between model complexity and predictive performance. Depending on the decision boundary of the classification problem, more rules can yield a better predictive performance. Rule induction pipelines often have a bias for smaller rule sets. This can make the rule set more consumable and help to avoid overfitting, but can also make it harder to tightly approximate complex decision boundaries. The reference learner xgboost on the other hand creates a model that is a non-trivial combination of a large number of (by default 100) trees. That can better approximate complex decision boundaries, but also creates a model complexity that is considered non-interpretable in general. So whereas it depends on the complexity of the decision boundary intrinsic to the data set how pronounced the trade-off is, it depends on the rule induction pipeline how model complexity and predictive performance are actually traded off. Thus, the benchmarking should help answer how pronounced the trade-off is in practice as well as how the trade-off is resolved by different pipelines.

Selection of Pipelines. We aimed at designing the benchmarking code to make it easy to add new data sets and algorithms. For the current, initial version of the benchmarking, we chose algorithms that were easily available in Python providing an interface that is similar to a sklearn classifier interface. Our selection includes: (i) a RIPPER [8] implementation that has a built-in brute-force binarizer (referred to as NATIVE), (ii) an implementation of BRCG [9] that uses beam search to shorten training time. BRCG has won the FICO explainable machine learning challenge;[2] (iii) CORELS [10], which is the latest in a series of discrete optimization-based approaches that learn rule lists. CORELS has demonstrated its benefits in crime prediction use case among others [10]; (iv) a supervised TREES and a QUANTILE binarizer that work with BRCG and CORELS, (v) the sklearn implementation of the decision tree learner CART [6], and (vi) the differentiable learner R2N [15] that allows to learn rule sets with linear predicates based on its own built-in binarizer (referred to as NATIVE).

Note that we use off-the-shelf code, mostly with their standard settings to test the readiness of the technology for application within our aforementioned scope. Although we also include a few alternative non-standard settings, we do not engage in any performance optimization at this point, simple or complex.

3.2 A Core Data Set Suite

With the aforementioned scope, we compiled a *core data set suite* that represents typical business problems such as transaction and insurance fraud detection, loan approval, customer churn prediction, and others, see column 2 of Table 1.

The performance of a given classification pipeline (with fixed hyper-parameters) can strongly depend on data set characteristics such as imbalance, noise, complexity of the decision boundary, density of the training data, etc., cf. Section 4.3ff. We therefore chose for the core suite only data sets that are (i) natural, i.e., non-synthetic, (ii) represent a prediction problem within a business use case and (iii) we leave the data set in its original state (only trivial modifications allowed). If the original target label is a numerical value (regression), we deliberately choose one or more thresholds for the original target to convert it into a classification problem. For example, in the *bike* data set, the target is the number of bikes that were rented out during a particular hour of the day. We chose two thresholds for this target: the mean bike demand and 75% of the maximal demand.

The core data suite currently contains 17 classification problems based on 15 data sets. The data sets are public taken from the UCI repository, OpenML and other sources. Table 1 shows some characteristics of classification problems of the core suite. The number of examples in the data sets ranges from 506 to more than 280 000 rows, where most are medium-sized, i.e., between 5000 and 50 000. Some data sets are purely numerical, one is purely categorical, most have a mix of both. The imbalance (positive ratio) varies from almost perfectly balanced (*heloc*) to extremely imbalanced (*fraud detection*). In Table 1, we also report the predictive performance of xgboost as our proxy for noise in the data set.

---

[2] https://community.fico.com/s/explainable-machine-learning-challenge.

Table 1. Overview over the data sets in the core suite, ordered by xgboost f-score (xgb f); pos. ratio: ratio of positive label value per row.

data set	use case	rows	columns	numerical features	categorical features	pos ratio	xgb f
orange churn	churn	50000	213	174	38	0.0734	0.05
fraud oracle	insurance fraud	15420	33	8	24	0.0599	0.45
taiwan credit	credit	30000	24	14	9	0.2212	0.47
german credit	credit	1000	21	7	13	0.3000	0.47
bike 75	demand prediction	8760	14	9	4	0.0070	0.50
bank marketing	product recommendation	4118	21	10	10	0.1095	0.51
orange up	product recommendation	50000	213	174	38	0.0736	0.56
compas	recidivism	7210	8	0	7	0.4508	0.61
heloc	credit	10459	24	23	0	0.4781	0.68
telco churn 2	churn	2000	14	9	4	0.5000	0.71
adult	income prediction	32561	13	4	8	0.2408	0.71
house	price prediction	22784	17	16	0	0.2960	0.82
telco churn	churn	3333	20	16	3	0.1449	0.84
fraud detection	transaction fraud	284807	31	30	0	0.0017	0.84
boston	price prediction	506	14	13	0	0.4130	0.88
electricity	price sensitivity	45312	9	8	0	0.4245	0.89
bike mean	demand prediction	8760	14	9	4	0.4022	0.92

4 Experimental Results

The charts in this section visualize results from a single run of the benchmarking where every pipeline receives the same subset of the data as training data and is evaluated against the complement of the training data. We have validated all observations mentioned in Sects. 4.1 and 4.2 in 4 additional runs of the entire benchmarking, each run using a different 7:3 random split for each data set.

4.1 General Performance

Predictive Performance. In Fig. 2, plot *maxRI* shows the best predictive performance (f-score) of *any* rule induction pipeline per classification problem against the reference xgboost. Rule induction demonstrates a performance that is comparable, and at times even superior, on our core data suite across a majority of problems. Apart from the data set *fraud oracle*, the difference of f-score w.r.t. xgboost is not larger than 0.09.

Figure 3, lower section, shows the predictive performance (f-score) of all pipelines in their *standard* settings (binarizer and hyper-parameters, default setting or documented standard) in relation to xgboost. Changes to these settings will be discussed in Sect. 4.2. As the standard setting for CART, we chose a maximum depth of 4, cf. Section 4.2.

For f-scores of 0, the pipelines have indeed returned an empty rule set (**if** false **then** pos. value **else** neg. value), which has no recall but can have a high accuracy when the data set is imbalanced. We observe that for each of the pipelines, there is at least one data set where the pipeline has a substantial under-performance w.r.t. xgboost. However, for all data sets, except *fraud oracle* (and in one other run also *bike 75*), there

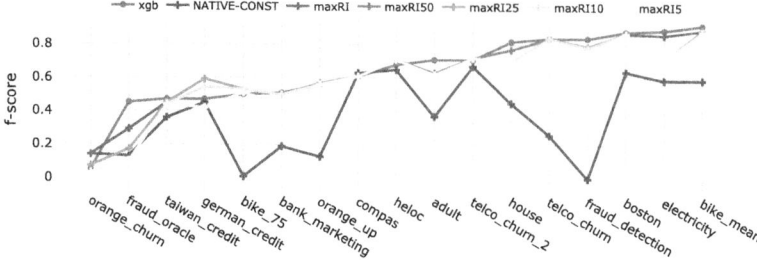

Fig. 2. Predictive performance (f-score) of rule induction compared to xgboost (xgb) and constant classifier (NATIVE-CONST = **if** true **then** pos. value), maxRI–best performance of *any* rule induction pipeline (standard or non-standard configuration), maxRIk–best performance of any rule induction pipeline with k rules or less.

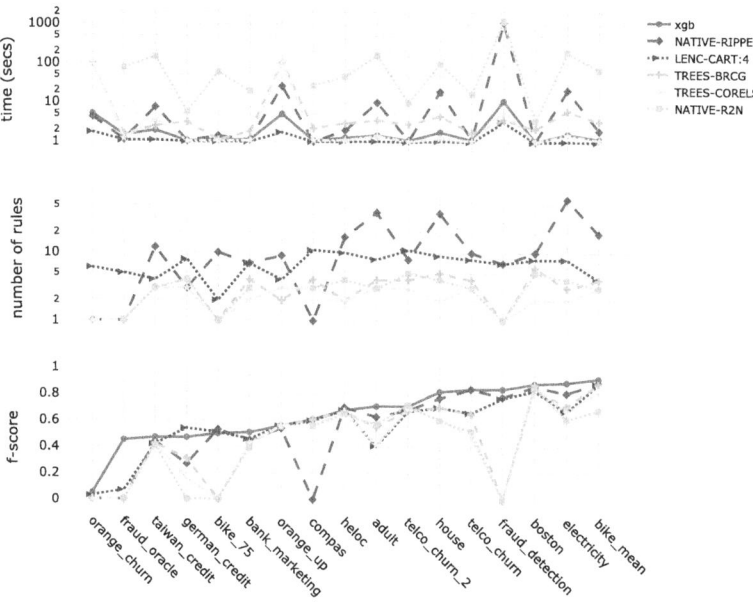

Fig. 3. Bottom: Predictive performance (f-score) for pipelines with standard settings. Middle: Number of rules (log scale) corresponding to the performance in the bottom section. Top: Corresponding training time (log scale). Missing data point means computation failure due to memory overflow or time-out (30 mins). LENC = label encoding, NATIVE = built-in binarizer.

is at least one pipeline that performs close to xgboost. In fact, two pipelines, RIPPER and CART:4 suffice to get close to xgboost for most data sets (besides *fraud oracle*, the largest under-performance is 0.09). For those two data sets, non-standard settings will help, cf. Figure 2 and Sect. 4.2.

The online version of the benchmarking [3], which contains full result tables and more charts, also lists recall and precision as well as balanced accuracy for each performance. The picture for balanced accuracy is similar to that of f-score.

Model Complexity. We measure model complexity in terms of (i) the number of rules per rule set and (ii) the sum of the number of predicates over all rules of the rule set. Figure 4 shows an example of a rule set, which was generated by BRCG on the *bike mean* data set. It has three rules and a sum of 12 predicates.

```
if
    ([Hour <= 1.5] AND [Rainfall_mm <= 0.25] AND [Temperature_C > 18.25]) OR

    ([Functioning Day == True] AND [Hour > 6.5] AND [Humidity_percent <= 80.5] AND
        [Seasons == Autumn]) OR

    ([Functioning Day == True] AND [Hour > 6.5] AND [Humidity_percent <= 86.5] AND
        [Rainfall_mm <= 0.25] AND [Temperature_C > 9.55])

then 1 (= bike demand above average)
```

Fig. 4. Rule set produced by BRCG on the *bike-mean* data set.

Since the average number of predicates per rule has a limited range between 2 and 6 for our pipelines in standard settings, we focus henceforth on the number of rules; sum, average and maximal number of predicates are provided in the online version [3]. The plots maxRI k for $k \in \{50, 25, 10, 5\}$ in Fig. 2 show the best f-score of any rule induction pipeline that was achieved with not more than k rules. We see that for many of the data sets of our suite, an f-score close to xgboost can be achieved with 5 rules or less. A prominent exception is the *electricity* data set, for which more than 50 rules are needed.

The middle section of Fig. 3 shows that CART:4 produces between 2 and 12 rules, BRCG less than CART:4 and CORELS produces, with one or two exceptions, not more than BRCG. The number of rules produced by RIPPER varies significantly.

Trade-off Model Complexity vs. Predictive Performance. Fig. 2 shows for some data sets that more rules can yield a higher performance, e.g., for the *electricity* data set. Looking at the *electricity* data set in Fig. 3, we see that RIPPER achieves a higher predictive performance than, for example BRCG and CORELS with a higher number of rules. A similar situation regarding RIPPER, BRCG and CORELS occurs also for *house, telco churn, heloc* and *adult*. On the other hand, there exist examples, e.g., the *bike mean* data set where RIPPER produces more rules than BRCG and CORELS with only a minor benefit.

Training Time. The top section in Fig. 3 shows the training time in seconds for the pipelines with recommended settings in logarithmic scale. While the times for CART are competitive with xgboost, CORELS, BRCG and RIPPER have satisfactory running times with the possible exception of the *fraud detection* data set, which is very large. R2N performs one order of magnitude slower due to an additional loop, viz. a cooling schedule around the back-propagation, cf. [15], which could still be deemed acceptable

4.2 Alternative Pipeline Configuration

In this section, we present some results for pipelines in non-standard configurations.

CART. Fig. 5 shows the results of alternative CART configurations where the tree depth is restricted to 6 nodes and where it is unrestricted. Whereas the number of rules always grows with lifting the restriction, the f-score does not always grow accordingly.

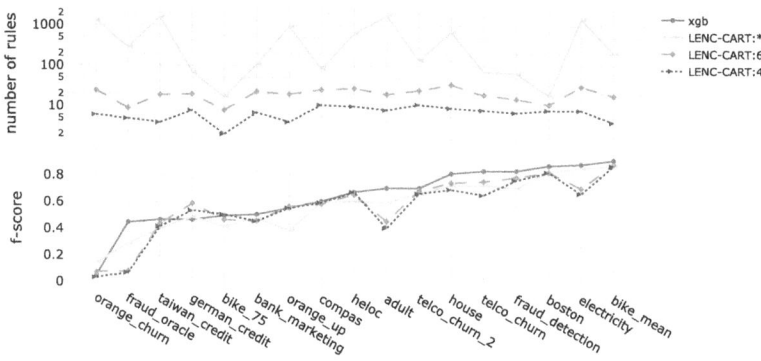

Fig. 5. Bottom: Predictive performance (f-score) for CART pipelines: CART:k tree depth restricted to k nodes, * is unrestricted. Top: Number of rules (log scale) corresponding to the performance in the top section.

BRCG. Figure 6 shows the results of alternative BRCG configurations, using the QUANTILE binarizer (default: 10 quantiles), the TREES2 binarizer (increasing max depth of the tree from 4 to 5 as well as using BRCG2, which decreases the parameters for the cost of rules and predicates by a factor of 10 with respect to BRCG. All of theses changes increase the search space, which is reflected by the increased training time (note the log scale). Significant performance improvements over the standard settings are obtained for a few data sets including *german credit*, *adult* and *fraud detection*.

Other pipelines. Changes similar to BRCG have been applied also to CORELS with fewer and less pronounced improvements. Adding an additional TREES and QUANTILE binarizer to RIPPER leads to worse results with the exception of a few striking improvements in some runs from the TREES binarizer, e.g., for *bike 75* and *fraud oracle*. Increasing the number of bits that a new rule need to gain in RIPPER from 64 to 256 also created performance improvements for some data sets. For full results, see the online version [3].

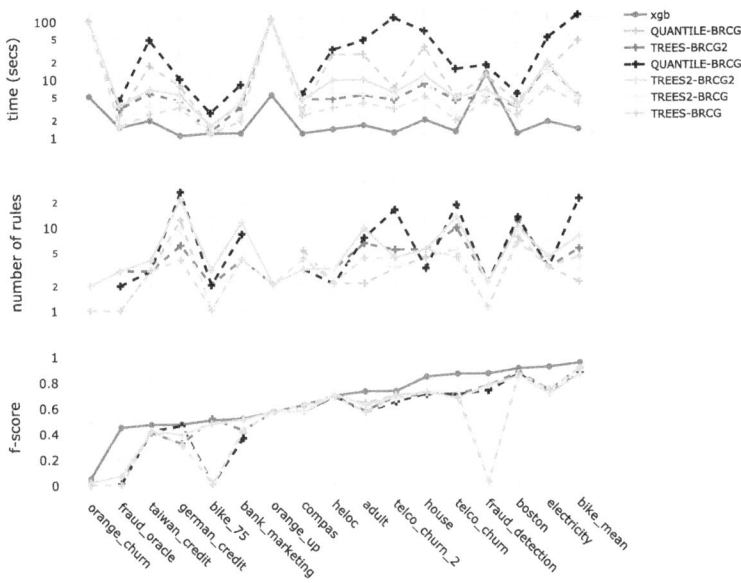

Fig. 6. f-score, number of rules (log scale) and training time (log scale) for BRCG-based pipelines: TREES: supervised binarizer with one tree of maximal depth 4; TREES2: supervised binarizer with one tree of maximal depth 5; BRCG2 = cost of rules and predicates reduced by a factor of 10 w.r.t. BRCG.

4.3 Effect of Imbalance and Noise

Imbalance. The data sets *fraud detection, fraud oracle,* and *bike 75* have a high imbalance, cf. Table 1 and BRCG and CORELS with standard settings do not learn a non-empty rule sets in those cases, cf. Figure 3.

To separate the effect of imbalance from the effect of other data set characteristics such as noise and a complex decision boundary, we have set up an experiment with a suite of synthetic data sets. The synthetic imbalance suite consists of 13 data sets, starting with a positive ratio of 0.5 and increasing the positive ratio from one data set to the next by a factor of 2. So the imbalance is increased exponentially while other characteristics are kept constant: data set size (100 000 rows over 3 numerical features populated randomly), label complexity that satisfies the same simple rule set which has the following single rule **if** $x_0 < 0.5$ **then** 1 **else** 0, and no noise is added.

Figure 7 shows the predictive performance on the synthetic imbalance suite. The first data set has only 7 positive out of 100 000 examples. Hence it is difficult for any pipeline to learn the precise threshold. With twice as many positive examples, xgboost, CART:4, RIPPER and BRCG2 henceforth perform perfectly, reflecting the absence of noise. All other rule induction pipelines deliver perfect or almost perfect performance from a lower point of imbalance.

Noise. No rule induction pipeline with standard settings produces any recall on the data set *fraud oracle*, which has on top of imbalance (positive ratio of 0.06, also a

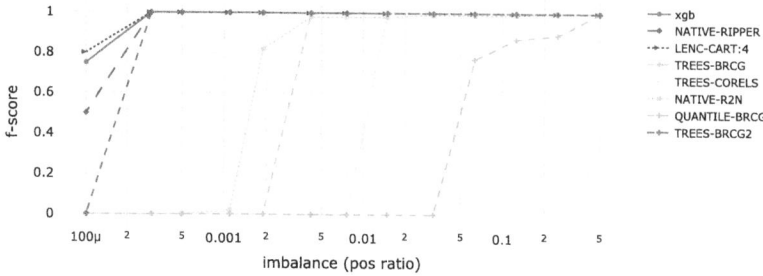

Fig. 7. f-score over log scale pos. ratio on the synthetic imbalance suite.

high noise level (f-score of xgboost 0.45). To separate the effect of noise, we created a suite of synthetic data sets with the same rule as the imbalance suite (now 50 000 rows) but with approximately constant positive ratio of 0.5 and with linearly increasing label noise.

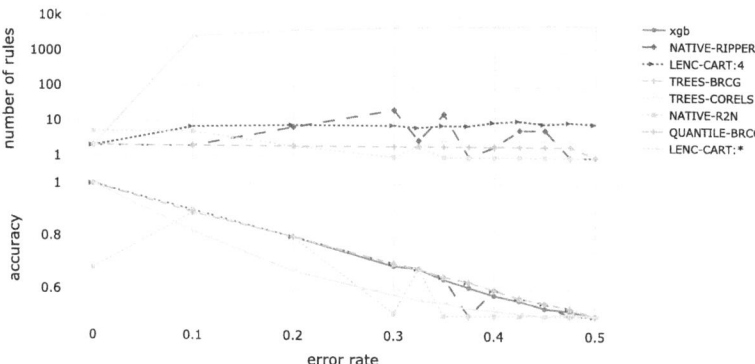

Fig. 8. Accuracy and number of rules over error rate on the synthetic noise suite.

Figure 8 shows the accuracy of the rule sets generated. While xgboost looses accuracy almost perfectly linearly with added noise, CART, BRCG and CORELS follow xgboost very closely and perform even slightly better than xgboost for this simple rule set, supposedly because of their bias towards short rule sets. Our RIPPER implementation performs similar except for high noise when its performance suffers from dropouts.

The upper section of Fig. 8 shows that RIPPER and CART produce, under noise, more rules than necessary for optimal performance (which is 2, one rule that was used for creating the label and the default rule). CART:∗ produces excessively many rules that yield sub-optimal accuracy (overfitting).

4.4 Complex Rule Sets

Since RIPPER achieves sometimes a substantially higher predictive performance than the other rule induction pipelines at the cost of longer rules and longer rule sets, we have set up a series of experiments to study the effect of the complexity of the decision boundary on the predictive performance. We consider the following three kinds of complexity: *disjunctive, conjunctive*, and *linear* complexity.

Disjunctive Complexity. In this experiment, we subdivide the unit interval into $2k$ intervals of equal width and assign each sub-interval alternately the label values 1 and 0. Hence the positive value 1 can be characterized with a set of k rules of the form **if** $c_i \leq x \leq c_{i+1}$ **then** 1. Note that dropping each of these k rules leads to an equal drop of predictive performance.

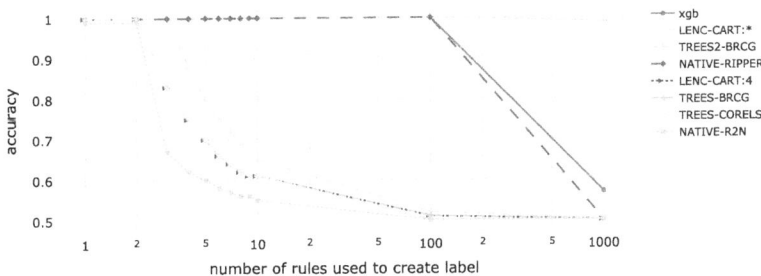

Fig. 9. Predictive performance (accuracy) on a disjunctive complexity suite.

Figure 9 shows the results. Unlike CART:*, xgboost degrades after 100 rules, which is the default setting for the number of trees it uses. RIPPER performs similar to xgboost. All other pipelines degrade quickly in performance after 2 rules, which shows their bias to produce small sets of rules.

Conjunctive Complexity. In this experiment, we generate data sets with a single rule of increasing length, i.e., with an increasing number of conjuncts. In order to keep the contribution of each conjunct equal, we use a common threshold c for each conjunct, i.e., a conjunct is of the form $x_i \leq c$ and the rule is of the form $\bigwedge_{i=1}^{k}(x_i \leq c)$. If we used the same threshold c, e.g., $c = 0.5$, for each data set and just use a different number k of conjuncts, the imbalance increases exponentially and some pipelines would be affected by strong imbalance as in the imbalance experiment above. To keep the imbalance approximately constant (at 0.5), we can populate the value for features x_i, $i = 1, \ldots k$ uniformly random in [0, 1] and use a threshold $c = 0.5^{\frac{1}{k}}$.

Figure 10 shows the results. BRCG and CORELS find precise thresholds but stop at some point to produce additional conjuncts (TREES-BRCG produces here a maximum of 4 conjuncts). The resulting degradation in performance is regular. Increasing the capacity of the binarizer (from TREES depth 4 to TREES2 depth 5) results in a maximum number of conjuncts of 5, hence the increased performance of TREES2-BRCG with

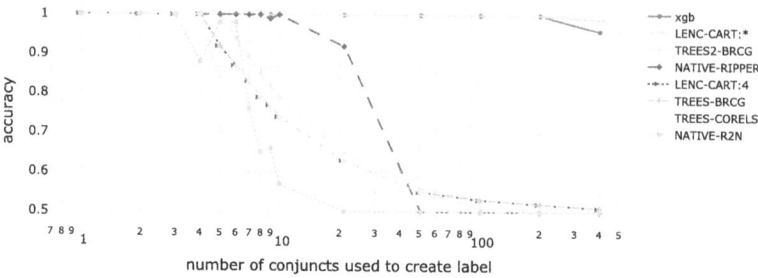

Fig. 10. Predictive performance (accuracy) on a conjunctive complexity suite.

respect to TREES-BRCG. Note that in contrast to BRCG and CORELS, RIPPER suddenly loses performance between 20 and 50 conjuncts.

Linear Complexity. Finally, we conduct an experiment where features are combined not in a conjunctive, but in a linear way. More precisely the label for data set k is defined by $\sum_{i=1}^{k} x_i \leq 0.5$.

Our results show (available online [3]) that R2N is the only pipeline in our selection that can find linear predicates, which allows it to marginally surpass the performance of xgboost. However, we also see again the inconsistency of R2N. Note that linear predicates might be considered harder to read compared to simpler predicates using thresholds only. The other pipelines need to approximate the linear, i.e., high-dimensional hyperplane decision boundary with a series of hyper-rectangles. With increasing bias towards shorter rule sets, that results in increasing loss of accuracy.

5 Conclusions and Outlook

5.1 Discussion of Experimental Results

Recommendations for Pipeline Selection. Fig. 3 suggests that often a selection of a few pipelines with standard settings will yield good results. If the priority is on predictive performance, the combination of RIPPER and CART:4 yields good predictive performance for almost all cases. Our RIPPER implementation generally yields a good predictive performance, but Figs. 3 and 8 suggest that, in the presence of higher noise, we risk more drop-outs (no recall). Note that the noise level can be approximately calculated by running xgboost before rule induction.

Figure 5 shows that the capacity restriction of CART is important—unrestricted CART suffers from too many rules. Figure 8 also shows the overfitting of unrestricted CART in the presence of noise, which also manifests to some extent in Fig. 5 for the data sets where restricted CART performs better than unrestricted CART. Even though CART:4 produces overall good results, Fig. 5 also shows that the optimal restriction of course depends on the data set. Therefore and because CART has short training times, CART is a promising candidate for automated hyper-parameter optimization.

When we are more interested in short rule sets and less in optimal predictive performance, BRCG consistently delivers short rule sets that often also perform well. CORELS tends to yield even shorter rule sets than BRCG—however, sometimes at the cost of lower predictive performance. Note that also rules from BRCG and CORELS are also significantly shorter compared to CART rules, cf. [3]. However, Figs. 3 and 7 suggest that their standard settings might not work in cases of very high imbalance. In that case, BRCG2 can be a good option, cf. Figures 6 and 7.

If after these recommended pipeline selections, there is still a large performance gap to xgboost, the reason might be a combination of noise and a complex decision boundary. A hint for a complex decision boundary could be a relatively high under-performance of CART:4 w.r.t. xgboost, e.g., for the *electricity, adult* and *fraud oracle* data sets. Figure 5 suggests the generic approach to find the k such that CART:k yields optimal performance, i.e., to gradually lift the restriction on CART. Unrestricted CART however does still not produce minimal model complexity, cf. e.g. Figures 3 and 8.

R2N might help in case of linear interactions between features, cf. Section 4.4, last paragraph, but it also performs very inconsistently with the current settings. Also RIPPER re-configurations have improved the RIPPER performance on *electricity, adult* and *fraud oracle*, cf. [3].

Open questions. Some performance gaps on some data sets are not yet well explained such as RIPPER on *compas*. Also a reliable selection strategy for those cases when a performance gap to xgboost remains after trying standard settings requires further study. It is an open question whether it is feasible to create a single pipeline that achieves a consistent performance with respect to the reference within acceptable training time. Moreover, the ideal pipeline would receive a single parameter that tightly controls the trade-off between performance and model complexity.

5.2 Limitations and Outlook

Limitations of Current Benchmarking. The current benchmarking for our scope is foremost limited by the data sets, which cover a range of different characteristics, but might still miss out on other data distribution characteristics that may be present in other natural data sets. We have assessed to the best of our ability that all data sets are plausibly natural, i.e., non-synthetic. However, provenance traceability is often limited. The feature names and categorical values in the orange data set appear pseudonymized, which does not affect the reported results. A single data set, viz. *fraud detection* has used stronger methods to preserve privacy, most likely a PCA transformation, which supposedly changes at least model complexity results compared to the original data. We have not yet found an alternative clear text natural data set on transaction fraud.

In the selection of pipelines, we are currently most notably missing a pipeline from the random forest extraction family, but there are also more algorithms from the other families that could be tried to complete the picture. It is also worthwhile to compare different implementations of the same algorithm, e.g., the *rulelearn* implementation and the long-standing WEKA implementation of RIPPER.

The benchmarking results were obtained on an Apple 8-core M2 processor with 24 GB of memory. A larger system would allow us to fill in some results that are currently missing, e.g. some non-standard settings for BRCG and CORELS on large data sets such as *orange up*, which caused memory overflow. Also, we have limited training time by 30 min for the core suite. Providing more space and time would allow us to assess whether additional non-standard settings for R2N, BRCG, and CORELS that result in a substantially larger search space will lead to better and more consistent results.

Additional metrics characterizing concepts of stability and redundancy for rule sets could further differentiate induction approaches in a generic way.

Future Work. Besides overcoming some of the above mentioned limitations, we want to extend the benchmarking to multi-class classification and regression. Rule-based regression models prominently include *score cards*, e.g. *credit score cards*, which can be represented in the popular standard DMN (Decision Model and Notation).

Recent work [19] has also increased the promise of using rule mining in multi-perspective process mining to obtain insights and explanations for process outcomes and deviances. We are also interested in investigating the comparative benefits of different rule mining pipelines for that use case.

References

1. DMN meets machine learning. https://www.trisotech.com/dmn-meet-machine-learning/
2. EU Artificial Intelligence Act. https://artificialintelligenceact.eu
3. Rule induction benchmark online. https://github.com/hvoelzer/rulebenchmark
4. Arya, V., Bellamy, R.K.E., Chen, P.Y., Dhurandhar, A., Hind, M., Hoffman, S.C., Houde, S., Liao, Q.V., Luss, R., Mojsilović, A., Mourad, S., Pedemonte, P., Raghavendra, R., Richards, J., Sattigeri, P., Shanmugam, K., Singh, M., Varshney, K.R., Wei, D., Zhang, Y.: One explanation does not fit all: A toolkit and taxonomy of AI explainability techniques (2019), https://arxiv.org/abs/1909.03012
5. Bénard, C., Biau, G., Veiga, S.D., Scornet, E.: SIRUS: Stable and Interpretable RUle Set for classification. Electronic Journal of Statistics **15**(1), 427–505 (2021)
6. Breiman, L., Friedman, J.H., Olshen, R.A., Stone, C.J.: Classification and regression trees (1984)
7. Chen, T., Guestrin, C.: XGBoost: A scalable tree boosting system. In: KDD. p. 785-794 (2016)
8. Cohen, W.W.: Fast effective rule induction. In: Machine Learning Proceedings, pp. 115–123. Morgan Kaufmann, San Francisco (CA) (1995)
9. Dash, S., Günlük, O., Wei, D.: Boolean decision rules via column generation. In: NeurIPS. pp. 4660–4670 (2018)
10. Elaine, A., Nicholas, L.S., Daniel, A., Margo, S., Cynthia, R.: Learning certifiably optimal rule lists for categorical data. J. Mach. Learn. Res. **18**(234), 1–78 (2018)
11. Freitas, A.A.: Comprehensible classification models: a position paper. SIGKDD Explor. **15**(1), 1–10 (2013)
12. Fürnkranz, J., Widmer, G.: Incremental reduced error pruning. In: Machine Learning Proceedings 1994, pp. 70–77 (1994)
13. Fürnkranz, J., Gamberger, D., Lavrač, N.: Foundations of Rule Learning. Springer (2012)
14. Grinsztajn, L., Oyallon, E., Varoquaux, G.: Why do tree-based models still outperform deep learning on typical tabular data. In: NeurIPS (2022)

15. Kusters, R., Kim, Y., Collery, M., de Sainte Marie, C., Gupta, S.: Differentiable rule induction with learned relational features. In: Proc. of the 16th Int. Workshop on Neural-Symbolic Learning and Reasoning as part of IJCLR. CEUR Workshop Proceedings, vol. 3212, pp. 30–44 (2022)
16. Qiao, L., Wang, W., Lin, B.: Learning accurate and interpretable decision rule sets from neural networks. In: AAAI. pp. 4303–4311 (2021)
17. Rudin, C.: Stop explaining black box machine learning models for high stakes decisions and use interpretable models instead. Nature Machine Intelligence **1**(5), 206–215 (2019)
18. Speh, C.: Evaluation of different rule learning algorithms. Technische Universität Darmstadt, Tech. rep. (2019)
19. Völzer, H., Zerbato, F., Sulzer, T., Weber, B.: A fresh approach to analyze process outcomes. In: ICPM 2023. pp. 97–104. IEEE (2023)
20. Wang, T., Rudin, C., Doshi-Velez, F., Liu, Y., Klampfl, E., MacNeille, P.: A bayesian framework for learning rule sets for interpretable classification. J. Mach. Learn. Res. **18**, 70:1–70:37 (2017)

Revising Defeasible Theories via Instructions

Mihai Pomarlan[1](✉)[iD], Maria M. Hedblom[2][iD], Laura Spillner[3][iD], and Robert Porzel[3][iD]

[1] Applied Linguistics Department, University of Bremen, Bremen, Germany
`pomarlan@uni-bremen.de`
[2] Jönköping Artificial Intelligence Laboratory, Jönköping University, Jönköping, Sweden
`maria.hedblom@ju.se`
[3] Digital Media Lab, University of Bremen, Bremen, Germany
`{spillner,porzel}@tzi.de`

Abstract. Progress in AI raises agent alignment problems. In this paper, we look at the problem of instructing an agent, i.e. informing it about a regularity in the world it did not previously know. We study an idealized case: agents reasoning with logical theories. The idealization helps to understand the space of possibilities of the problem, and illustrates potential pitfalls and solutions. We believe non-monotonic theories more plausibly approximate human practical and commonsense reasoning so our agents here also use non-monotonic inference. However, instructing a non-monotonic theory does not always result in better alignment. One main cause of this phenomenon is humans omitting the kind of information used by a non-monotonic inference system to resolve conflicts between its parts. We illustrate this with theories induced from a dataset consisting of situated objects. We argue that obtaining non-monotonic theories that respond better to instruction requires additional restrictions on the formalism and theory update procedure.

Keywords: Defeasible Logic · Model Reconciliation · Belief Revision

1 Introduction

Chatbots deployed today often ask the user to patiently correct them when they say weird or wrong things. This is reasonable. A chatbot might need to be informed about a user's preferences, or the user can handle a new situation better, or maybe the agent has some mistaken idea about the world. Whether an AI agent deployed today can hold its end of the bargain – reliably learn from the user's instruction – is another matter.

Several difficulties arise. The case of Microsoft's chatbot Tay shows that an AI agent should not trust everything it hears [28]. Another consideration is whether an agent is at all competent to reason about the world and update a theory about it, and it is not clear current AI agents can do so reliably. Still, let us assume that both our agent and its human user are logical agents: they each have a theory about the world which can be manipulated via a formalized procedure to yield conclusions. Let the human be trustworthy and truthful. This simplification shows what we can expect, under ideal conditions, of the artificial agents we hope to teach via the kind of interactions we use between humans.

A human would not recite everything they know, and will not give a robotic assistant a lecture. Instead, a human might state a rule in a particular situation where the artificial agent needs a correction (see Fig. 1). The agent must accommodate this rule into its theory and use it after in relevantly similar situations. The agent's updated theory should be better, from the user's perspective: it should make fewer mistakes and disagree less with the human's conclusions. If the human and agent use monotonic theories, this seems to be the case.

However, we argue non-monotonic methods are better suited to approximate human commonsense inference [1,24]. Practical situations require decisions with partial information, which makes deductive validity an unrealistic requirement: monotonic deduction has to either be satisfied with conclusions that are too weak, or too strongly held despite additional evidence.

Consider a mother telling her child that dirty dishes go in the dishwasher. Only later she might add that very dirty dishes must first be rinsed, paper cups must be put in the trash etc. There are many exceptions but they do not need attention often. This example illustrates the use of non-monotonic inference, as well as what the child has when receiving an instruction: their knowledge of the situation and the rule stated by the mother to apply in such a situation.

However, our hypothetical artificial agent using non-monotonic inference may introduce new errors in its theory when being told a new rule. This is because the formal mechanism by which one conclusion overrules another is underspecified by the instruction. We will illustrate how this happens in a realistic scenario when using defeasible logic (see Sect. 3): a defeasible theory ("Student") is liable to disagree more with a reference theory ("Teacher") despite receiving instructions from Teacher (Sect. 6). We look at how the number of situations in which Student and Teacher disagree changes with number of instructions received, and we focus on disagreements that reappear in situations for which Student has already received instructions. We then show an approach to eliminate the reintroduction of disagreements between Teacher and Student over situations where Student has already received instructions; empirically, this approach also reduces the introduction of new disagreements (Sect. 7).

2 Related Work

Our instructability problem as defined in Sect. 4 is a subcase of **model reconciliation** but unlike previously considered model reconciliation scenarios [3,25–27], in the instructability scenario the information flows from the human, and the focus is on the persistence of updates to the instructed agent.

Non-monotonic reasoning is tightly connected to work on belief revision. In the AGM model[1] of belief revision, the three primary different operations (expansion, revision, contraction) are based on non-monotonic reasoning [6]. Argument

---

[1] Named after the authors: Alchourròn, Gärdenfors and Makinson.

theory change (ATC) is a belief revision system for reasoning in changing knowledge bases, useful in hypothetical reasoning, dialogues etc. [20].

Other work includes knowledge acquisition based on non-monotonic dialogue systems (e.g. [21]), where agents pursue goals such as inquiries, negotiations, or persuasion. The agent theories are fixed, unlike the instructability case.

Theory revision for defeasible logic requires some adaptation of the AGM postulates [2] but has also been extensively researched for applications of defeasible logic to reasoning in the legal domain: modelling "legal dynamics" (e.g. what happens to past consequences of a law once it is abrogated) [12], modelling legislative dialog [13]. Further work considered "strategic" revisions where an agent either must find a subset of their theory to support a preferred conclusion (even when the agent's theory does not support this conclusion) [7,10] or revise a rule priority order so that the preferred conclusion is established [8]; NP-hardness results for these variants have been established. Our instructability problem however does not require an agent to lie by omission; a Teacher agent truthfully reports the conclusion of their theory, together with a subset of it that is an argument for that conclusion. Unlike the legal reasoning case, for instructability Student must simply accept Teacher's stated conclusion from the point of instruction onwards, with no consideration of past consequences and no negotiation from the Student's side. We will discuss in Sect. 4 why the hardness results for the strategic variants do not also cover instructability.

3 Defeasible Logic: a Brief Introduction

Defeasible logic is a family of non-monotonic logics introduced by Donald Nute [22] and further developed by David Billington [1]. Inference in propositional defeasible logic (the Billington variant) takes time linear in theory size [17] and, slightly modified, scales well to large knowledge bases [18]. It has found applications in legal inference [11] and robotics [15]. We refer the reader to [15] for an overview of defeasible logic variants. For a simpler exposition, we chose to work here with a version using only defeasible rules, ambiguity blocking, and individual defeat.

A defeasible logic theory is a set of (named) rules, each rule consisting of a conjunction of literals (the antecedent) and a consequent conclusion, and a priority relation between the rules. Each literal is a, possibly negated, proposition. We will use $r.\mathbf{ant}$ to refer to the antecedent of a rule r, and $r.con$ to refer to its conclusion. The expression below

  r : small , heavy $\Rightarrow$ metal

is a defeasible rule named r where $r.\mathbf{ant}$ is "small and heavy" and $r.con$ is "metal". A rule supports its conclusion, and opposes literals incompatible with it. A literal and its negation are always incompatible. There are also mutex sets: any two literals in a mutex set are incompatible. An expression $r > s$ means rule r has higher priority (is stronger) than s.

Inference proceeds by adding conclusions to a provability chain. A conclusion is a decorated literal $+\partial q$ ("defeasibly provable that q") or $-\partial q$ ("no defeasible proof of q"). A $+\partial q$ can be added to the chain at position P_n if:

- q is a fact, OR
- there is a rule r with $r.con = q$ for which the following conjunction is true:
  - for every literal $a \in r.\mathbf{ant}$, there exists $k < n$ such that $+\partial a = P_k$ AND
  - for every rule s such that q and $s.con$ are incompatible, EITHER there is b in $s.\mathbf{ant}$ such that there is $j < n$ such that $-\partial b = P_j$, OR $r > s$

If all literals in a rule antecedent are facts or $+\partial$, the rule is said to be **applicable**. The condition under which $-\partial q$ can be added to the chain at position P_n is the strong negation of the condition for $+\partial q$:

- q is not a fact, AND
- for every rule r with $r.con = q$ the following disjunction is true:
  - there is some literal $a \in r.\mathbf{ant}$ and $k < n$ such that $-\partial a = P_k$ OR
  - there is a rule s with q and $s.con$ incompatible, such that for every b in $s.\mathbf{ant}$ there is $j < n$ such that $+\partial b = P_j$, AND $r \not> s$

Defeasible logics are coherent ($+\partial q$ and $-\partial q$ will never be inferred together), consistent if the facts are consistent, and allow for undecided conclusions (neither $+\partial q$ nor $-\partial q$ gets added to the provability chain). It is usual to require transitivity of the rule priority relation, which provides further good meta-logical properties: Cut and Cautious Monotony (CM) [19][2]. If $(\mathbf{T}, >_{\mathbf{T}})$ is a theory (set of defeasible rules and rule priority relations), $\mathbf{f}$ is a set of facts, and $\vdash$ is "entails":

- Cut: if $((\mathbf{T}, >_{\mathbf{T}}), \mathbf{f} \vdash p)$ and $((\mathbf{T}, >_{\mathbf{T}}), \mathbf{f} \cup \{p\} \vdash q)$ then $((\mathbf{T}, >_{\mathbf{T}}), \mathbf{f} \vdash q)$
- CM: if $((\mathbf{T}, >_{\mathbf{T}}), \mathbf{f} \vdash p)$ and $((\mathbf{T}, >_{\mathbf{T}}), \mathbf{f} \vdash q)$ then $((\mathbf{T}, >_{\mathbf{T}}), \mathbf{f} \cup \{p\} \vdash q)$

In this paper, we will restrict ourselves to stratified theories. A theory is stratified if there exists a function L from literals in the theory to integers, such that whenever a, b are in a mutex set, $L(a) = L(b)$ and for every rule $a_1, a_2, ...a_n => c$ we have $L(c) > L(a_k)$ for all $k \in 1, .., n$.

We call a priority relation **arbitrary** if it is impossible to say, given only two rules, which one, if any, ranks higher. A restriction on the priority relation that makes it non-arbitrary is specificity: $s > r$ if and only if $s.\mathbf{ant}$ is more specific than $r.\mathbf{ant}$. We will use specificity as simplified to: $s > r$ if and only if $r.\mathbf{ant} \subsetneq s.\mathbf{ant}$. A priority relation restricted to specificity is transitive.

4   The Instructability Problem

Consider two agents, "Teacher" and "Student", who use defeasible logic to think about some aspects of the world. Teacher is trustworthy and truthful. When Teacher and Student come to different conclusions it is the Teacher who must be believed. A procedure is needed which allows Student to update their own theory to come to better agreement with Teacher. We will hereafter identify an agent with its theory and refer to a theory as Teacher or Student theory.

---

[2] Cut and Cautious Monotony have been put forth by Gabbay [5] as desirable properties if a non-monotonic formal system is to be regarded a logic. This proposal has since entrenched itself.

Fig. 1. Visual demonstration of an instruction scenario.

Let then $H(\mathbf{f},(\mathbf{T},>_\mathbf{T}),c) = \mathbf{R}$ be a partial function which, given a Teacher theory made of a set of rules $\mathbf{T}$ and a priority relation $>_\mathbf{T}$, and a set of facts $\mathbf{f}$ such that $(\mathbf{T},>_\mathbf{T}),\mathbf{f} \vdash c$ (i.e., $(\mathbf{T},>_\mathbf{T})$ infers $+\partial c$ from facts $\mathbf{f}$), selects a subset of rules $\mathbf{R}$ from $\mathbf{T}$ such that for all $\mathbf{R}'$ subsets of rules from $\mathbf{T}$, and $>_{\mathbf{R}\cup\mathbf{R}'}$ the priority relations between rules in $\mathbf{R}\cup\mathbf{R}'$, $(\mathbf{R}\cup\mathbf{R}',>_{\mathbf{R}\cup\mathbf{R}'}),\mathbf{f} \vdash c$.

Unlike strategic argumentation [7,10], Teacher has a trivial choice for the function H: return the entire set of rules $\mathbf{T}$. To avoid returning the whole theory, a heuristic H_{P-1} is to work backwards down the chain of reasoning that produced $+\partial c$, and add all rules that were necessary to support c and defeat their opponents. This heuristic will in general not guarantee either minimality of the returned set nor stability of the argument in the sense of [9]. For stratified shallow theories with individual defeat where a literal appears either only in antecedents or only in conclusions (as is the case for most theories induced from data), then H_{P-1} can return the rule applicable in $\mathbf{f}$ that defeats all its applicable opposing rules. Because $(\mathbf{T},>_\mathbf{T}),\mathbf{f} \vdash c$, such a rule must exist.

Let $U(\mathbf{f},(\mathbf{S},>_\mathbf{S}),\mathbf{R},c) = (\mathbf{S}',>_{\mathbf{S}'})$ be a partial function which given a set of facts $\mathbf{f}$, a set of rules $\mathbf{R}$ such that $\mathbf{R},\mathbf{f} \vdash c$ and a Student theory $(\mathbf{S},>_\mathbf{S})$, returns a new Student theory such that $(\mathbf{S}',>_{\mathbf{S}'}),\mathbf{f} \vdash c$. Note the absence from the parameters of the priority relation $>_\mathbf{R}$: humans would often not assert priority relations between the rules they state and all conceivable defeated counterarguments.

The instructability problem then refers to choosing a pair of functions H, U such that for every Teacher $(\mathbf{T},>_\mathbf{T})$, Student $(\mathbf{S},>_\mathbf{S})$ and facts $\mathbf{f}$, if $(\mathbf{T},>_\mathbf{T}),\mathbf{f} \vdash c$ then given $H(\mathbf{f},(\mathbf{T},>_\mathbf{T}),c) = \mathbf{R}$ we have that $U(\mathbf{f},(\mathbf{S},>_\mathbf{S}),\mathbf{R},c),\mathbf{f} \vdash c$. In short, if Teacher believes c holds in $\mathbf{f}$, then Student must come to believe this as well. This basic desideratum is **effectiveness**.

However, the most important desideratum for instructability is **persistence**: if Student was taught that c holds in $\mathbf{f}$, and assuming the Teacher does not change, then Student should still believe this whatever other instructions Student receives from Teacher. This can be expressed as: for every sets of facts $\mathbf{f}, \mathbf{f}'$, where $H(\mathbf{f}, (\mathbf{T}, >_T), c) = \mathbf{R}$, $H(\mathbf{f}', (\mathbf{T}, >_T), c) = \mathbf{R}'$, $U(\mathbf{f}, (\mathbf{S}, >_\mathbf{S}), \mathbf{R}, c) = (\mathbf{S_U}, >_\mathbf{S_U})$, and $U(\mathbf{f}', (\mathbf{S_U}, >_\mathbf{S_U}), \mathbf{R}', c') = (\mathbf{S}', >_{\mathbf{S}'})$, we have $(\mathbf{S}', >_{\mathbf{S}'}), \mathbf{f} => c$. Persistence differs from case stability as described in [9] because neither Teacher's case $\mathbf{R}$ nor the Student update is required to infer c from *all* supersets of facts $\mathbf{f}$. Instead, Student is only required to infer c from $\mathbf{f}$.

The persistence requirement makes instructability different from previously considered model reconciliation problems [3,25–27]. It differs from AGM belief revision [6] and the interactive dialogues between logical agents [21] in that Student's theory should change at the level of regularities it expects of the world, i.e. at the level of axioms or rules, not merely facts/defaults. The difference is made obvious if considering the adapted version of the AGM belief revision postulates for defeasible logic due to Billington [2], which operate by inserting/removing assertions of facts/defaults, rather than rules that are applicable to other situations. Billington's postulates can be straightforwardly adapted to describe a procedure that Student can use to update the rules in its theory, however as we will empirically show in Sect. 6, this procedure is not sufficient to guarantee the persistence desideratum of instructability.

For space reasons, we refer readers to [2] for the formal specification of revision postulates. We informally summarize here the postulates for theory revision: 1) the revised theory infers a set of conjunction-closed conclusions; 2) revision to add a non-contradicting conclusion to the theory results in that conclusion being added; 3) and 4) together: revision and expansion are the same if the conclusion to add was not contradicted by the original theory; 5) attempting to revise so as to introduce a conclusion contradictory to itself or to facts will have no effect; 6) revision to insert a conjunction of conclusions does not depend on the order in which the conjuncts are written; 7) and 8) together: revision to add conclusion c followed by expansion to add d is same as revision to add c and d.

5 An Illustrative Test Case: Situated Objects and Their Qualities

The problem of object quality inference described in [16] is: given a partial description of an object, estimate the likeliest values for its unknown qualities. The authors make a dataset publicly available. The problem is relevant for robotics: some qualities are not easy to perceive but significant for how to handle an object, e.g. temperature – not all robotic platforms come equipped with temperature sensors at the gripper – and fragility. Other qualities of an object may require effort to discover, such as searching for an object to find its location.

Liu et al. investigate this problem with the methods of classical machine- and deep learning [16]. But since their dataset consists of 1456 fully symbolic entries, it got our attention as an opportunity to also use it with logical methods, such as defeasible logic. An entry into this dataset is a "situated object", which is a list of quality values. An object can have fixed qualities, such as type, color, or shape, and situation-dependent qualities such as temperature or cleanliness.

For our experiments[3] we produced defeasible logic theories via theory induction on the situated object dataset. The induced rules have conclusions about the same quality, e.g. an object's temperature. In Sect. 7 we discuss how to apply a theory update procedure to more general theories.

To induce a theory, the dataset is randomly split into training and testing sets of entries and each entry is split into the conclusion and everything else. Quality values associated with the same quality are mutually exclusive.

We have implemented two rule induction heuristics. One is HeRO, published by Governatori et al. [14], adapted for defeasible theories with mutex sets. HeRO produces theories where the priority relation is a total order. It is impossible, just by looking at two rules with incomparable antecedents, to tell which has higher priority than the other in a HeRO theory, therefore we use the theories it induces as exemplars of defeasible theories with arbitrary priority relations.

The other theory induction method we implemented is a greedy heuristic that adds the best rule that is slightly more specific than some other rule already in the theory. Best means that, after adding the rule to the theory, the most as yet incorrectly decided training cases are corrected. Slightly more specific means the length of the antecedent of an added rule r is one more than the length of the antecedent of a rule s already present in the theory, and $s.\mathbf{ant} \subset r.\mathbf{ant}$.

6 Instructing Defeasible Theories with Arbitrary Priority Relation

We used the situated object dataset [16] to have a realistic scenario from which to induce theories. To induce a theory, we shuffle the dataset. The first 70% of entries (∼1000 entries) are training data, and use HeRO [14] to induce defeasible theories. We repeat this procedure to induce 10 different defeasible theories for the **temperature** quality of a situated object. The theories are 85% or more accurate on the test set, and the rule counts are about 50 rules, i.e. the theories compress the training set well. Any two of the induced theories, even if different, start in good agreement with each other. Some of the rules induced by HeRO seem quite natural (e.g., $inRefrigerator => cold$), but others are likely artifacts of the small dataset and its peculiarities (e.g. $translucent => roomTemperature$).

Teacher will use the heuristic $H_{P^{-1}}$ described in Sect. 4. The update procedure U: if Teacher asserts a rule r must be used to adjudicate a situation **f**, then Student will place it in its theory just above the highest priority rule Student

---

[3] Code for rerunning the experiments: https://github.com/mpomarlan/ruleml2024,

knows to apply to **f**; call this rule s. If $r.\mathbf{ant} = s.\mathbf{ant}$, then s is deleted from Student. This update procedure obeys the AGM postulates as adapted to defeasible logic [2], certainly for a shallow stratified theory that can only infer at most one conclusion from a set of facts. Postulates 4, 5, and 6 of AGM hold because Teacher is truthful and only one conclusion is added by the update on one set of facts. Postulates 1, 2, and 3 hold because the update procedure adds Teacher's conclusion to Student's beliefs, and no further inference happens.

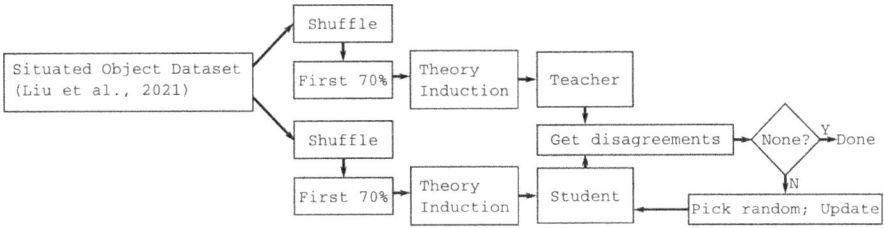

Fig. 2. Overview of the theory training and testing procedure.

To study the effects of updates on Student theories, we generate 100 samples of running an instruction protocol. Each sample is generated thusly: first, two theories are randomly selected and assigned Teacher and Student roles. A list of disagreements is constructed by seeing which situations from the Teacher's training set result in a definite conclusion for the Teacher, and a different conclusion for the Student. One disagreement is selected at random and the Student theory receives an update based on it. The list of disagreements is updated and the process repeats until Teacher and Student are in full agreement or 200 instruction steps are performed. An overview of our experimental pipeline is given in Fig. 2. For each sample run of an instruction protocol, we record step counts until agreement, maximum "backslides", and forgotten instructions. A backslide is an increase in the number of disagreements. A forgotten instruction is a case when Student reverts to a wrong conclusion for a situation, despite receiving an instruction about it previously. If an instruction is forgotten it is not counted as forgotten again until both Teacher restates it and Student forgets it once more.

We observe that even though the update procedure obeys AGM and Teacher and Student start in fairly good agreement, reaching complete agreement is difficult. A typical run is shown in Fig. 3: while agreement is eventually reached, instruction steps often introduce more disagreements than they solve. In more than half of the runs there are at least 20 forgotten instructions, as a histogram of forgetting events shows in Fig. 4. The number of steps needed for agreement tends to be large; in a third of the runs the theories did not come into agreement within 200 steps.

7 Instructing Defeasible Theories with Priority Based on Specificity

We now investigate instructability with the priority relation restricted to specificity (an antecedent is more specific if it is a superset of another).

We use the situated object dataset to induce ten defeasible theories for the **temperature** quality. To induce a theory, the dataset is shuffled and the first 70% entries (∼1000 entries) are used as a training set. The resulting theories tend to be small, with ∼90 rules[4]. To generate one sample of the instructability protocol, we select a random pair of theories where the first becomes Teacher, then randomly select disagreements and run updates on the disagreements until the theories agree entirely on the Teacher's training set. Disagreement means difference to a Teacher's definite conclusion. We have generated 100 samples of running instruction protocols to a full agreement for which we record the number of disagreements after each instruction step, the number of forgotten instructions, and the maximum number of backslides (increases in the number of disagreements from one step to another). Teacher again uses H_{P-1} as defined in Sect. 4. The update procedure U is specified in Algorithm 1. Note that, since for shallow theories with individual defeat the R set is a singleton, we have the update procedure just take that one rule as argument. We will also omit the priority relation from the arguments, since in this case it can be recovered from rule specificity.

Figure 5 shows a typical case of how the number of disagreements varies between Teacher and Student as more instruction steps are performed. Full agreement is reached quickly, with the number of steps always smaller than the number of rules in either theory and smaller than the initial disagreements. No instruction is forgotten. Of the 100 samples, one contained a maximum backslide of 1, i.e. one instruction step introduced one new disagreement.

While we cannot offer theoretical justifications for some of the empirically observed properties (convergence in very few steps, near-absence of backslides), we will next prove the Update Algorithm 1 meets our Persistence requirement.

Claim (Effectiveness): *Immediately after $Update(\mathbf{f}, \mathbf{S}, r, c)$, theory S uses rule r to adjudicate $\mathbf{f}$.*

The proof is immediate: all the rules that would apply to $\mathbf{f}$ and would indicate other conclusions are either weaker than r because their antecedents are less specific, or removed. □

Claim. *Let the Teacher theory be stable in time and decisive on a set of situations $\mathbf{F}$. Then, no rule from the Teacher theory added to the Student via Updates based on members of $\mathbf{F}$ (i.e. no update of the form $Update(\mathbf{f}, \mathbf{S}, r, c), \mathbf{f} \in \mathbf{F}$) will ever be removed by subsequent calls to Updates based on members of $\mathbf{F}$.*

Proof. To be removed, a rule s would have to apply to a situation where the teacher theory prefers the conclusion of another rule r. Since rule s is a rule in

---

[4] We can stop induction once the number of rules is the same as in HeRO theories; this does not change our results regarding backslides, convergence etc.

Algorithm 1. Theory update from rule and set of facts

   procedure UPDATE(**f**, **S**, r, c) ▷ Update theory **S** knowing that rule r should apply to a set of facts **f**
Require: r.ant ⊆ **f**
Require: r.con = c
     AddRule(**S**, r)
     for s ∈ **S** do
        if (s.con ≠ r.con) AND (s.ant ⊆ **f**) then
           if (s.ant − r.ant ≠ ∅) OR (s.ant = r.ant) then
               RemoveRule(**S**, s) ▷ Remove applicable rules contradicting and not defeated by r
           end if
        end if
     end for
   end procedure

the Teacher's theory, and given the specificity constraint on the priority relation, the Teacher can only prefer r if its antecedent includes that of s (s not being in the Teacher's theory would have been another reason to prefer r). However, to be removed by Update, s must have an antecedent that includes, or is incomparable to, that of r – contradiction. □

Claim (Persistence): *Assuming a stable Teacher theory, then any definite conclusion for a particular situation **f** taught to the Student theory via an Update will be preserved after any subsequent updates with definite conclusions as well.*

Proof. Suppose Student theory received an $Update(\mathbf{f}, \mathbf{S}, s)$, indicating Teacher uses s to adjudicate **f**. The previous claim establishes that rule s will remain in Student after subsequent updates. Suppose Student changes its mind about situation **f** because of an update and now either uses rule r to decide, or r and s are in unresolvable conflict. r must come from Teacher via Update, but then Teacher would have used it to adjudicate **f** – contradiction. □

Claim (Concise Convergence): *Let S be a Student theory. Assuming a stable Teacher theory T, then at most $N = \|T\| + \|S\|$ calls to Update are sufficient to produce full agreement.*

Proof. We assume that all updates are necessary, i.e. they are triggered by sets of facts where Teacher and Student disagree. The minimal effect an update can have is to add one rule from Teacher to Student (and such a rule will never be deleted) and/or remove a rule from Student. So after N updates, Student will have all the rules in the Teacher theory, and older rules from Student in unresolvable conflict with Teacher rules will have been removed. □

Monotonic convergence between the Student and Teacher cannot be guaranteed by our Update procedure; it remains possible that Student agrees with the Teacher on some situation **f** because it has a rule for it, a rule not present in the Teacher theory, and for that rule to be removed by an Update. However, at least for theories that start in near agreement, such cases appear rare.

So far we have considered shallow defeasible theories: all rules have consequents in the same mutex set. We can generalize the instructability update protocol for more complex theories where chains of inference are longer, i.e. where intermediary conclusions are established which then function as premises for other rules. In such a case, Teacher must provide a set of rules to prove their conclusion. Let this set of rules be denoted $\mathbf{R}$, $\mathbf{f}$ be the set of facts of the situation in which an instruction happens, and q be Teacher's conclusion. Then:

- $\mathbf{R}$ only contains rules from the Teacher's theory
- $\mathbf{R}, \mathbf{f} \vdash q$
- For any other subset of rules from the Teacher $\mathbf{R}'$, $\mathbf{R} \cup \mathbf{R}', \mathbf{d} \vdash q$

Under these conditions, Student can update their theory while achieving the previously established claims of Effectiveness, maintenance of Teacher rules, Persistence, and Concise Convergence by wrapping the update procedure in the algorithm described in Listing 2.

Algorithm 2. Wrapping updates for longer inference chains

    procedure UPDATEWRAPPER($\mathbf{f}, \mathbf{S}, \mathbf{R}, q$) ▷ Update theory $\mathbf{S}$ knowing that rules $\mathbf{R}$ should apply undefeated to set of facts $\mathbf{f}$
        while $\mathbf{R} \neq \emptyset$ **do**
            $r \leftarrow findApplicable(\mathbf{R}, \mathbf{f})$
            $Update(\mathbf{f}, \mathbf{S}, r)$
            $\mathbf{R} \leftarrow \mathbf{R} - \{r\}$
            $\mathbf{f} \leftarrow \mathbf{d} \cup \{r.con\}$
        end while
    end procedure

In Listing 2, $findApplicable$ is a function which, given a set of rules $\mathbf{R}$ and a set of facts $\mathbf{d}$, returns a rule applicable to $\mathbf{d}$.

Claim (Correctness): Algorithm 2 has Effectiveness, maintenance of Teacher rules, Persistence when used on defeasible theories where not all rules have conclusions in the same mutex set.

Proof (sketch). The idea is to repeatedly apply the reasoning of *Claim: Persistence)*. If Teacher supplies a set of rules R for an inference chain from a situation, a subset of these (say, R_0) must have antecedents included in the known facts of the situation. Student can incorporate these rules into their theory through the Update Algorithm 1. The new rules support conclusions which may render other rules from R applicable and the Update procedure can repeat, because Cautious Monotony ensures that if we had started from a situation equal to the original one plus the conclusions of R_0, we would arrive at the same total set of conclusions. □

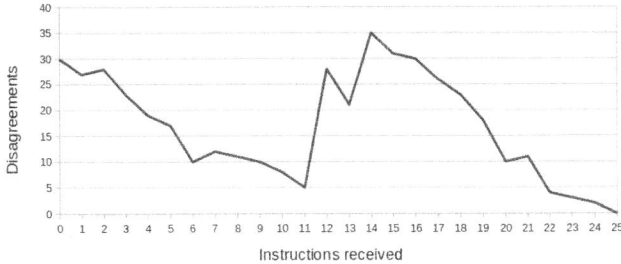

Fig. 3. A typical evolution of the disagreement between "Teacher" and a "Student" as a function of number of instructions received by Student. Arbitrary priority relation.

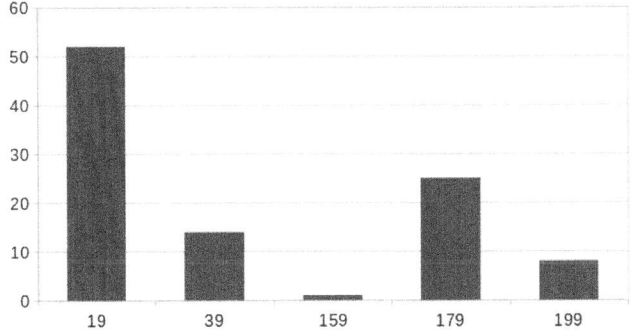

Fig. 4. Arbitrary priority relation. Histogram of forgotten instructions for 100 episodes. Y axis are numbers of episodes, X axis are bins for forgotten instruction counts (a bin N, following a bin M, means at least $M+1$ and at most N instructions were forgotten throughout the instruction steps).

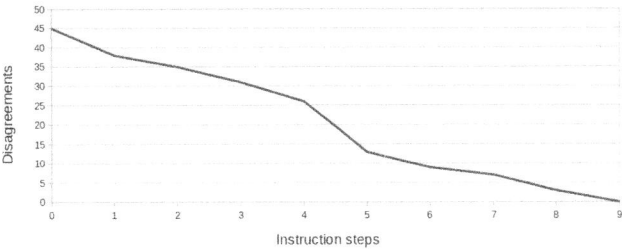

Fig. 5. A typical evolution of the disagreement between a Teacher theory and a Student theory as a function of the number of instructions received by the student. Both theories have a priority relation that is based on antecedent specificity.

8 Conclusions

We have defined the Instructability Problem as the problem of updating a Student agent's logical theory about the world based on an argument and a conclusion that a trustworthy Teacher asserts to hold about a particular situation.

The ultimate goal of instructability is for Student and Teacher to come to the same conclusions in future situations, and it is desired to come to such an agreement quickly and without forgetting previously received instructions. We aim for instructability to be a simplified, but somewhat realistic model of humans instructing each other.

We have shown that AGM postulates as adapted to defeasible logic, and as applicable to an instructability scenario, are insufficient to achieve some desirable properties for an instruction protocol, namely that Student should not forget instructions. This is because the priority relation of defeasible logic is not communicated in human instructions. If the priority relation is arbitrary, i.e. it is not possible to tell how two rules compare just by looking at them, then the Student in general cannot correctly assign priorities to rules coming from Teacher's instructions and it would seem Student is forced to remember the instructions it receives as pairs of the form (set of facts, conclusion), rather than hope for a more concise theory, or risk forgetting some of the instructions it receives.

Instead, a priority relation based on rule specificity allows instructability protocols with good properties because there is no ambiguity about rule priority. We show an algorithm for theory update in this case, experimentally indicating that it achieves agreement between Teacher and Student in very few steps compared to the worst possible case and prove that it avoids the instruction forgetting problem, i.e. displays a property we called Persistence, without Student having to explicitly memorize situations where it received instructions.

We have made several restrictions for our analysis. Many of these can be relaxed with a slight adjustment of the instruction protocol. We assumed Teacher is decisive, and that defeasible logic uses individual defeat to resolve conflicts. If Teacher is allowed to list all rules it uses to arrive at a conclusion (or, give applicable undefeated rules for all conclusions it finds support for in case no definite conclusion is reached) from a set of facts, then Update and UpdateWrapper algorithms are straightforward to adjust so as to maintain their claimed properties of Effectiveness, Persistence, and Concise Convergence even when Teacher is indecisive and team defeat is used. Specificity as a way to decide rule priority can also be replaced, as long as this replacement is common knowledge between Teacher and Student, and it is a criterion that can decide for any pair of rules which, if any, should have priority.

In future work, we intend to evaluate instructability of an artificial agent that uses defeasible logic also from a human user perspective. There is a debate in previous literature as to whether humans employ specificity considerations in their inferences. Ford and Billington observe that humans have trouble maintaining consistency when told to reason according to a formal non-monotonic system, and while some aspects of the formal system may improve performance, considerations of specificity do not [4]. Schurz meanwhile disputes both conclusions [23] and instead claims that humans can reason consistently and are helped in doing so by specificity playing a role in reasoning. Which set of results is more relevant for human-agent interaction remains an interesting problem.

References

1. Billington, D.: Defeasible logic is stable. J. Log. Comput. **3**(4), 379–400 (1993)
2. Billington, D., Antoniou, G., Governatori, G., Maher, M.: Revising nonmonotonic theories: the case of defeasible logic. In: Burgard, W., Cremers, A.B., Cristaller, T. (eds.) KI 1999. LNCS (LNAI), vol. 1701, pp. 101–112. Springer, Heidelberg (1999). https://doi.org/10.1007/3-540-48238-5_8
3. Dung, H.T., Son, T.C.: On model reconciliation: how to reconcile when robot does not know human's model? In: Lierler, Y., Morales, J.F., Dodaro, C., Dahl, V., Gebser, M., Tekle, T. (eds.) Proceedings 38th International Conference on Logic Programming, ICLP 2022 Technical Communications/Doctoral Consortium, Haifa, Israel, 31st July–6th August 2022. EPTCS, vol. 364, pp. 27–48 (2022). https://doi.org/10.4204/EPTCS.364.4, https://doi.org/10.4204/EPTCS.364.4
4. Ford, M., Billington, D.: Strategies in human nonmonotonic reasoning. Comput. Intell. **16**(3), 446–468 (2000)
5. Gabbay, D.M.: Theoretical foundations for non-monotonic reasoning in expert systems. In: Apt, K.R. (ed.) Logics and Models of Concurrent Systems. NATO ASI Series, vol. 13, pp. 439–457. Springer, Heidelberg (1985). https://doi.org/10.1007/978-3-642-82453-1_15
6. Gärdenfors, P.: The dynamics of belief systems: Foundations vs. coherence theories. Rev. Int. Philos. **44**(172 (1)), 24–46 (1990)
7. Governatori, G., Maher, M.J., Olivieri, F., Rotolo, A., Scannnapieco, S.: Strategic argumentation under grounded semantics is NP-complete. In: Bulling, N. (ed.) EUMAS 2014. LNCS (LNAI), vol. 8953, pp. 379–387. Springer, Cham (2015). https://doi.org/10.1007/978-3-319-17130-2_26
8. Governatori, G., Olivieri, F., Cristani, M., Scannapieco, S.: Revision of defeasible preferences. Int. J. Approximate Reasoning **104**, 205–230 (2019). https://doi.org/10.1016/j.ijar.2018.10.020, https://www.sciencedirect.com/science/article/pii/S0888613X18301336
9. Governatori, G., Olivieri, F., Rotolo, A., Cristani, M.: Inference to the stable explanations. In: Gottlob, G., Inclezan, D., Maratea, M. (eds.) Logic Programming and Nonmonotonic Reasoning LPNMR 2022. Lecture Notes in Computer Science, vol. 13416, pp. 245–258. Springer, Cham (2022). https://doi.org/10.1007/978-3-031-15707-3_19
10. Governatori, G., Olivieri, F., Scannapieco, S., Rotolo, A., Cristani, M.: Strategic argumentation is np-complete. ArXiv abs/1312.4287 (2013). https://api.semanticscholar.org/CorpusID:2078686
11. Governatori, G., Rotolo, A.: Changing legal systems: legal abrogations and annulments in Defeasible Logic. Log. J. IGPL **18**(1), 157–194 (2009). https://doi.org/10.1093/jigpal/jzp075
12. Governatori, G., Rotolo, A., Olivieri, F., Scannapieco, S.: Legal contractions: a logical analysis. In: Proceedings of the International Conference on Artificial Intelligence and Law, pp. 63–72 (2013). https://doi.org/10.1145/2514601.2514609
13. Governatori, G., Rotolo, A., Riveret, R., Villata, S.: Modelling dialogues for optimal legislation. In: ICAIL 2019 - 17th International Conference on Artificial Intelligence and Law, pp. 229–233. ACM Press, Montreal (2019). https://doi.org/10.1145/3322640.3326731, https://hal.science/hal-02381105
14. Johnston, B., Governatori, G.: Induction of defeasible logic theories in the legal domain. In: Proceedings of the International Conference on Artificial Intelligence and Law (2003)

15. Lam, H.P.: On the Derivability of defeasible logic. Ph.D., School of Information Technology and Electrical Engineering, The University of Queensland (2012)
16. Liu, W., Bansal, D., Daruna, A.A., Chernova, S.: Learning instance-level n-ary semantic knowledge at scale for robots operating in everyday environments. In: Shell, D.A., Toussaint, M., Hsieh, M.A. (eds.) Robotics: Science and Systems (RSS), pp. 529–547 (2021)
17. Maher, M.J.: Propositional defeasible logic has linear complexity. Theory Pract. Logic Program. **1**(6), 691–711 (2001). https://doi.org/10.1017/S1471068401001168
18. Maher, M.J., Tachmazidis, I., Antoniou, G., Wade, S., Cheng, L.: Rethinking defeasible reasoning: a scalable approach. Theory Pract. Logic Program. **20**(4), 552–586 (2020). https://doi.org/10.1017/S1471068420000010
19. Maier, F., Nute, D.: Well-founded semantics for defeasible logic. Synthese **176**(2), 243–274 (2010). https://doi.org/10.1007/s11229-009-9492-1
20. Moguillansky, M.O., Wassermann, R., Falappa, M.A.: Inconsistent-tolerant base revision through argument theory change. Log. J. IGPL **20**(1), 154–186 (2012)
21. Moubaiddin, A., Obeid, N.: Partial information basis for agent-based collaborative dialogue. Appl. Intell. **30**(2), 142–167 (2009)
22. Nute, D.: Defeasible reasoning: a philosophical analysis in prolog. Aspects Artif. Intell. **1**, 251–288 (1988)
23. Schurz, G.: Non-monotonic reasoning from an evolution-theoretic perspective: ontic, logical and cognitive foundations. Synthese **146**, 37–51 (2005)
24. Shoham, Y.: Nonmonotonic reasoning and causation. Cogn. Sci. **14**(2), 213–252 (1990)
25. Son, T.C., Nguyen, V., Vasileiou, S.L., Yeoh, W.: Model reconciliation in logic programs. In: Faber, W., Friedrich, G., Gebser, M., Morak, M. (eds.) JELIA 2021. LNCS (LNAI), vol. 12678, pp. 393–406. Springer, Cham (2021). https://doi.org/10.1007/978-3-030-75775-5_26, https://api.semanticscholar.org/CorpusID:234475630
26. Sreedharan, S., Hernandez, A.O., Mishra, A.P., Kambhampati, S.: Model-free model reconciliation. In: Proceedings of the Twenty-Eighth International Joint Conference on Artificial Intelligence, IJCAI-19, pp. 587–594. International Joint Conferences on Artificial Intelligence Organization (2019). https://doi.org/10.24963/ijcai.2019/83
27. Vasileiou, S., Previti, A., Yeoh, W.G.S.: On exploiting hitting sets for model reconciliation. In: AAAI Conference on Artificial Intelligence (2020). https://api.semanticscholar.org/CorpusID:229297869
28. Wolf, M.J., Miller, K.W., Grodzinsky, F.S.: Why we should have seen that coming: comments on microsoft's tay "experiment," and wider implications. ORBIT J. **1**(2), 1–12 (2017). https://doi.org/10.29297/orbit.v1i2.49, https://www.sciencedirect.com/science/article/pii/S2515856220300493

FaithEL: Strongly TBox Faithful Knowledge Base Embeddings for $\mathcal{EL}$

Victor Lacerda[1(✉)], Ana Ozaki[1,2], and Ricardo Guimarães[3]

[1] University of Bergen, Bergen, Norway
victor.botelho@uib.no, anaoz@uio.no
[2] University of Oslo, Oslo, Norway
[3] Zivid AS, Oslo, Norway

Abstract. Knowledge base embeddings map both TBox and ABox axioms into vector spaces. Recently, there have been various approaches for embedding normalized $\mathcal{EL}$ knowledge bases (KBs). However, none of these approaches show whether TBox axioms of a given KB match those that hold in the embedding. Embedding models that exactly match with the TBox part of the KB are called in the literature strongly faithful TBox models. Here we present an implementation of a strongly faithful TBox embedding method for normalized $\mathcal{EL}$ knowledge bases.

Keywords: Knowledge Bases · Knowledge Base Embeddings · Geometric Models · Description Logic

1 Introduction

Knowledge Base Embeddings (KBEs) [1,4,6,7,10–14] have emerged as a way to combine the strengths of traditional knowledge bases (KBs) with machine learning. The logic-based formalism behind KBs provides a clear semantics to a domain subject and a way of reasoning precisely about the domain. On the other hand, embeddings allow for representing data in vector spaces, where similarities between data points can be studied depending on their position in the vector space, contributing to the discovery of new facts based on data patterns.

Even though the $\mathcal{EL}$ description logic [2] and its variants have received the bulk of attention in previous works on KBEs [6,7,10,13,14], no method has solved the problem of representing the TBox part $\mathcal{T}$ of KBs in such a way that if an axiom holds in their geometrical representation then it is a logical consequence of $\mathcal{T}$, a property called *strong TBox-faithfulness* [11]. In this work we present *FaithEL*, an embedding method[1] that is able to faithfully represent the TBox component of KBs written in the normalized $\mathcal{EL}$ description logic, covering a gap in the current literature. In a nutshell, our embedding method receives a normalized $\mathcal{ELH}$ KB $\mathcal{K}$ as input, creates a canonical model (Sect. 2.1), and then uses this construction to create a geometric interpretation that is a strongly

---
[1] https://github.com/victorlacerdab/FaithEL_method/.

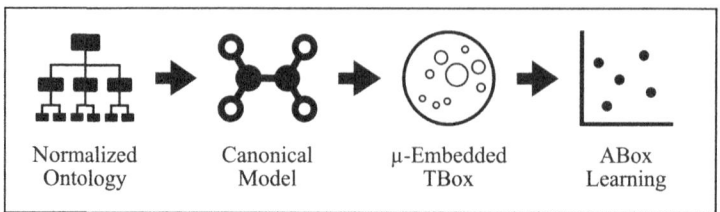

Fig. 1. The step-by-step method for achieving Strongly TBox Faithful and Weakly ABox Faithful embeddings.

TBox-faithful model of $\mathcal{K}$. Finally, our method employs an optimizer to learn the ABox part (Fig. 1) and some additional parameters (Sect. 3). We implement our method and perform experiments using a prototypical family KB (Sect. 4). Our endeavours to create strongly TBox-faithful models come with challenges, which we discuss in Sect. 5.

2 Preliminaries

2.1 The Description Logic $\mathcal{ELH}$

Syntax. Let N_C, N_R, and N_I be countably infinite and pairwise disjoint sets of *concept names*, *role names*, and *individual names*, respectively. $\mathcal{ELH}$ concepts C, D are built according to the syntax rule $C, D ::= \top \mid A \mid (C \sqcap D) \mid \exists r.C$ where $A \in N_C$ and $r \in N_R$. $\mathcal{ELH}$ *concept inclusions* (CIs) are of the form $C \sqsubseteq D$, *role inclusions* (RIs) are of the form $r \sqsubseteq s$, *concept assertions* are of the form $A(a)$, and *role assertions* are of the form $r(a, b)$, where $A \in N_C$, $a, b \in N_I$, $r, s \in N_R$, and C, D range over $\mathcal{ELH}$ concepts. CIs, RIs, and assertions are called *axioms*. A TBox is a finite set of CIs and RIs and an ABox is a finite set of (concept and role) assertions. A *normalized* $\mathcal{ELH}$ TBox is one that only contains CIs of the following forms: $A_1 \sqcap A_2 \sqsubseteq B$, $\exists r.A \sqsubseteq B$, and $A \sqsubseteq \exists r.B$, where $A_1, A_2, A, B \in N_C$ and $r \in N_R$. We say that an $\mathcal{ELH}$ concept is in *normal form* if it is of the form A, $\exists r.A$, or $A \sqcap B$, with $A, B \in N_C$ and $r \in N_R$. An $\mathcal{ELH}$ KB is the union of an $\mathcal{ELH}$ TBox and an ABox. It is in *normal form* if its TBox part is a normalized $\mathcal{ELH}$ TBox. We denote with $N_C(X), N_R(X), N_I(X)$ the set of concept, role, individual names occurring in a TBox, ABox, or KB X.

Semantics. The classical semantics of $\mathcal{ELH}$ is given by interpretations, as usual. An *interpretation* is a pair $(\Delta^\mathcal{I}, \cdot^\mathcal{I})$ where $\Delta^\mathcal{I}$ is a non-empty set, called *domain*, and $\cdot^\mathcal{I}$ is a function that maps each $A \in N_C$ to some $A^\mathcal{I} \subseteq \Delta^\mathcal{I}$, each $r \in N_R$ to some $r^\mathcal{I} \subseteq \Delta^\mathcal{I} \times \Delta^\mathcal{I}$, and each $a \in N_I$ to some $a^\mathcal{I} \in \Delta^\mathcal{I}$. The function $\cdot^\mathcal{I}$ extends to complex $\mathcal{ELH}$ concepts as follows $\top^\mathcal{I} = \Delta^\mathcal{I}$ and

$$(C \sqcap D)^\mathcal{I} = C^\mathcal{I} \cap D^\mathcal{I} \quad (\exists r.C)^\mathcal{I} = \{d \in \Delta^\mathcal{I} \mid \exists e \in \Delta^\mathcal{I} : (d, e) \in r^\mathcal{I}, e \in C^\mathcal{I}\}.$$

An interpretation $\mathcal{I}$ *satisfies*: a CI $C \sqsubseteq D$ iff $C^\mathcal{I} \subseteq D^\mathcal{I}$, an RI $r \sqsubseteq s$ iff $r^\mathcal{I} \subseteq s^\mathcal{I}$, a concept assertion $A(a)$ iff $a^\mathcal{I} \in A^\mathcal{I}$, and a role assertion $r(a, b)$ iff $(a^\mathcal{I}, b^\mathcal{I}) \in r^\mathcal{I}$.

An interpretation $\mathcal{I}$ *satisfies* a KB $\mathcal{K}$ iff it satisfies all axioms in $\mathcal{K}$. $\mathcal{K}$ *entails* an axiom α, written $\mathcal{K} \models \alpha$, iff every interpretation that satisfies $\mathcal{K}$ also satisfies α.

Canonical Model. We employ a definition of a *finite* canonical model that is suitable for constructing our strongly TBox-faithful models [8] later. This is a canonical model for CI/RI implication. It is a non-trivial adaptation of other definitions in the literature (see [9]) because here we falsify CIs/RIs that do not follow from a KB. Let $\mathcal{K}$ be a normalized KB with TBox $\mathcal{T}$ and an empty ABox:

$\Delta_u^{\mathcal{I}_\mathcal{K}} := \{c_A \mid A \in N_C(\mathcal{K}) \cup \{\top\}\}$ and
$\Delta^{\mathcal{I}_\mathcal{K}} := \Delta_u^{\mathcal{I}_\mathcal{K}} \cup \{c_{A \sqcap B} \mid A, B \in N_C(\mathcal{K})\} \cup \{c_{\exists r.B} \mid r \in N_R(\mathcal{K}), B \in N_C(\mathcal{K}) \cup \{\top\}\}$.

Definition 1. *The* canonical model $\mathcal{I}_\mathcal{K}$ *of* $\mathcal{K}$ *is defined as*

$A^{\mathcal{I}_\mathcal{K}} := \{c_D \in \Delta^{\mathcal{I}_\mathcal{K}} \mid \mathcal{T} \models D \sqsubseteq A\}$, *and*
$r^{\mathcal{I}_\mathcal{K}} := \{(c_{\exists s.B}, c_B) \in \Delta^{\mathcal{I}_\mathcal{K}} \times \Delta_u^{\mathcal{I}_\mathcal{K}} \mid \mathcal{T} \models s \sqsubseteq r\}$
$\cup \{(c_D, c_B) \in \Delta^{\mathcal{I}_\mathcal{K}} \times \Delta_u^{\mathcal{I}_\mathcal{K}} \mid \mathcal{T} \models D \sqsubseteq A, \; \mathcal{T} \models A \sqsubseteq \exists r.B, \text{ for some } A \in N_C(\mathcal{K})\}$,

for all $A \in N_C$, $r \in N_R$, *and where* D *is a concept in normal form.*

Conjecture 1 ([8]). Let $\mathcal{K}$ be a normalized $\mathcal{ELH}$ KB. The following holds

– for all $\mathcal{ELH}$ CIs α in normal form over $N_C(\mathcal{K}) \cup N_R(\mathcal{K})$, $\mathcal{I}_\mathcal{K} \models \alpha$ iff $\mathcal{K} \models \alpha$;
– and for all RIs α over $N_R(\mathcal{K})$, $\mathcal{I}_\mathcal{K} \models \alpha$ iff $\mathcal{K} \models \alpha$.

Proof Intuition. The elements in the domain of the canonical model are of the form c_D and we ensure that $c_D \in D^{\mathcal{I}_\mathcal{K}}$. We include c_D in the extension of a concept name A iff $\mathcal{T} \models D \sqsubseteq A$ (see definition of $A^{\mathcal{I}_\mathcal{K}}$). So intuitively all CIs of the form $D \sqsubseteq A$ hold in $\mathcal{I}_\mathcal{K}$ iff $\mathcal{T} \models D \sqsubseteq A$. Regarding CIs of the form $A \sqsubseteq \exists r.B$, we ensure that those elements c_D in the extension of A are also connected via r to c_B iff this follows from $\mathcal{T}$ (see second line of the definition of $r^{\mathcal{I}_\mathcal{K}}$). We deal with RIs in the definition of $r^{\mathcal{I}_\mathcal{K}}$. □

2.2 Geometric Models and Model Faithfulness

We go from classical interpretations of the $\mathcal{ELH}$ description logic to geometric interpretations, using definitions from previous works [3,4]. Let m be a natural number and $f \colon \mathbb{R}^m \times \mathbb{R}^m \mapsto \mathbb{R}^{2 \cdot m}$ a fixed but arbitrary linear map where:

1. the restriction of f to $\mathbb{R}^m \times \{0\}^m$ is injective;
2. the restriction of f to $\{0\}^m \times \mathbb{R}^m$ is injective;
3. $f(\mathbb{R}^m \times \{0\}^m) \cap f(\{0\}^m \times \mathbb{R}^m) = \{0^{2 \cdot m}\}$;

and 0^m denotes the vector $(0, ..., 0)$ with m zeros. For example, the concatenation function is a linear map (linear transformation) satisfying 1, 2, and 3. A linear map that satisfies Points 1, 2, and 3 is an *isomorphism preserving linear map*.

Definition 2 (Geometric Interpretation). *Let f be an isomorphism preserving linear map and m a natural number. An m-dimensional f-geometric interpretation η of (N_C, N_R, N_I) assigns to each $A \in N_C$ a region $\eta(A) \subseteq \mathbb{R}^m$, $r \in N_R$ a region $\eta(r) \subseteq \mathbb{R}^{2 \cdot m}$, and $a \in N_I$ a vector $\eta(a) \in \mathbb{R}^m$. We now extend the definition for arbitrary $\mathcal{ELH}$ concepts:*

$$\eta(\top) := \mathbb{R}^m, \quad \eta(C \sqcap D) := \eta(C) \cap \eta(D), \text{ and}$$
$$\eta(\exists r.C) := \{v \in \mathbb{R}^m \mid \exists u \in \eta(C) \text{ with } f(v,u) \in \eta(r)\}.$$

An m-dimensional f-geometric interpretation η satisfies: a CI $C \sqsubseteq D$ iff $\eta(C) \subseteq \eta(D)$, an RI $r \sqsubseteq s$ iff $\eta(r) \subseteq \eta(s)$, an assertion $A(a)$ iff $\eta(a) \in \eta(A)$, an assertion $r(a,b)$ iff $f(\eta(a), \eta(b)) \in \eta(r)$. We write $\eta \models \alpha$ iff η satisfies an axiom α. Also, we say that η is a model of $\mathcal{K}$ if it satisfies all axioms in $\mathcal{K}$.

Definition 3 (Faithfulness, adapted from [11]). *Let $\mathcal{K}$ be a satisfiable knowledge base. Given an m-dimensional f-geometric model η of $\mathcal{K}$, we say that:*

– *η is a strongly TBox-faithful model of $\mathcal{K}$ iff for all TBox axioms τ with symbols in $N_C(\mathcal{K}) \cup N_R(\mathcal{K})$: $\eta \models \tau$ iff $\mathcal{K} \models \tau$. Also, η is a strongly ABox-faithful model of $\mathcal{K}$ iff for all assertions α: $\eta \models \alpha$ iff $\mathcal{K} \models \alpha$.*

Example 1. Let $\mathcal{K}$ be a KB with TBox $\mathcal{T} := \{A \sqsubseteq B, B \sqsubseteq C\}$ and an empty ABox. Let η be a 1-dimensional f geometric interpretation such that $\eta(A) = [0,1]$, $\eta(B) = [0,2]$, and $\eta(C) = [-1,3]$, where square brackets denote a closed interval in $\mathbb{R}$. Then, η is a strongly TBox faithful model of $\mathcal{K}$. Let η' be a geometric interpretation such that $\eta'(A) = \eta(A)$, $\eta'(B) = \eta(B)$, and $\eta'(C) = \eta(B)$. Even though η' is a geometric model of $\mathcal{K}$, it is *not* a strongly TBox-faithful geometric model of $\mathcal{K}$ since η' also satisfies $C \sqsubseteq B$, which is not entailed by $\mathcal{K}$.

The defining feature of our FaithEL method is that it is able to produce strongly TBox faithful embeddings for $\mathcal{ELH}$ KBs, a property that is not guaranteed in previous works for normalized $\mathcal{ELH}$. Our method is *not* strongly ABox faithful. Guaranteeing strong ABox-faithfulness is uninteresting since KBEs are often used for link prediction, where it is desirable to infer new assertions based on patterns present in the data. A geometric interpretation that is a strongly TBox-faithful model can be seen as a counterpart of a canonical model (see Conjecture 1). We further explore this correspondence in the next section.

3 The FaithEL KB Embedding Method

We adopt a hybrid method for embedding KBs. The TBox part of the KB is created beforehand. We first create convex regions in a way that makes the geometric interpretation a strong TBox-faithful model, using the definition of the canonical model (Definition 1). Then, we learn the ABox part and some additional parameters associated with the TBox part. We now give the details of the FaithEL embedding method.

3.1 TBox Embedding Method

To ensure that our embedding is strongly TBox-faithful w.r.t. the KB $\mathcal{K}$ in normal form, we first build its canonical interpretation, $\mathcal{I}_\mathcal{K}$, according to Definition 1. This definition presupposes a normalized KB, and a finite canonical model. We then map each $d \in \Delta^{\mathcal{I}_\mathcal{K}}$ to a vector, according to the following function.

Definition 4. *Let $\mathcal{I}_\mathcal{K}$ be the canonical model of $\mathcal{K}$. We define a map $\mu \colon \Delta^{\mathcal{I}_\mathcal{K}} \mapsto \mathbb{R}^{\mathsf{d}}$, where d corresponds to $|N_C(\mathcal{K})| + |N_R(\mathcal{K})| \cdot |\Delta^{\mathcal{I}_\mathcal{K}}|$. Assume w.l.o.g. a fixed ordering in the indexing system for vector positions, where indices 0 to $|N_C(\mathcal{K})| - 1$ correspond to the indices for concept names; and k to $k + (|N_R(\mathcal{K})| \cdot |\Delta^{\mathcal{I}_\mathcal{K}}|) - 1$ correspond to the indices for role names together with an element $d \in \Delta^{\mathcal{I}_\mathcal{K}}$. By $v[A]$, and $v[r,d]$ we mean the value of the position in a vector v corresponding to A, and r together with an element d, respectively. For example, $v[A] = 1$ denotes the value of v in the position corresponding to A (according to the indexing system) has value 1. We now define μ using binary vectors. For all $d \in \Delta^{\mathcal{I}_\mathcal{K}}$, $a \in N_I$, $A \in N_C$, and $r \in N_R$:*

- *$\mu(d)[A] = 1$ if $d \in A^{\mathcal{I}_\mathcal{K}}$, otherwise $\mu(d)[A] = 0$, and*
- *$\mu(d)[r,e] = 1$ if $(d,e) \in r^{\mathcal{I}_\mathcal{K}}$, otherwise $\mu(d)[r,e] = 0$.*

We then apply the mapping μ to all elements $d \in \Delta^{\mathcal{I}_\mathcal{K}}$, which allows us to calculate the *vertex set* $\hat{\mathbf{V}}^{\mathbf{A}}$ for every concept name $A \in N_C$. That is, the vectors obtained from this mapping correspond to vertices for the convex regions we create. The *vertex set* $\hat{\mathbf{V}}^{\mathbf{r}}$ for each role name r is also defined as expected, using concatenation, denoted $\oplus$, as the linear map f of Definition 7.

Definition 5. *The vertex set $\hat{\mathbf{V}}^{(\cdot)}$ of concept names and roles is defined as:*

$$\hat{\mathbf{V}}^{\mathbf{A}} := \{\mu(d) \mid \mu(d)[A] = 1\}, \quad \hat{\mathbf{V}}^{\mathbf{r}} := \{\mu(d) \oplus \mu(e) \mid \mu(d)[r,e] = 1\}.$$

Definition 6. *The centroid $\mathbf{c}(\cdot)$ of a set of points is defined as:*

$$\mathbf{c}(\hat{\mathbf{V}}^{(\cdot)}) = \frac{1}{N} \sum_{n=1}^{N} v_n, \quad \text{for } v_n \in \hat{\mathbf{V}}^{(\cdot)}. \tag{1}$$

The convex geometric interpretation $\eta^*_{\mathcal{I}_\mathcal{K}}$ of each concept and role name is given by taking the *convex hull* $(\cdot)^*$ of each of the vertex sets defined above.

Definition 7. *We denote by $\eta^*_{\mathcal{I}_\mathcal{K}}$ the convex hull of the geometric interpretation $\eta_{\mathcal{I}_\mathcal{K}}$ and define $\eta^*_{\mathcal{I}_\mathcal{K}}$, for all concept names $A \in N_C$ and role names $r \in N_R$:*

$$\eta^*_{\mathcal{I}_\mathcal{K}}(A) := (\hat{\mathbf{V}}^{\mathbf{A}})^*; \quad \eta^*_{\mathcal{I}_\mathcal{K}}(r) := (\hat{\mathbf{V}}^{\mathbf{r}})^*.$$

An intuitive way of thinking about the resulting embeddings is that, since the vertices that define the regions associated with geometric interpretations are binary vectors, these regions are subsets of the d-dimensional unitary hypercube. This embedding method, along with the definition of geometric interpretation, is guaranteed to be a strongly TBox-faithful model of the TBox part of the KB.

Conjecture 2 ([8]). Let $\mathcal{K}$ be a normalized $\mathcal{ELH}$ KB and let $\mathcal{I_K}$ be the canonical model of $\mathcal{K}$. The d-dimensional convex $\oplus$-geometric interpretation of $\mathcal{I_K}$ is a strongly TBox faithful model of $\mathcal{K}$.

Proof Intuition. The proof follows a two-step procedure. We first prove that for all classical interpretations $\mathcal{I}$ and all (possibly) non-convex geometric interpretations η built using the mapping μ and with $\oplus$ as the linear map f, it is the case that $\mathcal{I} \models \alpha$ iff $\eta \models \alpha$, where α is a CI or an RI in normal form. The second step is to take the convex hull η^* of η and prove that $\mathcal{I} \models \alpha$ iff $\eta^* \models \alpha$. Since, by Conjecture 1, is is true that $\mathcal{I_K} \models \alpha$ iff $\mathcal{K} \models \alpha$, we conclude the statement. □

3.2 ABox Embedding Method

For the ABox, we rely on a supervised learning method, where training samples are concept/role assertions, associated with the concept/role's centroid acting as a golden label. The produced model is not strongly ABox-faithful (only TBox). This allows for downstream tasks such as link prediction, one of the main motivations for the study of KBEs.

Let $\mathcal{K}$ denote an $\mathcal{ELH}$ KB, with a, r and A denoting, respectively, individuals, role names and concept names appearing in $\mathcal{K}$. We associate with each $a \in N_I(\mathcal{K})$ a parameter θ^a, to each $r \in N_R(\mathcal{K})$ a pair of parameters (θ_h^r, θ_t^r), and to each concept name $A \in N_C(\mathcal{K})$ a parameter θ^A in the model. The individual parameters θ^a are initialized according to a normal distribution, where the mean is the center of the n-dimensional hypercube and the standard deviation is a hyperparameter σ. This procedure is made to avoid that all individuals are initialized identically. The moving parameters for concept names, θ^A, and roles, (θ_h^r, θ_t^r), are initialized with the centroids $\mathbf{c}(\cdot)$ of their respective vertex sets. Thus, the number of parameters in the model is given by $(|N_I(\mathcal{K})| + |N_C(\mathcal{K})| + 2 \cdot |N_R(\mathcal{K})|)*\mathsf{d}$.

One can imagine the parameters for concept and role names are 'weights' for the regions which are part of the learning.

We define two loss functions, one for concept assertions $A(a)$, denoted $\mathcal{L}(A, a)$, and one for role assertions, denoted $\mathcal{L}(r, a, b)$. By $\mathbf{d}(\cdot, \cdot)$ we denote the point-wise squared distance between two vectors, which is equivalent to the Mean Squared Error (MSE) loss function for n-dimensional vectors.

Concept Assertion. A concept assertion has the form $A(a)$, and it geometrically means that $\eta^*_{\mathcal{I_K}}(a) \in \eta^*_{\mathcal{I_K}}(A)$. In order to optimize this assertion, we minimize the following loss function:

$$\mathcal{L}(A, a) = \left(\mathbf{d}(\theta^a, \mathbf{c}(\hat{\mathbf{V}}^\mathbf{A})) + \mathbf{d}(\theta^A, \theta^a) + \mathbf{d}(\theta^A, \mathbf{c}(\hat{\mathbf{V}}^\mathbf{A})) \right). \quad (2)$$

Role Assertion. A role assertion has the form $r(a, b)$ and it means, geometrically, that $\eta^*_{\mathcal{I_K}}(a) \oplus \eta^*_{\mathcal{I_K}}(b) \in \eta^*_{\mathcal{I_K}}(r)$. Instead of having only a single parameter associated to $\eta^*_{\mathcal{I_K}}(r)$, we rely on *two* parameters, θ_h^r and θ_t^r, acting as *head* and *tail* parameters, respectively. The main motivation for not having a single parameter associated with roles is giving greater flexibility to the model. If we have a symmetric relation, the only way that $\theta^a \oplus \theta^b$ and $\theta^b \oplus \theta^a$ could approximate a single moving parameter θ^r would be by becoming the same point.

$$\mathcal{L}(r,a,b) = \bigg(\mathbf{d}(\theta^a \oplus \theta^b, \mathbf{c}(\hat{\mathbf{V}}^\mathbf{r})) + \mathbf{d}(\theta^a \oplus \theta^r_t, \mathbf{c}(\hat{\mathbf{V}}^\mathbf{r})) \\ + \mathbf{d}(\theta^r_h \oplus \theta^b, \mathbf{c}(\hat{\mathbf{V}}^\mathbf{r})) + \mathbf{d}(\theta^r_h \oplus \theta^r_t, \mathbf{c}(\hat{\mathbf{V}}^\mathbf{r})) \bigg). \tag{3}$$

The loss of an ABox $\mathcal{A}$ is the average of the losses of the assertions in $\mathcal{A}$.

Negative Sampling. We employ negative sampling as done in previous approaches for embedding EL KBs [6,7,10,13,14]. That is, for role assertions, we take either the head or the tail of a triple in the data and replace it by another element, checking whether the new (corrupted) triple is not in the original data. For concept assertions, the procedure replaces the individual name by another one that forms an assertion not present in the original data. For conciseness, we omit the negative sampling term on the loss functions above. For the loss function applied to concept assertions we add a term where we maximize the distance between θ^a and the vector $\theta^{a'}$ associated with a corrupted individual, and likewise for role assertions, for both θ^a_h and θ^a_t.

Parameter Constraints. In order to incentivize θ^A, θ^r_h, θ^r_t to stay within the regions related to their geometric interpretations, we add a radius hyperparameter and constraint operation to the optimization method that is applied to all θ^A, θ^r_h, and θ^r_t. After every epoch of training, we clip any role or concept parameters whose distance to its region's centroid is greater than the desired radius.

4 Proof of Concept

We test our model using the *Family* KB in [5] (consisting of 469 individuals, 9 concept names, and 6 role names) and use the following two scoring functions defined below to evaluate the data:

$$\mathbf{Score}(A,a) = \mathbf{d}(\theta^a, \theta^A) + \mathbf{d}(\theta^a, \mathbf{c}(\hat{\mathbf{V}}^\mathbf{A})) \tag{4}$$

$$\mathbf{Score}(r,a,b) = \mathbf{d}(\theta^a \oplus \theta^b, \mathbf{c}(\hat{\mathbf{V}}^\mathbf{r})) + \mathbf{d}(\theta^a \oplus \theta^r_t, \mathbf{c}(\hat{\mathbf{V}}^\mathbf{r})) + \mathbf{d}(\theta^r_h \oplus \theta^b, \mathbf{c}(\hat{\mathbf{V}}^\mathbf{r})). \tag{5}$$

For the evaluation, we use the *hits at k* (h@k) metric, which we define as usual:

$$\text{h@k}(r_1,...,r_n) = \frac{1}{n} \sum_{i=1}^{n} \mathbb{I}(r_i \leq k)$$

where r_i denotes the rank of an assertion as scored by (Eq. 4 and Eq. 5), k is a given parameter, and the indicator function $\mathbb{I}$ is defined as $\mathbb{I}(x \leq y) = 1$ for $x \leq y$, and 0 otherwise. The metric ranges from 0 to 1, and higher is better.

Table 1. The results of h@k for Concept and Role Assertions on the *Family* dataset.

Concept Assertions						
Epochs	1	5	25	50	75	100
h@1	0.000	0.000	0.286	0.286	**0.429**	0.000
h@3	0.286	0.286	0.571	0.571	**0.571**	0.571
h@10	0.571	0.714	0.857	1.000	**1.000**	1.000
Role Assertions						
Epochs	1	5	25	50	75	100
h@1	0.008	0.008	0.000	0.000	0.000	0.011
h@3	0.008	0.008	0.027	0.027	0.031	0.031
h@10	0.011	0.031	0.080	0.096	0.100	0.107

The results are presented in Table 1. Concept assertions were considerably easier to predict in our method. Since the regions connected to the geometric interpretation of concepts lie in the unitary hypercube, we initialize the parameters for individuals, θ_n^a according to a normal distribution with a mean equal to the center of the unit hypercube and $\sigma = 0.7$ to prevent them from being initialized at the same point. In order to weigh how far the negatively sampled individual parameter $\theta^{a'}$ is allowed to move, we have a hyperparameter ψ. We experimentally found that setting ψ lower than 1 leads to better results (we used $\psi = 0.7$ in the table), likely due to how sensitive the model is to big changes during the optimization of the negative sampling term. To test the embedding method's capabilities on RIs, we added the role inclusion Sibling ⊑ relatedTo. We excluded the axiom Mother ⊓ Father ⊑ ⊥, since our $\mathcal{ELH}$ fragment does not have ⊥.

5 Discussion and Future Work

We describe the FaithEL embedding method and provide an implementation as a proof of concept. Our method has a limitation, which is associated with the formal guarantee of strong-TBox faithfulness. The difficulty is that the number of dimensions depends on the size of the domain of the canonical model, which can be large even for relatively small KBs. There are three main ideas that merit further investigation: a) limiting the movement of the parameters related to concept names and roles by checking whether they are inside or outside the regions connected to their geometric interpretations directly, without relying on a radius hyperparameter; b) increasing the number of parameters per role in order to inject greater flexibility into the method; c) devise a fair way to compare FaithEL to other existing methods.

Acknowledgments. The first and second authors are supported by the Norwegian Research Council, project 316022. This work was partly supported by the Research

Council of Norway through its Centre of Excellence Integreat - The Norwegian Centre for knowledge-driven machine learning, project number 332645.

References

1. Abboud, R., Ceylan, I., Lukasiewicz, T., Salvatori, T.: BoxE: a box embedding model for knowledge base completion. In: Larochelle, H., Ranzato, M., Hadsell, R., Balcan, M.F., Lin, H. (eds.) Advances in Neural Information Processing Systems, vol. 33, pp. 9649–9661. Curran Associates, Inc. (2020). https://doi.org/10.5555/3495724.3496533
2. Baader, F., Horrocks, I., Lutz, C., Sattler, U.: An Introduction to Description Logic, 1st edn. Cambridge University Press (2017). https://doi.org/10.1017/9781139025355
3. Bourgaux, C., Ozaki, A., Pan, J.Z.: Geometric models for (temporally) attributed description logics. In: Homola, M., Ryzhikov, V., Schmidt, R.A. (eds.) DL. CEUR Workshop Proceedings, vol. 2954. CEUR-WS.org (2021)
4. Gutiérrez-Basulto, V., Schockaert, S.: From knowledge graph embedding to ontology embedding? An analysis of the compatibility between vector space representations and rules. In: Thielscher, M., Toni, F., Wolter, F. (eds.) KR, pp. 379–388. AAAI Press (2018). https://doi.org/10.4230/OASIcs.AIB.2022.3
5. Imenes, A., Guimarães, R., Ozaki, A.: Marrying query rewriting and knowledge graph embeddings. In: Fensel, A., Ozaki, A., Roman, D., Soylu, A. (eds.) RuleML+RR 2023. LNCS, vol. 14244, pp. 126–140. Springer, Cham (2023). https://doi.org/10.1007/978-3-031-45072-3_9
6. Jackermeier, M., Chen, J., Horrocks, I.: Dual box embeddings for the description logic EL++. In: Proceedings of the ACM on Web Conference, pp. 2250–2258. WWW, Association for Computing Machinery (2024). https://doi.org/10.1145/3589334.3645648
7. Kulmanov, M., Liu-Wei, W., Yan, Y., Hoehndorf, R.: EL embeddings: geometric construction of models for the description logic EL++. In: Proceedings of IJCAI (2019). https://doi.org/10.24963/ijcai.2019/845
8. Lacerda, V., Ozaki, A., Guimarães, R.: Strong faithfulness for ELH ontology embeddings (2023). https://arxiv.org/abs/2310.02198. Under review at Transactions on Graph Data and Knowledge (TGDK)
9. Lutz, C., Wolter, F.: Deciding inseparability and conservative extensions in the description logic EL. J. Symb. Comput. **45**(2), 194–228 (2010). https://doi.org/10.1016/j.jsc.2008.10.007
10. Mondal, S., Bhatia, S., Mutharaju, R.: EmEL++: embeddings for EL++ description logic. In: Martin, A., Hinkelmann, K., Fill, H., Gerber, A., Lenat, D., Stolle, R., van Harmelen, F. (eds.) AAAI-MAKE. CEUR, vol. 2846 (2021)
11. Özçep, Ö.L., Leemhuis, M., Wolter, D.: Cone semantics for logics with negation. In: IJCAI (2020)
12. Pavlovic, A., Sallinger, E.: ExpressivE: a spatio-functional embedding for knowledge graph completion. In: ICLR (2023)
13. Peng, X., Tang, Z., Kulmanov, M., Niu, K., Hoehndorf, R.: Description logic EL++ embeddings with intersectional closure. CoRR abs/2202.14018 (2022). https://arxiv.org/abs/2202.14018
14. Xiong, B., Potyka, N., Tran, T.K., Nayyeri, M., Staab, S.: Faithful embeddings for $\mathcal{EL}$++ knowledge bases. In: Sattler, U., et al. (eds.) ISWC 2022. LNCS, vol. 13489, pp. 22–38. Springer, Cham (2022). https://doi.org/10.1007/978-3-031-19433-7_2

RDF Surfaces as a First-Order Language for the Semantic Web

Dörthe Arndt[1,4](✉), Jos De Roo[2], Patrick Hochstenbach[2,3], Rebekka Martens[1], Femke Ongenae[2], and Mathijs van Noort[2]

[1] Computational Logic Group, Technische Universität Dresden, Dresden, Germany
doerthe.arndt@tu-dresden.de
[2] IDLab, Ghent University - Imec, Ghent, Belgium
[3] Ghent University Library, Ghent University, Ghent, Belgium
[4] ScaDS.AI, Dresden/Leipzig, Germany

Abstract. Inspired by the idea of RDF Redux, an RDF extension suggested by Pat Hayes, RDF Surfaces were recently developed and further specified by a W3C community group. The idea of RDF Surfaces is to add negation and explicit existential quantification to RDF and thereby gain the expressivity of first-order logic. RDF Surfaces come with a syntax and even with first implementations, but the semantics has so far only been defined informally. In this paper we aim to close this gap: we map RDF Surface graphs to first-order logic formulae and thereby define their semantics. We show that, restricted to RDF graphs, this semantics preserves simple entailment. That is, each RDF graph which entails another in its first-order translation, also entails this graph according to RDF's simple entailment and vice versa. To test whether this semantics fully meets the informal specification, we furthermore provide rs2fol, an implementation which follows our mapping and translates RDF Surfaces in N3-based syntax to first-order logic in TPTP syntax. We apply this implementation on the various examples collected on the Web page of the RDF Surfaces reasoner EYE, run them with the theorem prover Vampire and compare the results with those of EYE. With the exception of a different understanding of lists – EYE treats these as first-class citizens – results of both approaches coincide. We thus provides a tool for entailment checking which is conform to the current specification. This tool will help future developers of RDF Surfaces reasoners to test their derivations for correctness and the community as a whole to better understand the logic and – if needed – to refine or even restrict it.

Keywords: RDF Surfaces · FOL · Reasoning · RDF · Semantics

1 Introduction

RDF [6] can be seen as the most basic, but also most important, logic of the Semantic Web. The majority of other logical Web frameworks – for example OWL with its different profiles [3], Notation3 Logic (N3) [30], and SPARQL [11] – are based on (parts of) RDF. Most of these frameworks are compatible with RDF on a syntactic level. However, this does not hold for the semantics. For instance, OWL's description logic based direct semantics [20] and its RDF-based semantics [21], which directly extends RDF semantics, are not fully compatible. And while there is the possibility to include entailment regimes in SPARQL, it mainly connects to RDF through subgraph matching. These observations motivated Pat Hayes to re-think RDF. In his ISWC 2009 keynote talk [12] he proposed RDF Redux as an improved version of RDF. RDF Redux is a direct extension of RDF, which adds explicit existential quantification and negation to RDF with simple interpretations. As RDF already supports the conjunction of atomic formulae, it becomes as expressive as first-order logic (FOL) by these additions and thus also covers, for example, $SHOIN$ [1], the formal base of OWL DL. Following this idea, an W3C community group was formed[1] and RDF Surfaces were developed [15,17]. A Web logic with a concrete realisation in an N3-based syntax. Reasoning on this framework is supported by the EYE reasoner [7], which also hosts many examples discussed in the community group on its Web page [8], by Latar [14] and by Tension [27]. These implementations rely on an informal specification of the logic. The formal semantics of RDF Surfaces has not been defined yet.

In this paper we fill this gap. Following the informal descriptions and specifications detailed by Hochstenbach et al. [17], we define the abstract syntax of RDF Surfaces and map the formulae we retrieve directly to first-order logic. Our work builds upon the work of De Bruijn and Heymans who provided a mapping from RDF to first-order logic that preserves simple entailment [4]. Just as De Bruijn and Heymans, we understand graphs as conjunctions of triple statements where the blank nodes are assumed to be existentially quantified. As plain RDF does not include negation and explicit quantification – the aspects RDF surfaces adds to RDF – these two are not covered by De Bruijn and Heymans. We map RDF Surfaces to FOL and preserve simple entailment in same manner De Bruijn and Heymann do with their mapping from RDF to FOL. By doing so, we provide the first formal semantics for RDF Surfaces. To test whether our mapping is in line with the informal specification of the logic, we furthermore implemented rs2fol, a Kotlin program, which employs our mapping to translate concrete N3 representations of RDF Surfaces to TPTP syntax [25] – a standard format for first-order theorem provers – and performs entailment checking using the prover Vampire [19]. In our evaluation, we use this program to reason over the examples collected on the Web page of EYE [8]. These reflect the common expectations on the logic as they mainly contain use cases discussed in the community group and tests sent in by users. We compare our reasoning results to those of EYE, the most advanced among the different rs2fol reasoners. In a second round, we use our own test cases originated from FOL with rs2fol and EYE to exemplify how the development of RDF Surfaces and its reasoners can benefit from rs2fol.

The remainder of the paper is structured as follows: In Sect. 2, we explain the idea of RDF Surfaces in more detail and provide an example. After that, in Sect. 3, we introduce RDF Surfaces in a more formal way. In Sect. 4, we then define our mapping from RDF Surfaces to first-order logic which we implemented

---

[1] https://www.w3.org/community/rdfsurfaces/.

in our tool `rs2fol` which we describe in Sect. 5. This is followed, in Sect. 6, by the practical evaluation of our work. In Sect. 7, we discuss related work and end our paper with a conclusion (Sect. 8).

2 Idea and Examples

Before formally introducing the necessary concepts, we provide an informal introduction to RDF Surfaces to make the reader familiar with the general idea. As RDF Surfaces extends RDF with simple interpretations, we start by providing a triple:[2]

$$:\text{socrates a :Human .} \tag{1}$$

Informally speaking, this triple can be interpreted as *"Socrates is a human."*, or, in FOL (making use of the predicate tr to represent triples):[3]

$$tr(socrates, type, Human) \tag{2}$$

Applying RDF's simple entailment [13], we can replace the constant `:socrates` by a blank node:

$$\_:\text{x a :Human .} \tag{3}$$

which informally means *"There exists a human."*, or in FOL:

$$\exists x.tr(x, type, Human) \tag{4}$$

With RDF Surfaces, we make this implicit quantification explicit. Instead of Triple 3, we thus write:

$$(\_:\text{x}) \text{ log:onPositiveSurface } \{ \_:\text{x a :Human . } \} \text{ .} \tag{5}$$

We furthermore have the possibility to state negative information. If we write

$$(\_:\text{x}) \text{ log:onNegativeSurface } \{ \_:\text{x a :Human . } \} \text{ .} \tag{6}$$

this means that no humans exist, or in FOL[4]:

$$\neg \exists x.tr(x, type, human) \tag{7}$$

As this construct adds negation and explicit quantification, we can now express first-order operators. To state universal quantification, we use nested negation. The equivalence of

$$\forall x.tr(x, likes, cheese) \equiv \neg(\exists x.\neg tr(x, likes, cheese))$$

---

[2] To save space, we omit the prefix declarations in this paper.
[3] An alternative representation would be $type(socrates, human)$. We use the triple notation following [4] because RDF Surfaces allow variables in predicate position, more on that in Sect. 4.
[4] Note that this construct makes the previous one only syntactic sugar. Triple 5 could also be written as `() log:onNegativeSurface {(_:x) log:onNegativeSurface { _:x a :Human.}.}`. We include positive surfaces to improve readability.

expressing the fact that *"everyone likes cheese"*, can thus be expressed in RDF Surfaces as follows:

(_:x) log:onNegativeSurface {   (8)
    () log:onNegativeSurface { _ :x :likes :cheese . } . } .

Similarly, we can express disjunction. The statement *"socrates likes cheese or wine"* can be written in FOL as follows:

$$tr(socrates, likes, cheese) \lor tr(socrates, likes, wine) \quad (9)$$
$$\equiv \neg(\neg tr(socrates, likes, cheese) \land \neg tr(socrates, likes, wine))$$

This leads to the RDF Surface:

() log:onNegativeSurface {   (10)
    () log:onNegativeSurface { :socrates :likes :cheese . } .
    () log:onNegativeSurface { :socrates :likes :wine . } .
} .

The idea is, thus, that by the simple addition of negation and explicit existential quantification to RDF, we are able to express first-order formulae in a Semantic Web format. As a last example to illustrate the idea, we translate the rule that *"all humans are mortal"*, that is

$$\forall x. tr(x, type, human) \to tr(x, type, mortal) \quad (11)$$
$$\equiv \neg \exists x. (tr(x, type, human) \land \neg tr(x, type, mortal))$$

to RDF Surfaces:

(_:x) log:onNegativeSurface {   (12)
    _:x a :Human .
    () log:onNegativeSurface {
        _:x a :Mortal .
    } .
} .

RDF Surfaces thus also cover classical rules as for example present in N3 or SWRL [18]. More complicated constructs like disjunction in the conclusion of rules allow us to cope, for example, with the union operator of OWL DL [29]. RDF Surfaces provides a framework to express FOL in a Semantic Web format.

3 RDF Surfaces

After our informal introduction of RDF Surfaces and the idea behind our mapping, we next introduce the logic in a more formal way. Our definitions are inspired by Hochstenbach et al. [17]. The abstract syntax of RDF Surfaces is an extension of RDF's abstract syntax, more precisely, of generalised RDF [5]:

Definition 1. *The set $T = B \cup L \cup \mathrm{IRI}$ of RDF terms consists of the union of the sets B of blank nodes, L of literals, and IRI of IRIs. We call a triple $t \in T \times T \times T$ a generalised RDF triple. A set of generalised RDF triples is called a* generalised RDF graph.

The reason to use generalised RDF instead of the regular recommendation is mainly that we want to avoid that the consequences of our reasoning cannot be expressed – rules could produce triples with literals in subject position – and that the logic should be strong enough to express frameworks like N3 or SPARQL where variables in predicate position are allowed.[5] Generalised RDF triples can now form part of a Hayes triple:

Definition 2. *A* Hayes triple *(H-triple) is a triple of the form $\langle Gr, s, H \rangle$ where Gr is a (possibly empty) set of blank nodes, called graffiti; $s \in \{\mathrm{nS}, \mathrm{pS}\}$ is the surface type; and H is a (possibly empty) graph, that is a set of generalised RDF triples and H-triples. We call H a* Hayes graph *(H-graph).*

Connecting our abstract syntax to the concrete example provided in Formula 5, we note that there, the list (_:x) is the graffiti,[6] pS (for positive surface) is the surface type, and the graph containing Triple 3 is the H-graph. The definition of H-graphs is recursive, H-graphs can be nested. Formula 10 above is an example of such a nesting. Note that with the introduction of explicit quantification, blank nodes can now represent free variables. From an RDF Surfaces point of view, the blank node _:x occurs as a free variable in Triple 3. We introduce the concept of free variables in a more formal way:

Definition 3. *Let H be an H-graph, $t = \langle t_1, t_2, t_3 \rangle$ a generalised triple, $h = \langle Gr, s, H \rangle$ an H-triple, and B the set of blank nodes. We recursively define the set fr of free variables occurring in H, t and h as follows:*

$$\mathrm{fr}(t) = \{t_1, t_2, t_3\} \cap B$$
$$\mathrm{fr}(h) = \mathrm{fr}(H) \setminus Gr$$
$$\mathrm{fr}(H) = \bigcup_{x \in G} \mathrm{fr}(x)$$

For technical reasons – RDF Surfaces aims to support plain RDF – RDF Surfaces semantics assumes the existential closure when interpreting H-graphs containing free variables. That is, Triple 3 is understood as Formula 4 above and the following surface (which is a slight variation of Formula 6)

$$() \; \texttt{log:onNegativeSurface} \; \{ \; \texttt{\_:x a :Human.} \}. \tag{13}$$

means

$$\exists x. \neg tr(x, type, human) \tag{14}$$

---

[5] Note, however, that due to SPARQL's non-monotonicity and built-in functions, RDF Surfaces will most likely only be suitable to cover parts of it.

[6] Note that N3 does not support the use of sets, therefore, a list was chosen in the concrete syntax.

or in words *"there exists something which is not a human"*. Having introduced the syntax of RDF Surfaces, we provide the mapping to first-order logic in the next section.

4 Mapping RDF Surfaces to First-Order Logic

For our definitions, we briefly recap first-order logic and its semantics. For a more detailed discussion, we refer to the standard textbooks (e.g., Ebbinghaus et al. and Enderton [9,10]). The syntax of first-order logic is defined as follows:

Definition 4. *Given the disjoint sets V of variables, F of function symbols, R of relation symbols, where each element of $R \cup F$ has a fixed arity $n \geq 1$, and C of constants. We define the set $\mathcal{T}$ of FOL terms as follows:*

- *each $v \in V$ is a term,*
- *each $c \in C$ is a term,*
- *if $t_1, \ldots, t_n \in \mathcal{T}$ and $f \in F$ has arity n, then $f(t_1, \ldots, t_n)$ is a term.*

The set $\mathcal{F}$ of first-order formulae is then defined as:

- *if $t_1, \ldots, t_n \in \mathcal{T}$ and $r \in R$ has arity n, then $r(t_1, \ldots, t_n) \in \mathcal{F}$,*
- *if $\phi, \psi \in \mathcal{F}$ then $(\phi \wedge \psi) \in \mathcal{F}$,*
- *if $\phi \in \mathcal{F}$, then $\neg \phi \in \mathcal{F}$,*
- *if $v \in V$ and $f \in \mathcal{F}$ then $\exists x.f \in \mathcal{F}$.*

Note that our definition omits the connectives $\vee, \rightarrow$ and $\leftrightarrow$ as these can be seen as syntactic sugar – $\phi \vee \psi$ can, for example, be expressed as $\neg(\neg\phi \wedge \neg\psi)$. We chose this definition to emphasize the strong connection between FOL and RDF Surfaces. For the same reason, we also omit the universal quantifier: $\forall x.\phi$ can be expressed as $\neg \exists x.\neg \phi$.

For this syntax, we now also briefly recap the semantics:

Definition 5. *A structure $\mathfrak{A}$ for the sets F, R and C consists of a non-empty set $\mathcal{A}$, the domain, and of a mapping $\mathfrak{a}$ such that $\mathfrak{a}(c) \in \mathcal{A}$ for all $c \in C$, $\mathfrak{a}(r) \in 2^{\mathcal{A}^n}$ for all $r \in R$ with arity n, and $\mathfrak{a}(f)$ maps to an n-ary function in $\mathcal{A}$ if $f \in F$ and f has arity n.*
An assignment *is a mapping $\beta : V \rightarrow \mathcal{A}$, for $a \in \mathcal{A}$ and $x \in V$, we write $\beta\frac{a}{x}$ to indicate a mapping which behaves as β with the exception that it maps x to a. We call a pair of $\mathfrak{I}(\mathfrak{A}, \beta)$ an* interpretation.
We define $x^{\mathfrak{I}}$ as follows:

- *$c^{\mathfrak{I}} = \mathfrak{a}(c)$ for $c \in C$,*
- *$x^{\mathfrak{I}} = \beta(x)$ for $x \in V$,*
- *$(f(t_1, \ldots, t_n))^{\mathfrak{I}} = (\mathfrak{a}(f))(t_1^{\mathfrak{I}}, \ldots, t_n^{\mathfrak{I}})$.*

Let ϕ and ψ be formulae. We recursivly define:

- *$\mathfrak{I} \models r(t_1, \ldots, t_n)$ iff $\langle t_1^{\mathfrak{I}}, \ldots, t_n^{\mathfrak{I}} \rangle \in \mathfrak{a}(r)$,*
- *$\mathfrak{I} \models \phi \wedge \psi$ iff $\mathfrak{I} \models \phi$, and $\mathfrak{I} \models \psi$,*

- $\mathfrak{I} \models \neg \phi$ iff $\mathfrak{I} \not\models \phi$,
- $\mathfrak{I} \models \exists x \phi$ iff there exists an $a \in \mathcal{A}$ such that $\mathfrak{I}\frac{a}{x} \models \phi$.

This definition allows us to introduce the concepts of satisfiability and entailment:

Definition 6. *We call a formula ϕ satisfiable if there exists an interpretation $\mathfrak{I}$ such that $\mathfrak{I} \models \phi$, in this case we call $\mathfrak{I}$ a model of ϕ. We say that a formula ϕ entails a formula ψ, written as $\phi \models \psi$, if for each interpretation $\mathfrak{I}$ with $\mathfrak{I} \models \phi$ also $\mathfrak{I} \models \psi$ holds.*

As RDF does not support functions, these will also not play a role in our translation presented in this section. However, they will be used in our evaluation (Sect. 6.2) when we talk about lists. For this reason, they are included here. We now come to the definition of our mapping, which takes a formula in RDF Surfaces and translates it to FOL just as indicated by the examples in Sect. 2. This mapping relies on a term mapping $\ell : T \to V \cup C$, where each blank node is mapped to a variable, and each IRI and each literal is mapped to a constant. For simplicity, we assume this mapping to be injective. Note, however, that the mapping can be modified for literals such that these map to their canonical representation. This would allow us to handle datatype reasoning.

Definition 7. *Given an H-Graph G and an injective term mapping $\ell : T \to V \cup C$. We recursively define the translation mapping m from H-graphs to FOL as follows:*

- *for each generalised RDF triple $\langle s, p, o \rangle$: $m(\langle s, p, o \rangle) = tr(\ell(s), \ell(p), \ell(o))$;*
- *for each positive H-triple $\langle (b_1, \ldots b_n), \mathrm{pS}, H \rangle$:*
  $m(\langle (b_1, \ldots b_n), \mathrm{pS}, H \rangle) = \exists \ell(b_1) \ldots \exists \ell(b_n) m(H);$
- *for each negative H-triple $\langle (b_1, \ldots b_n), \mathrm{nS}, H \rangle$:*
  $m(\langle (b_1, \ldots b_n), \mathrm{nS}, H \rangle) = \forall \ell(b_1) \ldots \forall \ell(b_n) \neg (m(H));$
- *for each H-graph H: $m(H) = \bigwedge_{t \in H} m(t)$.*

Note that the translation function can produce FOL formulae containing free variables. We interpret these formulae as existentially closed, that is, given an H-graph H with a set of free variables $\mathrm{fr}(H) = \{x_1, \ldots, x_n\}$, we translate H via m and add quantifiers, such that $\exists \ell(x_1) \ldots \exists \ell(x_n) m(H)$. As a shortcut for the existential closure we will from now on write $\exists \mathbf{x}.m(H)$.

Our mapping relies on a term mapping ℓ. Note that the concrete choice of ℓ is not relevant for our purposes as long as ℓ is fixed and injective. We therefore omit ℓ from now on and assume it to be arbitrary but fixed and injective. We now use our mapping m to define the semantics of RDF Surfaces:

Definition 8. *Let H and G be H-graphs. We say that H is h-satifiable, if there exists a first-order interpretation $\mathfrak{I}$ such that $\mathfrak{I} \models \exists \mathbf{x}.m(H)$. We say, that H h-entails G, written as $H \models_h G$ if for each first-order interpretation $\mathfrak{I}$, it holds that $\mathfrak{I} \models \exists \mathbf{x}.m(G)$ if $\mathfrak{I} \models \exists \mathbf{x}.m(H)$. If $\mathfrak{I} \models_h G$, we call $\mathfrak{I}$ an h-model of G.*

Before evaluating the accuracy of our mapping with the existing examples for RDF Surfaces reasoning, we would like to briefly discuss how h-entailment behaves for generalised RDF graphs, that is, for graphs not containing H-triples. Recall that the semantics of these graphs is defined as follows [13]:

Definition 9. *A simple interpretation I is a structure consisting of:*

- *a non-empty set* IR *of resources,*
- *a set* IP, *called the set of properties,*
- *a mapping* IEXT : IP $\to 2^{\text{IR} \times \text{IR}}$,
- *a mapping* IS : IRI $\to$ (IR $\cup$ IP),
- *a partial mapping* IL : $L \to$ IR.

For a ground graph (a graph without blank nodes) G, we recursively apply I as follows:

- *If* $l \in L$: $I(l) = \text{IL}(l)$,
- *if* $c \in \text{IRI}$: $I(c) = \text{IS}(c)$,
- *if* $\langle s, p, o \rangle$ *a ground triple:* $I(\langle s, p, o \rangle) = \text{true}$ *iff* $\langle I(s), I(o) \rangle \in \text{IEXT}(I(p))$,
- *if G is a ground graph:* $I(G) = \text{true}$ *iff* $I(t) = \text{true}$ *for all triples* $t \in G$.

For a mapping $A : B \to \text{IR} \cup \text{IP}$, *we define*

$$[I + A](x) = \begin{cases} A(x), & \text{if } x \in B, \\ I(x) & \text{else.} \end{cases}$$

If G is a generalised RDF graph then $I(G) = \text{true}$ *iff there exists a mapping A such that* $[I + A](G) = \text{true}$.

This definition allows us, to define simple entailment and satisfiability:

Definition 10. *We call a generalised RDF graph G simply satisfiable if there exists an interpretation such that* $I(G) = \text{true}$. *We say that a graph G simply entails a graph F, written as* $G \models_s F$, *if for all interpretations I with* $I(G) = \text{true}$, *we also have* $I(F) = \text{true}$.

If we apply the mapping specified in Definition 7 on only generalised RDF graphs, we get a conjunction of triples in which the blank nodes are existentially quantified. The graph

$$\texttt{:socrates :knows \_:x. \_:x :name"Plato"}. \tag{15}$$

becomes

$$\exists x (tr(socrates, knows, x) \land tr(x, name, Plato)) \tag{16}$$

For these basic graphs, we can directly transform simple RDF interpretations to first-order interpretations and vice versa while preserving the truth:

Lemma 1. *Let G be a generalised RDF graph, then the following holds:*

G is simply satisfiable   iff   G is h-satisfiable.

Proof. If $G = \{\langle s_i, p_i, o_i\rangle | 1 \leq i \leq m\}$ is a generalised RDF graph, $\exists \mathbf{x}.m(G)$ is of the form
$$g = \exists \ell(x_1)\ldots \exists \ell(x_n) \bigwedge_{1 \leq i \leq m} tr(\ell(s_i), \ell(p_i), \ell(o_i))$$
Note that this FOL formula contains one single predicate symbol, namely tr. We show both directions separately.

"$\Leftarrow$": Let $\mathfrak{I}$ be an FOL interpretation of g such that $\mathfrak{I} \models g$. We construct a simple interpretation $I = (\text{IR}, \text{IP}, \text{IEXT}, \text{IS}, \text{IL})$ for G as follows: $\text{IR} := \mathcal{A}$, $\text{IP} := \{p \in \mathcal{A} | \exists s, o \in \mathcal{A} : \langle s, p, o\rangle \in \mathfrak{a}(tr)\}$, $\text{IEXT}(p) := \{\langle s, o\rangle | \langle s, p, o\rangle \in \mathfrak{a}(tr)\}$, $\text{IS}(c) := \mathfrak{a}(\ell(c))$ if c is an IRI and $\text{IL}(l) := \mathfrak{a}(\ell(l))$, if l is a literal. To see, that $I(G) = \text{true}$, we need to take a closer look at the blank nodes occurring in G. As $\mathfrak{I} \models \exists \ell(x_1)\ldots \exists \ell(x_n)m(G)$, there exist $a_1,\ldots,a_n \in \mathcal{A}$ such that $\mathfrak{I}\frac{a_1}{\ell(x_1)}\ldots\frac{a_n}{\ell(x_n)} \models m(G)$. We define A such that $A(x_i) := a_i$, for $1 \leq i \leq n$. With that A we get $[I + A](G) = \text{true}$.

"$\Rightarrow$": Let $I = (\text{IR}, \text{IP}, \text{IEXT}, \text{IS}, \text{IL})$ such that $I(G) = \text{true}$. To construct a model $\mathfrak{I}$ for g, we define: $\mathcal{A} := \text{IR} \cup \text{IP}$, $\mathfrak{a}(t) := I(\ell^{-1}(t))$ if t is a constant. Note that this mapping is well-defined because ℓ is injective and because if $I(G) = \text{true}$, then $\text{IL}(l)$ is defined for all literals occurring in G. For tr we set $\mathfrak{a}(tr) := \{\langle s, p, o\rangle | \exists p \in \text{IP} : \langle s, o\rangle \in \text{IEXT}(p)\}$. As $I(G) = \text{true}$, there exists furthermore a mapping $A : B \to \text{IR} \cup \text{IP}$, such that $[I + A](G) = \text{true}$. We use the values of that mapping to obtain $\mathfrak{I}\frac{A(x_1)}{\ell(x_1)}\ldots\frac{A(x_n)}{\ell(x_n)} \models m(G)$. We thus get $\mathfrak{I} \models \exists \ell(x_1)\ldots \exists \ell(x_n)m(G)$. □

As a direct consequence of that lemma, we get the theorem below, which means that if we limit h-entailment to RDF graphs, it behaves just as simple entailment:

Theorem 1. *For two generalised RDF graphs G and F the following holds:*
$$G \models_s F \quad \text{iff} \quad G \models_h F$$

Proof. Let $G \models_s F$ and $\mathfrak{I} \models \exists \mathbf{x}.m(G)$. Then, according to Lemma 1, we can construct a simple interpretation I for G such that $I(G) = \text{true}$. According to our assumption, we then also find a simple interpretation I' such that $I'(F) = \text{true}$. We again apply Lemma 1 and obtain a model $\mathfrak{I}' \models \exists \mathbf{x}.m(F)$. The other direction follows with the same argumentation. □

5 Implementation

In the previous section, we introduced a mapping from RDF Surfaces to FOL and used this to define their semantics. In addition to the fact that this helps us to better understand this new Web logic, we also have a practical advantage: FOL is supported by a wide range of tools performing reasoning. To make use of this tooling, but also to further test our mapping, we developed `rs2fol`, a Kotlin program which translates RDF surfaces to first-order logic and then uses a first-order theorem prover to perform entailment checking. In this section, we explain our implementation in detail. All code is available at https://github.com/RebekkaMa/rs2fol.

`rs2fol` directly implements the translation function m introduced in Definition 7 and converts RDF Surfaces, expressed in N3 syntax [17] – the syntax used in our motivational examples (Sect. 2) – into first-order logic formulae, written TPTP format [25]. TPTP is a very common input format for first-order theorem provers, and we chose it to be able to connect to different tools. In TPTP, facts are marked as *axioms*. For example, Formula 1 (*"Socrates is a human."*) is represented as:

$$\text{fof(formula1,axiom,triple('socrates','type','Human'))}. \qquad (17)$$

To test for whether or not a formula is a logical consequence of the others, potential consequences are marked as *conjecture*. If we, for example, want to know whether Formula 3 (*"There exists a human."*) is a logical consequence of the previous one, we add

$$\begin{array}{l}\text{fof(formula3,conjecture,}\\\qquad\text{? [X] : (triple(X,'type','Human')))}.\end{array} \qquad (18)$$

The question mark in this example indicates an existential quantifier.

`rs2fol` takes these translations and hands them over to a theorem prover. By using TPTP as representation format for FOL, we made our implementation compatible with different reasoning tools. Currently, `rs2fol` employs Vampire [19], which we have chosen for its persistently convincing results in prover competitions [26] and its good technical support. With Vampire we have two options. We either test whether one or more of the conjectures follow from the axioms (entailment checking) or, of no conjecture is given, it tests for satisfiability of the axioms. Employing Definition 8, that means that our implementation `rs2fol` performs h-entailment and h-satisfiability checking. Assuming that the calculus of Vampire is sound and complete and that our definition of the mapping actually meets the expectations informally stated about RDF surfaces, we provided the first sound and complete entailment checker for h-entailment.[7]

6 Evaluation

In the previous section, we introduced `rs2fol`, our tool to perform h-entailment checking according to our definition. We already discussed that h-entailment truly extends RDF's simple entailment. As a next step, we would like to use `rs2fol` to evaluate whether our definition is in line with the informal specification. To do so, we perform two tests: (1) we check whether our proposed transformation from RDF Surfaces to first-order logic is correctly implemented,

---

[7] Note, however, that FOL entailment- and satisfiability checking is known to be undecidable. That is a limitation which is unavoidable for RDF Surfaces given its complexity.

(2) being sure that rs2fol works as expected, we evaluate whether rs2fol supports the test cases for RDF Surfaces which exist so far. For (1), we considered a calculus, adopted from [9], and created test in the N3-based syntax reflecting the different derivation rules. For (2) we compared the reasoning results of the EYE reasoner to those of rs2fol on the example cases provided on EYE's Web page [8]. Below, we discuss the two data sets, the tests performed, and the respective test results separately. Afterwards we discuss tests we created motivated by these results.

6.1 Validity of the Implementation

From the point of view of first-order logic, RDF Surfaces is equipped with conjunction (two statements on a single surface), negation (the negative surface type), and existential quantification (blank node graffiti on a negative surface). We consider a first-order logic syntax with operators $\wedge$, $\neg$ and $\exists$. Via equivalences $\phi \vee \psi \equiv \neg(\neg\phi \wedge \neg\psi)$, $\phi \to \psi \equiv \neg(\phi \wedge \neg\psi)$ and $\forall \mathbf{x}.\phi \equiv \neg(\exists \mathbf{x}.\neg\phi)$, it follows that said logic has full first-order expressivity.

rs2fol translates h-graphs to first-order formulae. The theoretical validity of this transformation follows from Theorem 1. In order to additionally verify the validity of our implementation itself, we verify whether the output of rs2fol behaves as intended; we consider a set of calculus rules for FOL, taken from Ebbinghaus et al. [9], but adapted to accommodate for the syntactical difference of $\wedge$ instead of $\vee$:

$$\frac{\Gamma \phi}{\Gamma' \phi} \text{ for } \Gamma \subseteq \Gamma', \qquad \frac{}{\Gamma \phi} \text{ for } \phi \in \Gamma, \qquad \frac{\Gamma \psi \phi, \Gamma \neg \psi \phi}{\Gamma \phi}, \tag{19a}$$

$$\frac{\Gamma \neg \phi \psi, \Gamma \neg \phi \neg \psi}{\Gamma \phi}, \qquad \frac{\Gamma \phi, \Gamma \psi}{\Gamma (\phi \wedge \psi)}, \qquad \frac{\Gamma \phi \chi}{\Gamma (\phi \wedge \psi) \chi}, \tag{19b}$$

$$\frac{\Gamma \phi \frac{t}{x}}{\Gamma \exists x \, \phi}, \qquad \frac{\Gamma \phi \frac{y}{x} \psi}{\Gamma \exists x \phi \, \psi} \tag{19c}$$

Each of the rules in Eqs. 19b–19c of the calculus was encoded into RDF Surfaces. We translated the premises and a negation of the consequent[8] and performed satisfiability checking with rs2fol to detect that the positive consequent is entailed by the succedent. This was the case for all our files. While this alone can not be seen as proof that rs2fol's h-entailment checking is indeed complete and correct, we see this as a strong indication that the translation itself works. In terms of logical correctness and completeness, the implementation relies on Vampire and its underlying calculus.

6.2 Conformance to the Informal Semantics

After verifying that the code of rs2fol works as intended, we utilize rs2fol to answer the following question: Does our definition of h-entailment fully reflect

---

[8] The test files are available at https://github.com/RebekkaMa/rs2fol/tree/master/examples/sequent-calculus/minimal-example.

the informal semantics? Of course, this question is difficult to answer because it lies in the nature of an informal specification with different contributors, that expectations on the logic differ. However, there are implementations available which indicate the implementer's intuition and there exist test cases. For our tests, we chose to work with the reasoner EYE [28], a Notation3 engine that also supports RDF Surfaces reasoning. We chose that reasoner because it is the most advanced among the current implementations. As test files, we chose the test folder [8] on EYE's web page which does not only contain the test cases invented by the developers of EYE, but also cases that were discussed in the W3C community group or sent in by users. In this sense, the test cases reflect how the informal semantics is supposed to work.

In our tests, we compared the reasoning results of the EYE reasoner with those of rs2fol. At the time of testing, the test folder contained 97 files,[9] among these, 43 files included special features like customized built-in predicate or unusual syntax that are specific to EYE and were therefore excluded. To the remaining 54 files we used for testing we added one modified example, peano_short.n3s, derived from one of the unsupported files by reducing and removing unsupported elements.[10] The reason for that addition was that we wanted to include a file containing RDF list structures and these were not present in other files. EYE does not only perform entailment checking, but also has a query function that produces logical consequences of the input. We tested whether the output produced by the reasoner is h-entailed by the formulae. Our tests use a Bash script that systematically processes each of the 55 RDF Surfaces files. For each file, the script initially invokes EYE (version 10.16.4) to obtain the reasoning results. Subsequently, it executes rs2fol (version 1.0.0) which converts the currently processed file into a TPTP axiom and EYE's reasoning result into a TPTP conjecture formula. These two formulae are then passed to Vampire (version 4.7) for actual consequence checking.

We executed this script and observed that rs2fol confirmed all entailments performed by EYE with the exception of peano_s.n3s, the file we added. Further investigation showed that the reason for the disagreement was indeed the presence of lists: RDF's list construct heavily depends on blank nodes. In RDF, the list notation in the RDF triple

$$(\text{:a :b}) \text{ a rdf:List .} \tag{20}$$

is syntactic sugar for

$$\_\text{:b1 a rdf:List .}\_\text{:b1 rdf:first :a; rdf:rest }\_\text{:b2 .} \tag{21}$$
$$\_\text{:b2 rdf:first :b; rdf:rest rdf:nil .}$$

In contrast to that, N3 understands lists as first-class citizens [2], and given that EYE is also an N3 reasoner, it follows this interpretation. For list interpretations

---

[9] A snapshot is available at https://github.com/eyereasoner/rdfsurfaces-tests/tree/94eb1b74c70b51f34f67b15d59e8e02ebaf4a96b.

[10] Our tests folder is available at https://github.com/RebekkaMa/rs2fol/tree/master/examples/rdfsurfaces-tests.

supporting this interpretation, two lists having the same first and rest elements are interpreted equally, even if the lists themselves are represented by different blank nodes. In our test, two such lists where produced by different formulae and were thus equal in EYE but not for rs2fol.

It was rather easy to modify the translation rs2fol performs to make it understand lists the same way as EYE does. We added a binary first order function list and represented lists through nested functions, (:a :b) from above becomes list(a,list(b,nil)), and sucessfully repeated the test with the modification. However, RDF surfaces were introduced as a minimal extension or RDF with simple entailment [17] and this means that lists need to either be in line with the semantics of this framework or the difference should be reflected in the model. If we go for the first approach, it still needs to be clarified where exactly the blank nodes introduced by the use of ()-lists like the one exemplified in Formula 20 need to be placed. Our original implementation assumes this to be on the next surrounding surface of the list, but further tests are needed. We expect similar issues to happen with RDF-star given that – at least at the time of writing – it also adds syntactic sugar relying on blank nodes.

6.3 Universal Quantification

Motivated by the previous findings on lists, we performed a few more tests. Primary goal of these tests were to spot differences between rs2fol and EYE, as a secondary goal, we wanted to see how rs2fol entailment checking can help developers to spot incompleteness in their reasoning results. We extended the examples using the sequent rules from Sect. 6.1 to get more complex examples[11]. We observed that EYE and rs2fol agree in the mayority of cases, but we could spot differences in examples where unrestricted universal statements are derived through reasoning and then need to be applied. To illustrate this problem, we display a small example in Listing 1. Applying our mapping from Definition 4, the h-graph in the listing has the following FOL representation:

$$tr(bob, is, laughing) \land \neg tr(sue, is, happy) \quad (22)$$
$$\land \neg(\exists x \exists y \; tr(x, is, laughing) \land \neg tr(y, is, happy))$$

which is equivalent to

$$tr(bob, is, laughing) \land \neg tr(sue, is, happy) \quad (23)$$
$$\land \forall x \forall y \; tr(x, is, laughing) \to tr(y, is, happy)$$

It is easy to see that this formulae do not have a model, or in other words, that $tr(sue, is, happy)$ is a logical consequence of $tr(bob, is, laughing)$ and $\forall x \forall y \; tr(x, is, laughing) \to tr(y, is, happy)$. Currently, the reasoning process in EYE is able to correctly derive $\forall y \; tr(y, is, happy)$, but it does not apply this

---

[11] The test folder is available at: https://github.com/RebekkaMa/rs2fol/tree/master/examples/sequent-calculus/combined-rules.

```
1  :bob :is :laughing .
2
3  () log:onNegativeSurface { :sue :is :happy . } .
4
5  (_:x _:y) log:onNegativeSurface {
6         _:x :is :laughing .
7         () log:onNegativeSurface { _:y :is :happy . } .
8  } .
```

Listing 1. Example: If someone is laughing, everybody is happy. Bob is laughing and sue is not happy. This should lead to a contradiction which can be detected by `rs2fol` but in this format not (yet) by EYE.

universal fact to the instance *sue*. The reason seems to be in the algorithm it applies, which relies on materialization and needs to carefully select which facts it produces to avoid infinite productions. The reasoner itself provides special surfaces, to allow the user to guide the reasoning process. This observation leads to interesting discussions: while we defined semantics for h-entailment, we did not discuss how reasoning should work in practice and how and for which use cases it should be optimized. Do we want a logic with a control aspect similar to the idea of the cut operator in Prolog? Do we want to introduce fragments allowing performant reasoning? This discussion should be held in the community, but with our implementation, we provided a tool which will be very helpful in this regard as it can be used to spot shortcomings in implementations which should then be carefully inspected.

7 Related Work

Before concluding our paper, we would like to place our contribution into context. As mentioned in the beginning of this paper, the initial idea leading to the development of RDF Surfaces was given by Pat Hayes in a keynote talk at ISWC 2009 [12]. In this talk he discussed RDF in the context of the Semantic Web and the shortcomings he encounters. He collected his requirements on a WeB LOGIC (BLOGIC) and made a suggestion, RDF Redux. This logic supports existential quantification, conjunction and negation just as RDF Surfaces. The suggestion of Pat Hayes was inspired by Existential graphs, in particular Beta graphs, which have been invented by Charles Sanders Peirce (1839–1914) [23] and further developed by John Sowa [24]. The idea behind this logical framework is to provide reasoning with a graphical calculus. An interesting aspect here is that graphs are put into contexts which, according to Hayes, also happens with data in the Web. And there, we can still see a connection to RDF Surfaces which otherwise neglects the visual aspect. The mapping in this paper was inspired by the work of De Bruijn and Heymans who mapped plain RDF to F-logic [4] – an FOL based framework for knowledge representation with the goal to better understand its semantics. Similarly, Michael Schneider who is the editor of OWL's RDF-based semantics [21] provided in collaboration with Geoff Sutcliffe a mapping from that semantics (back then OWL-full) to TPTP [22], in order to perform reasoning. The definition of the full-profile as well as the mapping can be seen as an attempt to combine RDFS with DL. In that sense, RDF Surfaces provides an alternative approach which extends RDF simple entailment to FOL in order to get compatibility with description logic.

8 Conclusion

In this paper we mapped RDF Surfaces to first-order logic and thereby provided a definition of its formal semantics. We evaluated this semantics in two ways: (1) we proved that it supports RDF simple entailment, that is, if two RDF graphs entail each other under simple entailment, they also h-entail each other and that if they h-entail each other they also simply entail each other. (2) We tested whether our definition is in-line with the informal semantics. To perform this test, we developed `rs2fol`, a tool which executes our mapping and then uses the theorem prover Vampire to perform entailment checking. Here, we used `rs2fol` to verify the reasoning results of the reasoner EYE on different examples. Our tests showed that `rs2fol` and EYE agree in most cases, but we could also spot differences. One important point was that neither our definitions nor previous work [15–17] define how concepts which introduce blank nodes through syntactic sugar should handle these. EYE treats lists as first-class citizens. This makes them easier to process and that could also be an option for RDF Surfaces, it would, however, means that RDF Surfaces would deviate from the original RDF. In this context, it will also be challenging to integrate RDF-star, once RDF 1.2. is released. Another point we observed was that the results of EYE differ from those of `rs2fol` in cases where unrestricted universally quantified facts are derived which need to be applied to data. The reason for this finding was most likely that EYE is currently under development and does not yet fully support RDF Surfaces. It is, however, an open question whether it is really useful to fully support the whole logic with a reasoner as this comes with a price: first-order reasoning is not decidable and even for decidable cases often very slow. Given its expressivity, RDF Surfaces will have the same problem, so it makes sense to optimize for the most common use cases or to provide other measures to guide the reasoning. EYE does this by having extra surface types. Such things as well as possible profiles imposing restrictions need to be discussed in the community.

Apart from the obvious, testing the accuracy of our semantics, our experiments also showed the potential of our tool `rs2fol`. With `rs2fol`, we were able to spot cases of incompleteness in EYE's reasoning. `rs2fol` can furthermore be used to detect incorrect derivations which are far more problematic in the context of the Web where reasoning results are normally exchanged and used for applications. An entailment checker which relies on a well-established theorem prover like `rs2fol` with its underlying tool Vampire can help to prevent this problem from happening. Reasoning results can be checked independently. Developers can use `rs2fol` to evaluate their reasoning engines. `rs2fol` will furthermore help to refine the theory of RDF Surfaces. As changes to the semantics can easily be implemented in our mapping, their impact to existing use cases can be checked and the members of the community can better understand the compromises they make in terms of the semantics.

We are convinced that both of our contributions, the definition of the semantics of RDF Surfaces as well as the development of a tool for practical entailment checking will help the community bring RDF Surfaces further and to tackle the open challenges ahead of us.

References

1. Baader, F.: The Description Logic Handbook: Theory, Implementation and Applications. Cambridge University Press, Cambridge (2007)
2. Berners-lee, T., Connolly, D., Kagal, L., Scharf, Y., Hendler, J.: N3Logic: a logical framework for the world wide web. Theory Pract. Log. Program. 8(3), 249–269 (2008). https://doi.org/10.1017/S1471068407003213
3. Bock, C., et al.: OWL 2 web ontology language. W3C Recommendation (2012). http://www.w3.org/TR/owl2-syntax/
4. de Bruijn, J., Heymans, S.: Logical foundations of (e)RDF(S): complexity and reasoning. In: Aberer, K., et al. (eds.) ASWC/ISWC -2007. LNCS, vol. 4825, pp. 86–99. Springer, Heidelberg (2007). https://doi.org/10.1007/978-3-540-76298-0_7
5. Cyganiak, R., Wood, D., Lanthaler, M.: RDF 1.1 concepts and abstract syntax. http://www.w3.org/TR/2014/REC-rdf11-concepts-20140225/
6. Cyganiak, R., Wood, D., Lanthaler, M.: RDF 1.1: concepts and abstract syntax (2014). http://www.w3.org/TR/2014/REC-rdf11-concepts-20140225/
7. De Roo, J.: Euler yet another proof Engine - EYE. https://josd.github.io/eye/
8. De Roo, J., Hochstenbach, P., Arndt, D.: RDF surfaces tests (2024). https://github.com/eyereasoner/rdfsurfaces-tests
9. Ebbinghaus, H., Flum, J., Thomas, W.: Mathematical Logic. Undergraduate Texts in Mathematics. Springer, New York (1996). https://books.google.de/books?id=VYLA8m7cqYcC
10. Enderton, H.B.: A Mathematical Introduction to Logic. Elsevier, Amsterdam (2001)
11. Harris, S., Seaborne, A.: SPARQL 1.1 query language. W3C recommendation, W3C (2013). https://www.w3.org/TR/2013/REC-sparql11-query-20130321/
12. Hayes, P.: BLOGIC (2009). https://de.slideshare.net/PatHayes/blogic-iswc-2009-invited-talk. ISWC 2009 invited talk
13. Hayes, P., Patel-Schneider, P.F.: RDF 1.1 semantics. W3C Recommendation (2014). https://www.w3.org/TR/rdf11-mt/
14. Hochstenbach, P.: Latar. https://github.com/phochste/Latar, https://github.com/phochste/Latar
15. Hochstenbach, P., De Roo, J.: RDF surfaces primer (2023). https://w3c-cg.github.io/rdfsurfaces/
16. Hochstenbach, P., De Roo, J., Verborgh, R.: RDF surfaces: computer says no. In: Proceedings of the 1st Workshop on Trusting Decentralised Knowledge Graphs and Web Data (2023). https://arxiv.org/pdf/2305.08476.pdf
17. Hochstenbach, P., et al.: RDF surfaces: enabling classic negation on the semantic web (2024), https://arxiv.org/pdf/2406.10659. Submitted to Semantic Web Journal

18. Horrocks, I., et al.: SWRL: a semantic web rule language combining OWL and RuleML. W3C Mem. Submission **21**(79), 1–31 (2004)
19. Kovács, L., Voronkov, A.: First-order theorem proving and VAMPIRE. In: Sharygina, N., Veith, H. (eds.) CAV 2013. LNCS, vol. 8044, pp. 1–35. Springer, Heidelberg (2013). https://doi.org/10.1007/978-3-642-39799-8_1
20. Motik, B., Patel-Schneider, P.F., Cuence Grau, B.: OWL 2 web ontology language direct semantics. W3C Recommendation (2012). https://www.w3.org/TR/owl2-direct-semantics/
21. Schneider, M.: OWL 2 web ontology language RDF-based semantics. W3C Recommendation (2012). https://www.w3.org/TR/owl2-rdf-based-semantics/
22. Schneider, M., Sutcliffe, G.: Reasoning in the OWL 2 full ontology language using first-order automated theorem proving. In: Bjørner, N., Sofronie-Stokkermans, V. (eds.) CADE 2011. LNCS (LNAI), vol. 6803, pp. 461–475. Springer, Heidelberg (2011). https://doi.org/10.1007/978-3-642-22438-6_35
23. Sowa, J.: Knowledge Representation: Logical, Philosophical and Computational Foundations. Brooks/Cole (2000)
24. Sowa, J.: Reasoning with diagrams and images: observation and imagination as rules of inference. J. Appl. Log. **5**(5), 987 (2018)
25. Sutcliffe, G.: The TPTP problem library and associated infrastructure. From CNF to TH0, TPTP v6.4.0. J. Autom. Reason. **59**(4), 483–502 (2017)
26. Sutcliffe, G.: The CADE ATP system competition. https://tptp.org/CASC/ (2024)
27. Van Herwegen, J.: Tension.js. https://github.com/joachimvh/tension.js,https://github.com/joachimvh/tension.js
28. Verborgh, R., De Roo, J.: Drawing conclusions from linked data on the web: the EYE reasoner. IEEE Softw. **5**, 23–27 (2015). https://doi.org/10.1109/MS.2015.63
29. W3C OWL Working Group: OWL 2 Web Ontology Language. w3c Recommendation (2012). https://www.w3.org/TR/owl2-overview/
30. Woensel, W.V., Arndt, D., Champin, P.A., Tomaszuk, D., Kellogg, G.: Notation3 language (2023). https://w3c.github.io/N3/reports/20230703/

Ambiguities in Defeasible Logic: A Computational Efficient Framework and Algorithm

Guido Governatori[1,2](✉) and Francesco Olivieri[3]

[1] Charles Sturt University, Bathurst, NSW, Australia
ggovernatori@csu.edu.au
[2] Central Queensland University, Rockhampton, QLD, Australia
[3] Brisbane, QLD 4000, Australia

Abstract. We present a Defeasible Logic variant able to incorporate two different and conflicting facets of non-monotonic reasoning: ambiguity blocking and ambiguity propagation. The resulting logic is conservative about the two notions. We investigate the logical properties and we present efficient algorithms for the logic.

1 Introduction

An important feature of non-monotonic logics is their ability to handle conflicts, a situation where contradictory conclusions can be derived. Different strategies and mechanisms have been devised to solve, and to address conflicts and prevent the reasoning from collapsing: in fact meaningful conclusions can be drawn even when we have a conflict. However, in some cases, it is not possible (and sometimes not even advisable) to solve a conflict. In this situation, we can say that we have an ambiguity.

More specifically, a conclusion is ambiguous if there is a chain of reasoning supporting it, there is also a chain of reasoning supporting the opposite, but there is no mechanism to resolve the conflict. Here, we abstain from asserting the conclusion and its opposite. This is a common feature in sceptical non-monotonic formalism, but then, there is a clash of options. What about if the ambiguous conclusions are not the final statements of our arguments and are just some intermediate steps to obtain further conclusions? What should we do with other propositions following/depending on them?

Here, we have two alternatives: (i) we propagate the ambiguity to propositions depending on propositions already deemed as ambiguous; or (ii) we block the ambiguity, and we treat ambiguous conclusions as conclusions that do not hold.

F. Olivieri—Independent Researcher.

Let us consider an example. Suppose we have the following two rules[1]

$$\cdots \Rightarrow a \qquad \cdots \Rightarrow \neg a$$

Here, we have one applicable rule for a and one applicable rule for its opposite $\neg a$. If no mechanism to solve the conflict is available, then, in a sceptical framework, we can assert neither of the two conclusions. Hence, a and $\neg a$ are both ambiguous. Suppose that we have two more rules

$$a \Rightarrow b \qquad \cdots \Rightarrow \neg b$$

where the rule for $\neg b$ is applicable and it does not depend on a or $\neg a$. On the other hand, b depends on a, we need a to hold to be able to make the rule for b applicable.

As we alluded to above, we have two options. Let us examine them in turn.

Ambiguity Propagation. In the ambiguity propagation approach, every proposition depending on an ambiguous proposition is ambiguous as well. Moreover, every proposition opposite of an ambiguous proposition is ambiguous, unless there is a mechanism to solve the ambiguity. An alternative view is to build arguments (just chaining rules), and an argument is ambiguous if it contains an ambiguous proposition. Furthermore, an argument attacked by an ambiguous argument is ambiguous. This is the approach adopted by non-monotonic frameworks characterised by the Grounded semantics [7,11].

Looking at the rules given above, b depends immediately on a (having a as an element of its antecedent) and thus it is ambiguous. Moreover, $\neg b$ is ambiguous as well since it is attacked by b which is ambiguous.

Ambiguity Blocking. In this approach, a proposition is ambiguous if there is an applicable rule for it and there is an applicable rule for the opposite (hence, the notion is symmetric). On the contrary to ambiguity propagation, ambiguous propositions behave as propositions that do not hold. Accordingly, the rule $a \Rightarrow b$ is not applicable. Hence, the applicable rule $\cdots \Rightarrow \neg b$ is not attacked by an applicable rule; thus, $\neg b$ is not ambiguous, and we can conclude it. Ambiguity blocking is supported by frameworks like [1,8,17–19,21,26].

The two options are somehow incompatible but have their own use in real-life applications, for instance in the legal domain. Let us consider the following example.

Suppose you have a legal system adopting the *presumption of innocence* principle. Thus, by default, a defendant is regarded as innocent (or not guilty).

Suppose that a piece of evidence A suggests that the defendant in a legal case is not responsible, while a second piece of evidence B indicates that he/she is responsible; moreover, the sources are equally reliable. According to the

---

[1] We use '$\cdots \Rightarrow c$' to indicate a rule whose antecedent is assumed to hold, when we do not care about the actual content of the antecedent. Also, we say that the rule is applicable, in other terms, provided there are no other rules opposing it, the rule would allow us to asset its conclusion c.

underlying legal system, a defendant is presumed innocent (i.e., not guilty) unless responsibility has been proved (beyond reasonable doubt).

The above scenario is encoded by the following rules:

$r_1 : EvidenceA \Rightarrow \neg Responsible$
$r_2 : EvidenceB \Rightarrow Responsible$ $r_3 : Responsible \Rightarrow Guilty$
$r_4 : \Rightarrow \neg Guilty$

where r_3 is stronger than r_4. Given both *EvidenceA* and *EvidenceB*, the literal *Responsible* is ambiguous. There are applicable rules (r_1 and r_2) for and against the literal, with no way to adjudicate between them. As a consequence, r_3 is not applicable, and so there is no applicable rule arguing against the presumption of innocence (rule r_4). In an ambiguity blocking setting, we obtain a $\neg Guilty$ verdict; the ambiguity about responsibility is blocked from applying to *Guilty*. In contrast, in an ambiguity propagating setting, the ambiguity of *Responsible* propagates to *Guilty*, and thus the literals *Guilty* and $\neg Guilty$ are ambiguous too; hence an undisputed conclusion cannot be drawn. When we look at the example above, is it appropriate to say that we have reached a not guilty verdict without any reasonable doubt? The evidence supporting that the defendant was responsible has not been refuted. This example supports the contention of Governatori [9] that ambiguity propagating inference is a more appropriate representation of proof beyond a reasonable doubt.

Let us extend the scenario. Suppose that the legal system allows for compensation for wrongly accused people. A person (defendant) has been wrongly accused if the defendant is found innocent, where innocent is defined as $\neg Guilty$. In addition, by default, people are not entitled to compensation. The additional elements of this scenario are modelled by the rules:

$r_5 : \neg Guilty \Rightarrow Compensation$
$r_6 : \Rightarrow \neg Compensation$

where r_5 is stronger than r_6.

In the full scenario, the defendant is not found innocent, and so is not entitled to compensation.

If we take a purely ambiguity blocking stance then, since we are not able to determine whether there was responsibility, the defendant is not guilty, and then the defendant is entitled to compensation. On the other hand, in a purely ambiguity propagating setting, *Guilty* and $\neg Guilty$ are ambiguous, and this makes *Compensation* and $\neg Compensation$ ambiguous; we are in a position where we cannot decide whether the defendant is entitled or not to compensation. Accordingly, both choices are unsatisfactory: either the defendant receives compensation despite not being found innocent or no decision is made about compensation.

What we want is a regime where we can reason about guilt in an ambiguity propagating way, but then reason about compensation in an ambiguity blocking way. This can be achieved by replacing rule r_5 with

$r'_5 : BeyondReasonableDoubt(\neg Guitly) \Rightarrow Compensation$

where *BeyondReaonableDoubt* is a label indicating the proof standard used to conclude *Guilty*.

The logic we present in this paper is based on the approach proposed in [10] but with a proof-theoretic formulation instead of a meta-program description of the logic. In addition, we provide an efficient algorithm, and we investigate the computational complexity of the resulting logic.

Our agenda is: Sect. 2 presents the logical apparatus and discusses its properties. Section 3 advances the algorithms for the computation of the theory extension and proves their computational properties. Section 4 discusses related works and future lines of research.

2 Logic

Defeasible Logic [1,21] (DL) is a constructive non-monotonic formalism. In non-monotonic systems, more accurate conclusions can be obtained when more pieces of information become available. Throughout the years, many variants of DL have been proposed for the modelling of different application areas: agents [6,13], legal reasoning [2,12,16] and business processes [5,22,23].

The logic has at its heart a constructive proof theory. The key notion is the notion of derivation. As usual, a derivation is a sequence of expressions either given or derived from previous steps according to the appropriate inference rules (or proof conditions in Defeasible Logic parlance). A characteristic of Defeasible Logic is that the elements of a derivation carry more information; more specifically, each step of a derivation consists of three elements: a logical formula, the indication of how the formula has been derived (either as a positive proof or as a refutation), and the strength of its derivation.

The strength and derivation type are encoded in so-called proof tag. Notice that the constructive proof theory of the logic allows us to justify and explain every step of a derivation by indicating what rules (corresponding to norms) or facts are required/responsible for the step.

In this paper, we extend the language of Defeasible Logic by allowing in the language components of the proof theory. Thus formulas can be annotated with what we call proof labels. The idea is that when we have an annotated formula in the antecedent of a rule, the label specifies the standard according to which the formula has to be proved for the rule to be applicable.

We start by defining the language of a defeasible theory.

Definition 1. *Let* PROP *be a set of propositional atoms, and* Lab *be a set of arbitrary labels (the names of the rules). Accordingly,* Lit = PROP $\cup \{\neg l \mid l \in$ PROP$\}$ *is the set of* literals. *The* complement *of a literal l is denoted by $\sim l$: if l is a positive literal p then $\sim l$ is $\neg p$, and if l is a negative literal $\neg p$ then $\sim l$ is p.*

Definition 2 (Defeasible Theory). *A defeasible theory D is a tuple $(F, R, \succ)$, where F is the set of* facts, *R is the set of* rules, *and $\succ$ is a binary relation over R, called* superiority relation.

Specifically, the set of facts $F \subseteq$ Lit denotes simple pieces of information that are always considered true, like "Sylvester is a cat", formally $cat(Sylvester)$. The set of rules R contains three *types* of rules: *strict rules*, *defeasible rules*, and *defeaters*. The *superiority relation* $\succ \, \subseteq R \times R$ is a relation to solving conflicts in case of potentially contradicting information, that is when we have applicable rules for a conclusion and its complement. The superiority relation gives the relative strength of conflicting rules. Accordingly, in general, it is not an order, and it is not transitive.

We shall refer to a defeasible theory as simply a theory. A theory is *finite* if the set of facts and rules are finite.

Definition 3 (Rule). *A rule $r \in R$ is an expression $r \colon A(r) \hookrightarrow C(r)$, such that:*

1. *$r \in$ Lab is the unique name of the rule;*
2. *$A(r) \subseteq$ Lit is a (possibly empty) set of the* antecedents[2];
3. *$\hookrightarrow \, \in \{\rightarrow, \Rightarrow, \rightsquigarrow\}$ denotes, resp., strict rules, defeasible rules, and defeaters;*
4. *$C(r) \in$ Lit is the consequent, a literal.*

We use some abbreviations on rule sets. The set of strict rules in R is R_s, the set of defeasible rules is R_d, and the set of strict and defeasible rules is R_{sd}; $r \in R[p]$ if $C(r) = p$.

A strict rule is a rule in the classical sense: whenever the premises are indisputable, so is the conclusion. The statement "All Computing Scientists are humans" is formulated through the strict rule

$$CScientist(X) \rightarrow human(X)$$

as there is no exception to it. As in [1], we consider only a propositional version of this logic, and we do not take into account function symbols.

Defeasible rules represent statements that can be defeated by contrary evidence: the defeasible rule

$$CScientist, PaperAccepted \Rightarrow TravelConference$$

thus represents the statement "Computing scientists travel to the city of the conference". Defeaters are special rules whose only purpose is to prevent the derivation of the opposite conclusion: the statement "During pandemic travels might be prohibited" is better represented by the defeater

$$Pandemic \rightsquigarrow \neg TravelConference$$

as we simply want to "block" the derivation of travelling.

Finally, we introduce the notion of annotated literal [10].

---

[2] We shall interchangeably use *antecedent* to refer to the whole set of literals $A(r)$, or *antecedents* for the elements in it.

Definition 4 (Annotated Literal). *Let Π be a set of proof labels and $l \in$ Lit a literal. An* annotated literal *is an expression*

$$\lambda l,$$

where the annotation $\lambda = \pm\mu$ is such that the sign $\pm \in \{+,-\}$ and the proof label $\mu \in \Pi$.

The meaning of an annotated literal is that the literal is provable, or refuted, with the "strength" indicated by the proof tag. If the sign is $+$ the literal is provable with strength μ, and if it is $-$ the literal is refuted with strength μ. Defeasible Logic is a constructive logic, thus $-\mu l$ means that 'It is provable that it is not possible to prove l with strength μ'.

In this paper, we deal with the following set of proof labels:

$$\Pi = \{\Delta, \partial, \delta, \sigma\}.$$

The precise meaning of these proof labels will be provided by the formal definitions of derivations in this section. They have the following intuitive meanings:

- Δ: there is a monotonic proof (a proof that uses facts and strict rules only);
- ∂: there is a defeasible derivation that blocks ambiguities;
- δ: there is a defeasible derivation that propagates ambiguities;
- σ: there is a defeasible "credulous" derivation (essentially, ignoring unresolved conflicts).

In the body of a rule, we have two types of literals: *normal* literals and *annotated* literals. For a rule to be applicable, the normal literals must be provable with whatever conditions are required to prove the conclusion with a given strength. On the contrary, annotated literals specify their required strength independently of what type of conclusion we want to achieve.

Example 1. Consider the following rule

$$r: a, +\partial b, -\delta\neg c \Rightarrow d$$

The rule is a defeasible rule for d; moreover, $A(r) = \{a, +\partial b, -\delta\neg c\}$. The intuitive meaning of rule r is that:

If – literal a holds (according to the normal conditions to infer the conclusion of the rule), and
  – b is positively proved using the ambiguity blocking standard, and
  – $\neg c$ is refuted with the ambiguity propagation standard;
Then We are able to defeasibly infer d.

We will use the term *conclusions* and tagged formulas interchangeably.
The definition of proof is also the standard in DL.

Definition 5 (Proof). *Given a defeasible deontic theory D, a proof P of length m in D is a finite sequence $P(1), P(2), \ldots, P(m)$ of tagged modal formulas, where the proof conditions given in the rest of the paper hold.*

Given a proof P, $P(1..n)$ denotes the first n steps of P; we also use the notational convention $D \vdash \pm \mu l$, meaning that there is a proof P for $\pm \mu l$ in D.

Provability and refutability of a literal are based on the notions of rules being *applicable* or *discarded*. Informally, a rule is applicable when all normal elements in the rule's antecedent are provable and all annotated literals in the body are provable according to the specification of their annotations; a rule is discarded if one of the normal elements of the body is not provable, or at least one of the annotated literals in the body is not provable according to the specification of its annotation.

The intuitions above are formalised by the following definitions.

Definition 6 (Applicable). *A rule r for p is #-applicable at step $n+1$ of a derivation P, with $\# \in \{\Delta, \partial, \delta, \sigma\}$, iff $\forall a \in A(r)$:*

1. *if $a \in \mathrm{Lit}$, then $+\#a \in P(1..n)$;*
2. *if $a = \lambda b$ with $\lambda = +\mu$, then $+\mu a \in P(1..n)$;*
3. *if $a = \lambda b$ with $\lambda = -\mu$, then $-\mu a \in P(1..n)$.*

Accordingly, for the rule in Example 1 to be Δ-applicable we need to have a proof where we have $+\Delta a$, $+\partial b$ and $-\delta \neg c$.

Definition 7 (Discarded). *A rule r for p is #-discarded at step $n+1$ of a derivation P, with $\# \in \{\Delta, \partial, \delta, \sigma\}$, iff $\exists a \in A(r)$:*

1. *if $a \in \mathrm{Lit}$, then $-\#a \in P(1..n)$;*
2. *if $a = \lambda b$ with $\lambda = +\mu$, then $-\mu a \in P(1..n)$;*
3. *if $a = \lambda b$ with $\lambda = -\mu$, then $+\mu a \in P(1..n)$.*

Whenever clear from the context, we shall simply say that a rule is applicable/discarded and omit the 'for (literal) p'.

Note that the positive and negative proof conditions (and the notions used inside them) can be obtained from each other by applying the *strong negation principle* to the definition of applicability. The strong negation principle applies the function that simplifies a formula by moving all negations to an innermost position in the resulting formula, replacing the positive tags with the respective negative tags, and the other way around, see [14]. Positive proof tags ensure effective decidable procedures to build proofs; the strong negation principle guarantees that the negative conditions provide a constructive and exhaustive method to verify that deriving the given conclusion is impossible.

We now introduce the proof conditions for definite derivations and refutations (corresponding to monotonic forward-looking chaining of rules), sceptical defeasible derivations and refutations, and supported and unsupported (corresponding to credulous derivations and refutations ignoring unresolved conflicts). The proof conditions correspond to inference rules and establish conditions under which we can append an element at the end of a proof based on what has been previously proved. While the logic is constructive, proofs are not deterministic. Given a sequence of proved elements, it is possible to extend it in multiple ways, provided that the conditions of the proof conditions are satisfied.

Definition 8 (Definite derivation).

If $P(n+1) = +\Delta p$ then either
(1) $p \in F$, or
(2) $\exists r \in R_s[p]$ such that r is Δ-applicable.

Definition 9 (Definite refutation).

If $P(n+1) = -\Delta p$ then
(1) $p \notin F$ and
(2) $\forall r \in R_s[p]$ then r is Δ-discarded.

Intuitively, the idea behind definite derivations is that there is a chain of (definitely) applicable strict rules, where a rule is definitely applicable where all the literals in its body are definitely provable and the annotated literals are provable with the required strengths and modes. Conversely, to refute a literal in the definite sense, we have to show that it is impossible to prove it using only facts and strict rules; we must hence have that all rules for that conclusion are definitely discarded.

Defeasible derivations in Defeasible Logic have an argumentation-like structure, where the first step is to provide an argument (i.e., an applicable rule) for the conclusion we want to prove; then we have to look at all possible attacks to it (i.e., rules for the opposite conclusion); finally, we have to rebut the attacks, either to undercut them, or to counterattack with a stronger argument. Therefore, before advancing the definitions for defeasible provability/refutability, we have to first define what is a rule being defeated and undefeated.

Definition 10 (Defeated). *A rule r is* defeated *at step $n+1$ of a derivation P for p iff $\exists s \in R[\sim p]$ such that s is applicable and $s \succ r$.*

The notion of defeated consists of identifying rules stronger than rules for the opposing conclusion.

Definition 11 (Undefeated). *A rule r is* defeated *at step $n+1$ of a derivation P for p iff $\forall s \in R[\sim p]$ then s is discarded or $s \not\succ r$.*

The schemas for ambiguity blocking and ambiguity propagation have the same structure, but for ambiguity propagating, we make it easier to attack an argument and harder to rebut.

We start with defeasible provability and refutability for ambiguity blocking.

Definition 12 ($+\partial$).

If $P(n+1) = +\partial p$ then either
(1) $+\Delta p \in P(1..n)$, or
(2) the following conditions hold
    (.1) $-\Delta \sim p \in P(1..b)$, and
    (.2) $\exists r \in R_{sd}[p]$ such that
        (.1) r is ∂-applicable, and
        (.2) $\forall s \in R[\sim p]$ either
            (.1) s is ∂-discarded, or (.2) s is defeated.

The notion is standard in DL: we prove a literal if all rules supporting the opposite are either discarded or defeated. We note that ambiguity blocking equates unsupported with discarded (where, in general, discarded is a stronger notion since it accounts for unresolved conflicts, while unsupported does not).

Definition 13 ($-\partial$).

If $P(n+1) = -\partial p$ then
(1) $-\Delta p \in P(1..n)$ and
(2) one of the following conditions holds
    (.1) $+\Delta \sim p \in P(1..b)$, or
    (.2) $\forall r \in R_{sd}[p]$,
        (.1) r is ∂-discarded, or
        (.2) $\exists s \in R[\sim p]$ such that
            (.1) s is ∂-applicable and (.2) s is undefeated.

Before moving on the case of ambiguity propagation, we have to introduce some auxiliary proof conditions: the proof conditions for the notion of support.

Definition 14 ($+\sigma$).

If $P(n+1) = +\sigma p$ then either
(1) $+\Delta p \in P(1..n)$ or
(2) $\exists r \in R[p]$ such that
    (.1) r is σ-applicable and
    (.2) $\forall s \in R[\sim p]$ then either
        (.1) s is δ-discarded or (.2) $s \not\succ r$.

A literal is supported if all its attacks are either discarded or not stronger.

Definition 15 ($-\sigma$).

If $P(n+1) = -\sigma p$ then
(1) $-\Delta p \in P(1..n)$ and
(2) $\forall r \in R[p]$ then either
    (.1) r is σ-discarded or
    (.2) $\exists s \in R[\sim p]$ such that
        (.1) s is δ-applicable and (.2) $s \succ r$.

Definition 16 ($+\delta$).

If $P(n+1) = +\delta p$ then either
(1) $+\Delta p \in P(1..n)$, or
(2) the following conditions hold
    (.1) $-\Delta \sim p \in P(1..b)$ and
    (.2) $\exists r \in R_{sd}[p]$ such that
        (.1) r is δ-applicable, and
        (.2) $\forall s \in R[\sim p]$ then either
            (.1) s is σ-discarded, or (.2) s is defeated.

For ambiguity propagation, the first main difference is Condition (2.2.2.1), where the attacking rules are rebutted if unsupported (σ-discarded). While support is a weaker notion than applicable, unsupported is stronger than discarded. Accordingly, the proof condition makes it easier to attack an argument and harder to rebut it.

Definition 17 ($-\delta$).

If $P(n+1) = -\delta p$ then
(1) $-\Delta p \in P(1..n)$, and
(2) one of the following conditions holds
    (.1) $+\Delta \sim p \in P(1..b)$, or
    (.2) $\forall r \in R_{sd}[p]$ either
        (.1) r is δ-discarded, or
        (.2) $\exists s \in R[\sim p]$ such that
            (.1) s is σ-applicable and (.2) s is undefeated.

Definition 18. *Assume two theories D and D'. The set of positive and negative conclusions of D is the extension $E(D) = (+\Delta, -\Delta, +\partial, -\partial, +\delta, -\delta, +\sigma, -\sigma)$, where $\pm\# = \{p \mid p \text{ appears in } D \text{ and } D \vdash \pm\#p\}$, $\# \in \{\Delta, \partial, \delta, \sigma\}$ and we use symbol $\vdash$ to indicate that there is a derivation of p from D.*

D and D' are equivalent iff $E(D) \equiv E(D')$, they have the same extension.

Example 2. Let us see how to recast the scenario we discussed in Sect. 1. It has been argued that the legal proof standards correspond to various ways in which a conclusion can be proved in Defeasible Logic [9], where ambiguity propagating corresponds to the *beyond reasonable doubt* proof standard, ambiguity blocking to the *preponderance of evidence* or *clear and convincing case* standard, and positive support to the *scintilla of evidence* standard. Accordingly, we can use the following formalisation

$$r_1: EvidenceA \Rightarrow Responsible$$
$$r_2: EvidenceB \Rightarrow \neg Responsible$$
$$r_3: Responsible \Rightarrow Guilty$$
$$r_4: \Rightarrow \neg Guilty$$
$$r_5: +\delta \neg Guilty \Rightarrow Compensation$$
$$r_6: \Rightarrow \neg Compensation$$

with $r_4 \succ r_3$ and $r_5 \succ r_6$.

In the case where we have $EvidenceA$ and $EvidenceB$, we have $-\partial Responsible$, $-\partial \neg Responsible$, $-\delta Responsible$, $-\delta \neg Responsible$, from which we then obtain $-\partial Guilty$, $-\delta Guilty$, $-\delta \neg Guilty$ and $+\partial \neg Guilty$. Hence, rule r_5 is not applicable, and we conclude $+\partial \neg Compensation$ and $+\delta \neg Compensation$.

Furthermore, assume that the legal system contains the additional provision that if the case has some merits (there are some doubts whether he/she was responsible, so there is some scintilla of evidence) then the defendant has to pay for their own legal proceeding fees. The rule corresponding to the provision is:

$$r_7: +\sigma Guilty \Rightarrow PayOwnLegalProceedingsFees$$

Here, in the first instance, we derive $+\sigma Responsible$, and then we conclude $+\sigma Guilty$. Thus, r_7 is δ- and ∂-applicable.

Another interesting application of the logic is provided by the following scenario.

Example 3. Suppose you have a set of sensors deployed in a working environment. The sensors send a signal when there are some abnormal readings indicating some possible faults with the sensor (or a critical situation). Simultaneously, it is possible to run some diagnostics to check if the system works correctly (no faulty signals). Suppose now that you have some abnormal readings indicating a fault, but the diagnostic reports no problems (so no fault). Given the conflict between the two sources of information, the procedure is to send an inspection to the site to check if there are problems.

$$r_1: abnormalReading \Rightarrow fault$$
$$r_2: negativeDiagnostic \Rightarrow \neg fault$$

The two rules above alone are not able to determine when both are applicable whether to perform an on-site inspection, and we are left when an ambiguity that we cannot solve. However, if we add the rule

$$-\delta fault, -\delta \neg fault, +\sigma fault \Rightarrow inspection$$

the ambiguity is detected, $+\sigma fault$ indicates that the failure is not vacuous, and then it triggers the derivation of *inspection*.

2.1 Formal Properties

A theory is *coherent* if it is not possible to derive and refute the same conclusion; a theory is *consistent* if it is not possible to derive a conclusion and its opposite.

Theorem 1 (Coherence). *Assume a theory D and a literal $p \in$ Lit. It is impossible that $D \vdash +\#p$ and $D \vdash -\#p$, with $\# \in \{\Delta, \partial, \delta, \sigma\}$.*

Proof. The result follows from Theorem 1 of [14] by proving that *if* the proof conditions for a positive proof tag, and the corresponding negative ones, are the strong negation of each other, *then* no theory can prove both $+\#x$ and $-\#x$ for any conclusion x. It is immediate to verify that all pairs of proof conditions defined in this paper obey the principle of strong negation.

Theorem 2 (Consistence). *Assume a theory D and a literal $p \in$ Lit. If there are no cycles in the transitive closure of the superiority relation, then $D \vdash +\#p$ and $D \vdash +\#\neg p$, $\# \in \{\partial, \delta, \sigma\}$, only if $D \vdash +\Delta p$ and $D \vdash +\Delta \neg p$.*

Proof. The proof follows the schema of [3].

Theorem 3 (Inclusion). *For any theory D,*

$$+\Delta \subseteq +\delta \subseteq +\partial \subseteq +\sigma \text{ and } -\sigma \subseteq -\partial \subseteq -\delta \subseteq -\Delta.$$

Proof. We can easily replicate the proof in [4,10].

3 Algorithms

Our algorithms compute the extension of a defeasible theory fetched as input. The idea behind them is to compute, at each iteration step, a *simpler yet equivalent* theory than the one we had at the previous step. By "simpler theory", we mean that, by proving and refuting literals, we can progressively perform two actions that preserve the theory extension:

1. **Simplify the antecedents** of the rules by removing proved elements. Assume rule '$r: a, +\delta b \Rightarrow c$' and we prove $+\partial a$: then ∂-applicability of r does not depend any longer on a, and we can "rewrite it" as '$r: +\delta b \Rightarrow c$'.
2. **Eliminate (discarded) rules** from the theory itself. Assume again rule '$r: a, +\delta b \Rightarrow c$', but now we refute b, i.e., $-\delta b$; r is δ-discarded and can neither support c, nor attack $\neg c$; we can hence remove r from the rule set '$R \setminus \{r\}$'.

We describe first Procedures PROVE and REFUTE as their inside operations will help understanding the main algorithm.

Procedure Prove

Input: Literal l, proof tag #

1. $\#^+ \leftarrow \#^+ \cup \{l\}$;
2. if $\# = \Delta$ then PROVE($l, \square$), with $\square \in \{\partial, \delta, \sigma\}$
3. $HB \leftarrow HB \setminus \{l\}$;
4. $R^\square \leftarrow \{A(r) \setminus \{+\#l\} \hookrightarrow C(r) \,|\, r \in R^\square\}$;
5. $R^\square \leftarrow R^\square \setminus \{r \in R^\square | -\#l \in A(r)\}$;
6. $\succ^\delta \leftarrow \succ^\delta \setminus \{(r,s), (s,r) \in \succ^\delta | -\#l \in A(r)\}$ with $\square \in \{\delta, \sigma\}$;
7. $\succ^\partial \leftarrow \succ^\partial \setminus \{(r,s), (s,r) \in \succ^\delta | -\#l \in A(r)\}$ with $\square \in \{\partial\}$;

Procedure PROVE is invoked when a literal l is proved with strength #. If the literal was strictly proved, it is also defeasibly proved and supported (Line 2). We simplify the rules of the theory by removing $+\#l$ from rules' antecedent (Line 4), remove those rules with $-\#l$ in their antecedent (Line 5), and finally update the superiority relation (Lines 6, 7).

Procedure Refute

Input: Literal l, proof tag #

1. $\#^- \leftarrow \#^- \cup \{l\}$;
2. $HB \leftarrow HB \setminus \{l\}$;
3. if $\# \in \{\partial, \delta, \sigma\}$ then $-\Delta \leftarrow -\Delta \cup \{l\}$
4. $R^\square \leftarrow \{A(r) \setminus \{-\#l\} \hookrightarrow C(r) |\, r \in R^\square\}$, with $\square \in \{\partial, \delta, \sigma\}$;

Procedure REFUTE is invoked when a literal l is disproved with strength $\#$. If l was $\#$-refuted, $\# \in \{\partial, \delta, \sigma\}$, then it is also strictly refuted (Line 3). We update the rules' antecedent (Line 4).

Algorithm 1: COMPUTEEXTENSION

Input: A theory $D = (F, R, \succ)$
Output: The extension $E(D)$ of D

1. $\pm \Delta \leftarrow \emptyset;\ \pm \partial \leftarrow \emptyset;\ \pm \delta \leftarrow \emptyset;\ \pm \sigma \leftarrow \emptyset$;
2. $HB = \{l \in \text{Lit} \mid l \in F \vee l \text{ appears in } D\}$;
3. **for** $l \notin HB$ **do** $-\# \leftarrow -\# \cup \{l\}$, with $\# \in \{\Delta, \partial, \delta, \sigma\}$
4. $R^{\square} \leftarrow \{\{+\square l \mid l \in A(r) \text{ and } l \neq \lambda p\} \cup \{\lambda p \mid l \in A(r) \text{ and } l = \lambda p\} \hookrightarrow C(r) \mid r \in R_{de} \cup R_{dft}\}$, with $\square \in \{\partial, \delta, \sigma\}$;
5. $\succ^{\square} \leftarrow \succ$, with $\square \in \{\delta, \partial\}$
6. **for** $r \in R^{\sigma}$ **do** $r_{sup} \leftarrow \{s \in R^{\sigma} \mid s \succ r\}$
7. **for** $l \in HB$ **do** $R^{\square}[l]_{infd} \leftarrow \emptyset$, with $\square \in \{\partial, \delta\}$
8. **repeat**
9. $\quad \#^{\pm} \leftarrow \emptyset$, with $\# \in \{\Delta, \partial, \delta, \sigma\}$;
10. $\quad$ **for** $l \in HB$ **do**
11. $\quad\quad$ **if** $\exists r \in R_s[l] \mid A(r) = \emptyset$ **then** PROVE(l, Δ)
12. $\quad\quad$ **if** $R^{\sigma}[l] = \emptyset$ **then**
13. $\quad\quad\quad$ REFUTE(l, σ);
14. $\quad\quad\quad$ $r_{sup} \leftarrow r_{sup} \setminus \{s \in R^{\sigma} \mid l \in A(s)\}$;
15. $\quad\quad\quad$ $\succ^{\delta} \leftarrow \succ^{\delta} \setminus \{(r, s), (s, r) \in \succ^{\delta} \mid l \in A(r)\}$
16. $\quad\quad$ **if** $R^{\delta}[l] = \emptyset$ **then**
17. $\quad\quad\quad$ REFUTE(l, δ);
18. $\quad\quad\quad$ $\succ^{\delta} \leftarrow \succ^{\delta} \setminus \{(r, s), (s, r) \in \succ^{\delta} \mid l \in A(r)\}$;
19. $\quad\quad$ **if** $\exists r \in R^{\sigma}[l] \mid A(r) = \emptyset$ and $r_{sup} = \emptyset$ **then**
20. $\quad\quad\quad$ REFUTE$(\sim l, \delta)$ PROVE(l, σ);
21. $\quad\quad$ **if** $\exists r \in R^{\delta}[l] \mid A(r) = \emptyset$ **then**
22. $\quad\quad\quad$ $R^{\delta}[\sim l]_{infd} \leftarrow R^{\delta}[\sim l]_{infd} \cup \{s \in R^{\delta}[\sim l] \mid r \succ s\}$;
23. $\quad\quad\quad$ **if** $r \in R^{\delta}{}_{sd}[l]$, $r_{sup} = \emptyset$ and $R^{\sigma}[\sim l] \setminus R^{\delta}[\sim l]_{infd} = \emptyset$ **then**
24. $\quad\quad\quad\quad$ PROVE(l, δ) REFUTE$(\sim l, \delta)$ PROVE(l, σ) REFUTE$(\sim l, \sigma)$;
25. $\quad\quad$ **if** $R^{\partial}[l] = \emptyset$ **then** REFUTE(l, ∂)
26. $\quad\quad$ **if** $\exists r \in R^{\partial}[l] \mid A(r) = \emptyset$ **then**
27. $\quad\quad\quad$ $R^{\partial}_{infd}[\sim l] \leftarrow R^{\partial}_{infd}[\sim l] \cup \{s \in R^{\partial}[\sim l] \mid (r, s) \in \succ\}$;
28. $\quad\quad\quad$ **if** $\exists r \in R^{\partial}_{sd}[l]$, $A(r) = \emptyset$ and $R^{\partial}[\sim l] \setminus R^{\partial}_{infd}[\sim l] = \emptyset$ **then**
29. $\quad\quad\quad\quad$ PROVE(l, ∂) REFUTE$(\sim l, \partial)$;
30. $\quad$ $+\# \leftarrow \#^{+}$ and $-\# \leftarrow \#^{-}$, with $\# \in \{\Delta, \partial, \delta, \sigma\}$;
31. **until** $(\delta^{+} = \emptyset$ and $\delta^{-} = \emptyset$ and $\sigma^{+} = \emptyset$ and $\sigma^{-} = \emptyset)$ or $(R^{\sigma} = \emptyset$ and $R^{\delta} = \emptyset)$;
32. **return** $E(D) = (+\Delta, -\Delta, +\partial, -\partial, +\delta, -\delta, +\sigma, -\sigma)$

The main Algorithm 1 COMPUTEEXTENSION starts by initialising: the $\#$ sets for the extension (Line 1), and the Herbrand Base HB used to properly cycle over literals (Line 2). If a literal does not appear in HB, then it belongs to the negative theory extension (Line 3).

As they require different level of support to prove the conclusion with their mode (∂ from δ from σ), we create three rule support sets ($R^\square$s at Line 4). To empower the notion of support, we create the r_{sup} sets containing the rules stronger of each rule (**for** cycle at Line 5). Sets $R[]_{infd}$ will store the rules supporting l, that are defeated by an *applicable* rule for $\sim l$ (Line 7).

We now enter the main **repeat-until** cycle on literals on the HB. If there exists a strict rule that is applicable, $A(r) = \emptyset$, then we invoke PROVE with Δ (**if** at Line 10).

if there are no rules σ-supporting l, we invoke REFUTE on σ and update r_{sup} by removing those rules now σ-discarded (Lines 13–15).

if there are no rules δ-supporting l, we invoke REFUTE on δ and update the superiority relation by removing those rules now δ-discarded (Lines 16–18).

if it exists a σ-applicable rule r such that there are no applicable rules for the opposite defeating it ($r_{sup} = \emptyset$), then we invoke REFUTE on $\sim l$ and δ, and PROVE on l and σ (Lines 20).

if it exists a δ-applicable rule r, we update $R^\delta_{infd}[\sim l]$, with all those rules s defeated by r (Line 22). The **if** at Line 23 checks both conditions that no applicable rule for $\sim l$ defeats r (i.e., $r_{sup} = \emptyset$), and that all rules for $\sim l$ are defeated (i.e., $R^\delta[\sim l] \setminus R^\delta_{infd}[\sim l] = \emptyset$); in case, we invoke PROVE on l and δ as well as σ, and, symmetrically, REFUTE on $\sim l$.

if there are no ∂-rules for l, we invoke REFUTE on ∂. **if** there is a ∂-applicable rule, symmetric to the case before we update R^∂_{infd}, and, finally, if all ∂-rules for $\sim l$ are defeated by ∂-applicable rules for l, we invoke PROVE on l and REFUTE on $\sim l$.

3.1 Computational Properties

The *size* of a theory D, $\Sigma(D)$, is the number of occurrences of literals plus the number of occurrences of rules plus 2 for every superiority tuple. Thus, theory $D = (F = \{a,b\}, R = \{r\colon a \Rightarrow c,\ s\colon +\delta b \rightsquigarrow \neg c\}, \succ = \{(r,s)\})$ has size $2 + 6 + 2 = 10$.

For space reasons, some parts of the proofs are only sketched.

Theorem 4. *Algorithm 1* COMPUTEEXTENSION *terminates in* $O(\Sigma^2)$.

Proof. Procedures PROVE and REFUTE terminate, with complexity $O(\Sigma)$, as the size of the input theory is finite, and they modify finite sets.

Termination of Algorithm 1 COMPUTEEXTENSION is thus bound to termination of the **repeat-until** cycle at Lines 8–31, as all other cycles loop over finite sets of elements of the order of $O(\Sigma)$. Given that both HB and R are finite sets, and given that, every time a literal is proved/refuted, it is removed from the corresponding set, the algorithm eventually empties such sets, and, at the next iteration, no modification to the extension can be made. This proves the termination of Algorithm 1 COMPUTEEXTENSION. Since the operations in the inner **for** cycle directly decrease, iteration after iteration, the number of the remaining repetitions of the out-most **repeat-until**, and vice versa, the **repeat-until** is in $O(\Sigma)$. Therefore, Algorithm 1 COMPUTEEXTENSION is in $O(\Sigma^2)$.

Theorem 5. *Algorithm 1* COMPUTEEXTENSION *is correct and complete, i.e., $D \vdash +\#l$ iff $l \in +\#$ of Algorithm 1, $\# \in \{\Delta, \partial, \delta, \sigma\}$.*

Proof. Removing literals from sets of antecedents respects applicability conditions of Definition 6; removing rules from the rule set is also in accordance with discardability conditions of Definition 7, and definitions of all positive and negative proof tags.

The proof follows the schemata of the ones in [13], and consists in proving that the extensions of: (i) the original theory D, and (ii) of the simpler theory D' are the same. Suppose that $D \vdash +\partial l$ at $P(n)$. Thus, if R' of D' is obtained from R of D as '$R' = \{A(r) \setminus \{+\partial l\} \hookrightarrow C(r) \,|\, r \in R\} \setminus \{s \in R \,|\, -\partial {\sim} l \in A(s)\}$', then for every $l \in \text{Lit}$, $D \vdash \pm \partial l$ iff $D' \vdash \pm \partial l$. The proof that the transformation above produces theories equivalent to the original one is by induction on the length of derivations and contrapositive.

4 Conclusions and Related Work

The debate between ambiguity propagation and ambiguity blocking was a prominent topic at the dawn of research in non-monotonic reasoning (see [20]), where the two approaches conflict [25]. Accordingly, most (sceptic) non-monotonic frameworks opt for one of the two options (see the references we provided in Sect. 1 for some of the approaches adopting ambiguity blocking and systems characterised by the grounded semantics for ambiguity propagation). It has been argued [9] that there are practical applications where the integration of both approaches is need (see the motivating example in Sect. 1 and its formalisation in Example 2). Though, the issues of combining them in a conservative way has been by far neglected with the exception of [10,15]. [10] presents a meta-program description of the logic and does not provide an (efficient) algorithm and does not discuss the computational complexity, while [15] addresses the issue of deontic ambiguities depending on ambiguity blocking and ambiguity propagation. Similarly, no algorithms or complexity analysis are discussed. We plan to fill the gap and to extend the algorithm to the defeasible deontic logics of [15,24] to fully understand the effects of the combination of the two ways to address ambiguity in deontic/normative settings.

References

1. Antoniou, G., Billington, D., Governatori, G., Maher, M.: Representation results for defeasible logic. ACM Trans. Comput. Log. **2**(2), 255–287 (2001)
2. Bhuiyan, H., Olivieri, F., Governatori, G., Islam, M.B., Bond, A., Rakotonirainy, A.: A methodology for encoding regulatory rules. In: Workshop on MIning and REasoning with Legal texts. CEUR Workshop Proceedings, vol. 2632. CEUR-WS.org (2019)
3. Billington, D.: Defeasible logic is stable. J. Log. Comput. **3**(4), 379–400 (1993)
4. Billington, D., Antoniou, G., Governatori, G., Maher, M.J.: An inclusion theorem for defeasible logics. ACM Trans. Comput. Log. **12**(1), 6 (2010)

5. Cristani, M., Olivieri, F., Tomazzoli, C.: Automatic synthesis of best practices for energy consumptions. In: IMIS, pp. 154–161. IEEE Computer Society (2016)
6. Dastani, M., Governatori, G., Rotolo, A., van der Torre, L.: Programming cognitive agents in defeasible logic. In: Sutcliffe, G., Voronkov, A. (eds.) LPAR 2005. LNCS (LNAI), vol. 3835, pp. 621–636. Springer, Heidelberg (2005). https://doi.org/10.1007/11591191_43
7. Dung, P.M.: On the acceptability of arguments and its fundamental role in nonmonotonic reasoning, logic programming and n-person games. Artif. Intell. **77**(2), 321–358 (1995)
8. Gordon, T.F., Prakken, H., Walton, D.: The Carneades model of argument and burden of proof. Artif. Intell. **171**(10–11), 875–896 (2007)
9. Governatori, G.: On the relationship between Carneades and defeasible logic. In: ICAIL 2011, pp. 31–40. ACM (2011)
10. Governatori, G., Maher, M.J.: Annotated defeasible logic. Theory Pract. Log. Program. **17**(5–6), 819–836 (2017)
11. Governatori, G., Maher, M.J., Antoniou, G., Billington, D.: Argumentation semantics for defeasible logic. J. Log. Comput. **14**(5), 675–702 (2004)
12. Governatori, G., Olivieri, F., Rotolo, A., Scannapieco, S.: Computing strong and weak permissions in defeasible logic. J. Philos. Log. **42**(6), 799–829 (2013)
13. Governatori, G., Olivieri, F., Scannapieco, S., Rotolo, A., Cristani, M.: The rationale behind the concept of goal. TPLP **16**(3), 296–324 (2016)
14. Governatori, G., Padmanabhan, V., Rotolo, A., Sattar, A.: A defeasible logic for modelling policy-based intentions and motivational attitudes. Log. J. IGPL **17**(3), 227–265 (2009)
15. Governatori, G., Rotolo, A.: Deontic ambiguities in legal reasoning. In: ICAIL 2023, pp. 91–100. ACM (2023)
16. Governatori, G., Rotolo, A., Sartor, G.: Logic and the law: Philosophical foundations, deontics, and defeasible reasoning. In: Handbook of Deontic Logic and Normative Reasoning, vol. 2, pp. 655–760. College Publications, London (2021)
17. Grosof, B.N., Labrou, Y., Chan, H.Y.: A declarative approach to business rules in contracts: courteous logic programs in XML. In: ACM Conference on Electronic Commerce, pp. 68–77 (1999)
18. Maier, F.: Interdefinability of defeasible logic and logic programming under the well-founded semantics. TPLP **13**(1), 107–142 (2013)
19. Maier, F., Nute, D.: Well-founded semantics for defeasible logic. Synthese **176**(2), 243–274 (2010)
20. Makinson, D.: General patterns in nonmonotonic reasoning. In: D. Gabbay, C.H., Robinson, J. (eds.) Handbook of Logic in Artificial Intelligence and Logic Programming, vol. 3, pp. 35–110. Oxford University Press (1994)
21. Nute, D.: Defeasible logic. In: Handbook of Logic in Artificial Intelligence and Logic Programming, vol. 3. Oxford University Press (1987)
22. Olivieri, F., Cristani, M., Governatori, G.: Compliant business processes with exclusive choices from agent specification. In: Chen, Q., Torroni, P., Villata, S., Hsu, J., Omicini, A. (eds.) PRIMA 2015. LNCS (LNAI), vol. 9387, pp. 603–612. Springer, Cham (2015). https://doi.org/10.1007/978-3-319-25524-8_43
23. Olivieri, F., Governatori, G., Cristani, M., van Beest, N., Colombo-Tosatto, S.: Resource-driven substructural defeasible logic. In: Miller, T., Oren, N., Sakurai, Y., Noda, I., Savarimuthu, B.T.R., Cao Son, T. (eds.) PRIMA 2018. LNCS (LNAI), vol. 11224, pp. 594–602. Springer, Cham (2018). https://doi.org/10.1007/978-3-030-03098-8_46

24. Olivieri, F., Governatori, G., Cristani, M., Rotolo, A., Sattar, A.: Deontic meta-rules. J. Log. Comput. **34**, 261–314 (2024)
25. Touretzky, D.S., Horty, J.F., Thomason, R.H.: A clash of intuitions: the current state of nonmonotonic multiple inheritance systems. In: IJCAI, pp. 476–482 (1987)
26. Wan, H., Kifer, M., Grosof, B.N.: Defeasibility in answer set programs with defaults and argumentation rules. Semant. Web **6**(1), 81–98 (2015)

Legally-Guided Automated Decision-Making System Using Language Model Agents for Autonomous Driving

Ya Wang[1,2](✉), Daniel Barta[1], Julian Hesse[1], Philip Buchwald[1], and Adrian Paschke[1,2](✉)

[1] Fraunhofer Institute for Open Communication Systems, Kaiserin-Augusta-Allee 31, 10589 Berlin, Germany
{ya.wang,adrian.paschke}@fokus.fraunhofer.de
[2] The Free University of Berlin, Kaiserswerther Straße 16-18, 14195 Berlin, Germany

Abstract. Recent advances in language models have facilitated the development of agent-based systems. Despite their encouraging results in various reasoning tasks, these systems often operate as "black boxes", raising concerns about potential illegal behavior due to opaque decision-making processes. This concern is particularly critical in autonomous driving, where precise decision-making requires a thorough understanding of traffic scenes and strict adherence to established norms. In this paper, we propose a legally-guided automated decision making system (LAD) that employs language models to dynamically retrieve facts for related rules through context-based query generation while delegating decision-making to a symbolic solver. In our experiments, we demonstrate that this neuro-symbolic system, with a limited number of formalized traffic rules, provides a more accurate, interpretable, and traceable solution for rule-compliant decision-making compared to pure language models.

Keywords: Neurosymbolic System · Large Language Model Agent · Ontological Reasoning · Rule Compliance · Autonomous Driving

1 Introduction

The emergence of large language models (LLMs) has made automated problem-solving through agents increasingly feasible [40,45]. Recent works have explored the potential of LLM-based agents in various fields, such as education [8,20], software development [15,31], and chemical engineering [5,27]. Although enhancing language models with external tool usage and planning capabilities has led to significant breakthroughs in various tasks, they still struggle with complex

---

The original version of the chapter has been revised. A typo in the second author's name has been corrected. A correction to this chapter can be found at https://doi.org/10.1007/978-3-031-72407-7_18

This work has been partially funded by German Federal Ministry for Economic Affairs and Climate Action within the project "KI Wissen" (19A20020J), the Deutsche Forschungsgemeinschaft (DFG, German Research Foundation) project RECOMP (DFG-GZ: PA 1820/5-1), and the Institute of Applied Informatics (InfAI).

reasoning, often exhibiting logical inconsistencies and hallucinations [12,21,33]. This could raise legal concerns, especially due to the "black box" nature of these models in automated decision-making. These issues become even more critical in safety-focused domains like autonomous driving, where compliance with legal norms and road safety is paramount. Existing studies have improved the reasoning capabilities of language models by integrating them with symbolic solvers [28,37], resulting in high accuracy in specific domains and a more reliable reasoning process. Additionally, using human feedback for training and prompting rules into models are common approaches to enhance rule compliance in decision-making [19]. However, these methods may not guarantee that a model's decisions strictly adhere to established norms. Inspired by the automated rule compliance checking [4,14], we propose a neuro-symbolic system that externally assesses the decisions made by language models, evaluating them against existing rules to ensure legal compliance. More specifically, our system is structured into four distinct layers, as illustrated in Fig. 1. The first layer, the data input layer, contains raw data characterizing the scenario involving the agent and rules, such as written legislation and legal precedents. The second layer links the data to an ontology with comprehensive domain-specific knowledge, converting both scenario and rule data into a machine-interpretable format. The third layer acts as an evidence collector, querying facts according to rules that either prohibit or mandate the agent's decision. The final layer accepts the facts and relevant rules, using a symbolic solver to derive the ultimate decision. To reduce the workload on the symbolic solver, we design multiple LLM-based agents to collaborate, ensuring efficient derivation of reliable and traceable rule-compliant decisions.

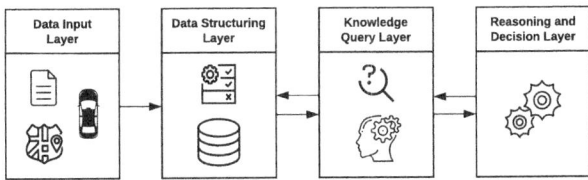

Fig. 1. Overview of the multi-layered architecture for legally-guided automated decision making system.

2 Preliminaries

2.1 Problem Formulation

Consider a traffic scene represented by a set of facts $\mathcal{T}$, consisting of n objects $\{o_1, o_2, \ldots, o_n\}$. Each object o_i is associated with a set of properties $\mathcal{P}_i = \{p_{i1}, p_{i2}, \ldots, p_{im}\}$, where m denotes the number of properties per object. Given an agent within the traffic scene, its possible decisions are within a set of actions $\mathcal{A} = \{a_1, a_2, ..., a_k\}$. These actions are either explicitly or implicitly regulated by a set of traffic rules $\mathcal{R}$. Each rule in $\mathcal{R}$ takes the form $\Phi \rightarrow \Psi$, stipulating that the occurrence of condition Φ mandates or prohibits the outcome of actions Ψ. The task is to find a subset of actions, denoted as $A \subseteq \mathcal{A}$, which, upon execution by an agent in the traffic scenario, adheres to the entirety of traffic regulations specified in $\mathcal{R}$. Formally, given the traffic scene $\mathcal{T}$ and the rule set $\mathcal{R}$, the task is to derive driving actions A when the current scene fulfills the rule condition:

$$\forall (\Phi \to \Psi) \in \mathcal{R}, (\mathcal{T} \models \Phi) \Rightarrow (A \models \Psi),$$

where $\models$ represents the satisfaction relation, indicating that if a traffic scene $\mathcal{T}$ satisfies the condition Φ, then it must also guarantee the outcome Ψ, thus adhering to the traffic rules. The central challenge of this task lies in the non-direct evaluability of rule conditions by given facts, necessitating the integration of world and mathematical-physical knowledge to infer the new facts required for grounding the rules. Moreover, the already significant computational complexity inherent in deductive reasoning systems is magnified in traffic scenes due to the extensive number of rules, predicates, predicate arguments, and facts involved. This complexity demands the design of an agent capable of actively and efficiently navigating the search space, requiring a thorough understanding of the traffic scene and applicable traffic rules for effective decision-making.

2.2 Legal Norms Formalization

Legal norms are generally classified into two categories. First, constitutive norms establish the system's terminology and framework. Second, prescriptive norms specify the normative outcomes applicable under defined conditions [6,32]. The latter is further classified into three modalities: obligations, prohibitions, and permissions, often structured as 'if-then' statements, aligning well with the logical structures required by reasoning systems [3,4]. Formalizing legal norms into machine-interpretable formats is challenging, characterized by Westhofen et al. [43] as a congruence problem between the legal interpretation and the system implementation, primarily due to the vagueness, abstract expressions, exceptions, and potential conflicts within the norms. Building on legal theory elements, Chitashvili et al. [7,34] introduce an intuitive normal form structure to represent traffic norms, aimed at facilitating collaboration between computer scientists and legal experts. Specifically, they propose a four-dimensional framework-space (R_ϕ), time (T_ϕ), subject (S_ϕ), and action (O_ϕ)-to structure legal norms (ϕ). R_ϕ defines where the rule applies. T_ϕ specifies the duration or activation moments. S_ϕ indicates who is bound by the rule. O_ϕ describes what is obligated, prohibited, or permitted. We adopt this structure and extend it with a fifth dimension, exceptions (E_ϕ), which refers to prioritized exceptional rules that apply in specific cases, overriding standard rules. In terms of modalities, we focus mainly on formalizing obligations and prohibitions, incorporating permissions only when they provide actionable guidance under exceptional circumstances. Starting from the legal text, we analyzed the rules and represented them in the form $R_\phi \wedge T_\phi \wedge S_\phi \wedge E_\phi \to O_\phi$. Each dimension contains detailed descriptions, which serve as a preparation for the process of translating general norm structures into specific logic sentences (see Section A.1 in the external report for more details[1]).

2.3 Ontology-Based Traffic Scene Representation

Ontology is a commonly used method for modeling domain-specific knowledge, providing a formal and explicit specification of a shared conceptualization that allows for consistent and unambiguous knowledge exchange and management [1]. Ontology-based traffic scene modeling [16,24] has attracted considerable interest, because it allows for modeling complex real-world situations and supports automated reasoning while remaining accessible for human interpretation of traffic scenes. An ontology is often described as a knowledge base $\mathcal{KB} = (\mathcal{TB}, \mathcal{AB})$ with two main components: the TBox and the ABox [10]. The TBox $\mathcal{TB}$, or Terminological Box, describes the hierarchical structure of classes, including object and data properties, axioms, and logical constructs. The ABox $\mathcal{AB}$, or Assertional Box, contains the specific instances and facts derived from situational knowledge, usually represented as a graph in RDF [38]. In traffic scene representation, the TBox functions as the backbone and schema, while the ABox holds the real-world data and facts mapped to the TBox concepts. A major advantage of using ontologies is their support for reasoning capabilities when coupled with a solver, enabling a range of inference services such as subsumption, satisfiability, and equivalence checks for the TBox, as well as instance entailment, classification, retrieval, and consistency checks for the ABox. The development of an ontology is often started by searching for existing ontologies [26]. The OpenX ontology developed by ASAM [36], provides a comprehensive foundation with common definitions, properties, and relationships in road traffic. We use the OpenX ontology as our backbone, extending it with additional concepts and relationships specific to our use cases. Especially, we introduce multiple legal terms to support rule formalization (see Section A.2 in the external report for more details).

3 Legal Rule-Compliant Decision-Making Systems in Autonomous Driving

3.1 Traffic Scene Understanding and Reasoning

Driving in complex traffic scenes demands diverse recognition and reasoning skills. These skills align with the dual-system theory from "Thinking, Fast and Slow" [9]. System 1 is fast and intuitive, while system 2 is slower and more logical. On highways and other simple conditions, system 1 usually dominates. In more complex scenarios, such as dealing with inoperative vehicles on the street, system 2 tends to dominate and often requires a more comprehensive grasp of traffic patterns and normative reasoning. Consider a situation where an ego vehicle is constrained on the right by a solid white line and faces an obstacle blocking its lane. Although traffic rules generally prohibit crossing a solid line, an exception allows

---
[1] The link to the external report.

for overtaking when the obstacle's removal timeframe is uncertain and there's no oncoming traffic. This scenario illustrates how understanding the traffic context informs the correct application of rules and helps determine suitable actions. To showcase our approach's applicability in rule-compliant decision making, we develop a system to handle the scenarios containing inoperative vehicles. Specifically, we categorize driving decisions in these scenarios into primary and secondary actions. The primary action space A_p, designed to help a vehicle escape challenging situations, includes a set of maneuvers: A_p = {Overtake(X), MakeUTurn(X), Pass(X), Wait(X)}, where X indicates the inoperative vehicle to which the action applies. Note that the action "Pass" is differentiated from "Overtake" by its execution within the same lane. The secondary action space, represented as A_s = {SpeedLimit(X), KeepSafeLateralDistance(X), LaneChangeTo(X), Cross(X)}, where X denotes the specific value or road elements, contains actions that are contingent upon the primary actions. The primary driving actions are explicitly or implicitly governed by the rules of prohibition and exception, while the secondary driving actions are mainly governed by obligation rules, which mandate the subsequent actions to be taken, such as maintaining lateral distance when overtaking. Modern vehicles are commonly equipped with numerous electronic control units (ECUs) for environment perception, providing a rich data source for traffic rule-based reasoning. We assume that the required information for rule evaluation, such as road infrastructure and traffic conditions, can be inferred or accessed via the Controller Area Network (CAN) within the vehicle. Our goal is to use this information, presented as key-value pairs, to derive primary and secondary actions that comply with traffic rules.

3.2 Multi-agent Supported Decision Making

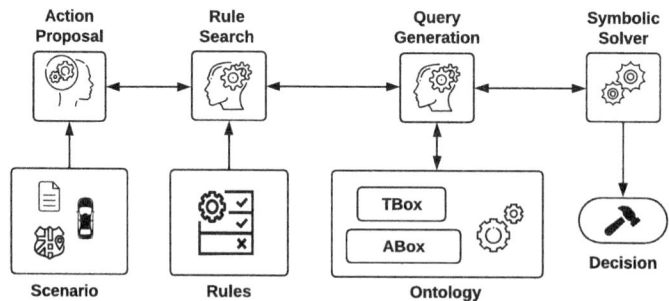

Fig. 2. Multi-agent collaboration on rule-compliant decision making.

Our system is designed with multiple agents working collaboratively to derive rule-compliant actions. As depicted in Fig. 2, the process begins with the first agent proposing an action based on its interpretation of scenario data. The second agent takes this proposed action and key features in the scene, using them to identify applicable rules. The third agent receives these formalized rules and generates context-specific queries, seeking answers from the ontology. At last, the identified rules and facts are processed through a symbolic solver to evaluate the consistency of the actions. Notably, the interaction among agents, as well as between agents and data sources, enables an iterative decision-making process.

Rule Formalization and Search. Working closely with legal experts, we gather traffic norms from various sources, including written legislation, legal precedents, and court decisions. We then analyze these rules and convert them into a normal form structure with detailed descriptions across five dimensions. To translate the rules into executable programs, we represent them in predicate logic, limiting them to a maximum of two arguments and avoiding explicit quantifiers to maintain simplicity and coherence. This formalization enables efficient querying within the description logic-based ontology and ensures reasoning through a Prolog-based solver [44]. In total, we formalized 25 rules with different modalities for our traffic scenarios. Benefiting from the clear and more implementable representation of traffic rules in the normal form structure, the translation into predicate logic can be semi-automated by prompting a language model with logical syntax and legal terms from the ontology, followed by a thorough review. The search for related rules is carried out by a semantic search agent, which maps rules into an embedding space using text embedding models. The agent then queries the rules based on proposed actions and key features extracted from the traffic scene.

Data Mapping. The key-value pairs representing scenario data lacks the semantic meaning required for direct evaluation of traffic rule predicates, such as "hasOncomingTraffic(X, Y)". To address this, new facts must be inferred based on the understanding of spatial configurations, object counts and their interrelationships. While LLMs can parse basic scenario data using their common sense knowledge, they struggle with domain-specific contexts. We overcome this by integrating LLMs with our ontology, which contains hierarchical classes, properties, axioms, and rules to enable deterministic inference and precise evaluation of traffic rules. We adapt the OpenX ontology to better suit our requirements by reducing its scope and then extending it to maintain its utility while optimizing query performance. The refined version has a total of 396 axioms, along with 113 classes, 35 object properties, 6 data properties, and 2 SWRL [39] rules within the TBox. We use the Owlready2 library [18] to map scenario data into the ABox, making it accessible for a variety of queries, such as examining the state of objects, and exploring spatial relationships among traffic participants.

Legal knowledge Reasoning. We use Prolog Solver for legal knowledge reasoning. Prolog is a declarative language derived from a subset of first-order logic, operating under the Closed World Assumption (CWA) to maintain decidability. In our pipeline, any facts or rules not retrieved from prior agents are considered false. The rule compliance of the proposed primary action is validated using available information through the Prolog query with backward chaining. Once the action is deemed consistent, it is added to the knowledge base. Subsequently, possible secondary actions are iteratively queried and derived. As Prolog doesn't inherently support deontic logic reasoning for different modalities of rules, we devise a mechanism to manage exceptional rules as a priority when assessing the current scene for possible rule exceptions. We then assign truth values to the "exception" dimension of corresponding rules. An action is deemed rule-compliant when it aligns with both prohibition and obligation rules.

SPARQL Query Generation. Query generation connects common-sense knowledge from LLMs with domain-specific ontology expertise. While other studies and applications [13,35] have used LLMs to generate SQL queries by providing syntax, schema, and examples, our approach follows a similar principle, guiding LLMs step-by-step through SPARQL syntax and structure. In our application, we explored using rule context and ontology segments for query generation. We propose three methods for query generation in predicate evaluation for a rule, each providing a different level of flexibility and contextual information.

1. **Zero-Informed:** This method focuses on unary predicates, specifically designed for class hierarchical reasoning, characterized by a invariable and consistent query structure. It generates queries aimed at searching for instances that belong to the class required by the rule evaluation.
2. **Rule-Informed:** This method generates queries based on the context of the evaluated rule, which can be answered by the ontology reasoning. For example, given the context of the rule that states a solid lane marking on the left that connects to the ego lane and requires generating a query about the predicate *LeftConnectedTo(X, Y)*, this method would incorporate the information about X as the ego lane type and Y as the solid line type into the query construction. This method limits the range of possible answers derived from the ontology.
3. **Ontology-Informed:** This method targets queries that can not directly inferred from the ontology. It incorporates additional ontological information, including comments about the predicate and available predicates, to construct the query.

These three query generation methods offer increased context and flexibility but reduced semantic correctness. In our work, most queries use the first two methods, while only two queries use the third (see examples in Section B.1 in the external report for more details).

3.3 Legally-Guided Automated Decision Making (LAD) Algorithm

We propose the Legally-Guided Automated Decision Making (LAD) Algorithm, which combines language models with symbolic reasoning to derive rule-compliant actions. As presented in Algorithm 1, it takes as input a TBox $\mathcal{TB}$, a traffic scene $\mathcal{T}$, a set of traffic rules $\mathcal{R}$, and possible actions $\mathcal{A}$. It outputs primary A_p and secondary A_s actions that comply with the corresponding rules I_p and I_s. The process begins by mapping data to an ABox $\mathcal{AB}$. Together with the traffic rules, this forms a knowledge base $\mathcal{KB}$, which is then ready for querying. Basic facts about the current scene are then extracted from this knowledge base. In the first loop of N trials, the language model $\mathcal{LM}$ proposes a primary action $\hat{a}_p$ and identifies relevant scene features $\hat{ft}$ based on the blockage of the front vehicle. It then searches for all rules related to the proposed action and the identified features. In the second loop, for each relevant rule $\hat{r}_i$, the algorithm evaluates which rule predicates are not currently supported by the available facts. For each absent predicate, the language model generates queries, which are used to retrieve new facts from the knowledge base through ontology reasoning. Upon identifying a candidate primary action $\hat{a}_p$, the symbolic solver $\mathcal{SL}$ verifies the action's consistency with the rules through backward chaining. If the action is found to be compliant, the loop terminates, marking the action as the primary compliant action. If not, the process iterates, updating the prompts for the language model to refine the action proposal. After determining the primary action, the algorithm employs the symbolic solver to derive secondary actions that are compliant with the rules. Our algorithm reduces the workload for the symbolic solver by suggesting candidate actions, pinpointing the most relevant rules, and extracting the necessary facts though context-based query generation. This approach significantly narrows the search space for rule evaluation, while offering more interpretable and traceable results compared to purely language-based models.

Algorithm 1. Legally-Guided Decision Making through Language Model Agents

Input: TBox $\mathcal{TB}$, traffic scenario $\mathcal{T}$, traffic rules $\mathcal{R}$, possible actions $\mathcal{A}$
Output: Primary and secondary actions $\{A_p, A_s\}$, compliant with the rules $\{I_p, I_s\}$
Hyperparameter: Number of trails N, Language model $\mathcal{LM}$, Symbolic solver $\mathcal{SL}$

1: $A_p, A_s, I_p, I_s \leftarrow \emptyset$
2: $\mathcal{AB} \leftarrow f(\mathcal{TB}, \mathcal{T})$ ▷ Mapping data into ABox
3: $\mathcal{KB} = \{\mathcal{AB}, \mathcal{R}\}$ ▷ Build knowledge base with rule sets ready for query
4: $facts \leftarrow query(\mathcal{KB})$ ▷ Retrieve basic available facts
5: **for** $n = 1, \ldots, N$ **do** ▷ Iterate N trials for LLM primary action proposal
6:   $\hat{a}_p, \hat{ft} \leftarrow \mathcal{LM}(\mathcal{AB}, \mathcal{T}, facts, prompts)$ ▷ Output candidate action and scene features
7:   $\hat{\mathcal{R}} \leftarrow \text{SEARCH}(\mathcal{R}, \hat{a}_p, \hat{ft})$ ▷ Search for all related rules
8:   **for** $\hat{r}_i$ in $\hat{\mathcal{R}}$, $i = 1, \ldots d$ **do**
9:     $\mathcal{AP} \leftarrow \text{EVALUATE}(\hat{r}_i, facts)$ ▷ Identify rule predicates absent from facts
10:     **for** p_j in $\mathcal{AP}$, $j = 1, \ldots k$ **do**
11:       $q \leftarrow \mathcal{LM}(p_j, \hat{r}_i, prompts)$ ▷ Generate queries for absent predicates
12:       $new\_facts \leftarrow query(\mathcal{KB}, q)$ ▷ Retrieve new facts with ontology reasoning
13:       $facts \leftarrow facts \cup new\_facts$
14:     **end for**
15:   **end for**
16:   $c, a_p, i_p \leftarrow SL(facts, \hat{a}_p, \hat{\mathcal{R}})$ ▷ Verify action consistency via backwards chaining
17:   **if** c is True **then**
18:     $A_p \leftarrow A_p \cup a_p$
19:     $I_p \leftarrow I_p \cup i_p$
20:     **break** ▷ Stop loop when primary action found
21:   **else**
22:     $\text{UPDATE}(prompts, a_p)$ ▷ Update prompts for next iteration
23:   **end if**
24: **end for**
25: $A_s, I_s \leftarrow SL(facts, A_p, \hat{\mathcal{R}})$ ▷ Derive secondary actions
26: **return** A_p, A_s, I_p, I_s

4 Experiment

Regulating language model behavior often involves embedding explicit rules through prompting. In contrast, our method restricts its output by employing ontology-based fact retrieval to evaluate rules via query generation. While agent-based language models [15,46,47] have demonstrated higher accuracy in decision-making, our experiment aims to assess whether our approach delivers more accurate, reliable, and traceable rule-compliant decisions compared to rule-prompting methods.

4.1 Dataset

Despite the availability of diverse datasets in autonomous driving, there are few designed specifically for rule compliance assessment. In our experiment, we create a compact synthetic dataset consisting of 60 randomly generated two-lane road scenarios. Each scenario contains detailed information about traffic participants, road infrastructure, environmental factors, and applicable traffic rules, all stored in key-value pairs in JSON format.

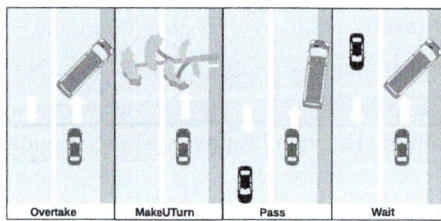

Fig. 3. Examples of driving scenarios, classified by primary decision types.

These scenarios are equally distributed across four classes based on primary actions (see Fig. 3): Overtake, MakeUTurn, Pass and Wait. Each class encompasses various scenarios, including differences in the number, size, type, location, and speed of vehicles, road markings, traffic signs, weather conditions, and congestion levels, all of which may influence driving actions. Annotations within the dataset cover primary decisions and required secondary decisions to fulfill applicable traffic rules. Our data generation follows principles of flexibility, extensibility, and scalability through random sampling for variables considering physical and rule constraints, supplemented by thorough manual review. While our dataset, programmatically configured, may not fully reflect real-world driving complexities, it aims to test our hypotheses and serve as an example for collaboration between legal experts and computer scientists in dataset creation (see examples in Section B.2 in the external report for more details).

4.2 Baselines and Metrics

Language models primarily trained on large natural language corpora [2], have limited understanding of specific key-value data structures. While targeted prompts can help, the results may not always be reliable. To maximize the reasoning potential of our baseline models, we implement a rule-based approach that programmatically generates narratives for each scenario from key-value pairs, enabling language models to derive rule-compliant actions from these textual descriptions. We use Few-shot-CoT [23, 42] as our baseline method, enabling complex reasoning by prompting detailed intermediate reasoning steps. To guide decision-making, we provide four representative examples that follow different reasoning paths involving traffic rules. For a fair comparison of reasoning abilities, we exclude the rule search part by specifying applicable traffic rules as natural language text in the baseline models and as logical forms in our method. We use GPT-3.5-Turbo and GPT-4-Turbo as laungage models for both methods. To evaluate the accuracy of derived actions, we use precision P, recall R, and the $F1$ score as our metrics in each scenario. A True Positive is counted when both the predicate and its argument are correctly predicted. Subsequently, we calculate the average and standard deviation for each metric across all classes and methods.

4.3 Results

As presented in Table 1, our method, NeSy-LAD, outperforms the Few-shot-CoT baseline models across GPT-3.5 and GPT-4, with significant gains in precision, recall, and F1 Score. The NeSy-LAD with GPT-4 achieved the best performance, exhibiting a 13.75% increase in precision, a 7.25% increase in recall, and a 10.54% increase in F1 score compared to the Few-shot-CoT with GPT-4. Remarkably, even when utilizing GPT-3.5, NeSy-LAD still outperforms the Few-shot-CoT with GPT-4 by 0.75%, which indicates that integrating ontology-based fact retrieval with a symbolic solver offers a significant advantage over the approach directly prompting rules for the decision-making. GPT-4 generally outperforms GPT-3.5 across both methods. Notably, in the Few-shot-CoT approach, GPT-4 demonstrates a recall that is 12.5% higher than the GPT-3.5 implementation. To explore the performance of these two methods across various scenario categories, we plotted the average F1 scores for both in Fig. 4 (left). Our method demonstrates higher F1 scores in the "Wait", "Pass", and "MakeUTurn" classes, with the exception of the "Overtake" class. The Few-shot-CoT approach tends to favor the "Overtake" action to escape these challenging scenarios, whereas our method relies more on the rule evaluation. Particularly, in the "Wait" and "Pass" classes, which involve a higher number of rules and predicates (Fig. 4, left), our method achieved very high F1 scores. The errors in our approach for the class of "Overtake" stem mainly from incorrect query

Table 1. Comparison of performance between Few-shot-CoT and NeSy-LAD.

Metric	Few-shot-CoT	Few-shot-CoT	NeSy-LAD	NeSy-LAD
	GPT-3.5	GPT-4	GPT-3.5	GPT-4
Precision	79.64 ± 3.29%	82.08 ± 5.45%	85.50 ± 3.01%	**95.83 ± 1.85%**
Recall	73.83 ± 2.85%	86.33 ± 2.47%	84.31 ± 3.81%	**93.58 ± 4.39%**
F1 Score	76.13 ± 3.30%	84.15 ± 7.91%	84.90 ± 6.82%	**94.69 ± 6.24%**

generation, including both semantic and syntactic inaccuracies. Semantic errors are more common, largely due to the misuse of the rule context and available predicates from the ontology for query generation. The errors in the Few-shot-CoT approach arise from several sources: omitted traffic rules, inconsistencies between the reasoning process and conclusions, and an inability to accurately capture the semantic meaning of the rules. For example, the action "Wait" is mostly regulated implicitly by the prohibition of "Overtake" or "MakeUTurn" in traffic rules, which Few-shot-CoT may not capture. With respect to interpretable and traceable reasoning, our approach provides detailed insights into evaluated rules and generated queries for unary and binary predicates (Fig. 4, right), offering a more reliable and trustworthy process than Few-shot CoT.

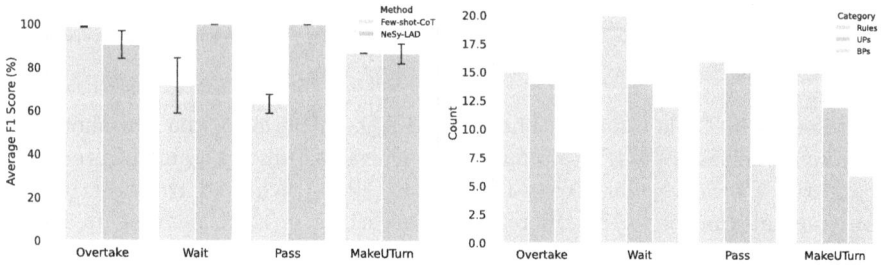

Fig. 4. Comparison of average F1 scores (left), and distribution of the average number of evaluated rules and generated queries for unary (UPs) and binary (BPs) predicates across all classes (right).

4.4 Discussion

Despite the significant results, we acknowledge certain limitations in our experiment and approach. First, we tested only a limited set of rules and predicates, which may not fully represent the language model's query generation capabilities. To scale the approach, future work should explore more efficient mechanisms that utilize various contexts or consider fine-tuning the model for SPARQL query generation. Secondly, the symbolic solver treats facts as either true or false, operating entirely on the Closed World Assumption, which contradicts real-world situations. Meanwhile, it doesn't account for probabilities, and misidentified rules and facts from other agents could lead to incorrect conclusions. Lastly, our system is heavily dependent on formalized rules in an executable format. We argue that legislation regarding automated agents should address both implementability for systems and interpretability for humans, which calls for collaboration between computer scientists and legal experts. This lays the groundwork for the safe and lawful deployment of agents in real-world applications. Our LAD system integrates traffic rules explicitly into a symbolic solver, providing an interpretable and traceable decision-making process for humans. This setup allows for flexible and rapid rule updates as regulations evolve. Additionally, our system's modular design allows different modules to be replaced with varying techniques. For instance, the ontology query part can be replaced with knowledge graph embeddings, and the symbolic solver can be substituted with a neural-based reasoner. Though our system was originally designed for decision-making in autonomous driving, it can be adapted to other domains requiring scene recognition and rule compliance. In conclusion, our approach provide a scalable and adaptable framework that can serve as a foundational solution for a wide range of applications, enabling reliable and interpretable rule-compliant decision making in diverse contexts.

5 Related Works

While neural systems handle unstructured, noisy data well, symbolic systems excel in logical deduction and interpretability [11,49]. Combining neural networks with symbolic solvers leverages the strengths of both. Yi et al. [48] propose a disentangled system that uses neural models to create structured representations first and then employs a symbolic program to derive answers. This approach demonstrates advantages in reasoning accuracy and transparency, despite decoupling reasoning from perception. Manhaeve et al. [22] attempted to address this issue by creating a unified differentiable framework and introducing a novel logical language called DeepProbLog. However, this method may encounter challenges related to scalability, training convergence, and interpretability because of its end-to-end design. Recent advance in LLMs have taken the processing of unstructured data to a new level, but complex logical reasoning still remains a challenge [21]. To address this, Pan et al. [28] integrated LLMs with symbolic solvers, achieving improved accuracy across benchmarks. Trinh et al.'s AlphaGeometry [37] utilized LLMs to propose innovative constructs guiding symbolic solvers in solving Olympiad-level geometry problems. Our work takes a similar approach, leveraging LLMs to propose potential solutions that help reduce the problem complexity for symbolic solvers. Additionally, we use LLMs to generate queries for fact retrieval, aiding in rule compliance checks. Aligning the behavior of automated agents with established norms is crucial for safe deployment in real-world applications [17,30]. Ontology-based rule compliance checking has been widely studied and applied in various fields because it offers notable benefits in interpretability, traceability, and determinism [29,50]. Automated vehicles are designed to strictly follow traffic rules but can struggle with situations requiring deep normative reasoning, like exceptional cases where decision flexibility is needed. Previous solutions [25,41] involved ontology-based frameworks with manually defined rules and queries. Hanif et al. [4] proposed an automatic regulatory framework with a defeasible deontic logical solver to enable vehicles to comply with rules through reasoning over driving environment and legal information. Our work builds on these methods, integrating language model-based agents into rule-compliant decision-making. This combination of LLMs and symbolic solvers creates a more robust and interpretable framework for navigating complex traffic situations, balancing flexibility with precision for effective rule compliance.

6 Conclusion

In this paper, we present a framework that combines language models with a symbolic solver for rule-compliant decision-making in autonomous driving. Our approach regulates automated agents with formalized rules, providing an adaptable solution for safer and more interpretable automated decision-making. Despite its effectiveness in traffic scenarios, our system has limitations when dealing with complex rules and probabilistic reasoning. Future work should explore more implementable rule formats and develop more scalable query methods.

References

1. A translation approach to portable ontology specifications. Knowl. Acquisit. **5**(2), 199–220 (1993). https://doi.org/10.1006/knac.1993.1008
2. Achiam, J., et al.: GPT-4 technical report. arXiv preprint arXiv:2303.08774 (2023)
3. Athan, T., Governatori, G., Palmirani, M., Paschke, A., Wyner, A.: LegalRuleML: design principles and foundations. In: Faber, W., Paschke, A. (eds.) Reasoning Web 2015. LNCS, vol. 9203, pp. 151–188. Springer, Cham (2015). https://doi.org/10.1007/978-3-319-21768-0_6
4. Bhuiyan, H., Governatori, G., Bond, A., Rakotonirainy, A.: Traffic rules compliance checking of automated vehicle maneuvers. Artif. Intell. Law **32**(1), 1–56 (2024)
5. Bran, A.M., Cox, S., Schilter, O., Baldassari, C., White, A.D., Schwaller, P.: ChemCrow: augmenting large-language models with chemistry tools. arXiv preprint arXiv:2304.05376 (2023)
6. Bulygin, E.: On norms of competence. Law Philos. **11**(3), 201–216 (1992)
7. Chitashvili, M., Hermann, M., Sasdelli, D., Wüst, C.: A normal form for representing legal norms and its visualisation through normative diagrams. In: Proceedings of the 19th International Conference on Artificial Inteligence and Law (2023)
8. Dan, Y., et al.: EduChat: a large-scale language model-based chatbot system for intelligent education. arXiv preprint arXiv:2308.02773 (2023)
9. Daniel, K.: Thinking, fast and slow (2017)
10. De Giacomo, G., Lenzerini, M., et al.: TBox and ABox reasoning in expressive description logics. KR **96**(316-327), 10 (1996)
11. Garcez, A.D., et al.: Neural-symbolic learning and reasoning: a survey and interpretation. Neuro-Symb. Artif. Intell.: State Art **342**(1), 327 (2022)
12. Golovneva, O., et al.: ROSCOE: a suite of metrics for scoring step-by-step reasoning. arXiv preprint arXiv:2212.07919 (2022)
13. Gu, Z., et al.: Few-shot text-to-SQL translation using structure and content prompt learning. In: Proceedings of the ACM on Management of Data, vol. 1, no. 2, pp. 1–28 (2023)
14. Guo, D., Onstein, E., La Rosa, A.D.: A semantic approach for automated rule compliance checking in construction industry. IEEE Access **9**, 129648–129660 (2021)
15. Hong, S., et al.: MetaGPT: meta programming for multi-agent collaborative framework. arXiv preprint arXiv:2308.00352 (2023)
16. Hülsen, M., Zöllner, J.M., Weiss, C.: Traffic intersection situation description ontology for advanced driver assistance. In: 2011 IEEE Intelligent Vehicles Symposium (IV), pp. 993–999. IEEE (2011)
17. Kubica, M.L.: Autonomous vehicles and liability law. Am. J. Comp. Law **70**(Supplement_1), i39–i69 (2022)

18. Lamy, J.B.: Owlready: ontology-oriented programming in python with automatic classification and high level constructs for biomedical ontologies. Artif. Intell. Med. **80**, 11–28 (2017)
19. Leike, J., Schulman, J., Wu, J.: OpenAI alignment research (2024). https://openai.com/blog/our-approach-to-alignment-research. Accessed 21 Apr 2024
20. Liffiton, M., Sheese, B.E., Savelka, J., Denny, P.: CodeHelp: using large language models with guardrails for scalable support in programming classes. In: Proceedings of the 23rd Koli Calling International Conference on Computing Education Research, pp. 1–11 (2023)
21. Liu, B., et al.: LLM+ P: empowering large language models with optimal planning proficiency. arXiv preprint arXiv:2304.11477 (2023)
22. Manhaeve, R., Dumancic, S., Kimmig, A., Demeester, T., De Raedt, L.: DeepProbLog: neural probabilistic logic programming. In: Advances in Neural Information Processing Systems, vol. **31** (2018)
23. Min, S., et al.: Rethinking the role of demonstrations: what makes in-context learning work? (2022)
24. Mohammad, M.A., Kaloskampis, I., Hicks, Y., Setchi, R.: Ontology-based framework for risk assessment in road scenes using videos. Procedia Comput. Sci. **60**, 1532–1541 (2015)
25. Morignot, P., Nashashibi, F.: An ontology-based approach to relax traffic regulation for autonomous vehicle assistance. In: IASTED Multiconferences - Proceedings of the IASTED International Conference on Artificial Intelligence and Applications, AIA 2013, pp. 122–129 (2013). https://doi.org/10.2316/P.2013.793-024
26. Noy, N.: Ontology development 101: a guide to creating your first ontology (2001). https://api.semanticscholar.org/CorpusID:500106
27. Ogundare, O., Madasu, S., Wiggins, N.: Industrial engineering with large language models: a case study of ChatGPT's performance on oil & gas problems. In: 2023 11th International Conference on Control, Mechatronics and Automation (ICCMA), pp. 458–461. IEEE (2023)
28. Pan, L., Albalak, A., Wang, X., Wang, W.Y.: LOGIC-LM: empowering large language models with symbolic solvers for faithful logical reasoning. In: Findings of the Association for Computational Linguistics: EMNLP 2023, pp. 3806–3824 (2023). https://doi.org/10.18653/v1/2023.findings-emnlp.248
29. Pauwels, P., Zhang, S.: Semantic rule-checking for regulation compliance checking: an overview of strategies and approaches. In: 32rd International CIB W78 Conference (2015)
30. Prakken, H.: On the problem of making autonomous vehicles conform to traffic law. Artif. Intell. Law **25**, 341–363 (2017)
31. Qian, C., et al.: Communicative agents for software development. arXiv preprint arXiv:2307.07924 (2023)
32. Raz, J.: The Concept of a Legal System: An Introduction to the Theory of a Legal System. Oxford University Press, Oxford (1980)
33. Ribeiro, D., et al.: STREET: a multi-task structured reasoning and explanation benchmark. arXiv preprint arXiv:2302.06729 (2023)
34. Sasdelli, D., Trivisonno, A.T.G.: Normative diagrams as a tool for representing legal systems. Rev. Socionetw. Strategies **2**, 217–231 (2023)
35. Sun, R., et al.: SQL-PALM: improved large language modeladaptation for text-to-SQL. arXiv preprint arXiv:2306.00739 (2023)
36. Tao, J., et al.: ASAM OpenX ontology user guide (2021). https://www.asam.net/standards/asam-openxontology/

37. Trinh, T.H., Wu, Y., Le, Q.V., He, H., Luong, T.: Solving olympiad geometry without human demonstrations. Nature **625**(7995), 476–482 (2024). https://doi.org/10.1038/s41586-023-06747-5
38. W3C: Resource description framework (RDF) (2024). https://www.w3.org/RDF/. Accessed 21 Apr 2024
39. W3C: A semantic web rule language combining OWL and RuleML (SWRL) (2024). https://www.w3.org/submissions/SWRL/. Accessed 21 Apr 2024
40. Wang, L., et al.: A survey on large language model based autonomous agents. Front. Comput. Sci. **18**(6), 1–26 (2024)
41. Wang, Y., Grabowski, M., Paschke, A.: An ontology-based model for handling rule exceptions in traffic scenes. In: Proceedings of the International Workshop on AI Compliance Mechanism (WAICOM 2022), p. 87 (2022)
42. Wei, J., et al.: Chain-of-thought prompting elicits reasoning in large language models. In: Advances in Neural Information Processing Systems, vol. 35, pp. 24824–24837 (2022)
43. Westhofen, L., Stierand, I., Becker, J.S., Möhlmann, E., Hagemann, W.: Towards a congruent interpretation of traffic rules for automated driving-experiences and challenges, pp. 8–21 (2022)
44. Wielemaker, J.: SWI-prolog: a comprehensive prolog implementation (2024). https://github.com/SWI-Prolog/swipl-devel. Accessed 21 Apr 2024
45. Xi, Z., et al.: The rise and potential of large language model based agents: a survey. arXiv preprint arXiv:2309.07864 (2023)
46. Yang, H., Yue, S., He, Y.: Auto-GPT for online decision making: benchmarks and additional opinions. arXiv preprint arXiv:2306.02224 (2023)
47. Yao, S., et al.: ReAct: synergizing reasoning and acting in language models. arXiv preprint arXiv:2210.03629 (2022)
48. Yi, K., Torralba, A., Wu, J., Kohli, P., Gan, C., Tenenbaum, J.B.: Neural-symbolic VQA: disentangling reasoning from vision and language understanding. In: Advances in Neural Information Processing Systems (NeurIPS), pp. 1031–1042 (2018)
49. Yu, D., Yang, B., Liu, D., Wang, H., Pan, S.: A survey on neural-symbolic learning systems. Neural Netw. **166**, 105–126 (2023). https://doi.org/10.1016/j.neunet.2023.06.028
50. Zhong, B., Gan, C., Luo, H., Xing, X.: Ontology-based framework for building environmental monitoring and compliance checking under BIM environment. Build. Environ. **141**, 127–142 (2018)

Correction to: Legally-Guided Automated Decision-Making System Using Language Model Agents for Autonomous Driving

Ya Wang, Daniel Barta, Julian Hesse, Philip Buchwald, and Adrian Paschke

Correction to:
Chapter 17 in: S. Kirrane et al. (Eds.): *Rules and Reasoning*, **LNCS 15183,**
https://doi.org/10.1007/978-3-031-72407-7_17

The book was published with a typo in the second author's name in chapter 17. Correctly it should read "Daniel Barta". This has been corrected in the corresponding chapter accordingly.

The updated version of this chapter can be found at
https://doi.org/10.1007/978-3-031-72407-7_17

© The Author(s), under exclusive license to Springer Nature Switzerland AG 2024
S. Kirrane et al. (Eds.): RuleML+RR 2024, LNCS 15183, p. C1, 2024.
https://doi.org/10.1007/978-3-031-72407-7_18

Author Index

A
Arndt, Dörthe 200

B
Barta, Daniel 234
Betz, Patrick 32
Bisquert, Pierre 23
Bizarro, Pedro 50
Bravo, João 50
Buchwald, Philip 234

C
Calvanese, Diego 59, 108
Charoensit, Akira 23
Colin, Renaud 23
Corman, Julien 124

D
De Roo, Jos 200
Di Florio, Cecilia 91

G
Ghosh, Arka 108
Gomes, Ana Sofia 50
Governatori, Guido 217
Guimarães, Ricardo 191

H
Hedblom, Maria M. 176
Hesse, Julian 234
Hochstenbach, Patrick 200
Horn, Daniel 159

J
Jakubowski, Maxime 1

K
Kim, Yusik 159

L
Lacerda, Victor 191
Lüdtke, Stefan 32

M
Martens, Rebekka 200
Martins, Lucas 50
Meilicke, Christian 32, 75

N
Nutt, Werner 124

O
Olivieri, Francesco 217
Ongenae, Femke 200
Ott, Simon 75
Ottosson, Greger 159
Ozaki, Ana 191

P
Pano, Albulen 108
Paschke, Adrian 234
Peñaloza, Rafael 142
Pomarlan, Mihai 176
Porzel, Robert 176

R
Rotolo, Antonino 91

S
Savković, Ognjen 124
Soares, Carlos 50
Spillner, Laura 176
Stuckenschmidt, Heiner 32, 75

T
Tornil, Florent 23
Turhan, Anni-Yasmin 142

U
Ulliana, Federico 23

V
Van den Bussche, Jan 1
van Noort, Mathijs 200
Völzer, Hagen 159

W
Wandji, Romuald Esdras 59
Wang, Ya 234
Wenzel, Mario 14

X
Xiao, Guohui 108

Y
Yeche, Quentin 23

SPRINGER NATURE

GPSR Compliance

The European Union's (EU) General Product Safety Regulation (GPSR) is a set of rules that requires consumer products to be safe and our obligations to ensure this.

If you have any concerns about our products, you can contact us on ProductSafety@springernature.com

In case Publisher is established outside the EU, the EU authorized representative is:

Springer Nature Customer Service Center GmbH
Europaplatz 3
69115 Heidelberg, Germany

The manufacturer's authorised representative in the EU is Springer Nature Customer Service Centre GmbH, Europaplatz 3, 69115 Heidelberg, Germany. If you have any concerns regarding our products, please contact ProductSafety@springernature.com

Printed and bound by CPI Group (UK) Ltd, Croydon, CR0 4YY

25/03/2026

02078195-0011